Internet Agents:
Spiders, Wanderers, Brokers, and 'Bots

Fah-Chun Cheong

New Riders

New Riders Publishing, Indianapolis, Indiana

Internet Agents: Spiders, Wanderers, Brokers, and 'Bots
By Fah-Chun Cheong

Published by:
New Riders Publishing
201 West 103rd Street
Indianapolis, IN 46290 USA

Printed in the United States of America 1 2 3 4 5 6 7 8 9 0

CIP Data Available upon Request

Warning and Disclaimer
This book is designed to provide information about Internet agents. Every effort has been made to make this book as complete and as accurate as possible, but no warranty or fitness is implied.

The information is provided on an "as is" basis. The author and New Riders Publishing shall have neither liability nor responsibility to any person or entity with respect to any loss or damages arising from the information contained in this book or from the use of the disks or programs that may accompany it.

Publisher	Don Fowley
Publishing Manager	Jim LeValley
Marketing Manager	Ray Robinson
Managing Editor	Tad Ringo

Product Development Specialist
Julie Fairweather

Development Editor
Suzanne Snyder

Production Editor
Cliff Shubs

Copy Editors
Amy Bezek, Fran Blauw, Gail Burlakoff, Laura Frey, Lisa Wilson

Associate Marketing Manager
Tamara Apple

Acquisitions Coordinator
Tracy Turgeson

Publisher's Assistant
Karen Opal

Cover Designer
Jay Corpus

Cover Illustrator
Roger Morgan

Book Designer
Sandra Schroeder

Manufacturing Coordinator
Paul Gilchrist

Production Manager
Kelly D. Dobbs

Production Team Supervisor
Laurie Casey

Graphics Image Specialists
Jason Hand, Clint Lahnen, Laura Robbins, Craig Small, Todd Wente

Production Analysts
Angela D. Bannan
Bobbi Satterfield

Production Team
Heather Butler, Dan Caparo, Kim Cofer, Kevin Foltz, Erika Millen, Erich J. Richter, Christine Tyner, Karen Walsh

Indexer
Christopher Cleveland

About the Author

Fah-Chun Cheong consults with start-up companies around the San Francisco Bay Area in the application of agent technologies for electronic commerce on the World Wide Web and Internet.

Mr. Cheong received his B.S. in Electrical Engineering from The University of Texas at Austin in 1986, and his M.S. and Ph.D. degrees in Computer Science from the University of Michigan in 1988 and 1992, respectively. His Ph.D. research work is on the design and development of an experimental agent-oriented programming language and compiler system for heterogeneous distributed computing environments. He founded Agent Computing, Inc. in 1994, with a vision to develop innovative application-specific agent technologies for the Internet.

Trademark Acknowledgments

All terms mentioned in this book that are known to be trademarks or service marks have been appropriately capitalized. New Riders Publishing cannot attest to the accuracy of this information. Use of a term in this book should not be regarded as affecting the validity of any trademark or service mark.

Dedication

To my parents and sisters

Acknowledgments

This book might not have been written (well, at least not in 1995!) if Vinay Kumar had not invited me along to a dinner earlier this year at a sushi place in San Francisco with Jim LeValley, Publishing Manager for New Riders Publishing. I thank him for that and for the many interesting and insightful discussions on a variety of topics we have had over many cups of espresso.

A very big thank you to Kevin Hughes for reviewing drafts of this book. I am grateful to ex-colleagues at EIT and ex-EIT friends, especially Jeff Pan and Jim McGuire, for information in a variety of areas, most notably procurement agents, Web robots, and secure HTTP.

I would like to thank all the people on the Internet whose pioneering work in agents, spiders, wanderers, and Web robots has made an early book on this topic a possibility. Special thanks to all the authors of Web robots, spiders, and wanderers who have answered e-mail questionnaires on Internet agents; their insightful comments and responses have contributed much toward shaping the content of this book.

I am indebted to Roy Fielding for his libwww-perl and MOMspider source code, which, in a vastly simplified form, have now become the basis upon which WebWalker is built. Many thanks to Bruce Krulwich whose BargainFinder agent on the Web inspired the development of WebShopper for this book.

Martijn Koster has authored and maintained a number of marvelous Web pages on the net. Among his creations, I have found the List of Robots a comprehensive reference and an invaluable resource for much of this book.

The Stanford Libraries have proved invaluable to me on this project, as on others. I am extremely grateful that Stanford opens its Mathematics and Computer Science Library, and also the Engineering Library, to the surrounding community at large.

A very big thank you to the friendly, competent, and generally fantastic editorial staff at New Riders who prepared this book for publication. I am indebted to Jim LeValley for taking an interest in Internet agents, coming up with an initial plan for this book, and supplying me continuously with an unending stream of helpful sources and materials. I am especially thankful to Julie Fairweather for developing the book, coordinating the process to keep publication on schedule, and for helping with numerous screen-shots of the Web. Special thanks to Cliff Shubs for his excellent editing and his many thoughtful remarks on the book, and to Suzanne Snyder for helping with the development of the book. Many thanks go to Roger Morgan for designing the great spider on the front cover.

Contents at a Glance

Part I: Introduction

Part II: Web Robot Construction

Part III: Agents and Money on the Net

Part IV: Bots in Cyberspace

Part V: Appendices

Table of Contents

Part III: Agents and Money on the Net   183

8 Web Transaction Security   185

9 Electronic Cash and Payment Services   205

Part IV: Bots in Cyberspace   227

10 Worms and Viruses   229

G List of World Wide Web Spiders and Robots 375

Bibliography 387

Index 401

part

••

I

Introduction

The World of Agents

Welcome to the world of agents. On the Internet, agents can take on many different forms and perform interesting functions. Some agents have been deployed on the Net and are in use daily. The following are some common types of agents on the Internet that you probably have already encountered:

→ Web robots, spiders, and wanderers

→ Web commerce agents

→ Worms and viruses

→ MUD agents and chatterbots

Web robots, *spiders,* and *wanderers* are programs that traverse the World Wide Web information space. They move from one Web document to another by referencing the hyperlinks embedded in the Web pages. Web robots speak the native HyperText Transfer Protocol (HTTP) of the World Wide Web, using it to retrieve Web documents from servers. They crawl on the Web to discover new resources, to index the Webspace for keyword searching, and to seek out dead links in Webspace for automated maintenance.

Web commerce agents are the automated Web shoppers, bargain-hunters, and smart online buyers for comparison-shopping and automated procurement. They are also the automated online catalogs and electronic sales representatives for manufacturers and retailers. But more importantly, they are playing the emerging roles of brokers, bar-terers, traders, and middlemen that promise to facilitate commerce on the Internet and on the Web in the near future.

Worms and *viruses* are malicious agents that replicate themselves in an elusive way to travel from machine to machine, network to network. In the past, they were often hand-carried by humans on floppy disks. But for the future, the Internet, with its decentralized global connectivity, is increasingly a vulnerable new medium of transport. Such undercover dark agents of society are considered harmful and extremely dangerous to the well-being of our global computing and communications infrastructure.

MUD agents and *chatterbots* are automatons from the world of Multi-User Dungeons or Multi-User Dimensions in cyberspace. MUD agents provide useful services to human players, such as answering inquiries and giving directions, through a type-written natural-language interface. Chatterbots are conversational agents whose main job is to chat with human players. Unlike MUD agents, chatterbots are not specific to MUDs and can also exist outside of the MUD world.

The following chapters of this book examine various Web robots and spiders, and introduce some widely accepted operational guidelines for Web robots. Web commerce agents, although currently with few deployed examples, are introduced along with the World Wide Web. This book includes a chapter dedicated to discussing how one such spider for Web maintenance, WebWalker, can be constructed. This book also examines the operations of worms and viruses, as well as MUD agents and chatterbots.

The foundation technologies underlying Internet agents, such as transaction security, electronic cash, and payment services, are explained in detail along with examples of current commercial offerings on the Internet.

This book is about agents on the Internet, but for the sake of building a solid foundation for appreciating agents in general, the remainder of this chapter is dedicated to the pioneers of agent research who are currently busy constructing agents of the future. The next section discusses the concept of agents in general, and introduces a taxonomic agent framework for understanding various kinds of agents.

What are Agents?

The qualifying attributes of agenthood have for many years been the staple of lively philosophical discussions and the favorite subject of debates within the agent research community. Never before has a field of inquiry been so rich and diverse, yet fragmented, that its primary subject of inquiry remains shrouded in a perpetual rhetoric: *What exactly is an agent?*

Simply put, agents can be considered personal software assistants with authority delegated from their users. Early visionaries such as Nicholas Negroponte (1970, 1989) and Alan Kay (1984) were among the first to recognize the value of software personal assistants. They spoke of the idea of employing agents in the interface to delegate certain computer-based tasks. More recently, several computer manufacturers have adopted this idea to illustrate their vision of the interface for the future; for example, videos produced by Apple (1988). In the words of Ted Selker (1994) from IBM's Almaden Research Center, "Agents are computer programs that simulate a human relationship, by doing something that another person could otherwise do for you."

The Telescript agent programming language technology developed by General Magic, a start-up company in the Silicon Valley, supports the deployment of software agents as personal delegates across the network. General Magic defines an agent as a piece of Telescript program that is sent across the network (White 1994). The Telescript program encapsulates the user's instructions for performing all kinds of tasks in electronic venues on the network, which are called "places." Electronic mailboxes, calendars, markets, and gathering points, for example, are all places.

As illustrated in figure 1.1, people who dispatch Telescript agents can think of these agents as electronic extensions of themselves, capable of gathering information resourcefully, negotiating deals, and performing transactions on their behalf. These Telescript agents can be customized for an individual user's preferences, and also are intelligent in the sense that they can have contingency plans. In other words, Telescript agents can assess themselves, as well as the conditions of their surrounding environment when situated in different places, and act accordingly, perhaps changing from an original course of action to an alternative plan.

Figure 1.1

A Telescript agent from General Magic.

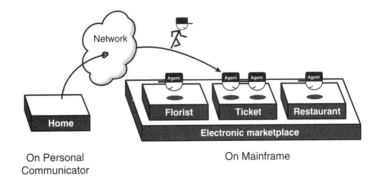

On Personal Communicator

On Mainframe

The definition of agents, however, usually deviates from such a simple one as delegated software programs given above. Agent research has drawn upon the ideas and results produced by people from diverse disciplines, including robotics, software engineering, programming languages, computer networks, knowledge engineering, machine learning, cognitive science, psychology, computer graphics—even art, music, and film. From this diversity of perspectives, not one definition, but a rich set of views on agents, has emerged.

In addition to being understood as delegated software entities, agents can also be studied along other important dimensions, such as coordination, knowledge, creativity, and emotion. The programming and social aspects of agents are also important considerations. The remaining sections of this chapter explore the concept of agents along these various dimensions.

Agents and Delegation

Agents are primarily human-delegated software entities that can perform a variety of tasks for their human masters. This section examines their roles as personal assistants, desktop agents, surrogate bots, and softbots.

Personal Assistants

Pattie Maes, an assistant professor with the Massachusetts Institute of Technology Media Lab, has been working to create agents that reduce work and information overload for computer users (1994). She believes that as computers and networks begin to reach a larger populace, the current dominant metaphor of direct manipulation (Schneiderman 1988), which requires the user to initiate all tasks explicitly and to monitor all events, might not be the most convenient for many new, untrained users. She favors an alternative, complementary style of interaction called "indirect management," (Kay 1990) which engages the user in a cooperative process with a computer program known as the intelligent personal assistant.

Maes's work has resulted in agents that provide personalized assistance for a variety of tasks, including meeting scheduling, e-mail handling, electronic news filtering, and the selection of books, music, and other forms of entertainment. In the process of constructing such agents, Maes has identified the following two problems:

→ **Competence.** How does an agent acquire the knowledge to decide when, with what, and how to help the user?

→ **Trust.** How do you ensure that users feel comfortable delegating tasks to an agent?

According to Maes, both problems can be solved with a machine-learning approach, where the agent learns about its user's habits through interactions over time. Specifically, a learning agent gradually acquires its competence by the following:

→ Observing and imitating the user

→ Receiving positive and negative feedback from the user

→ Receiving explicit instructions from the user

→ Asking other agents for advice

Over time, the agents become more helpful as they accumulate knowledge about how the user handles certain situations. Gradually, more tasks that initially were performed directly by the user can be taken care of by the agent. As shown in figure 1.2, Maes' agents use simple caricatures to convey their internal state to the user.

The user also is given time to gradually and incrementally build up a model of the agent's competencies and limitations. The particular learning approach adopted enables the agent to give explanations for its reasoning and behavior in language the user is familiar with. An example of this would be "I thought you might want to take this action because this situation is similar to this other situation we have experienced before." The user would have the opportunity to become more comfortable delegating tasks to the agents after using them for some time.

Figure 1.2

Simple caricatures convey agent "emotional" states to user.

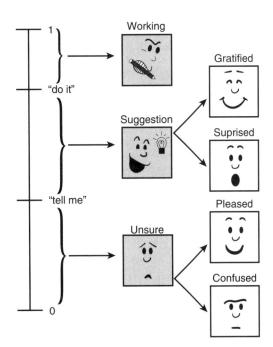

Envoy Desktop Agents

The Envoy Framework has been proposed by researchers at Brown University's Institute for Research in Information and Scholarship (IRIS) as an open architecture for agents on the desktop (PYFLHCM 1992). The framework supports agents that operate in conjunction with existing desktop user applications and assists users with the more tedious, repetitive, and time-consuming tasks. Envoy agents help users with tasks such as the following:

→ Sifting through incoming information

→ Monitoring information sources continuously

→ Searching data sources at regular intervals

→ Delegating tasks now for future execution

In the Envoy Framework shown in figure 1.3, a user specifies a mission for the Envoy by interacting with an Envoy-aware application. These Envoy-aware applications are called *operatives* because they are responsible for actually carrying out missions on behalf of the user. As the user's representative, the Envoy would schedule, track, and dispatch all missions the user has specified, and handle all communications with the operatives.

When an operative completes an assigned mission, it notifies the Envoy, which in turn notifies the user through a set of Envoy-aware applications called *informers*. The mission results can be a brief message, a short report, or an interactive report viewable from the native application interface. At any time, the user can view a mission summary listing all active missions, as well as reports generated by operatives responsible for those missions.

A *bureau chief* on the local area network maintains a record of each user's Envoy, as well as all Envoy-aware applications in the environment. New operatives or informers in the environment must first register with the bureau chief.

New Wave Desktop Agents

In contrast to the Envoy Framework, Hewlett-Packard's New Wave Agent (HP 1989) is a more limited form of desktop integration that automates

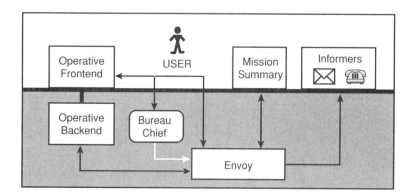

Figure 1.3

The Envoy Framework employs operatives, informers, and a bureau chief.

tasks users perform frequently. Application developers implement a defined set of protocols to make their applications agent-aware in the New Wave environment.

A New Wave user can specify routine tasks by demonstration. Say, for example, the user wants to start a database access application, download specific information into a spreadsheet, generate a graph from the spreadsheet data, copy the graph to a text document, and mail it to a group of users. All the user needs to do is turn on the recording feature and perform the desired sequence of actions interactively. The task is represented as a script document on the desktop and can be scheduled for execution using the calendar. The script also can be edited by the user if needed.

The integration of agent functionality into the desktop environment enables users to automate routine and repetitive tasks quite easily. Because tasks can be defined by example, the cognitive overhead of learning a scripting language is substantially reduced. A user needs only be sufficiently familiar with the language to make any necessary modifications to scripts. In addition, the calendar on the New Wave desktop provides an intuitive metaphor and convenient mechanism for scheduling agent tasks.

Surrogate Bots

Agents can relieve users of low-level administrative and clerical tasks, such as setting up meetings, sending out papers, locating information, tracking whereabouts of people, and so on. Research scientists at AT&T Bell Labs, Henry Kautz and Bart Selman, and MIT graduate student Michael Coen,

have built and tested an agent system consisting of *surrogate bots* that addresses the real-world problem of handling the communication involved in scheduling a visitor to their laboratory at AT&T Bell Labs (1994).

Kautz, Selman, and Coen have identified the following issues as important for successful deployment of agents: reliability, security, and ease-of-use. Users should be able to assume that the surrogate bots are reliable and predictable, and human users should remain in ultimate control.

They approach the problem in a bottom-up fashion by first identifying specific tasks that are both feasible using current technology and also truly useful to the everyday users. After this, a set of software surrogate bots are designed, implemented, and tested with real users.

Visitor Scheduling Bots

The job of scheduling visitors is quite routine, but it consumes a substantial amount of the host's time. The normal sequence of tasks are as follows:

1. Announce the upcoming visit by e-mail.

2. Collect responses from people who would like to meet with the visitor.

3. Put together a schedule that satisfies as many constraints as possible.

4. Send out the schedule to participants.

5. Possibly reschedule people at the last minute due to unforeseen events.

In their agent system, a specialized surrogate bot, the *visitorbot,* handles the visitor scheduling. For each individual user, there is a *userbot* whose job

is to mediate communications between the human owner and the visitorbot. Figure 1.4 shows the user-interface created by a userbot in response to a message from the visitorbot.

The task-specific visitorbot specifies what information needs to be transferred or obtained but not how the communication should take place. It is the responsibility of each userbot to consider its owner's preferences and to accordingly determine the preferred mode of communication: graphics, voice, fax, or e-mail.

The userbot has its own graphical window containing buttons the user can press to change the preferred mode of communication, or to suspend processing of messages until a later time. The window also contains buttons labeled with all the different *taskbots* known to the userbot. When the user presses one of these buttons, the userbot sends a help request message to the appropriate taskbot, thereby initiating an interaction between the user and the selected taskbot.

Internet Softbots

Oren Etzioni and Daniel Weld, both professors at the University of Washington at Seattle, have the long term goal of developing an agent-based interface that enables naive users to locate, monitor, and transmit information across the net. For the past three years, they have led the Internet Softbot project, which focuses on the problems of designing and building a software robot capable of effectively exploring the Internet (1994).

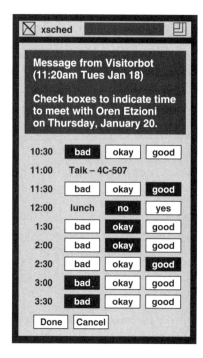

Figure 1.4

A window pops up to show a message from visitorbot.

The Internet Softbot uses a Unix shell and the World Wide Web to interact with a wide range of Internet resources. Softbot sensors are analogous to whiskers on a physical insect robot, and include Internet facilities such as archie, gopher, netfind, and others. Softbot effectors are analogous to the mechanical arms and legs on a physical robot, and include ftp, telnet, mail, and numerous file manipulation commands. The softbot is designed to incorporate new sensor and effector facilities into its repertoire of Internet-based tools as they become available.

According to Etzioni and Weld, the softbot supports a qualitatively different kind of human-computer interface. In addition to simply allowing the user to interact with the computer, the softbot behaves like an intelligent personal assistant. The user can make a high-level request, and the softbot uses search, inference, and knowledge to determine how to satisfy the request. Furthermore, the softbot is designed to be robust enough that it can tolerate and recover from ambiguity, omissions, and errors in human requests.

Softbot Planner

The planning component of softbot is called the *softbot planner*. It takes as input a logical expression which describes the user's goal in the form of a sentence in first-order predicate logic. For users unfamiliar with logical expressions, a graphical fill-in form that automatically translates to a softbot goal is available.

After searching a library of *action schemata* describing available information sources, databases, utilities, and software commands, a sequence of actions to achieve the goal is then generated. The softbot planner is able to decompose complex goal expressions into simpler components and solve them with divide-and-conquer techniques. Interactions between subgoals, which are usually problematic, are automatically detected and resolved.

The softbot planner relies on a logical model of the available Internet resources that tells it how these resources can be invoked or accessed, as well as the effect of doing so. Unlike traditional programs and scripts which are committed to a rigid flow of control determined by the programmer when the program was coded, the softbot planner synthesizes plans on demand when the program is run, based upon the user's goal. In the words of Etzioni and Weld, a softbot "is worth a thousand shell scripts."

Example Softbot Usage

With the Internet Softbot, for example, a user can quickly perform the task of "sending the budget memos to Mitchell at CMU" with ease (see fig. 1.5).

The softbot first disambiguates the reference to Mitchell at CMU by executing the command `finger mitchell@cmu.edu` and recording who the various Mitchells are at CMU. If necessary, it prompts the user to select the intended recipient. If it decides to send the memos, the softbot determines the correct e-mail address and reasons about the document format (for example, postscript if it contains figures and LaTeX source otherwise). Furthermore, if Mitchell is out of town (for example, as notified by reply e-mail from the "vacation" program), or if the memos are confidential (such as encrypted), it ensures delivery in a timely and secure manner.

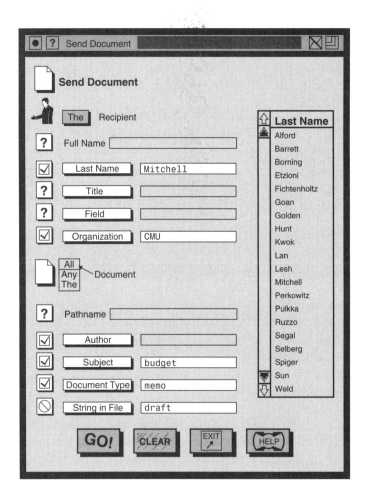

Figure 1.5

Softbot request form for sending a document.

Agents and Coordination

Agents can also facilitate work and coordinate tasks among people, machines, and other agents. This section describes conference-support agents such as GDS and M, and communicative agents based upon an agent communication language (ACL). The coordination, collaboration, and communication aspects of agents are emphasized.

Conference-Support Agents

Researchers at LUTCHI Research Centre at Loughborough University of Technology in England demonstrate that group support agents are viable for design tasks (ECJS 1994). They have constructed a Geographic Decision System (GDS) to provide multi-agent group support to design conferences.

GDS has a separation of function, which is achieved by partitioning the system into distinct components. A central communication bus serves as the backbone of the system, attached to which are the per-user presentation layers and dialog controllers, plus one of each of the following system-wide agents:

→ Conference agent

→ Group agent

→ Application agent

→ User agent

→ Floor agent

The *conference agent* controls initialization of the system. It interacts with the person who starts the conference to learn about the other participants, their locations, and any applications to be shared. A presentation layer and a dialog controller are then created for each participant. The conference agent next invokes other agents and starts the appropriate applications along with their respective application interface modules. Throughout the conference, the conference agent allows newcomers to join, members to leave, and different applications to be shared.

A separate *group agent* supports the customization of group options. It might be undesirable, for example, that every participant does have the ability to end the conference.

The *application agent* provides external software application services to the group. An example of such an external software system could be the geographic information system, which might be useful to the group in the design of road systems.

The application agent can intercept and modify messages from the dialog controllers to the application interface module by snooping on the communication bus.

The *user agent* intercepts all messages on the communication bus, which allows it to have master control of interaction with users. In other words, the user agent enables different members of the group to view data from different vantage points and to interact with it, and with one another, in different styles.

The *floor agent* works with the user agent to ensure that only one participant can enter data at a time. The floor agent understands different floor policies, such as moderated, first-come, or round-robin, and offers the capability to change the floor policy as needed.

Integrated Agents

Doug Riecken, a researcher from the AT&T Bell Laboratories, takes the position that it takes many integrated agents to create a software assistant (1994). In such an approach, many different reasoning processes, called a "society of agents," are integrated to realize a software assistant capable of performing a broad range of tasks. Riecken's efforts have resulted in the realization of *M*, a software assistant that helps the user classify, index, store, retrieve, explain, and present information in a desktop multimedia conferencing environment.

M's Architectural Design

M's architectural design is based upon the theory of integrating a variety of reasoning processes, or

agents, to form an intelligent assistant. Influenced by AI pioneer Marvin Minsky's "society of mind" theory (1985), M is built to accommodate the following types of reasoning capabilities:

→ Spatial (based upon properties of space)

→ Structural (based upon relationships between parts of some object)

→ Functional (based upon the functional purpose of some object)

→ Temporal (based upon properties related to time)

→ Causal (based upon events, actions, and state changes in objects)

→ Explanation-based (explanation of a situation through first principles)

→ Case-based (solving new problem by analogy of stored solutions to old ones)

M accomodates these capabilities by integrating various subsystem components, including a spreading activation semantic network for realizing K-lines/polynemes, a rule-based system, a set of blackboards for realizing transframes and pronomes, a scripting system, a history logfile system, and an I/O system.

M's Operation

M was used at the AT&T Bell Labs within a virtual meeting room that supports multimedia desktop conferencing. Participants collaborate using pen-based computers and with voice through telephones. The goal of the software assistant is to classify and index the changing state of the virtual meeting room.

In this virtual place, each user is supported by a personalized assistant, and the world is composed of electronic documents, electronic ink, images, markers, white boards, copiers, staplers, and so on. The assistants attempt to recognize and define relationships among objects based upon actions applied by the user to the world and the resulting new states of the world.

From observing that a user annotates two adjacent documents by drawing a circle to enclose them together, for example, M can infer and explain a plausible relationship between the two documents. Essentially, M applies the following reasoning capabilities:

→ Spatial reasoning to find out about the nearness of the two documents and the circle

→ Structural and functional reasoning about the circle enclosing two documents

→ Causal reasoning about the action of enclosing objects.

Riecken's underlying thesis is that an assistant for classifying and explaining actions applied to objects within a dynamic world should be functionally effective if it can simultaneously generate and test multiple domain theories in relation to a given goal.

When an event occurs, such as an individual annotating a document or moving a piece of paper, M's I/O system records who did what and archives it as an input record for processing. M attempts to generate and maintain simultaneous theories of the world by using a set of "blackboards" to which emerging theories of the world are posted. Thus, each blackboard serves as the working area to

expand and improve a given theory, and the set of blackboards are ranked based upon the strength of each theory.

According to Riecken, the integrated agents in M make possible a new framework for users to work together electronically. M improves the performance of participants in a virtual meeting room by allowing for added expressiveness while minimizing many computer-related actions.

Communicative Agents

Professor Michael Genesereth and his graduate student Steven Ketchpel at Stanford University have examined the practical issues of software interoperation from the viewpoint of an agent software architecture (GK 1994). They have coined the term *agent-based software engineering* to describe the approach of writing software applications as components called software agents.

These *software agents* interoperate by exchanging messages in a universally mandated agent communication language. Software agents differ from objects in object-oriented programming in that the meaning of an agent message is based upon a common language with agent-independent semantics, whereas the meaning of an object message can vary from one object to another.

Genesereth and Ketchpel have identified the following three issues that need to be addressed within the context of agent-based software engineering:

➜ What is an appropriate agent communication language?

➜ What is the best way to build agents capable of communicating in this language?

➜ What communication architectures are conducive to cooperation?

Agent Communication Language

Two popular approaches are used to design an agent communication language: a procedural approach or a declarative approach. In the procedural approach, communication can be thought of as the exchange of procedural directives. Individual commands, as well as entire programs, can be transmitted and executed at the recipient's end. Scripting languages, such as TCL, Apple Events, and Telescript, are based upon the procedural approach.

In the declarative approach, communication can be thought of as an exchange of declarative statements, such as definitions, assertions, or assumptions. The declarative approach, in the form of Agent Communication Language (ACL), was chosen by Genesereth and Ketchpel for their agent-based software engineering.

ACL was designed by researchers in the ARPA Knowledge Sharing Effort (NFFGPSS 1991). ACL is made up of three parts: a vocabulary, an inner language called Knowledge Interchange Format (KIF), and an outer language called Knowledge Query and Manipulation Language (KQML).

The vocabulary of ACL is listed in a large and open-ended dictionary of words appropriate for common application areas (Gruber 1991). KIF is a prefix version of first-order predicate calculus, capable of encoding simple data, constraints, rules, and quantified expressions, among other things. KQML is a

linguistic layer above KIF that provides contextual information for more efficient communications.

With a clear definition of the ACL, it is straightforward to write agent programs that abide by certain behavioral constraints in order to work together correctly. For the large number of existing legacy software, however, Genesereth and Ketchpel offer the following three approaches to agentification:

→ Implement a *transducer*, which mediates between an existing program and other agents.

→ Design a *wrapper* around an existing program to enable it to speak ACL.

→ Rewrite the original program, as a last resort.

Agent Communication Architecture

Several architectures have been proposed for organizing agents to enhance collaboration. In the *contract-net approach* (DS 1983), agents in need of services distribute requests for proposals to other agents, who evaluate those requests and submit bids to the originating agents. The originators use the bids in deciding to whom to award contracts.

In the *specification sharing approach*, agents advertise their individual capabilities and needs. This information is then used to coordinate agent activities.

Finally, in the *federated system approach*, agents do not communicate directly with one another but instead rely on system programs called *facilitators* to handle all communications with other agents (see fig. 1.6).

Already, agent architecture has been put to use in concurrent engineering for application-level interoperation, as reported by Cutkosky (1993). The long-range vision for agent technology, according to Genesereth and Ketchpel, is one in which any system can interoperate with any other system without the intervention of human users or their programmers.

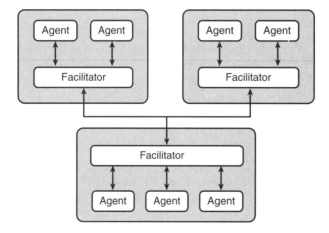

Figure 1.6

Federation of agents.

Agents and Knowledge

The knowledge component of agents serves many useful functions. This section discusses how agents can teach people new programming skills, learn about the calendar scheduling habits of human users, reason with common sense, and derive world knowledge from sensing the surrounding physical environment.

Teaching Agents

Ted Selker, manager of User Systems Ergonomics Research at IBM's Almaden Research Center, views agents as computer programs that simulate a human relationship. According to Selker, there can be two types of agents.

An *assistant-style agent* is one that builds a relationship with the user through a private interface. Using this interface, the agent can understand the user's needs to perform formerly complex or unknown tasks with computer-created macros. An *advisory-style agent*, on the other hand, is one that builds a user relationship with the explicit goal of educating the user.

Selker has built an advisory-style teaching agent called Cognitive Adaptive Computer Help (COACH) that helps users learn to program in the Lisp programming language (1994).

The COACH Agent

To use a computer language effectively, a student needs to understand both its syntax and its semantics.

The *syntax* includes language statements, as well as tokens such as keywords and acceptable variable names in Lisp. The syntax definition is used as a way to classify user progress and to guide instruction.

The *semantics* of the language includes learnable concepts in Lisp such as evaluation, iteration, stored variables, and so on. In addition, learnable concepts, all of which must be mastered to do a specific task, are further organized by COACH into basic sets. The COACH system also includes examples of these learnable concepts and a model of the particular student's understanding and ability to use each one. COACH has the user-interface shown in figure 1.7.

COACH watches the user's actions in order to build an adaptive user model of the user's experience and expertise. While the user is working on a task, aspects of the user's successes and failures are recorded. The system is proactive in that it can anticipate user needs and is capable of presenting help before it is requested. Both the user and the system can initiate help in a mixed-initiative interaction.

Several representations of language knowledge work together in COACH to create help for the user:

→ Subject frames, which consist of knowledge about the domain

→ Adaptive frames, which hold the recording of user experience relative to a domain

→ Presentation rule sets, which embody a model of teaching

→ A multi-level parser, which is the syntax definition of the domain

The defined network of relationships between the domain to be learned, the user's actions, and the state of the user model, forms the basis for selecting user help. The system chooses when to use example, description, and syntax style help depending upon the levels of user expertise, such as novice, intermediate, professional, or expert.

Field-Testing COACH

To test the hypothesis that an adaptive coaching paradigm improves productivity, a version of COACH without the automatic help and adaptiveness was created.

In a usability study conducted by Selker involving 19 programmers with no prior Lisp experience, users of the adaptive system wrote five times as many Lisp functions as those of the nonadaptive one. During the course, users of the adaptive system liked Lisp more than the other group, consulted the help screen more often, and rated COACH higher as a learning environment. Finally, at the end of the course, only 11 percent of the students from the adaptive group, as compared to a full two-thirds of students from the nonadaptive group, indicated they felt uncomfortable with Lisp (Selker 1994).

An adaptive teaching scenario concentrates on the user's individual needs by moving students toward an apprenticeship or learn-while-doing approach and away from syllabus-style classroom experience. An adaptive teaching paradigm is found to improve productivity.

The COACH system demonstrates that agent technology can successfully work in place of a human coach to give personalized instruction while a student is actually working out solutions.

Learning Agents

Researchers at Carnegie Mellon University (CMU), Mitchell, Caruana, Freitag, McDermott, and Zabowski, believe that machine learning plays an important role in future personal software assistants. They imagine a future where knowledge-based assistants "operate across the network as a kind of software secretary, providing services for work and home such as paying bills, making travel arrangements, submitting purchase orders, and locating information in electronic libraries" (MCFMZ 1994).

The Calendar Apprentice

The success of these agents will depend on knowing and learning about the particular user's habits and goals, and tailoring to them accordingly. The CMU researchers have built a calendar manager called Calendar Apprentice (CAP), which learns its user's scheduling preferences from experience—it is a learning apprentice that assists the user in managing a meeting calendar.

CAP provides an interactive editing and e-mail interface to an online calendar, and is capable of giving customized scheduling advice to each user. In approximately five user-years of experience (one user-year is equivalent to one user using CAP for one year), CAP has learned an evolving set of several thousand rules that characterize scheduling preferences for each of its users (JDMMZ 1991; DBMMZ 1992; MCFMZ 1994).

Traditionally, many programs provide simple parameters enabling users to explicitly customize the program's behavior. Text editors, for example, enable users to set default font types and sizes, while desktop window managers enable users to choose the default placement of icons and windows.

According to the CMU researchers, however, there are limits to this approach. Customizing an e-mail sorter to accommodate one's personal notion of an urgent message, for example, requires detailed articulation of a fairly subtle concept. Furthermore, even if users are willing to initially customize their assistants, they might be unwilling to continually update this knowledge. A message about a particular business contract, for example, might be quite urgent before an approaching deadline, but not necessarily as urgent after the deadline.

The approach adopted in CAP can be summarized as follows:

→ Provide a convenient interface (see fig. 1.8) that enables the user to perform the task—an editing and e-mail interface to an online calendar, for example.

→ Treat each user interaction as a training example of the user's habits. Each meeting scheduled by the user reflects preference for the duration, time, location, and so on, of this type of meeting.

→ Learn general regularities from this training data and use this learned knowledge to increase the services offered. An assistant could, for example, provide interactive advice to the user or offer to negotiate specific meetings on the user's behalf.

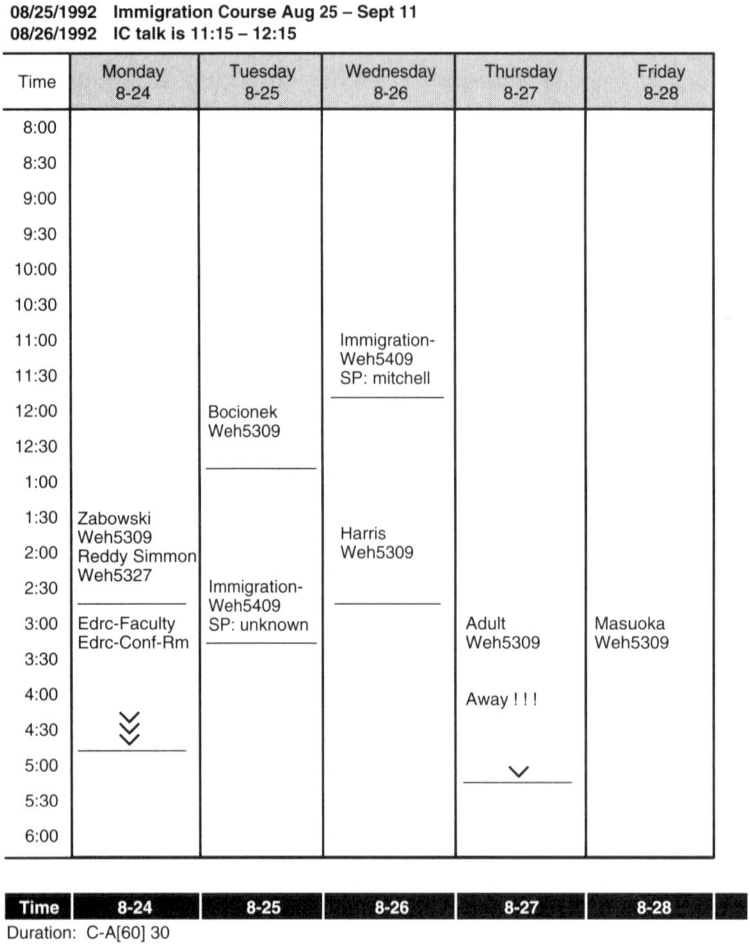

Time	Monday 8-24	Tuesday 8-25	Wednesday 8-26	Thursday 8-27	Friday 8-28
08/25/1992 Immigration Course Aug 25 – Sept 11					
08/26/1992 IC talk is 11:15 – 12:15					

08/25/1992 Immigration Course Aug 25 – Sept 11
08/26/1992 IC talk is 11:15 – 12:15

Time	Monday 8-24	Tuesday 8-25	Wednesday 8-26	Thursday 8-27	Friday 8-28
8:00					
8:30					
9:00					
9:30					
10:00					
10:30					
11:00			Immigration-Weh5409 SP: mitchell		
11:30					
12:00		Bocionek Weh5309			
12:30					
1:00					
1:30	Zabowski Weh5309		Harris Weh5309		
2:00	Reddy Simmon Weh5327				
2:30		Immigration-Weh5409 SP: unknown			
3:00	Edrc-Faculty Edrc-Conf-Rm			Adult Weh5309	Masuoka Weh5309
3:30					
4:00				Away ! ! !	
4:30					
5:00					
5:30					
6:00					

Time	8-24	8-25	8-26	8-27	8-28	

Duration: C-A[60] 30

Figure 1.8

The Calendar Apprentice user interface.

CAP Functionality

With CAP, users can edit the calendar by adding, deleting, moving, copying, and annotating meetings, and they can mark various calendar events as either tentative or confirmed. Other CAP commands instruct CAP to send e-mail meeting invitations or meeting reminders to the attendees as appropriate.

As time goes on, CAP learns the scheduling preferences of its user, and evolves gradually from a passive editing interface to a knowledgeable assistant capable of interacting more intelligently with the user and offloading the work of meeting negotiation from the user.

Currently, CAP learns rules that enable it to suggest the meeting duration, location, time, and date.

Each night, CAP automatically runs a learning algorithm to refine the set of rules it will use to provide advice on the following day. The learning algorithm is similar to ID3 (Quinlan 1986), which learns a decision tree from the most recent training data.

A *decision tree* organizes the problem of classifying an object into a series of questions about the object. Calendar meetings, for example, can be classified according to meeting location and based upon various "feature tests" at branch points. These feature tests can ask whether it is lunchtime or not (dining hall or conference room), as well as the attendee's department (EE building or CS building).

Field-Testing CAP

Results from field testing CAP within a small academic community at Carnegie Mellon University indicate that it is indeed possible for the system to learn rules that characterize scheduling preferences. The accuracy of learned advice varies significantly from feature to feature, and from user to user. It also is observed that the accuracy of CAP varies over time, reflecting the dynamic nature of the domain and the need for updating user-specific scheduling preferences. In particular, the periods of poorest performance correlate strongly with the semester boundaries in the academic year—when there are permanent scheduling changes.

Based upon CAP's performances, its creators at CMU conclude that "while rules learned by CAP are useful for providing interactive advice to be approved or overriden by the user, they are not sufficiently accurate to support autonomous negotiation of all meetings by the agent on the user's behalf" (MCFMZ 1994).

Rather than total automation of user workload, the CMU researchers foresee that a more likely scenario for practical software agents of the future is one of shared responsibility. Only the subset of situations for which the agent has high confidence will be handled autonomously, while difficult cases will always be referred to the user.

Common-Sense Agents

Douglas Lenat, principal scientist at Microelectronic and Computer Corporation (MCC), believes that agents need some common corpus of shared knowledge in order to communicate. According to Lenat, the past 20 years have witnessed numerous successes in which knowledge-based systems have been constructed and deployed. Amidst all these successes, however, there is constant failure as well. These systems cannot share knowledge and pool together their expertise and work together synergistically. In other words, these systems were *brittle* in the face of unanticipated situations (LGPPS 1990).

Lenat believes the primary impediment to achieving interesting agent behavior is lack of knowledge. He reasons that we would not need to work as hard to come up with clever algorithms, data structures, and architectures if we had a large database of knowledge to fall back on.

Backed by a 10-year, 25 million dollar grant in the Cyc project (as in enCYClopedia) that started in 1984, Lenat is boldly pioneering an attempt to assemble a massive knowledge base (on the order of tens of millions of axioms) spanning human consensus knowledge (LGPPS 1990; GL 1994).

Second Paradigm of Software Agents

In Lenat's view, there are two contrasting paradigms for software agents today. In the first paradigm, competence emerges from a large number of relatively simple agents integrated by some cleverly engineered architecture. An example of this first paradigm is SOAR (LNR 1987), whose forerunners were the early production systems like OPS5 (BFKM 1985).

In the second paradigm, competence emerges from the aggregate system possessing a large amount of useful knowledge. For real world tasks, this involves a dauntingly large amount of what might be called common-sense knowledge. In this second paradigm, the architecture is relatively unimportant. The archetype of this paradigm is Cyc, and its forerunners were the early expert systems.

The Cyc project intends to test seriously the second paradigm of software agents. Much of the constituent common-sense knowledge includes simple notions of time, space, causality, and events; human capabilities, limitations, goals, decision-making strategies, and emotions; familiarity with art, history, literature, and current affairs; and so forth.

The level of shared knowledge correlates directly to tasks performed by the intelligent agents. To be practical, Cyc has adopted the following maxim: "Share most of the meaning of most of the terms, most of the time" (GL 1994).

But how much shared knowledge is enough? The Cyc research so far seems to suggest that even relatively narrow tasks require a large fraction of common-sense knowledge to be shared. But fortunately, a wide range of tasks can use this same large body of shared knowledge.

Common Sense Knowledge in CYC

Lenat's approach is to express common-sense knowledge in a frame-based language (LGPPS 1990). The common-sense knowledge is represented by a more expressive predicate calculus (also called first-order logic) framework, which provides the following enhanced features:

→ Defaults representation (allowing one to talk about unstated facts)

→ Reification (allowing one to talk about propositions in the knowledge base)

→ Reflection (allowing one to talk about the act of working on some problem)

In order to answer most queries, Cyc has to do some sophisticated inference. Rather than relying upon a single general mechanism (such as resolution) for problem solving, Cyc makes extensive use of specialized mechanisms that employ different algorithms and data structures for frequently used classes of inferences.

The bulk of the effort in building the knowledge base involves identifying, formalizing, and entering microtheories of various topics such as money, buying, shopping, and so on. Cyc researchers follow a process that begins with a statement, in English, of the theory. To achieve an axiomatization of the theory, the necessary Cyc concepts are identified and made precise. To test whether the topic has been adequately covered, stories dealing with the topic are represented in Cyc. Questions that a human should be able to answer after reading the story are then posed to Cyc.

Within the next two years, Lenat expects that most knowledge entry will take place by semiautomated

natural language understanding. Humans will then be able to "take the role of tutors rather than brain surgeons" in feeding knowledge to Cyc (GL 1994).

Physical Agents

Rodney Brooks, an associate professor with the MIT Artificial Intelligence Laboratory, believes in approaching intelligence in an incremental manner, with strict reliance on robots interfacing to the real world through perception and action at every step along the way.

Brooks offers his "physical grounding hypothesis," which states that to build a system that is intelligent, it is necessary to have its representation directly based upon the physical world. He observes that the real world is its own best model. In other words, the real world is always up to date and always contains every detail there is to be known. He believes that the trick is for autonomous agents in the form of physical robots to sense it appropriately and often enough.

The traditional notion of intelligent systems held by AI workers has been that of a central system, with perceptual modules as inputs and action modules as outputs. The traditional methodology decomposes intelligence into functional units whose combinations provide overall system behavior.

Brooks argues that "human-level intelligence is too complex and too little understood to be correctly decomposed into the right subpieces at the moment and that, even if we knew the subpieces, we still would not know the right interfaces between them."

Brooks prefers an alternative decomposition of an intelligent system along the orthogonal directions of behavior-generating modules, each of which individually connects sensing to action, without going through a central information processor. The advantage of this approach is that it gives an incremental path from very simple systems to complex autonomous intelligent systems. Furthermore, the coexistence and cooperation of these behavior-generating modules sets the stage for the emergence of more complex behaviors.

Brooks' research approach has resulted in a successful series of mobile robots with insect-level intelligence that operate without supervision in standard office environments (Brooks 1990, 1991).

The Genghis Robot

An example of Brook's mobile robots is Genghis, a six-legged robot weighing one kg that walks under Brooks' *subsumption architecture* and has a highly distributed control system (1989). The robot can successfully walk over rough terrain. Genghis is made up of 12 motors, 12 force sensors, six pyroelectric sensors, one inclinometer, and two whiskers. Genghis also is capable of following certain moving objects, such as human beings, using its pyroelectric sensors.

Genghis has no central control system. Instead, a subsumption architecture enables successive layers of behavior-generating modules to implement various aspects of Genghis' walking behavior. Genghis uses force measurements to comply with rough terrain and to lift its feet over obstacles, and it uses inclinometer measurements to selectively inhibit rough terrain compliance when appropriate. It uses whiskers to lift feet over obstacles and uses the directionality of infrared radiation to modulate the backswing of particular leg sets so that it follows a moving source of radiation.

The resulting control system in Genghis is elegant in its simplicity. It directly implements walking through very many tight couplings of sensors to actuators, without a centralized information processor. Genghis' capability to walk is thus an emergent behavior derived from the interaction of many diverse system components without the supervision of a centralized control system.

Agents and Creativity

Agents can be creative too. This section explores how agents can offer creative ideas in architectural styles, jazz music, mathematics, and mechanical shape design. Agents also can perform automated configuration design from a catalog of physical parts.

Creative Agents

Margaret Boden, a professor at the University of Sussex's School of Cognitive and Computing Sciences, has investigated the practical question of whether agent systems might help further human creativity (1994). She has examined how creativity in its various forms might be scientifically understood in terms of the computational resources involved.

Creativity involves coming up with something novel, new, and different. This new idea, in order to be interesting, must be intelligible. No matter how different the new idea is, it must be understood in terms of what was already known before. The potential role of agents as they relate to creativity includes suggesting, identifying, or even evaluating differences between familiar ideas and novel ones.

According to Boden, not all creativity can be understood as a novel combination of familiar ideas. Creative ideas are present in architecture, musical compositions, literary genres, mathematical theorems, and engineering inventions. Some creative ideas actually help open up a whole new set of conceptual spaces previously unthought of. This means that when exploring the implications of radical scientific theories or of new musical genres, simple combination juggling would not cut it. A structured, disciplined, and sometimes even systematic search for the promised meanings is necessary.

One way to start thinking about the whole enterprise of creativity is to consider the notion of conceptual spaces. A *conceptual space* is a mental terrain, a style of thinking (Boden 1991). It is defined by a set of constraints demarcating the boundaries and dimensions of the relevant domain. Many creative achievements result from exploring conceptual spaces in systematic and imaginative ways. Agents can help map, explore, and perhaps even guide in the transformation of conceptual spaces.

Architectural Styles

In the architectural domain, for example, computational work on architectural styles suggests some ways in which agents might help a human architect. The architectural style of Frank Lloyd Wright's Prairie House can be captured in a computer program (HF 1992). Similarly, the stylistic essence of a Palladian villa (see fig. 1.9) can be explicitly described with a computationally inspired "space grammar" that begins with a rectangle from which internal rectangles are recursively generated according to some prescribed rules (KE 1981). This process is illustrated in figure 1.10.

Figure 1.9

Palladian villa floorplan.

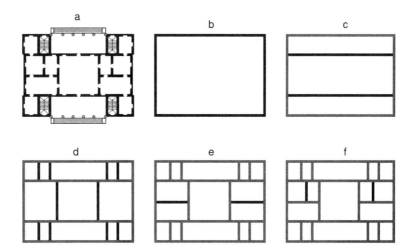

For a human architect or an architectural student who has little experience working on a particular architectural genre, an agent's timely advice or forbiddance on a piece of substructure design is especially valuable.

Jazz Dimensions

After the conceptual space of a specific domain is mapped, agents can explore it in interesting ways. In the jazz domain, for example, there are computer programs that help people improvise jazz (Hodgson 1990; Waugh 1992). These programs understand the various dimensions of the jazz musical space and can travel through it in many ways. If left to wander through the space by themselves, these programs improvise—on a given melody, harmony, and rhythm—by making random choices along many dimensions simultaneously. Working in this fashion, these programs often develop novel musical ideas that the professional jazz musicians find interesting and might want to explore further.

Mathematical Spaces

Agents can also guide in the transformation of conceptual spaces in surprising ways. The most well known example can be found in Douglas Lenat's program, Automatic Mathematician, whose transformations of the space of heuristics resulted in the discovery of two previously unknown theorems about prime numbers (1983).

Design Shapes

Researchers from the LUTCHI Research Centre at Loughborough University of Technology in England have studied how agents can assist design teams by providing support for *emergence*, a significant feature of the creative design process.

In particular, they have investigated the support of shape emergence in design communication, as well as how it can be handled by agents using pattern recognition methods. An emergent form displays characteristics not present in its source. The researchers' favorite example is the radical

transformation of the bicycle frame concept in the LotusSport bicycle, which uses a single-unit carbon fiber monocoque construction instead of the conventional steel-tube diamond frame (ECJS 1994).

Many psychological processes are involved in creative thinking, from combinational juxtaposition to the more complex exploratory-transformational reasoning to the highly unstructured emergent thinking. As we begin to understand more about the underlying computational aspects of such thought processes, we will be better equipped to build agents that could assist humans across a broader range of creative endeavours.

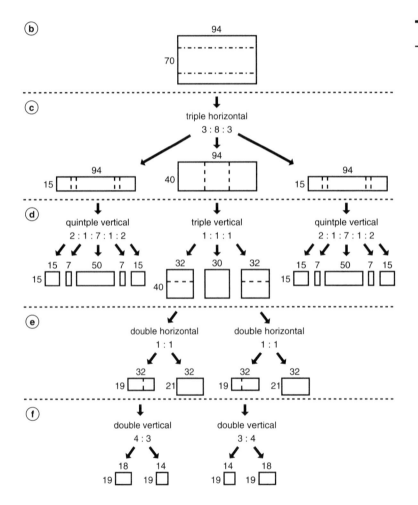

Automated Design Agents

Professor Bill Birmingham and graduate student Tim Darr of the University of Michigan have experimented with an approach of automated design-space exploration using the Automated Catalog-Design Service (ACDS) system (DB 1992; BDDWW 1993).

ACDS performs configuration design, where an artifact is designed by selecting parts from a catalog. The designer needs only to provide a high-level description of the design, including the functions to be performed, the interconnections of the components, and their specifications. In ACDS, the entire design space is reduced through a series of pruning operations until a set of feasible designs result.

ACDS is organized as a loosely-coupled network of different kinds of agents. It can self-organize based upon design specifications, such as the following:

→ Catalog agents

→ System agents

→ Constraint agents

Catalog Agents

Each catalog agent represents a set of physical parts. ACDS can support thousands of catalog agents, each of which could be the product line of a component manufacturer. Catalog agents are able to choose whether to participate in a particular design.

System Agents

The system agent provides a graphical interface that enables the user to specify the design for presentation to the ACDS network. The system agent translates the high-level design specifications into the network's representation and broadcasts it to relevant agents. These design specifications are needed for creating any necessary constraint agents for the design.

Constraint Agents

Constraint agents maintain consistency throughout the network by enforcing design constraints. Each constraint agent ensures that the evolving design space conforms to the constraint it represents when evaluating proposed bids of their parts from catalog agents. Constraint agents can thus direct the pruning of part catalogs to satisfy any violated constraints. This process of removing infeasible parts, bidding, and pruning continues until all constraints are satisfied or a determination is made that no solutions exist.

Agents and Emotion

Though it might seem surprising at first, agents can have "emotions," too. This section explores the role of emotions in agents and discusses how emotion can help animate faceless software agents into cartoon-like effable characters (but not to the extent of *anthropomorphizing* them to human-level intelligence and capabilities), making them more life-like.

Professor Joseph Bates of Carnegie Mellon University thinks emotions play an important role in the construction of believable agents (1994). He describes a believable agent not as one that has an honest or reliable character, but as one that provides an illusion of life in convincing ways so the audience wants to believe the agent is real.

According to Bates, believable agents are the interactive analog of believable characters discussed in the arts of fiction-writing and film-making. Emotion is the primary means of achieving this believability. An agent with demonstrated emotions helps people understand that the character really cares about its surrounding environment and that it truly has desires.

Art of Animation

Animation artists made great strides in advancing the state of the animation arts by constructing believable characters following the introduction of Disney's Mickey Mouse in the 1930's. Animation artists spoke of building characters "whose adventures and misfortunes make people laugh—and even cry" (TJ 1981).

According to Thomas and Johnson, two of Disney's nine earliest animators, "there is a special ingredient in (the arts of) animation that produces drawings that appear to think and make decisions and act of their own volition; it is what creates the illusion of life" (TJ 1981).

Artificial Intelligence

Many researchers in artificial intelligence (AI) have long sought to build robots or agents that seem to think, feel, and live. In addressing the 1985 American Association of Artificial Intelligence, Woody Bledsoe (1986), an AI pioneer at the University of Texas at Austin, spoke of his continuing dream to build a computer friend that could "understand, act, autonomously think, learn, enjoy, hate."

The AI researchers, in their search for the essential qualities of humanity, emphasize the computational aspects of re-creating capabilities such as reasoning, learning, and problem-solving on the computer. On the other hand, animation artists seek to reproduce life forms from nothing more than simple line drawings, inks, and celluloids that move frame by frame. The practical requirements of producing hundreds of thousands of such drawings forced animators to use extremely simple imageries, and to seek and abstract precisely that which is crucial.

Bates argued that, as a result, although the scientists might have been more effective in re-creating life with the help of a computer, it is the artists who have come closest to capturing the essence of humanity. The insights of character animators in their artistic inquiry might thus be key to building computational models of interactive agents that are believable.

The Oz Project

The Oz Project at Carnegie Mellon University is an experiment in how the work of programmers and animators could be combined to create visible, human-like entities with which humans could eventually work or play.

Bates is leading the Oz Project group to build a small, simulated world containing several real-time, interactive, self-animating creatures called Woggles.

The Woggles have names like Bear, Shrimp, and Wolf. As shown in figure 1.11, each Woggle is animated as a 3D oval or egg-shaped spherical entity with a pair of eyes, using the principles of traditional animation. At each moment, several Woggles are often seen moving, jumping, and gesturing socially on the screen.

Figure 1.11

Woggles have names like Bear, Shrimp, and Wolf.

In using emotions to construct believable agents, the Oz Project researchers needed to devise an internal representation of emotion inside the agent that was consistent with the appearance of its definite emotional state. The researchers developed a goal-directed, behavior-based architecture for action (Brooks 1986; LB 1983; Maes 1989). This action architecture is then coupled with a module for generating, representing, and expressing emotion (OCC 1988; BLR 1992).

The action system uses a minimalist notion of goals to manipulate a dynamically changing set of behaviors. The agents appraise surrounding events that occur with respect to their goals. This enables an agent to arrive at a clearly defined emotional state and to produce a definite emotional reaction to the event.

When a Woggle fails to reach an important goal, for example, and thinks the failure was caused by the action of another Woggle, it enters the angry state. In Woggles, each emotion is mapped in a personality-specific way to a behavioral feature of the Woggle. In this way, the emotional state of each Woggle can be made externally visible through its characteristic behaviors. In a fear state, for example, a Woggle whose fear is mapped to the aggressive feature behaves accordingly.

The believability of an interactive agent depends on the appearance of reactivity, emotions, goals, and situated social competence, among other things. In order to present a convincing illusion of life in agents, Bates suggests AI researchers should attempt a methodological emphasis on the emotional dimension of agents.

Agents and Programming

The programming aspects of agents are an important consideration, too. This section describes not so much the nuts and bolts of agent programming with traditional programming languages, but more the higher-level programming support offered for programming agents. KidSim handles agent programming without the use of a programming language, and Oasis offers explicit support for programming with distributed agents on a network of machines.

KidSim

David Smith, Allen Cypher, and Jim Spohrer from Apple Computer's Advanced Technology Group view the question of how to instruct agents as an end-user programming problem, currently an unsolved one in computer science. They believe computer scientists have not made programming easy enough for most people. They cite as evidence the fact that only a tiny fraction of computer users are able to program, although most can follow a recipe, give directions, make up stories, or plan trips—mental activities similar to those involved in programming (1994).

After observing that most computer users are proficient with some kind of editor or editor-like applications (such as drawing packages or painting programs), Smith, Cypher, and Spohrer decided to make programming as easy as editing. They have developed KidSim, for "Kids' Simulations," which is a toolkit that enables children to build symbolic simulations. The key idea in KidSim is the way in which children specify the behavior of agents, accomplished by combining two powerful techniques—graphical rewrite rules and programming by demonstration—into KidSim to improve the end-user's ability to program agents (SCS 1994).

Simulation Toolkit

In KidSim, kids can modify the programming of existing simulation objects and define new ones from scratch. A KidSim simulation primarily consists of the following components:

→ A game board, divided into finite squares like a checkerboard

→ A clock, whose time is divided into discrete (as versus continuous) ticks

→ One or more simulation objects representing agents

→ A copy box, the source of new simulation objects

→ A rule editor, for defining and modifying rules

The game board represents the simulation microworld. The clock starts and stops a simulation. The clock can be run backward to undo changes, encouraging kids to experiment and take chances. The copy box is a container that automatically makes copies of simulation objects placed inside it.

In KidSim, the active objects in simulations are agents. During each clock tick, agents move around on the game board and interact with one another. Agents have their own visual appearance, characteristic properties (such as name, age, height, hunger, fear, and so on) and rules of behavior.

Graphical Rewrite Rules

The behaviors of agents are specified with graphical rewrite rules using the rule editor. A *graphical rewrite rule* is a transformation of a game board region from one state to another. It consists of a "before" part and an "after" part. Each part is a small scene that might occur during the simulation run. A rule matches if its "before" part is the same as some area of the game board at some moment in time. When a rule matches, KidSim transforms the corresponding region of the game board to the scene in the "after" part of the rule using a recorded program.

Programming by Demonstration

This recorded program is obtained from *programming by demonstration*, a technique in which the user puts the system in "record" mode and continues to operate the system in the normal way. The user's actions are then faithfully recorded in an executable program and can be replayed later as needed (Smith 1977; Cypher 1993). KidSim uses graphical rewrite rules as visual reminders of recorded actions, thus solving the problem of users trying to understand what the agents are supposed to do.

As reported by Smith, Cypher, and Spohrer in 1994, the KidSim approach appears to solve the end-user programming problem for some types of simulations. Perhaps we can derive from this that a solution to the general end-user programming problem probably lies some distance further down the same path.

Oasis

While in graduate school at the University of Michigan, the author had the opportunity to design a new programming language, called Oasis (Object and Agent Specification and Implementation System), for experimentation with agent-oriented programming (Cheong 1992a).

Oasis Agents

Oasis explicitly supports the concept of agents in its model of computation. In Oasis, agents are coarse-grained, computational entities that are dynamically created by the Oasis runtime system. Oasis agents are implemented as Unix processes that are distributed across the heterogeneous network of workstations. A collection of agents can thus cooperate among themselves to effect computations in a parallel distributed fashion on the network.

Each agent supports multiple threads of control using a non-preemptive scheduler. These threads can synchronize among themselves on condition variables specified by the programmer in the agent program. The threads facility enables an agent to accept and initiate multiple remote procedure calls concurrently.

Oasis Objects

Oasis objects are information nuggets that are dynamically created by agents during computation. Oasis objects do not have an identity in the traditional sense of object-oriented databases. They can

thus be freely transferred, traded, or replicated among the agents during cooperative computations without the constraints and programming hassle of maintaining consistency through locking. Objects no longer needed are automatically recycled through a garbage collector which, unlike traditional garbage collectors, does not require the use of runtime tags. The Oasis runtime system provides full support for automatic marshaling of objects, including complex user-defined objects with pointers, for remote procedure calls.

Oasis Compiler System

The Oasis compiler system generates native machine code but is network transparent in the sense that Oasis programmers need not be aware of workstation heterogeneity in the computing environment. In other words, the Oasis programmer does not have to maintain separate versions of binary code for different machine architectures. This is possible because the generation of native code at individual target machines is delayed until just before the agent program is actually run.

Oasis has been used to program a group of agents that cooperatively solve the Traveling Salesman Problem (in about 100 lines of Oasis code). The solution proceeds in a parallel distributed fashion on a cluster of workstations, with respectable speedups on different problem sizes.

The Oasis compiler generates native code for four different processors: Sparc, Mips, PowerPC, and 680x0. Its runtime system has been ported to several Unix platforms, including Sun-OS on Sparcstations, Ultrix on Decstations, Aix on PowerPC's, and Nextstep on Nextstations. The Oasis source code is publicly available by FTP from the University of Michigan at the following address (Cheong 1993b):

```
ftp://ftp.eecs.umich.edu/software/oasis/
```

Agents and Society

Donald Norman, an Apple Fellow at Apple Computer, foresees that the major difficulties with agents in our society are that people might not be comfortable with the autonomous actions of agents.

Norman observes that a distinguishing feature of the new crop of agents, as compared with mechanical robots of an earlier era, is that they now possess computational power, when previously they were simply servo mechanisms and control devices. According to Norman (1994), agents now:

> [H]ave Turing-machine powers, they take over human tasks, and they interact with people in human-like ways—perhaps with a form of natural language, perhaps with animated graphics or video. Some agents have the potential to form their own goals and intentions, to initiate actions on their own without explicit instructions or guidance, and to offer suggestions to people. Thus, agents might set up schedules, reserve hotel and meeting rooms, arrange transportation, and even outline meeting topics, all without human intervention. Moreover, today's agents are simple in comparison to those that are being planned.

Control

Indeed, it is important that people feel in control of their computational systems as a result of these added powers. They must be comfortable with actions performed for them by their agents. This can be accomplished in part through a better understanding of the underlying agent technology and in part through confidence in the system. Some people will always want to know the actions of their agents.

Over Expectations

Norman cautions that the added computational power of agents easily can foster an overblown expectation in people's mind of their exaggerated capabilities. People have a tendency to *anthropomorphize*, to see human attributes in anything that is the least bit intelligent. When fueled by the enthusiasm of technology visionaries who sees far into the future and amplified by the inclination of researchers to show their agents in human form, people naturally, but falsely, build on expectations of human-like intelligence, understanding, and actions in such personified agents.

Safety

Safety plays a part in the feeling of control, as does the issue of privacy. Agents should not do things that jeopardize the physical, mental, and financial well-being of human users. This can be tricky given that malicious agents in the form of computer worms and viruses can arrive unannounced and wreak havoc on the system.

Privacy

The question of privacy is an even more complex topic. The idea of autonomous, intelligent agents having access to one's personal records, correspondence, and financial activities can be somewhat disconcerting. Moreover, with embedded agents in e-mail messages, it might be difficult to safeguard one's privacy from the action of foreign agents collecting a recipient's private information and transferring it back to the senders.

Agent technology promises deliverance to computer users, relieving them from the complexity of command languages and the tedium of direct manipulation with intelligent, agent-guided interactions. Agents also can enhance human performance by making people appear smarter, or hide complexity by automating actions that you do not know how or prefer not to do.

Along with such promises comes the potential for social mischief, loss of privacy, and technological alienation from feelings of loss of control. But all these problems can be solved, though, provided enough consideration is given in the early design stages of intelligent systems of which agents are a part.

Commercial Future of Agents

Much of the agents discussed in the preceding sections exist only in universities and research labs. They have not made it to the commercial mainstream, yet. But according to Irene Greif (1994),

Director of Workgroup Technologies at Lotus, two industry trends could influence the evolution of agent technology and push agents out of the labs and into the mainstream of PC software:

→ The move toward suites of internetworking desktop products

→ The growing population of mobile users

Product Suites

A suite is a set of desktop applications that has been integrated to reduce the cost of software ownership and to improve individual productivity. Greif expects that agents will make an impact on suite products through "task-oriented" conversations with the users.

User interfaces today, for example, converse with users in a stylized fashion in the form of dialog boxes. This communication will become more powerful if they can converse about richer database structures, such as explicitly represented models of tasks in the form of task descriptions, which are similar to work process descriptions used by workflow agents (MWFF 1992). Greif envisions that the next significant step in the user interface will be a move away from conversing through forms to conversing about task descriptions. When this happens, the interaction between users and agents will become more like a collaboration through explicit data structures that represent tasks.

Mobile Computing

In the area of mobile computing, agents will add a new richness to the user interface. As people change their locations and work environments more frequently, they will continue to expect the same level of support from mobile computing, despite the vastly different capacity of the connectivity model. Greif envisions a personalized agent that understands where you are, what you are doing, and how you can best be reached. It is a new kind of agent in that instead of finding and doing things for a user in the network, it actually is interacting with other agents on the user's behalf.

To illustrate, consider the following example of a mobile user who is accessible only by pager and wants to read news articles about certain companies. Greif explains:

> It might not make sense for any of these articles to be forwarded to her when she only has her pager and can't read anything. However, if her calendar shows that she's on her way to visit the XYZ Co., it might be worth sending a message to her pager that there is a news item about that company. From an icon in the pager screen, she should be able to easily send a request back to her agent to have the full article faxed to the hotel before her breakfast meeting.

Most agents find something, take an action, and then move on. The interesting thing to note here is that, in this case, the agent might have to deliver the same piece of information several times, and in different formats (as a brief note to her pager and the full article to the hotel computer).

Concluding Remarks

I do not have a separate category for intelligent agents. I think it would not do justice to agents described here to contemplate using a separate category of agents called *intelligent agents*, and to use this category for the purpose of taxonomic classification by including some in the category but excluding others.

Agents display their intelligence differently; some by being creative, some by being crafty and elusive (worms and viruses), some by being helpful (personal assistants and surrogate bots), and still others by being resourceful in their own ways (COACH). In addition, agents can use different means to achieve intelligence; some adopt heuristics (softbots), some others use constraints (ACDS), some depend on knowledge databases (Cyc), and yet others learn from experience (Calendar Apprentice).

I consider all of the agents described here as intelligent, but to different degrees. Whether they possess insect-level intelligence or command Cyc-style encyclopedic world knowledge, it does not really matter. A colony of simple autonomous insects sometimes can display more intelligent behavior than a complex omnicient robot. In my opinion, intelligence is simply too vague a term at the current state of the art in agent research to even be considered a useful taxonomic category for classifying and understanding the wide variety of agents in the world.

The following chapters take you on a tour to visit agents on the Internet: the Web robots, spiders, and wanderers; the Web shoppers and bargain-hunters; worms and viruses; as well as MUD agents and chatterbots. But first, the Internet, then the Internet agents.

The Internet: Past, Present, and Future

This chapter tracks the development history of networks in the U.S. that have led to the Internet as we know it today: the network of networks. We have relied on Peter Denning's excellent article for materials that relate to the first 20 years in the history of ARPAnet (Denning 1989).

In the 1950s, the U.S. Department of Defense was worried about the ability of U.S. forces to survive a nuclear first strike. Survival depended critically on

the durability of the communications network. Traditional telephone networks that used circuit switching technology were considered too fragile for the purpose. The Rand Corporation, a defense contractor, undertook a series of studies and came up with the recommendation that the communications network should be based upon a packet switching technology. With packet switching, instead of using fixed point-to-point connections between any pair of machines for communications, messages are divided into packets. These packets are independently routed between intermediate computers until they reach their final destination, whereupon the message is reassembled for final delivery.

About the same time, experiments were conducted around the world to investigate the new packet switching technology, which promised tremendous flexibility and reliability in connecting computers at various sites. The first packet-switching network was implemented at the National Physical Laboratory in England. It was quickly followed by ARPAnet in the U.S. in 1969.

Early Days of ARPAnet

In 1968, against the backdrop of the Cold War with Russia, the Defense Department's Advanced Research Projects Agency (ARPA) commissioned the Bolt Beranek and Newman (BBN) company to build the first Interface Message Processors (IMPs).

 MPs are dedicated network controlling computers that translate between messages and packets.

By the end of 1969, BBN had delivered the first four IMPs along with a packet-switching network protocol called the *Network Control Protocol* (NCP). The first IMP was installed at UCLA in the fall of 1969. By 1970, the first packet-switched computer network in the U.S. was created, with four operating nodes connecting UCLA, U.C. Santa Barbara, Stanford University, and the University of Utah. This was the beginning of the ARPAnet. If any one link in the network failed, packets could still be routed via the remaining links, thus providing the needed fault tolerance and reliability. By 1971, there were 15 nodes on ARPAnet. By 1973, ARPAnet had grown to 37 nodes (Denning 1989).

 Electronic mail very quickly became the major source of traffic on ARPAnet, although it was not mentioned among the original goals of ARPAnet.

The first public demonstration of ARPAnet was held in 1972, arranged by Robert Kahn of BBN, at the first International Conference on Computer Communications in Washington, D.C. It soon became clear that research networking was growing rapidly and that the ARPAnet needed to connect to other networks. A working group, chaired by Vinton Cerf of UCLA, was established to study the creation of a common protocol for internetwork communications.

In 1973, the newly renamed Defense Advanced Research Project Agency (DARPA) began a research program to investigate techniques and technologies for connecting various types of packet-switched networks together. This was called the Internetting

project, and the main internet that resulted from it was called the Internet (Cerf 1992).

In 1974, Vinton Cerf and Robert Kahn released the Internet Protocol (IP) and the Transmission Control Protocol (TCP), which define the way data are passed among machines in a packet-switched network. The first physical implementation of the Internet involved four networks: a packet satellite network, a packet radio network, the ARPAnet, and an Ethernet at the Xerox Palo Alto Research Center (QCM 1994).

Notable Computer Networks

Toward the end of the 1970s, various "community networks" began to emerge (QH 1986; QCM 1994). Notable examples include the following:

➜ CSNET, which connects computers in the computer science research community

➜ BITNET, which connects IBM machines in computing centers

➜ USENET, which connects Unix sites by UUCP or other means

➜ FidoNet, which connects MS-DOS PCs by phone lines

➜ Various internal corporate networks, for example, IBM VNET, DEC Easynet, Xerox Internet

By the late 1970s, the ARPAnet was serving a select number of research centers. However, not all universities had network connections. The University of Wisconsin discerned a need and decided to create a network for increased collaboration among computer science researchers. The Computer Science Research Network (CSNET) was thus formed in January 1981, funded in large part by the National Science Foundation. Most CSNET hosts didn't use TCP/IP; instead, many were connected by modems and phone lines and used dial-up protocols that permitted essentially one service: e-mail.

Vinton Cerf had suggested connecting ARPAnet and CSNET via a gateway using the TCP/IP protocols. It also was suggested that CSNET could exist as a collection of several independent networks sharing a gateway to the ARPAnet (Moore 1994a). This marked the beginning of the Internet as a collection of independent, free-standing networks that came to an agreement on how to communicate with each other. By 1982, researchers on CSNET could communicate with sites within CSNET and ARPAnet by e-mail with equal ease. In a limited sense, the Internet had taken a first step to becoming "the network of networks."

In May 1981, BITNET (Because It's Time Network) was formed. BITNET has a tendency to link computer centers together and was created to connect IBM mainframes at the City University of New York. BITNET was built using the Network Job Entry (NJE) protocol and software native to the IBM VM/370 operating system.

BITNET uses the Listserv mechanism for providing news services. *Listserv* was a program originally designed to act as a mailing-list server whose function is to distribute e-mail to users on a mailing list. Listserv can thus be considered a rudimentary form of Internet during the early evolution of the Internet. It's somewhat like the USENET newsgroup

concept. The difference is that the readers of a particular newsgroup need to first subscribe to the appropriate Listserv, and that news articles are sent directly via e-mail rather than broadcast throughout the network.

USENET (Users' Network) is not a physical network. It began in 1980 as a medium of communications between users of two machines, one at the University of North Carolina, the other at nearby Duke University. USENET newsgroups were invented to capture the flavors of both the ARPAnet-style mailing lists as well as the bulletin board services. The early USENET news distribution mechanism depended on Unix-to-Unix-Copy (UUCP) for transport of news articles over telephone links using a simple "flooding" algorithm (Horton 1983). When USENET became much larger, a more efficient protocol for delivering and accessing news, that is, the Network News Transfer Protocol (NNTP), was adopted

(KL 1986). In addition to UUCP, USENET news can be carried on BITNET, as well as the larger Internet.

 USENET has enjoyed immense popularity since its inception, reaching a large constituency and growing rapidly to encompass 2,000 machines in 1986.

FidoNet was invented in 1983 to connect personal computers running MS-DOS via modems and phone lines (see fig. 2.1). It was designed by Tom Jennings of San Francisco as an imitation of UUCP and USENET to link together Fido bulletin boards that had recently sprung up across the nation. The Fido protocols offer similar functions as that of UUCP but are completely different internally and more efficient. It allows users to send e-mail to each other and to create discussion groups just like USENET and BITNET. Starting in 1987, FidoNet

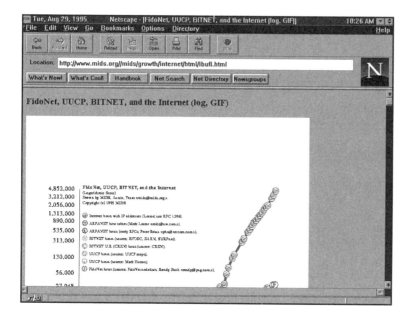

Figure 2.1

FidoNet, UUCP, BITNET, and the Internet. (Courtesy of MIDS, Austin, Texas)

could share traffic with USENET after the Unix-to-Unix-Copy (UUCP) software originally developed for the Unix platform was ported to MS-DOS.

 n o t e Interestingly, the name Fido is not an acronym but the common pet name for a family dog.

In 1989, BITNET and CSNET merged to become the Corporation for Research and Education Networking (CREN). But CSNET was subsequently retired when the NSFnet regional networks subsumed its functions.

Internet and NSFnet

The first pieces of the Internet began around 1980 when DARPA began converting machines attached to its research networks to the new TCP/IP protocols. The transition to Internet technology was completed in January 1983 when DARPA mandated that all computers connected to the ARPAnet use TCP/IP. At around the same time, the original ARPAnet was split into two networks: ARPAnet for continued research and MILNET for military operations.

To encourage adoption of the new protocols, DARPA had decided to make an implementation of the TCP/IP available at a low cost. At that time, the computer science departments at most universities were running a version of Unix available from the University of California at Berkeley as part of its Berkeley Software Distribution. DARPA funded BBN to implement the Internet protocols under Unix and Berkeley to integrate them with its distribution. With TCP/IP networking support built into BSD 4.2 Unix, DARPA could reach over 90 percent of the university computer science departments in the U.S. As the Internet grew, the original method of naming nodes became unwieldy. A hierarchical naming system that allowed each *domain* to select its internal address was introduced in 1984.

In 1984, the National Science Foundation started connecting its supercomputing centers with a high-bandwidth network called the NSFnet. The first NSFnet was built by the Cornell Theory Center and the National Center for Supercomputing Applications (NCSA). The NSFnet started out as a 56 Kbps network in 1986, primarily serving the NSF's six supercomputer centers. In its lifetime (1986 to 1995), NSFnet had undergone several iterations over the implementation of its backbone, upgrading to higher speed at each stage: in 1986 (DS-0, 56 Kbps), 1988 (T-1, 1.544 Mbps), and 1990 (T-3, 45 Mbps).

Merit, a non-profit network corporation based in Michigan, began managing the NSFnet backbone in July, 1988, after working in partnership with IBM and MCI to deliver the initial T1 backbone to NSFnet, which connected 13 sites. The NSFnet had become the backbone for the potpourri of networks known collectively as the Internet.

Beginning in 1986, the National Science Foundation (NSF) supplied seed money to support the mid-level regional networks that provided extensive connectivity for campus networks at educational institutions, government agencies, and commercial businesses. The NSFnet had thus played a key role in further accelerating the already rapid growth of the Internet.

In 1990, after 20 years of service, the ARPAnet was officially retired. ARPAnet's role was, for all

practical purposes, supplanted by the NSFnet. In the same year, NSF created the Advanced Network Services Inc. (ANS), a non-profit corporation jointly owned by Merit, IBM, and MCI. In 1990, ANS took over the operation of the NSFnet backbone, which by then was already operating at T3 speeds (45 Mbps) using circuits provided by MCI and router technology from IBM. By the end of 1991, all NSFnet backbone sites were connected to the new ANS-provided T3 backbone (Merit 1992).

NSF and AUP

The NSF and the ANS were very generous in sharing the network backbone. The NSFnet services are available to any Internet user as long as NSF's acceptable-use policy (AUP) is adhered to. The acceptable-use policy basically states the following general principle:

> NSFnet Backbone services are provided to support open research and education in and among US research and instructional institutions, plus research arms of for-profit firms when engaged in open scholarly communication and research. Use for other purposes is not acceptable.

In particular, the AUP states the following as unacceptable use:

→ Use for for-profit activities, unless covered by the General Principle or as a specifically acceptable use

→ Extensive use for private or personal business

In other words, nearly anyone can use the NSFnet backbone as long as it is not used for profit or used extensively for private or personal business.

In 1990, the Federal Networking Council, as part of the governing body of the Internet, made a radical policy change. It no longer required organizations that wanted to join the Internet to seek sponsorship by a U.S. government agency. This event marked the start of the "commercialization" of the Internet (Moore 1994b).

In 1992, in extending ANS's contract to run NSFnet, NSF considered itself a customer of ANS. As a result, the limitations outlined by the acceptable-use policy applied only to traffic from the NSF (Moore 1994b). The expectation was that different organizations on the Internet would formulate their own acceptable-use policies regarding their portions of the Internet. For all practical purposes, the floodgate had finally opened for commercial use of the Internet.

Growth of the Internet

NSFnet performance statistics have been collected, processed, and reported by the Merit Network since 1988. In December 1994, the numbers contained in Merit's statistical reports began to decrease, as NSFnet traffic began to migrate to the new NSF network architecture.

In the new architecture, traffic is exchanged at interconnection points called *NAPs* (*Network Access Points*). Each NAP provides a neutral interconnection point for network service providers.

On April 30, 1995, the NSFnet Backbone Service was successfully transitioned to the new network architecture, signaling the end of the NSFnet project.

By any measure, the growth of the Internet has been impressive. As illustrated in table 2.1, Merit recorded a 134 percent growth (from 6031 to 14,121) in networks configured for traversal of the NSFnet backbone from July 1992 to July 1993.

Mark Lottor, formerly at SRI but now at Network Wizards, used the ZONE program to determine the approximate number of Internet hosts and domains (see RFC 1296 (Lottor 1992)). His Internet Domain Survey of July 1993 shows 79 percent growth in Internet hosts in the year from July 1992. His October 1993 report shows 81 percent growth in hosts (see table 2.2) and 55 percent in domains from October 1992 to October 1993 (see table 2.3).

Table 2.1   History of NSFNet Growth by Networks

Date	Total Nets	Total Non-US
Jul 88	217	9
Jan 89	384	34
Jul 89	650	99
Jan 90	1,233	250
Jul 90	1,727	436
Jan 91	2,338	693
Jul 91	3,086	1,012
Jan 92	4,526	1,496
Jul 92	6,031	2,133
Jan 93	9,117	3,413
Jul 93	14,121	5,827
Jan 94	23,494	9,869
Jul 94	36,153	15,362
Jan 95	46,318	19,637

Table 2.2   Growth of Internet Hosts

Date	Hosts
Aug 81	213
Aug 83	562
Oct 85	1,961
Dec 87	28,174
Oct 89	159,000
Oct 90	313,000
Oct 91	617,000
Oct 92	1,136,000
Oct 93	2,056,000
Oct 94	3,864,000
Jan 95	4,852,000

Table 2.3 Growth of Internet Domains

Date	Domain
Jul 88	900
Jul 89	3,900
Oct 90	9,300
Jul 91	16,000
Oct 92	18,100
Oct 93	28,000
Oct 94	56,000
Jan 95	71,000

What do all these growth rates for networks, hosts, and domains mean? For one, the slowest growth seems to be in domains, which probably means that organizations join the net more slowly, but increase their host counts rapidly after they are connected (Quarterman 1993). For another, the fastest growth is in the number of networks configured for traversal of the NSFnet backbone (presumably a large fraction of all IP networks on the Internet), which probably indicates the important role played by NSFnet in connecting many previously isolated networks.

Most of these measures of Internet growth show sustained exponential growth (note the vertical scale is logarithmic). According to Matrix Information and Directory Service (MIDS) (see fig. 2.2), averaging across these figures gives us a rough count of approximately 100 percent annual growth (Quarterman 1993).

Another way to gauge the growth of Internet is by the volume of traffic. Table 2.4 shows the growth in traffic volume on the NSFnet backbone.

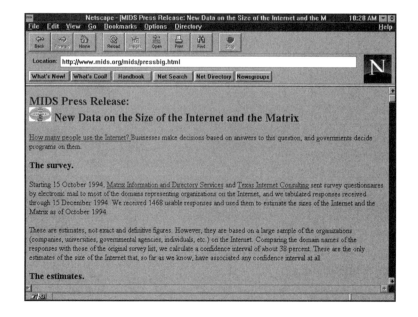

Figure 2.2

A press release on the MIDS home page.

Table 2.4 NSFnet Byte Traffic History (in billions of bytes)

Month	1991	1992	1993	1994	1995
Jan	NA	2,256	4,782	8,609	13,196
Feb	NA	2,371	5,015	9,303	9,790
Mar	1,268	2,761	6,053	11,226	11,218
Apr	1,402	2,848	6,219	11,587	5,316
May	1,442	3,061	5,845	12,187	NA
Jun	1,244	3,274	6,195	12,466	NA
Jul	1,594	3,373	6,389	12,764	NA
Aug	1,484	3,200	6,631	13,385	NA
Sep	1,769	3,315	7,022	14,990	NA
Oct	1,879	3,903	8,468	17,232	NA
Nov	1,959	4,651	8,483	17,781	NA
Dec	1,956	4,372	8,283	16,313	NA

How Big is the Internet?

According to Tony Rutkowski, Executive Director of the Internet Society, a commonly used method of estimating the total number of Internet users is to multiply the number of host computers by 10. In January 1995, for example, the ZONE program identified close to 5 million hosts, which is equivalent to about 50 million users.

A more detailed breakdown of such a measure of Internet users is provided by MIDS, a company that conducts ongoing investigations about the size, shape, and other characteristics of the Internet and other networks. Combining and processing data from a variety of sources, MIDS estimated the size of the Internet as of October 1994 to be as such:

→ 7.8 million users of 2.5 million computers (MIDS calls this the core Internet) that can provide interactive services such as remote login, file transfer or World Wide Web

→ 13.5 million users of 3.5 million computers that can use the interactive services supplied by the core Internet; for example, people who can use Mosaic or Lynx to browse the World Wide Web

→ 27.5 million users who can exchange electronic mail with other users on the Internet, as well as other networks

The following figures provide further details on the distribution of the Internet by geography, both international (see fig. 2.3 and table 2.5) and U.S. (see table 2.6), as well as by top-level domain names (see table 2.7).

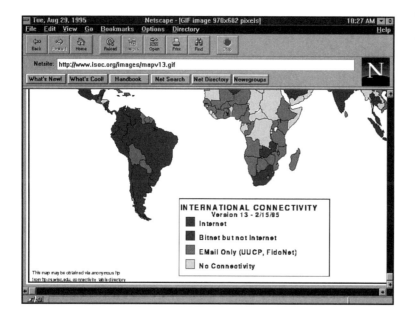

Figure 2.3

Global Connectivity Map. (Courtesy of Internet Society).

Total Code	Initial Country	Nets	Connection
DZ	Algeria	3	Apr 94
AR	Argentina	27	Oct 90
AM	Armenia	3	Jun 94
AU	Australia	1,875	May 89
AT	Austria	408	Jun 90
BY	Belarus	1	Feb 95
BE	Belgium	138	May 90
BM	Bermuda	20	Mar 94

Table 2.5

NSFNET International Connections and Nets

Total Code	Initial Country	Nets	Connection
BR	Brazil	165	Jun 90
BG	Bulgaria	9	Apr 93
BF	Burkina Faso	2	Oct 94
CM	Cameroon	1	Dec 92
CA	Canada	4,795	Jul 88 *
CL	Chile	102	Apr 90
CN	China	8	Apr 94
CO	Colombia	5	Apr 94
CR	Costa Rica	6	Jan 93
HR	Croatia	31	Nov 91
CY	Cyprus	25	Dec 92
CZ	Czech Republic	459	Nov 91
DK	Denmark	48	Nov 88
DO	Dominican Republic	1	Apr 95
EC	Ecuador	85	Jul 92
EG	Egypt	7	Nov 93
EE	Estonia	49	Jul 92
FJ	Fiji	1	Jun 93
FI	Finland	643	Nov 88
FR	France	2,003	Jul 88 *

continues

Total Code	Initial Country	Nets	Connection
PF	French Polynesia	1	Oct 94
DE	Germany	1,750	Sep 89
GH	Ghana	1	May 93
GR	Greece	105	Jul 90
GU	Guam	5	Oct 93
HK	Hong Kong	95	Sep 91
HU	Hungary	164	Nov 91
IS	Iceland	31	Nov 88
IN	India	13	Nov 90
ID	Indonesia	46	Jul 93
IE	Ireland	168	Jul 90
IL	Israel	217	Aug 89
IT	Italy	506	Aug 89
JM	Jamaica	16	May 94
JP	Japan	1,847	Aug 89
KZ	Kazakhstan	2	Nov 93
KE	Kenya	1	Nov 93
KR	South Korea	476	Apr 90
KW	Kuwait	8	Dec 92
LV	Latvia	22	Nov 92
LB	Lebanon	1	Jun 94

Total Code	Initial Country	Nets	Connection
LI	Liechtenstein	3	Jun 93
LT	Lithuania	1	Apr 94
LU	Luxembourg	59	Apr 92
MO	Macau	1	Apr 94
MY	Malaysia	6	Nov 92
MX	Mexico	126	Feb 89
MA	Morocco	1	Oct 94
MZ	Mozambique	6	Mar 95
NL	Netherlands	406	Jan 89
NC	New Caledonia	1	Oct 94
NZ	New Zealand	356	Apr 89
NI	Nicaragua	1	Feb 94
NE	Niger	1	Oct 94
NO	Norway	214	Nov 88
PA	Panama	1	Jun 94
PE	Peru	44	Nov 93
PH	Philippines	46	Apr 94
PL	Poland	131	Nov 91
PT	Portugal	92	Oct 91
PR	Puerto Rico	9	Oct 89
RO	Romania	26	Apr 93

continues

Total Code	Initial Country	Nets	Connection
RU	Russian Federation	405	Jun 93
SN	Senegal	11	Oct 94
SG	Singapore	107	May 91
SK	Slovakia	69	Mar 92
SI	Slovenia	46	Feb 92
ZA	South Africa	419	Dec 91
ES	Spain	257	Jul 90
SZ	Swaziland	1	May 94
SE	Sweden	415	Nov 88
CH	Switzerland	324	Mar 90
TW	Taiwan	575	Dec 91
TH	Thailand	107	Jul 92
TN	Tunisia	19	May 91
TR	Turkey	97	Jan 93
UA	Ukraine	60	Aug 93
AE	United Arab Emirates	3	Nov 93
GB	United Kingdom	1,436	Apr 89
US	United States	28,470	Jul 88 *
UY	Uruguay	1	Apr 94
UZ	Uzbekistan	1	Dec 94

Table 2.5, Continued

NSFNET International Connections and Nets

Total Code	Initial Country	Nets	Connection
VE	Venezuela	11	Feb 92
VN	Vietnam	1	Apr 95
VI	Virgin Islands	4	Mar 93
93	Total	50,766	

* Merit began managing the NSFNET backbone in July, 1988.

Table 2.6

NSFnet Networks by U.S. States, May 1995

State	Code	Total Nets
Alabama	AL	260
Alaska	AK	26
Arizona	AZ	186
Arkansas	AR	70
California	CA	4,832
Colorado	CO	696
Connecticut	CT	463
Delaware	DE	23
Florida	FL	770
Georgia	GA	445
Hawaii	HI	127
Idaho	ID	56
Illinois	IL	577

continues

State	Code	Total Nets
Indiana	IN	347
Iowa	IA	147
Kansas	KS	70
Kentucky	KY	82
Louisiana	LA	198
Maine	ME	103
Maryland	MD	1,178
Massachusetts	MA	2,005
Michigan	MI	540
Minnesota	MN	867
Mississippi	MS	109
Missouri	MO	303
Montana	MT	37
Nebraska	NE	156
Nevada	NV	40
New Hampshire	NH	175
New Jersey	NJ	1,208
New Mexico	NM	142
New York	NY	2,152
North Carolina	NC	677
North Dakota	ND	21
Ohio	OH	1,233

Table 2.6, Continued

NSFnet Networks by
U.S. States, May 1995

State	Code	Total Nets
Oklahoma	OK	136
Oregon	OR	593
Pennsylvania	PA	919
Rhode Island	RI	147
South Carolina	SC	240
South Dakota	SD	15
Tennessee	TN	353
Texas	TX	1,341
Utah	UT	141
Vermont	VT	68
Virginia	VA	1,964
Washington	WA	972
Washington DC	DC	744
West Virginia	WV	46
Wisconsin	WI	280
Wyoming	WY	28
Military, Asia	AA	10
Military, Europe	AE	92
Military, Pacific	AP	46
Military Unspecified	AX	8
(Unknown)	XX	6

Table 2.7 Host Distribution by Top-Level Domain Name, January 1995

com 1,316,966	it 30,697	gr 4,000	cn 569	li 27
edu 1,133,502	at 29,705	cl 3,054	ve 529	gb 27
uk 241,191	es 28,446	tr 2,643	bm 474	zw 19
gov 209,345	za 27,040	ru 1,849	in 359	am 19
de 207,717	dk 25,935	si 1,773	ph 334	jr 18
ca 186,722	be 18,699	th 1,728	ec 325	pa 17
mil 175,961	kr 18,049	my 1,606	kw 220	mo 12
au 161,166	tw 14,618	sk 1,414	id 177	dz 10
org 154,578	il 13,251	ee 1,396	uy 172	kz 7
net 150,299	hk 12,437	ar 1,262	pe 171	fj 5
jp 96,632	cz 11,580	co 1,127	eg 161	aq 4
fr 93,041	pl 11,477	hr 1,090	bg 144	md 3
nl 89,227	hu 8,506	int 904	lt 121	gl 3
se 77,594	mx 6,656	br 800	cy 88	fo 3
fi 71,372	ie 6,219	cr 798	pr 82	sa 2
ch 51,512	pt 5,999	lu 614	jm 76	gn 2
no 49,725	sg 5,252	lv 612	zm 69	by 2
us 37,615	su 4,963	ro 597	tn 57	az 1
nz 31,215	is 4,735	ua 574	ni 49	

Internet Society, IAB, and IETF

The Internet Society is an international organization for global cooperation and coordination for the Internet and its associated internetworking technologies and applications. Its principal purpose is

> [T]o maintain and extend the development and availability of the Internet and its associated technologies and applications—both as an end in itself, and as a means of enabling organizations, professions, and individuals worldwide to more effectively collaborate, cooperate, and innovate in their respective fields and interests.

The Internet Society (ISOC) (see fig. 2.4) was formed by a number of people with long-term involvement in the Internet Engineering Task Force (IETF) (see fig. 2.5). In 1990, it appeared that long-term support for the standards-making activity of the IETF, which had come primarily from research supporting agencies of the U.S. Government (notably ARPA, NSF, NASA, and DOE), might need to be supplemented in the future. As a result, one of its principal rationales was to provide an institutional home for and financial support for the Internet Standards process.

Figure 2.4

The Internet Society's home page.

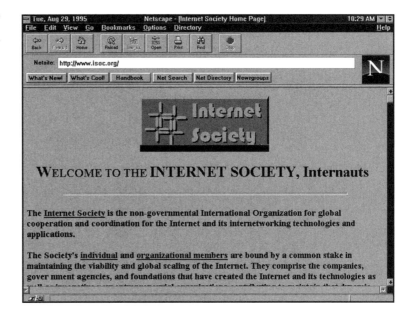

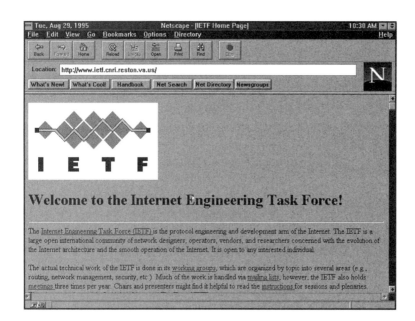

Figure 2.5

The IETF home page.

The Internet Society was announced in June 1991 at an international networking conference in Copenhagen and brought into existence in January 1992. In June 1992, at the annual meeting of the Internet Society, INET'92, in Kobe, Japan, the Internet Activities Board proposed to associate its activities with ISOC and was renamed the Internet Architecture Board (IAB).

The IAB is considered a technical advisory group of the ISOC. It is chartered to provide oversight of the architecture of the Internet and its protocols. Historically, the IETF and its sister organization, the Internet Research Task Force, had been considered two arms of the IAB. At the technical and developmental level, the Internet is made possible through creation, testing, and implementation of Internet Standards. These standards are developed by the Internet Engineering Task Force.

The IETF is a loosely self-organized group of people who make technical and other contributions to the engineering and evolution of the Internet and its technologies. The actual technical work of the IETF is done in its working groups, which are organized by topic into several areas (for example, routing, network management, and security).

The IETF produces a set of working documents, each called an RFC (Request for Comment). Some of these RFCs pass through the IAB Standards Process (Chapin 1992) to become Internet Standards. Internet Standards exist for all the basic TCP/IP protocols.

According to Vinton Cerf, the highest ISOC goal was to "keep the Internet going." Among the high priority activities associated with that goal was to provide support for the Internet Standards process carried out by the Internet Engineering Task Force.

Information Superhighway and the National Information Infrastructure

The first year of the Clinton administration saw the creation of the U.S. Advisory Council on the National Information Infrastructure as a new branch under the Commerce Department. Signed into President Clinton's executive order of 1993 was the national goal of creating an "information superhighway," the National Information Infrastructure (NII) which

> [S]hall be the integration of hardware, software, and skills that will make it easy and affordable to connect people with each other, with computers, and with a vast array of services and information resources.

The following executive summary was excerpted from the U.S. Federal government's NII Agenda for Action (see fig. 2.6). It mentions nine goals for the NII that bear striking resemblances to what the Internet can offer today, but there are important differences as well.

The National Information Infrastructure:
Agenda for Action Executive Summary

All Americans have a stake in the construction of an advanced National Information Infrastructure (NII), a seamless web of communications networks, computers, databases, and consumer electronics that will put vast amounts of information at users' fingertips. Development of the NII can help unleash an information revolution that will change forever the way people live, work, and interact with each other:

Figure 2.6

The Federal government's Agenda for Action home page.

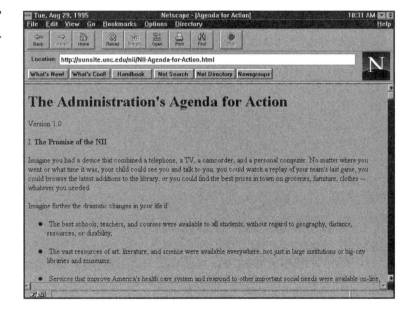

→ People could live almost anywhere they wanted, without foregoing opportunities for useful and fulfilling employment, by "telecommuting" to their offices through an electronic highway.

→ The best schools, teachers, and courses would be available to all students, without regard to geography, distance, resources, or disability.

→ Services that improve America's health care system and respond to other important social needs could be available online, without waiting in line, when and where you needed them.

Private sector firms already are developing and deploying that infrastructure today. Nevertheless, there remain essential roles for government in this process. Carefully crafted government action will complement and enhance the efforts of the private sector and assure the growth of an information infrastructure available to all Americans at reasonable cost. In developing our policy initiatives in this area, the Administration will work in close partnership with business, labor, academia, the public, Congress, and state and local government. Our efforts will be guided by the following principles and objectives:

→ Promote private sector investment, through appropriate tax and regulatory policies.

→ Extend the "universal service" concept to ensure that information resources are available to all at affordable prices. Because information means empowerment—and employment—the government has a duty to ensure that all Americans have access to the resources and job creation potential of the Information Age.

→ Act as a catalyst to promote technological innovation and new applications. Commit important government research programs and grants to help the private sector develop and demonstrate technologies needed for the NII, and develop the applications and services that will maximize its value to users.

→ Promote seamless, interactive, user-driven operation of the NII. As the NII evolves into a "network of networks," government will ensure that users can transfer information across networks easily and efficiently. To increase the likelihood that the NII will be both interactive and, to a large extent, user- driven, government must reform regulations and policies that may inadvertently hamper the development of interactive applications.

→ Ensure information security and network reliability. The NII must be trustworthy and secure, protecting the privacy of its users. Government action will also ensure that the overall system remains reliable, quickly repairable in the event of a failure and, perhaps most importantly, easy to use.

Introduction

➜ Improve management of the radio frequency spectrum, an increasingly critical resource.

➜ Protect intellectual property rights. The Administration will investigate how to strengthen domestic copyright laws and international intellectual property treaties to prevent piracy and to protect the integrity of intellectual property.

➜ Coordinate with other levels of government and with other nations. Because information crosses state, regional, and national boundaries, coordination is critical to avoid needless obstacles and prevent unfair policies that handicap U.S. industry.

➜ Provide access to government information and improve government procurement. The Administration will seek to ensure that Federal agencies, in concert with state and local governments, use the NII to expand the information available to the public, ensuring that the immense reservoir of government information is available to the public easily and equitably. Additionally, Federal procurement policies for telecommunications and information services and equipment will be designed to promote important technical developments for the NII and to provide attractive incentives for the private sector to contribute to NII development.

The time for action is now. Every day brings news of change: new technologies, like hand-held computerized assistants; new ventures and mergers combining businesses that not long ago seemed discrete and insular; new legal decisions that challenge the separation of computer, cable, and telephone companies. These changes promise substantial benefits for the American people, but only if government understands fully their implications and begins working with the private sector and other interested parties to shape the evolution of the communications infrastructure.

The benefits of the NII for the nation are immense. An advanced information infrastructure will enable U.S. firms to compete and win in the global economy, generating good jobs for the American people and economic growth for the nation. As importantly, the NII can transform the lives of the American people—ameliorating the constraints of geography, disability, and economic status—giving all Americans a fair opportunity to go as far as their talents and ambitions will take them.

Is the Internet the information superhighway that America is seeking? I think so. Since its inception as ARPAnet in 1969 and over the course of past twenty-five years, the Internet has demonstrated remarkable resilience, innovative adaptability, and spontaneous cooperation when faced with various challenges brought on by both changes in technology as well as its rapid growth.

I believe that the following NII issues can all be satisfactorily addressed and fully accommodated by the Internet—not in its present form, but in an advanced version of the Internet as it continues to evolve into the future:

→ Private sector investment

→ Universal availability

→ Technology innovation

→ Seamless interactivity

→ Security and reliability

→ Resource management

→ Intellectual property rights

→ Coordination

→ Government information access

World Wide Web: Playground for Robots

In the past couple of years, the World Wide Web has completely reshaped the Internet. The Web has transformed the Internet from an exclusive country club frequented by the "well-connected" and privileged few, to a huge public arena visited daily by people from all walks of life. It has done so by introducing graphical user interfaces to facilitate access to the Internet, allowing users to experience sights and sounds in an intuitive style of navigation. The World Wide Web has opened the Internet to the masses.

World Wide Web Development

The precursor of the World Wide Web was a small, home-brewed personal hypertext system developed at CERN, Geneva's European Laboratory for Particle Physics, for keeping track of personal information on a distributed project. The positive experience prompted development of what became the World Wide Web. In March 1989, Tim Bernes-Lee at CERN began circulating a proposal to build a "hypertext system" for easy sharing of information among geographically separated teams of researchers in the High Energy Physics community.

In October 1990, development on the World Wide Web was started and the project began to take shape. By Christmas of 1990, access to hypertext files and Internet news articles was demonstrated with the line-mode and graphical NeXTStep browsers. Before the end of 1991, the CERN newsletter announced the Web to the World. Other early browsers for the World Wide Web include Viola (Pei Wei, U.C. Berkeley), Mosaic (Marc Andreesen, Illinois NCSA), Cello (Thomas Bruce, Cornell University), as well as Lynx in full-screen character mode (Lou Montulli, University of Kansas).

Growth of the Web

Over time, the Web became immensely popular in part because of the browsers that made it easy for everyone on the Internet to roam, browse, and contribute to the Web information space. In April 1993, there were 62 registered Web servers on the Internet. By April 1994, the number of registered Web servers had grown to 829. By May 1994, the number increased to 1,248 (BLCLNS 1994).

The growth in World Wide Web traffic on the Internet is equally impressive. Since its start, World Wide Web traffic has grown at twice the rate of general Internet expansion. In 1994, World Wide Web traffic over the NSFnet, measured in bytes, grew an astounding 15-fold (1,500 percent)! Figure 3.1 plots the monthly traffic volume across the NSFnet T3 backbone from January 1993 through April 1995.

By July 1994, the Web had outgrown CERN's capability to deal with it as a single research laboratory dedicated to High Energy Physics. CERN began to transfer the Web project to a new group called the W3 Organization, a joint venture between CERN and MIT based in Cambridge, Massachusetts, for further development (see fig. 3.2). Between late 1994 and early 1995, this development venture blossomed into a collection of organizations and expertise called the World Wide Web Consortium.

 n o t e Currently, all "official" Web-related research and developments are undertaken or coordinated by the W3 Consortium.

Information Dissemination with the Web

The Web originally was conceived as a convenient way to disseminate information within an organization (BLCLNS 1994). The Web behaves like a

Figure 3.1

Monthly traffic in bytes across the NSFnet T3 backbone.

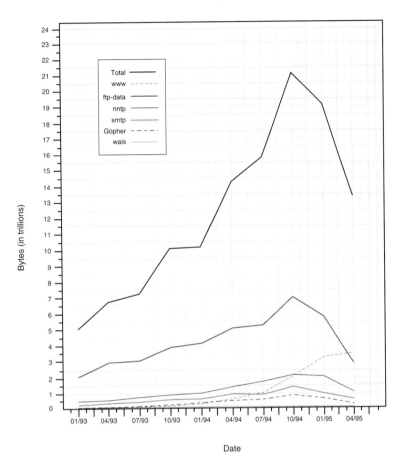

networked repository of information that pools together useful knowledge, allowing collaborators at remote sites to share their ideas, as well as information on all aspects of a common project. Figure 3.3 illustrates the Web information space of a typical research center.

As a tool for information distribution, the Web can provide users and customers with resources previously available only to manufacturers, suppliers, and distributors. The Web has become very popular over the past two years as a new medium of expression on the Internet due in part to its capability to provide a flexible and extensible way to interact with users over the Internet for a variety of purposes.

Information residing on the Web can be smoothly reshaped by alterations in hypertext links to represent the state of new knowledge in a constantly changing environment. Furthermore, the highly scalable design of the Web requires no centralized administration of information. These properties have

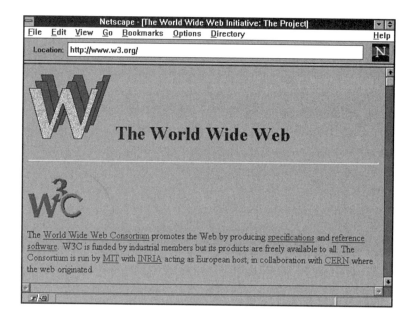

Figure 3.2

The W3C Home Page.

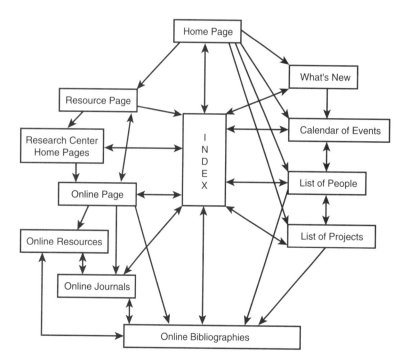

Figure 3.3

Web Information Space of a Research Center.

helped the Web to expand rapidly from its origins at CERN to the Internet, irrespective of boundaries of nations or disciplines.

Innovative Uses of the Web

Over the short span of a couple years, the Web has evolved to fulfill a great number of diverse needs on the Internet. It's a powerful medium for advertising and for delivery of online electronic catalogs and product information. It's also an important vehicle for setting up virtual storefronts in cyberspace. These virtual storefronts can be used for distributing software electronically, for browsing multimedia art galleries, for taking orders on various goods and services, for publishing electronic newspapers, or for "netcasting" radio and video programs. In short, the Web now has become a place of communications and learning, a new marketplace, and an exciting show ground for new information technologies.

Architecture of the World Wide Web

The World Wide Web organizes, transmits, and retrieves information of all types by using a combination of hypertext, graphics, and multimedia technologies, unified in a set of naming conventions, network protocols, and document formats, and realized by using a client-server architecture.

The World Wide Web architecture is illustrated in figure 3.4 and is designed to be highly scalable. Its content is the universe of network-accessible information, which the Web originators have termed "an embodiment of human knowledge."

Figure 3.4

Client-Server Architecture of World Wide Web.

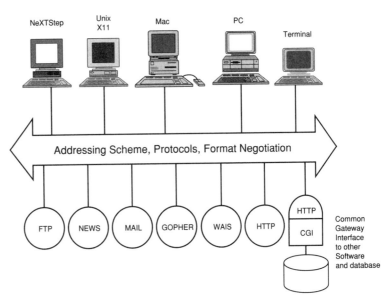

Besides the Web, there are other information systems like Gopher (AMLJTA 1993) and WAIS (DKMSSWSG 1990) that use a similar client-server architecture. These systems, however, play distinct roles and have different purposes. Gopher, which is sort of like a Web without full hypertext capability, uses a menu system that allows information to be organized in a hierarchy of directories. WAIS provides no navigation facilities and uses indexing exclusively to transport users into the desired location of the information space. Using the analogy of a book as an information space, Gopher often is described as its table of contents, WAIS the index pages, and World Wide Web the hypertext body where the bulk of the contents reside.

A body of software realizes the Web in a concrete form. This software architecture is composed of the following components that interoperate over the Internet:

→ Clients that allow users to navigate the Web or even interact with the server in interesting ways

→ Servers that allow Internet sites to publish information or export data to the world

→ Proxies that facilitate communications and provide access control for sites that must rely on an intermediary host for communication with the Internet (for example, sites behind a firewall)

Web Clients

A World Wide Web client program runs on a desktop computer and is capable of accessing different Web servers distributed across the Internet. With an interactive Web browser client, users can view hypermedia documents by following information links in the Web information space. The first prototype of a Web client is a hypertext browser/editor on NeXTStep, written by Tim Bernes-Lee at CERN. Currently, a multitude of commercial browsers, such as Netscape Navigator, are available on a variety of client platforms such as PC/Windows, Mac, Unix/X11.

In addition to providing basic browsing functions, Web clients can solicit user input through an onscreen fill-out form. This capability allows bidirectional information flow and is useful for enhanced interactivity. Web clients that also provide editing functions further allow online Web document construction in a dynamic environment.

Web Servers

A World Wide Web server program usually runs on a multitasking workstation that is powerful enough to handle multiple requests from clients from all over the Internet. The most common request is to "GET" a Web page for display on the client browser. The two most popular server software packages are from CERN (written by Tim Bernes-Lee) and NCSA (written by Rob McCool), and they are simply called CERN and NCSA. Favorite platforms for Web servers include various flavors of Unix, as well as Windows/NT. The Web pages that the client views reside on a file system and have addresses that reflect the directory path that leads to the file.

Besides serving hypertext documents, a Web server also has the capability to act as a gateway to other software or information sources such as a relational database. Using the Common Gateway Interface, the Web server invokes a program script that takes information provided by the client

(usually from a fill-out form that appeared in the client browser), processes it according to instructions in the script, and returns a Web page result to the client.

Web Proxies

A *proxy* actually is a Web server that usually runs on a *firewall* machine (that is, a machine that functions like a security barrier between the larger Internet and a smaller local area network within an organization). The proxy acts as an intermediary between Web clients inside the firewall and Web servers out on the Internet. When the proxy receives a request from an internal machine behind the firewall, it sends the request out to some Web server on the Internet and waits for the response. When the reply comes back from the Internet, it passes the result back to the internal client.

A proxy also can be used to cache Web documents, which is useful when multiple clients within an organization (not necessarily behind a firewall) make requests for the same Web pages. The proxy will store the result of first requests and simply pass on the stored Web page for subsequent requests, substantially reducing network response time for the clients. The proxy also can store pre-loaded popular Web pages for use in caching.

Web Resource Naming, Protocols, and Formats

The World Wide Web incorporates the idea of a boundless information world in which all objects have a reference by which they can be retrieved. Despite the many different protocols in existence, the World Wide Web implements a universal addressing system, the Universal Resource Identifier (URI), to make object referencing in this world possible. Various protocols and access algorithms are encoded as specific Universal Resource Locators (URL), conforming to the general URI addressing scheme.

Although the World Wide Web architecture encompasses many other preexisting Internet protocols (see fig. 3.4), the native and primary network protocol used between World Wide Web clients and servers is the HyperText Transfer Protocol (HTTP). HTTP enables World Wide Web clients and servers to communicate efficiently, providing performance and features not otherwise available.

World Wide Web also defines a HyperText Markup Language (HTML), which is a document format that every World Wide Web client is required to understand. It is used for the transmission and representation of basic items such as text, list, and menus, as well as various styles of inputs in a fill-out form.

URI and URL: Universal Resource Identifier and Locator

The Web is designed to include objects that can be accessed by using any number of protocols that are either already in existence, being invented for the Web, or to be invented in the future. To abstract the idea of a generic object, the Web uses the concepts of a universal set of objects, and of a universal set of names and addresses of objects. A Universal Resource Identifier (URI) (BL 1994) is a

member of this universal set of names and addresses. URIs are strings used as addresses of objects on the Web, which could be documents, menus, or images.

Access instructions for an individual object under a given protocol are encoded into an address string. A *Universal Resource Locator* or *URL* (BLMM 1994) is a form of URI that expresses an address that maps onto an access algorithm using network protocols.

Both URIs and URLs are integral to the architecture of the World Wide Web. They allow for easy addressability of an object anywhere on the Internet, which is essential for the Web architecture to scale and for the Web information space to be independent of network and server topology.

Common URI Syntax

Although the syntax for the rest of the URL might vary depending on the particular scheme selected, URL schemes that involve an IP-based protocol connecting to a specified host on the Internet use a common syntax for the scheme-specific data, which conforms to the following URI specification:

`scheme://user:password@host:port/url-path`

Some or all of the parts, such as *user:password@*, *:password*, *:port*, and */url-path*, might be excluded. The scheme-specific data starts with a double slash to indicate that it complies with the common Internet scheme syntax. The URL of the main page of the World Wide Web project, for example, is as follows:

`http://www.w3.org/hypertext/WWW/`

Where:

➜ The prefix `http` indicates the addressing scheme and defines the interpretation of the rest of the string

➜ The address `www.w3.org` identifies the HTTP server to be contacted

➜ The substring `hypertext/WWW/` identifies the document object to be accessed on the `www.w3.org` server

By default, the World Wide Web server listens to TCP port 80. The URI syntax, however, allows alternative ports to be specified. To designate an alternative port, for example, 8000, where an experimental Web server has been set up to listen on, the following URI is used:

`http://www.w3.org:8000/experiment/test`

Different network protocols use different syntaxes where appropriate. A small amount of common syntax, however, is enforced by URI to retain in the common model various forms and features usually encountered in many information systems. Hierarchical forms, for example, are useful for hypertext, where a large compound document can be split into many smaller interlinked documents. The common URI syntax reserves the forward slash character as a way of representing a hierarchical name space.

For query purposes, the question mark character is used as a separator between the address of an object and a query operation applied to it. In all cases, the client passes the path string to the server uninterpreted. A search on a text database, for example, might look like this:

`http://www.my.com/AboutUs/Index/Phonebook?john`

A reference to a particular part of a document might look like the following, where the fragment identifier string #smith is not sent to the server, but is retained by the client and used when the whole document has been retrieved:

```
http://www.my.edu/admin/people#smith
```

URLs for Various Protocols

URIs are universal. They encode members of a universal set of network addresses. A new URI scheme can be readily designed for any new network protocol that has some concept of objects. One can form an address for any object by specifying the set of protocol parameters necessary to access the object. If these protocol parameters for accessing the object are encoded into a concise string, with a prefix to identify the protocol and the encoding, one has a new URI scheme, also known as a Universal Resource Locator (URL). There are schemes for the following:

➜ HyperText Transfer Protocol (for example, `http://www.w3.org/hypertext/WWW`)

➜ Gopher protocol (for example, `gopher://gopher.micro.umn.edu/`)

➜ Wide Area Information Servers (for example, `wais://munin.ub2.lu.se:210/academic_e-mail_conf`)

➜ File Transfer Protocol (for example, `ftp://rtfm.ai.mit.edu/pub/usenet-by-group/news.answer/ftp-list`)

➜ Electronic mail address (for example, `mailto:webmaster@w3.org`)

➜ Usenet news (for example, `news://comp.infosystems.www.misc`)

➜ Reference to interactive sessions (for example, `telnet://downwind.sprl.umich.edu:3000`)

➜ Local file access (`file://localhost/etc/rc.local`)

Gopher and WAIS

Gopher and WAIS are two other information systems similar to WWW. Gopher is a hierarchical, menu-based, campus-wide information system that also provides a simple text search mechanism by means of a master index located on the Veronica server. The WAIS protocol is largely influenced by the z39.50 protocol used for networking library catalogs, and provides more sophisticated search capabilities using a master index.

HTTP: HyperText Transfer Protocol

HTTP is an Internet protocol for accessing Web servers (BLFN 1995). HTTP adopts a readable text-based style, similar to that of the File Transfer Protocol (FTP) and Network News Transfer Protocol (NNTP) that have been used on the Internet for many years. HTTP is not so much a protocol for transferring hypertext, as the name might suggest, but more a protocol for transferring information with the efficiency necessary for making hypertext jumps. The data transferred can be anything: for example, plain text, hypertext, images, audio, or video.

HTTP is a simple request and response protocol layered on top of TCP. There are essentially four steps to an HTTP transaction:

1. **Connect.** When a user clicks on a hyperlink, the client goes out to the Internet to locate the server machine specified in the URL, and attempts to establish connection with the server.

2. **Request.** Each HTTP request from the client begins with an operation code, called the *method*, followed by the URL of an object. The "GET" method retrieves the document URL. The "PUT" method updates the Web document, possibly with the help of a client editor. The "POST" method attaches a new document to the Web, or submits a filled-in form to the server for processing.

3. **Response.** The Web server attempts to fulfill the client's request and returns the result. A three-digit status code tells the client how the response was understood and attended to.

4. **Close.** The server terminates the connection after performing the requested action. Both client and server software must handle instances of unexpected or premature closings (for example, triggered by the Stop button on most browsers, or caused by machine crashes).

The entire process of an HTTP transaction can be observed from the status bar of most browsers. Using the Netscape Navigator, for example, you see the following:

```
Connect: Contacting http://www.w3.org...
Connect: Host contacted. Waiting for reply...
Transferring data...
Document: Done.
```

Statelessness in HTTP

HTTP is stateless, as evidenced by the fact that a network connection is made and broken for each HTTP operation. HTTP runs over a TCP connection that is held only for the duration of a single operation. When a user browses the Web, document objects are retrieved in succession from one, but sometimes multiple, servers on the Internet. The stateless model is simple and efficient because a hyperlink from one object could lead to an object that resides anywhere, maybe on the local server or some remote server.

Being a stateless protocol, HTTP does not understand the concept of a *session* (logical grouping of multiple consecutive transactions) and has no provision for remembering what has gone on before with particular client-server pairs. As far as the server is concerned, each HTTP request is handled anew and carries no history or knowledge from past transactions with the client. In cases where the server needs to track client interactions over several HTTP transactions, various gateway programming tricks have been invented to retain state variables in the server or to pass them around back and forth between client and server (DC 1995).

Format Negotiations

HTTP is capable of format negotiations. In addition to simply transferring HTML documents, HTTP can be used to retrieve documents in an unbounded and extensible set of formats. The client first sends a list of formats that it can handle, and the server replies with data in any of those formats that it can produce.

According to the original Web developers (BLCLNS 1994), this type of negotiation has the advantage of allowing proprietary formats to be used between consenting programs, without the need for standardization of those formats. Furthermore, this negotiation system introduces a hook for transporting future formats that have yet to be invented. Currently, this negotiation system is used for natural languages such as French or Japanese where available, as well as for compression forms such as x-compress or x-gzip.

When objects are in transit over the network, information about them (meta-information) is transferred in HTTP headers. By adopting an extension of the Multi-purpose Internet Mail Extensions (MIME) (BF 1993) for use in the set of headers, the Web developers made a design decision to facilitate integration of hypermedia mail, news, and information access.

By further adopting the convention that unrecognized HTTP headers and parameters are ignored, it has been easy to try new ideas on working production servers. This has allowed the protocol definition to evolve in a controlled way by the incorporation of tested ideas.

HTML: HyperText Markup Language

HTML is a common basic language for the interchange of hypertext (BLC 1995; Raggett 1995). It describes the structure and organization of a document. HTML is designed to be simple so that it can be easily produced by both people and programs.

The idea behind HTML is to format information online for efficient electronic distribution, search, and retrieval in such a way that it is independent of the appearance details of the document. This greatly expedites the writing and production of documents.

Conventional word processing formats dictate the appearance of documents when displayed, and thus do not interoperate across different word processors. HTML does not dictate, but merely suggests, appropriate presentations for documents. By focusing only on document structure, and not on final appearance, HTML allows Web browsers free rein to interpret and display an HTML-formatted document to the best of their capabilities.

Level of HTML Conformance

HTML is a markup language defined according to the Standard Generalized Markup Language (SGML) (Goldfarb 1990), an international standard (ISO 8879) for text information processing. A valid HTML document can be parsed by an SGML parser provided the SGML declarations also include a Data Type Definition (DTD) for HTML. HTML is an evolving standard with the following levels of conformance:

→ **Level 0.** The minimum set of elements making up an HTML document that all browsers recognize. It includes a core set of simple structure elements such as headings, paragraphs, hyperlinks, bulleted lists, ordered list, and menu, all of which are useful when structuring online documents.

→ **Level 1.** Level 0 features plus character formatting and inline images.

→ **Level 2.** Level 0 and Level 1 features plus Form interface for the entry of data by users.

→ **Level 3.** Level 0, 1, 2 features plus extensions for tables, figures, and mathematical formulas, stylesheets, and other features for control of layout.

 Currently, many browsers support a subset of the more advanced (and possibly not yet standard) HTML features, in addition to those of the more basic levels. This is due in part to intense competition among browser manufacturers for market share.

HTML Tags

HTML documents consist of a set of tags that specify the logical structure of the document, as well as suggestion of how it could be displayed. Most HTML elements are identified in a document as a start tag, which gives the element name and attributes, followed by the content, followed by the end tag (see fig. 3.5). As in the following tag, tags define the start and end of headings, paragraphs, lists, character highlighting, and hyperlinks:

```
<HTML>
<HEAD>
<TITLE> Sample HTML Example </TITLE>
</HEAD>

<BODY>
<H1> This is H1 Header </H1>
<H2> This is H2 header </H2>
<H3> This is H3 header </H3>
<H4> This is H4 header </H4>
```

```
<P>      This is a paragraph. End tags are not
         strictly needed for paragraphs, but they
         are allowed.

<P> Here is an unordered list:
<UL>
<LI> First item in an unordered list.
<LI> Second item in an unordered list.
</UL>

<P> Here is an ordered list:
<OL>
<LI> First item in an ordered list.
<LI> Second item in an ordered list.
</OL>

<P> You can include character highlighting in a
      paragraph:
             e.g. <I> italics </I> or <B> bold</B>.

<P> This is a hypertext link to the
<A href="http://www.w3.org/"> W3C home page </A>.
</BODY>
</HTML>
```

HTML exists as a markup language independent of HTTP or World Wide Web. HTML can be used in hypertext e-mail (as "text/html" MIME content type), news, and anywhere hypertext structure is needed. There is no requirement that file contents of Web pages be stored in HTML. Servers can store file contents in other formats or in variations on HTML that include extra information of local interest only. Upon requests from clients, HTML documents can be generated on-the-fly.

Forms and Imagemaps: Enhanced Web Interactivity

The power of the World Wide Web lies in its expressiveness. As originally conceived, the Web implements a distributed information space whose sole means of user interaction is hypertext navigation through mouse point-and-click. Fill-out forms and imagemaps are recent technical developments that substantially enrich the expressiveness of the Web by providing enhanced interactivity.

Fill-Out Forms

The HTML Form interface allows document creators to define HTML documents containing forms to be filled out by users. Features of a fill-out form include radio buttons, check boxes, menus (pull-down or otherwise), and text input, all of which are designed to accept user inputs. When a user fills out the form and presses a button indicating the form should be "submitted," the information on the form is sent to a server for processing. The server usually prepares an HTML document using the information supplied by the user and returns it to the client for display. Details are described in the next section on gateway programming.

Clickable Images

Imagemaps, originally invented in May, 1993, by Kevin Hughes, then of Honolulu Community

College, introduced interactive graphics to the World Wide Web. Imagemaps enable the use of clickable images, which are to graphics what hypertext links are to Web documents. In an imagemap, different parts of the image are linked to different places in the Web information space. When a user clicks on a certain part of an image, the corresponding Web document linked to that part will be fetched as though a normal hypertext link has just been activated. Imagemaps thus combine the freedom of graphics design with the navigational power of hypertext documents. The use of imagemap is best illustrated in the Virtual Tourist Web page, shown in figure 3.6, where a clickable world map (visible if you were to scroll down) provides an easy way for users to navigate different parts of the world.

Gateway Programming: Processing Client Input

The Common Gateway Interface (CGI) is key to providing advanced Web interactivity. It allows the Web to be connected to other software and databases by essentially functioning as a gateway. Using CGI, the user can execute a program remotely on the server, search for specific items in a database, or exchange information through an interface with other software. Gateway programs can be used to execute filter programs that generate HTML documents (from other native formats) on-the-fly, or to extract inventory and pricing information from commercial databases upon request.

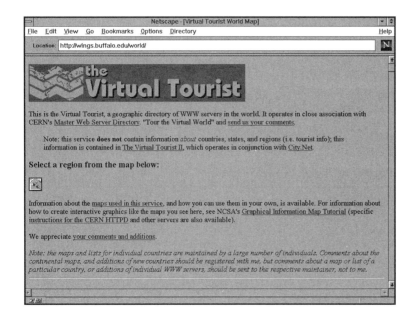

Figure 3.6

The Virtual Tourist Imagemap.

Mastery of gateway programming requires knowledge of either a scripting language (such as Perl or TCL) or a programming language (such as C/C++), an understanding of how input arguments are specified and extracted for processing, and the ability to properly format the output for display on client browsers.

Gateway programs usually are deposited under a directory called `/cgi-bin/` on most Unix machines, if using the CERN or NCSA Web servers. The pathname to the gateway program `/cgi-bin/qs` on the server `www.secapl.com`, for example, is included as part of its URL, as in the following:

`http://www.secapl.com/cgi-bin/qs`

Gateway Program Interaction

A link to the gateway program can be created in a Web page by embedding the gateway program's URL in an HTML anchor. The following are ways to invoke a gateway program (other than simply clicking on a specific hypertext link with an embedded gateway program URL):

→ Clicking on a specific location within an imagemap

→ Returning an ISINDEX query box

→ Submitting a fill-out form

Figure 3.7 illustrates how a gateway program can be triggered using a fill-out form. The following describes the detailed action sequence:

1. The client requests the URL `http://www.secapl.com/cgi-bin/qs` from the `www.secapl.com` server after the user clicks on the corresponding hyperlink in a Web page.

2. The server returns the requested URL `http://www.secapl.com/qs`, which is an HTML form (see fig. 3.8).

3. The user fills out the form with `msft` and clicks on the submit button.

4. The client sends the resulting filled-out form, now identified by URL `http://www.secapl.com/qs?msft`, to the server for processing.

5. The server executes gateway program `/cgi-bin/qs` using `msft` as input argument.

6. The formatted output, identified by URL `http://qs.secapl.com:85/cgi-bin/qsyy` is passed from the server back to the client and displayed as a Web page on the user's screen.

There are specific books that provide more comprehensive coverage of gateway programming (DR 1995).

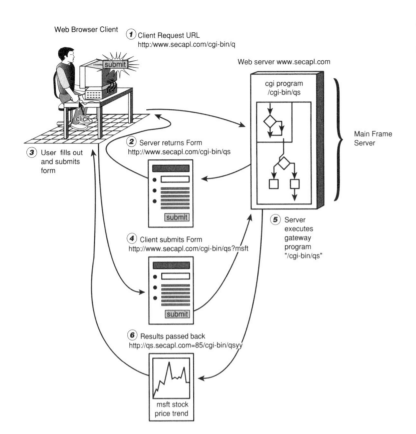

Figure 3.7

Invocation of a Gateway Program using Forms.

Web Browser Client ① Client Request URL
http:/www.secapl.com/cgi-bin/q

submit

Web server www.secapl.com

cgi program
/cgi-bin/qs

Main Frame
Server

click

③ User fills out
and submits
form

② Server returns Form
http://www.secapl.com/cgi-bin/qs

submit

⑤ Server
executes
gateway
program
"/cgi-bin/qs"

④ Client submits Form
http://www.secapl.com/cgi-bin/qs?msft

submit

⑥ Results passed back
http://qs.secapl.com=85/cgi-bin/qsyy

msft stock
price trend

The Next Step: Agents on the Web

Most of the commercial and entrepreneurial efforts had focused on the Web being a facilitator of electronic commerce, usually consummated in secure transactions involving digital cash or some other form of payment schemes over the Internet. Many such applications require the client and server to authenticate each other and exchange sensitive information confidentially. Current HTTP implementations have only modest support for the cryptographic mechanisms appropriate for such

transactions, but interesting developments are underway (see Chapters 8, "Web Transaction Security," and 9, "Electronic Cash and Payment Services").

Early Commerce Agents

The World Wide Web and Mosaic have been considered the "killer apps" for the Internet because they have made possible the innovative use of the medium on a grand scale. It is believed that the next step in the evolution of the Internet is to consider the Web as a natural platform for introducing

Figure 3.8

HTML form to be filled-out.

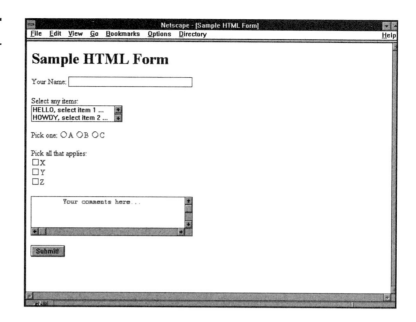

innovative "commerce agents" of all types that can provide many interesting services such as bargain-hunting, mortgage-rate locking, bartering, brokering, and stock tracking.

Virtual storefronts on the Web, complete with online catalogs and automated ordering services, already implement a rudimentary form of sales agents. In response, various bargain-finding and procurement agents came into being on the Web relying on the use of such facilities. For example, the BargainFinder agent developed by Dr. Bruce Krulwich, a research scientist at Andersen Consulting, is one such early prototype of commerce agents. BargainFinder has been deployed on the Web as a service since July 1995 and can be found at Andersen Consulting's Web site at `http://bf.cstar.ac.com/bf/`. BargainFinder allows users to search for CDs and compare prices among nine compact disc sources on the Internet.

However, the BargainFinder service has run into problems. BargainFinder was not welcome at some of the online CD stores (especially those that charge higher prices for their CDs!). In fact, three out of the nine stores that BargainFinder visits have taken actions to prevent BargainFinder from accessing their online inventory database. There are also problems with BargainFinder trying to cope with some of the more difficult data formats used by a few online CD stores. To make Web shopping technology more readily accessible, I have developed a WebShopper agent that is freely available to the public. WebShopper can be configured to run as either BookFinder or CDFinder, from anywhere on the Internet. As their names imply, BookFinder shops for books and CDFinder shops for CDs on the Web.

WebShopper is quite similar to BargainFinder; the major difference being that WebShopper does not perform price comparisons for the user as does the BargainFinder. Instead, WebShopper explores various online sources (whose URLs and related search parameters are specified in a WebShopper task file), and simply collects final results of the search for particular books or CDs. The user can then perform comparisons based not just on the price alone, but also on other relevant terms of sale like freight charges and refund policies. The complete listing of WebShopper agent code can be found in Appendix C. Sample task files used by BookFinder and CDFinder to shop for books and CDs can be found in Appendices D and E.

Web Agents of the Future?

It is likely that a new breed of sophisticated commerce agents will come to dominate the Internet of the future, with no less impact as when compared with what Mosaic does to the Web. It also is likely that the arrival of these Internet "killer bots" will radically transform the face of the Web, upset the established marketplace and institutions, and challenge people with new ways of interacting with the medium.

At the phenomenal rate of commercialization that the Internet and the Web is currently experiencing, I would not be surprised to find in the near future digital versions of any of the following commerce agents on the Web: travel agents, insurance agents, real estate and mortgage brokers, stock brokers, manufacturers' agents, or even specialty headhunters of the literary, theatrical, sports, and talent agents genre! No one knows for sure which way future events will be played out. There have been speculations, conjectures, grand visions, and more importantly, concrete plans. It is my hope that most readers will find the rest of this book useful and informative as a gentle introduction to the wonderful world of agents and related technologies. For the few who harbor greater ambitions, it is further hoped that this book shall lead you down the path of constructing interesting agents for the Internet and the Web.

The next few chapters begin the journey on Web robots, which are agents that roam the Web with the goal of automating specific tasks related to the Web. Specifically, Chapter 4, "Spiders for Indexing the Web," introduces the use of *spiders* and *wanderers* for discovering Web resources. Chapter 5, "Web Robots: Operational Guidelines," examines Web robots in general and explores issues of interest and offers guidelines to both robot writers and Webmasters. Chapter 6, "HTTP: Protocol of Web Robots," provides an in-depth treatment of the latest version 1.0 of the HTTP protocol whose mastery is required for Web robot construction. Finally, Chapter 7, "WebWalker: Your Web Maintenance Robot," illustrates the detailed construction of one such Web robot, called the WebWalker.

p a r t

· ·

Web Robot Construction

4

Spiders for Indexing the Web

The World Wide Web is decentralized, dynamic, and diverse; navigation is difficult, and finding information can be a challenge. The reason for this challenge is that users of the World Wide Web usually navigate to find resources by following hypertext links. As the Web continues to grow, users must traverse more links to find what they are looking for, making it impractical to just wander the Web searching for information. Users, therefore, have come to depend on search engines to help them find online resources.

There are a number of different search engines available on the Web, each using a different method to build its underlying database. On one end of the spectrum are search engines that rely entirely on individual servers to provide self-indexing information, such as Martijn Koster's Aliweb (Archie-like indexing for the Web) (1994). This approach requires people to write index files in a specific format and store these files on their servers. Many (and apparently most) server managers have not proven willing or able to make the required effort. As a result, databases produced by this method are invariably far from complete.

On the other end of the spectrum are proactive engines, which use *Web robots* such as WebCrawler and Lycos to index large portions of the Web. Web robots, also called *spiders* or *wanderers*, are software programs that traverse the World Wide Web information space by following hypertext links and retrieving Web documents by standard HTTP protocol. Web robots require no centralized decision making and no participation from individual Web site administrators—that is, the *Webmasters*—other than their compliance with the protocols that make the Web operate in the first place. Engines of this class tend to build more complete databases than those that rely on the voluntary efforts of cooperative Webmasters.

 n o t e Even the most comprehensive engines (such as Lycos) do not provide full indexing of the entire Web due to resource constraints. But by starting from the corpus of information that the spiders have discovered, and *recalled* by the search engine based upon user query, users can usually navigate much easier on the Web to find the *precise* information specific to their needs.

This chapter examines Web indexing spiders in general but focuses on two of the better known ones, the WebCrawler and Lycos spiders, that have come to dominate the Web. This chapter also discusses more advanced information gathering and dissemination architectures, such as Harvest and WebAnts, into which spiders of the future can be nicely integrated to work in a distributed and cooperative fashion.

Web Indexing Spiders

There are a variety of spiders that "crawl" around in the Web to collect information about what they find. Spiders make use of hyperlinks embedded in Web pages to automatically traverse the Web, moving from one HTML document to another by referencing the URL anchor. The information collected by spiders can be used for a variety of purposes, such as building an index for assisting users with keyword-oriented searching.

The World Wide Web Worm by Oliver McBryan, the first widely used spider, was made available in March 1994. It was an early ancestor to the newer species of spiders on the Web today. It builds an index of titles and URLs from its collection of over 100,000 Web documents and still provides the user with a search interface (shown in fig. 4.1) to its database.

Figure 4.1

World Wide Web Worm home page.

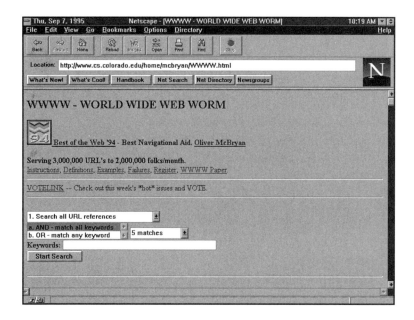

The World Wide Web Worm, as well as early spiders such as the Jumpstation (by Jonathan Fletcher), does not index the *content* of documents. Rather, only the HTML document titles and headers, as well as anchor text information outside the documents, are indexed.

These early spiders eventually became eclipsed by a subsequent generation of spiders that provide more powerful databases by indexing the full contents of documents. The Repository Based Software Engineering (RBSE) Spider arrived on the scene in February 1994 and was the first spider that indexed documents by content (Eichmann 1994). It was followed closely by Brian Pinkerton's WebCrawler, which began operation in April 1994.

According to Pinkerton, the reason for going to full-content indexing is that indexing by titles alone might not be adequate. Titles are an optional part

of an HTML document, and 20 percent of the documents do not have them. In addition, basing an index only on titles omits a significant fraction of documents from the index. Furthermore, titles don't always reflect the content of a document. Therefore, by indexing both titles and content, spiders such as the WebCrawler and Lycos capture more of what people want to know.

Web spiders often are criticized for being inefficient and wasteful of valuable Internet resources, even though they try to be *good citizens* on the Web (see Chapter 5, "Web Robots: Operational Guidelines," for more information on becoming citizens).

The triumph of the current generation of spiders over the earlier is mainly an issue of building high-quality, content-based indexes of Web documents. Given the phenomenal growth rate of the Web, the current generation of spiders will be hard-pressed

to keep up. A new generation of spiders will eventually supercede the current spiders by focusing on the increasingly important issues of performance and scalability.

These spiders of the future will use sophisticated information gathering and dissemination architecture, such as that offered by Harvest (BDHMS 1994) and WebAnts. On the horizon are a whole new generation of stronger, faster, and smarter spiders that can better survive the rapid growth of a dynamic and massive Web.

 n o t e A list of information resources about other interesting spiders can be found in Appendix G, "List of World Wide Web Spiders and Robots," or Martijn Koster's up-to-date *List of Robots* (1994c).

WebCrawler: Finding What People Want

The WebCrawler project was started by Brian Pinkerton at the University of Washington in Seattle. WebCrawler is a resource discovery tool for the World Wide Web that provides a fast way of finding resources by maintaining an index of the Web that can be queried for documents about a specific topic.

WebCrawler was announced and made available to the world in April 1994 with an initial database containing information on Web documents from 6,000 servers. It answers over 6,000 queries per day and is updated weekly. In 1995, WebCrawler was acquired by America Online and is now operated as a public service available free to the Web community. As of this writing, WebCrawler has a content index of about 100 MB that holds information on over 150,000 different documents that it has explored. In addition, WebCrawler knows of the existence of over 1,500,000 unique documents it has not visited.

WebCrawler is capable of performing the following functions:

➡ Building indexes of the Web

➡ Automatically navigating on demand

Ordinary users can access the centrally maintained WebCrawler Index using a Web browser such as Mosaic or Netscape Navigator. Privileged users can run the WebCrawler client itself, automatically searching the Web on demand, but this feature is not available to the general public. The WebCrawler uses an incomplete breadth-first traversal to create an index and relies on an automatic navigation mechanism to find the rest of the information. Both document titles and document content are indexed using a vector space model (Salton 1989).

Searching with WebCrawler

The database built by WebCrawler is available through the following search page on the Web (see fig. 4.2).

Figure 4.2

The WebCrawler search form.

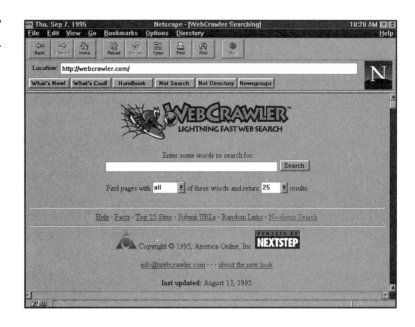

How WebCrawler Moves in Webspace

WebCrawler accesses the Web one document at a time, making local decisions in the Webspace about how best to proceed next. Unlike other centralized approaches to indexing and resource discovery, such as Aliweb (Koster 1994) and Harvest (BDHMS 1994), WebCrawler operates using only the infrastructure that makes the Web work in the first place: the ability of clients to retrieve documents from servers.

The WebCrawler design has the following characteristics:

→ It uses a content-based, full-text indexing system to provide a high-quality index. In a Web robot, there is no additional network load imposed by full-text indexing; the load occurs only at the server.

→ It uses a breadth-first search strategy to create a broad index, spreading the load among servers and ensuring that every server with useful content has at least several pages represented in the index.

→ It tries to include as many Web servers as possible. It does so in a friendly manner, such as not overloading Web servers with rapid-fire requests. It also respects the *Robot Exclusion Standard* (see Chapter 5), which is a way for Webmasters to communicate to compliant robots which areas of the Web are off-limits.

The discovery of new documents is important in the WebCrawler design due to the dynamic nature of the Web information space. WebCrawler discovers new documents by learning their identities in the form of Uniform Resource Locators (URLs). WebCrawler starts with a known set of documents, examines the outbound links from them, follows

one of the links that leads to a new document, then repeats the whole process. In other words, WebCrawler simply explores the Webspace as a large directed graph using a graph traversal algorithm that performs the following sequence of actions over and over:

1. Discovers a new document

2. Marks the document as having been retrieved

3. Deciphers any outbound links

4. Indexes the content of the document

WebCrawler Architecture

As illustrated in figure 4.3, the WebCrawler software architecture is made up of the following four components:

→ **The search engine.** This directs the WebCrawler's activities and is responsible for deciding which new documents to explore and for initiating their retrieval.

→ **The agents.** These are responsible for retrieving the documents from the network at the direction of the search engine.

→ **The database.** This handles the persistent storage of the document metadata, the links between documents, and the full-text index.

→ **The query server.** This implements the query service provided to the Internet.

WebCrawler's Search Engine

The WebCrawler search engine determines which documents and what types of documents to visit. Non-indexable files, such as pictures, sounds, PostScript, or binary data, are not retrieved. In addition, erroneously retrieved files are ignored during the indexing step. This sort of file-type discrimination is applied to both indexing and real-time search modes.

The search engine uses different discovery strategies when running the WebCrawler in indexing mode and when running it in real-time search mode. In indexing mode, the goal is to build an index of as much of the Web as possible within limited storage space. WebCrawler believes that the Web documents used to build the index should come from as many different servers as possible. It uses a modified breadth-first algorithm to ensure that

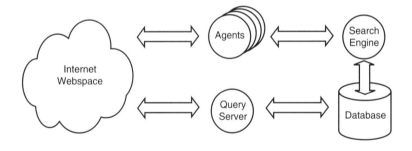

Figure 4.3

WebCrawler Software Architecture.

every server has at least one document represented in the index. These steps show how the algorithm works:

1. When a document on a new server is found, that server is placed on a list of servers to be visited right away.

2. One document from each of the new servers is retrieved and indexed before visiting any other documents.

3. When all known servers have been visited, indexing proceeds sequentially through a list of all servers until a new one is found, at which point the process repeats.

In real-time search mode, where the goal is to find documents that are most similar to a user's query, the WebCrawler uses a different search algorithm. The intuition behind the algorithm is that following links from documents that are similar to what the user wants is more likely to lead to relevant documents than following any link from any document. According to Pinkerton, this intuition roughly captures the way people navigate the Web; they find a document about a topic related to what they are looking for and follow links from there.

The algorithm works like this:

1. WebCrawler runs the user's query against its index to first come up with an initial list of similar documents.

2. From the list, the most relevant documents are noted, and any unexplored links from those documents are followed.

3. As new documents are retrieved, they are added to the index, and the query is re-run.

4. The results of the query are sorted by relevance, and new documents near the top of the list become candidates for further exploration.

5. The process is iterated either until the WebCrawler has found enough similar documents to satisfy the user or until a time limit is reached.

Searching for and finding documents by navigating from within other *similar* documents was first demonstrated and proven to work with the Fish search developed by Debra and Post at Eindhoven University of Technology (DP 1994). The Fish search offers a client-based search tool that is integrated with the Mosaic browser. The Fish search is reminiscent of schools of fish moving in the direction of food, hence its name. In the Fish search, each URL corresponds to a fish. After a document is retrieved, the fish spawns a number of children depending on whether the document is relevant and how many URLs are embedded in the document. The fish dies after following a number of links without finding any more relevant documents. Searches can be conducted by keywords, regular expressions, or by relevancy ranking with external filters. The WebCrawler extends this concept to initiate the search using the index, and to follow links in an intelligent order.

When people navigate, they choose links based on the *anchor text* (words that describe a link to another document) and tend to follow a directed path to their destination. When WebCrawler navigates and sees multiple links in a document, it evaluates each link for relevance based upon the similarity of the anchor text to the user's query. But anchor texts usually are short and do not adequately convey the

much needed relevance information as well as the full document text. To help the situation, Pinkerton noted that a thesaurus could be used to expand the anchor text.

WebCrawler's Agents

Agents are invoked by the search engine for the purpose of retrieving Web documents. Because waiting for servers and the network creates a search bottleneck, agents run in separate processes, and the WebCrawler employs up to 15 agents in parallel. For each new Web document to be retrieved, the search engine finds a free agent, and asks the agent to retrieve the URL representing the document. The agent either responds to the search engine with an object containing the document content or an explanation of why the document could not be retrieved. After the agent has responded, it becomes free again and may be given new work to do.

The agent program uses the CERN WWW library (libWWW), which supports access to several types of content through different protocols, including HTTP, FTP, and Gopher. As a practical matter, running agents in separate processes helps isolate the main WebCrawler process from memory leaks and errors in the agent and in libWWW.

WebCrawler's Database

The WebCrawler's database holds both the full-text index and the representation of the Web as a graph. The database is stored on disk and is updated as documents are added. To protect the database from system crashes, updates are made under the scope of transactions that are committed every few hundred documents.

WebCrawler uses NeXTStep's IndexingKit to build its full-text index, which is inverted to make queries fast: looking up a word produces a list of pointers to documents that contain that word. More complex queries are handled by combining the document lists for several words with conventional set operations. The index uses a vector-space model for handling queries (Salton 1989).

Words from a document are run through a "stop list" to prevent common words from being indexed, and they are weighted by their frequency in the document divided by their frequency in a reference domain. Words that appear frequently in the document and infrequently in the reference domain are weighted most highly, while words that appear infrequently in either are given lower weights. This type of weighting is commonly called *peculiarity weighting*.

The remainder of the database stores data about servers, documents, and links. Entire URLs are not stored; instead, they are broken down into objects that describe the server and the document. A link in a document is simply a pointer to another document. Each object is stored in a separate Btree on disk: documents in one, servers in another, and links in the last. Separating the data in this way allows the WebCrawler to scan the list of servers quickly to select unexplored servers or the least recently accessed server.

WebCrawler's Query Server

The query server implements the WebCrawler search service available via an HTML search form on the Web. This simple interface is powerful and can find related documents with ease. The query model it presents is a simple vector-space query

model based on the full-text database described earlier. Users enter keywords as their query, and the titles and URLs of documents containing some or all of those words are retrieved from the index and presented to the user as an ordered list sorted by relevance. In this model, relevance is the sum (over all words in the query) of the product of the word's weight in the document and its weight in the query divided by the number of words in the query.

 n o t e The WebCrawler is a useful Web searching tool. It does not place an undue burden on individual servers while building its index. WebCrawler adopts the standard for robot exclusion standard (see Chapter 5) and identifies itself as *WebCrawler* in the HTTP User-Agent request header field when traversing the Web.

Lycos: Hunting WWW Information

The Lycos project was headed by Dr. Michael Mauldin of the Center for Machine Translation at Carnegie Mellon University as an experiment in "best-first-search" within the Web information space. The Lycos home page is shown in figure 4.4.

According to Mauldin, the word Lycos came from the arachnid family Lycosidae, which are relatively large ground spiders that catch their prey by pursuit rather than in a web. These spiders also are noted for their speed and are especially active at night. Lycos lives up to its name by continuously "hunting" its prey (Web pages on servers) for information. The search results are then merged with the catalog on a weekly basis.

Figure 4.4

The Lycos home page.

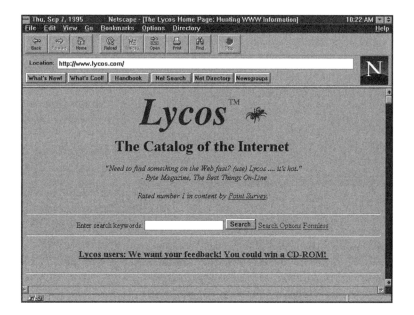

The Lycos spider is a fairly recent spider that was announced to the world in August 1994. It helps users locate Web documents containing specific user-supplied keywords. Due to the comprehensiveness of its database, Lycos quickly became very popular with Web users who needed to conduct full-content searches over the space of documents formed by the Web. By mid-July of 1995, Lycos accumulated the following:

→ 5,077,834 unique URLs

→ 1,177,750 documents (a total of 8,703,484,067 bytes)

→ 3,900,084 unexplored URLs with descriptions

→ 1,834,323,446 bytes of Lycos summaries

→ 1,078,127,917 bytes of inverted index

The Lycos database has grown rapidly, from 634,000 references in August 1994 to over 5.6 million unique URLs in August 1995. Lycos thus offers a huge database to locate documents matching any given query.

Searching with Lycos

The search interface provides a way for users to find documents that contain references to a keyword, and to examine a document outline, keyword list, and an excerpt (see fig. 4.5). The result of a sample search using Lycos to find relevant Web pages on Ebola can be seen in figure 4.6.

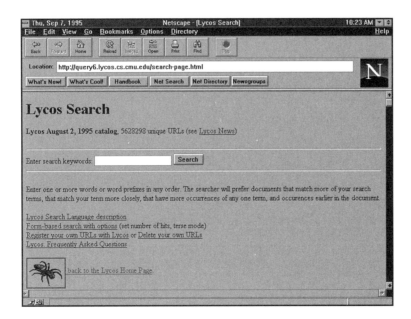

Figure 4.5

The Lycos search form.

Figure 4.6

A Lycos search for Ebola returns different match information.

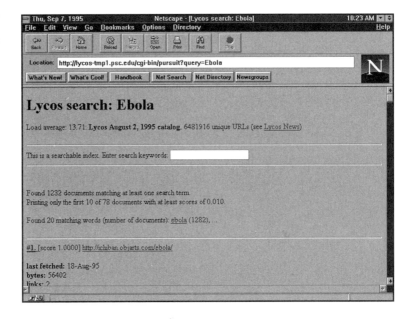

Lycos' Search Space

Lycos defines the Webspace to be any documents in the following spaces:

→ HTTP space

→ FTP space

→ Gopher space

Lycos can retrieve documents that it has not searched by using the text in the parent document as a description for the unexplored links (the highlighted text from each HTML hyperlink anchor is associated with the URL for that anchor). Lycos does not, however, search and index ephemeral, time-varying, or infinite virtual spaces. Therefore, Lycos ignores the following spaces:

→ WAIS databases

→ Usenet news

→ Mailto space

→ Telnet services

→ Local file space

Lycos also ignores files that start with "/dev/tty" or end with these extensions: AU, AVI, BIN, DAT, DVI, EXE, FLI, GIF, GZ, HDF, HQX, JPEG, LHA, MAC, MPEG, PS, TAR, TGA, TIFF, UU, UUE, WAV, Z, or ZIP.

Lycos Indexing

To reduce the amount of information that needs to be stored, Lycos extracts the following pieces of information from each document that it retrieves:

➜ Title

➜ Headings and subheadings

➜ 100 most important words

➜ First 20 lines

➜ Size in bytes

➜ Number of words

The 100 important words are selected using the *Tf*IDf* weighting algorithm, which considers word placement and frequencies, among other factors. Words, for example, are scored by how far into the document they appear. Thus, hits in the title or first paragraph are scored higher.

 In a collection of *N* documents, the *term frequency* (Tf) is the number of occurences of particular terms in the collection, and the *document frequency* (Df) is the number of documents in the collection in which particular terms occur. The idea of an *inverse document frequency* (IDf) is to measure how good particular terms are as a document discriminator—that is, to distinguish the few documents in which they occur from the many from which they are absent. A typical IDf factor is given by log(N/Df).

In the Tf*IDf weighting algorithm, the basic idea is that the best indexing terms are those that occur frequently in individual documents but rarely in the remainder of the collection. The importance, or *weight*, of a term is thus defined as the product of multiplying Tf, the term frequency, by *inverse document frequency* (IDf). In other words, weight = Tf × IDf = Tf × log(N/Df).

How Lycos Moves in Webspace

The Web-wandering component of Lycos originally was derived from a program called Longlegs, written by John Leavitt and Eric Nyberg at Carnegie Mellon University.

Lycos uses an innovative, probabilistic scheme to skip from server to server in Webspace. This avoids overloading any one server with a barrage of requests, and also allows Lycos to give preference to URLs deemed more informative. The basic steps of the algorithm are as follows:

1. When a URL resource is fetched, Lycos scans its contents for new URL references, which it adds to an internal queue.

2. To choose the next URL to explore, Lycos makes a random choice among the HTTP, Gopher, and FTP references on the queue based upon preferences.

Lycos prefers to seek out popular documents, that is, those that have multiple links into them. Lycos also has a slight preference for shorter URLs, which generally are top-level directories and documents closer to the "root" of the hierarchy (December 1994).

According to Mauldin, the Lycos philosophy is to keep a finite model of the Web that enables subsequent searches to proceed more rapidly. The idea is to prune the "tree" of documents and to represent the clipped ends with a summary of the documents found under that node. The 100 most important words lists from several documents can be combined to produce a list of the 100 most important words in the set of documents.

 Lycos currently maintains an index database to a huge collection of Web documents that is probably the largest among all known spiders. Lycos complies with the standard for robot exclusion, and identifies itself as "Lycos" by setting the HTTP User-Agent field in the request header. In this way, Webmasters can tell when Lycos has hit their server.

Harvest: Gathering and Brokering Information

Harvest is an integrated suite of customizable tools that provides a scalable, customizable architecture for gathering, indexing, caching, replicating, and accessing Internet information, which includes the Web as well (BDHMS 1994). The philosophy behind the Harvest system is that it gathers information about Internet resources and customizes views into what is "harvested."

The creators of the Harvest system recognize three types of problems with most current Internet information systems:

→ Most World Wide Web robots use expensive object retrieval protocols to gather indexing information and do not coordinate information gathering among themselves. Each World Wide Web robot gathers all the information it needs, without trying to share overlapping information with other robots.

→ Little support exists for customizing how different information formats and index/search schemes are handled.

→ Internet data and indices often become very popular and cause serious network and server bottlenecks.

According to Professor Michael Schwartz of the University of Colorado at Boulder, who is team leader for the project, Harvest can address the problem of how to make effective use of Internet information in the face of rapid growth in data volume, user base, and data diversity.

Harvest provides a very efficient means of gathering and distributing index information (with *Gatherers*), and supports the easy construction of many different types of indexes customized to suit the peculiarities of each information collection (with *Brokers*). In addition, Harvest also provides caching and replication support to alleviate bottlenecks.

 Harvest was deployed on the Internet in November 1994, and can be reached at `http://harvest.cs.colorado.edu`, as shown in figure 4.7.

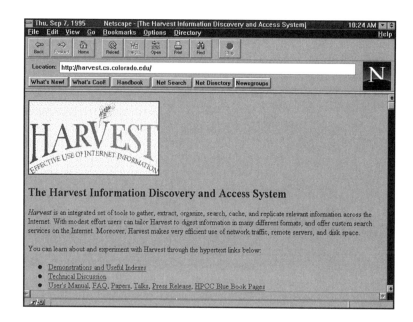

Figure 4.7

The Harvest home page.

Harvest enables Internet users to locate and summarize information stored in many different formats on machines around the world. The Harvest system interoperates with multiple information resources, including the World Wide Web. Harvest now has the capability, for example, to locate thousands of technical reports from around the world on a particular topic and then summarize the contents of each report.

n o t e   Harvest is not a spider; it is more than that. A spider can be a component, called a *Broker*, in the Harvest architecture.

Searching with Harvest

With the help of a spider to collect Web pages, Harvest can index the Web information space. For example, the Harvest WWW Home Pages Broker,

accessible through an HTML forms interface shown in figure 4.8, currently holds content summaries of more than 45,000 Web home pages. It uses WAIS as its backend searching and indexing engine.

The Harvest Home Pages Broker has a very flexible and powerful interface, providing Boolean search queries based on author, keyword, title, or URL reference. For example, searching for Ebola on the Harvest Home Pages Broker returns 12 matches.

Although the Harvest database of World Wide Web documents is currently not as extensive as that of other spiders, it has great potential for efficiently collecting a large amount of them.

Figure 4.8

*The Harvest WWW
Home Pages Broker
Query Interface.*

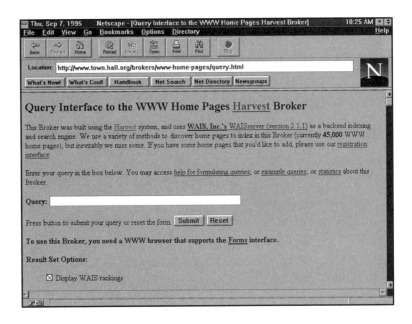

Harvest Architecture

In contrast to the individual gathering efforts in the current generation of Web spiders (see fig. 4.9), the Harvest architecture offers a big improvement. In the Harvest architecture, both the information-gathering efforts, as well as gathered results, can be shared.

 A Harvest Gatherer collects indexing information, while a Harvest Broker provides an incrementally indexed query interface to the gathered information.

As illustrated in figure 4.10, Harvest offers a flexible scheme consisting of Gatherers and Brokers

Figure 4.9

*Uncoordinated informa-
tion gathering by Web
robots.*

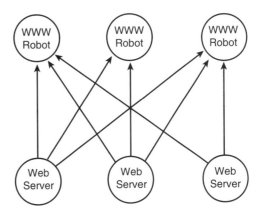

that can be arranged in various ways. This flexibility enables efficient use of network and server resources.

The Harvest architecture consists of the following subsystems:

→ Gatherer collects indexing information

→ Broker provides a flexible interface to gathered information

→ Index/Search subsystem allows the information space to be flexibly indexed and searched in a variety of ways

→ Object Cache stores contents of retrieved objects to alleviate access bottlenecks to popular data

→ Replicator mirrors index information of Brokers to alleviate server bottlenecks

Harvest Gatherer

The Gatherer provides an efficient and flexible way to collect indexing information. It solves two major problems that plague most current Web indexing systems:

→ Data collection inefficiencies

→ Duplication of implementation effort

Most current indexing systems cause excessive load on remote sites and generate excess network traffic. Retrieving via HTTP/Gopher/FTP requires heavyweight operations, like forking separate

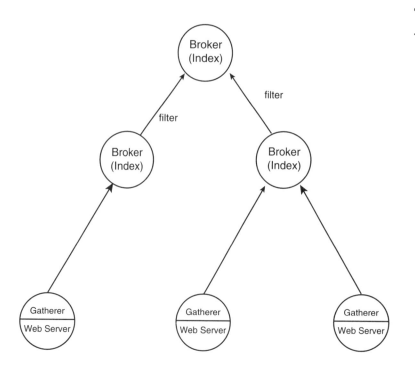

Figure 4.10

The Harvest approach to information gathering.

processes for each object, and entire objects often are retrieved when only a small part of the information actually is needed (for example, retaining only HTML anchors in an index).

Although the Gatherer can access an information Provider from across the network using the native HTTP, Gopher, or FTP protocols, this arrangement is primarily useful for interoperating with systems that do not run the Harvest software. The following are two important ways for Gatherers to achieve efficient use of network and server resources:

➜ A Gatherer can be run at the Provider site, saving a great deal of server load and network traffic.

➜ A Gatherer can feed information to many Brokers, saving repeated gathering costs.

The Harvest Gatherer provides efficient data collection through Provider site-resident software optimized for indexing. The Gatherer scans objects periodically, maintains a cache of indexing information (so that separate traversals are not required for each request), and allows a Provider's indexing information to be retrieved in a single stream (rather than requiring separate requests for each object). It minimizes network traffic by pre-filtering the contents and sending only incremental updates of indexing information in compressed form over the network.

The Gatherer avoids duplication of implementation efforts by providing enough flexibility to allow different indexes to be built. It uses a customizable content extraction system that allows users to customize what data are gathered, whether data are gathered locally (which is more efficient but requires

site cooperation), or remotely (which allows data to be gathered via the standard HTTP/Gopher/FTP protocols). The Gatherer extracts information in different ways depending on the file types. It can, for example, find author and title lines in Latex documents, and symbols in object code.

Harvest Broker

The Broker provides an indexed query interface to gathered information. Periodically, the Broker retrieves information from one or more Gatherers or other Brokers, and incrementally updates its index. The Broker's interface is independent of the indexer, and can be customized to include new indexers with minimal effort. The Broker also can be configured to expire and re-collect information at varying intervals from the specified Gatherers.

The Broker collects objects directly from another Broker using a bulk transfer protocol. The Broker keeps track of the unique identifiers and time-to-live's for each indexed object. When a query or update is received, it invokes the Index/Search Subsystem.

 A Broker can collect information from many Gatherers, to build an index of widely distributed information.

Brokers also can retrieve information from other Brokers, in effect cascading indexed views from one another, using the Broker's query interface to filter/refine the information from one Broker to the next.

Harvest provides a distinguished Broker instance called the Harvest Server Registry (HSR), which registers information about each Harvest Gatherer,

Broker, Cache, and Replicator in the Internet. The HSR is useful when searching for an appropriate Broker and when constructing new Gatherers and Brokers, to avoid duplication of effort. It can also be used to locate Caches and Replicators.

Harvest Index/Search Subsystem

Harvest defines a general Broker-Indexer interface that can accommodate a variety of back-end search engines to accommodate diverse indexing and searching needs. The backend is required to support Boolean combinations of attribute-based queries, and incremental updates. A variety of different backends can thus be used inside a Broker. Currently, Harvest supports WAIS, Glimpse, and Nebula; they all are optimized for different uses.

Glimpse supports space-efficient indexes and flexible interactive queries. Glimpse uses pointers to occurrence blocks of adjustable sizes, instead of pointing to the exact occurrence. It can thus achieve very space efficient indexes, typically 2–4 percent the size of the data being indexed, compared with 100 percent in the case of WAIS. As a concrete example, indexing the Computer Science technical reports from 280 sites around the world requires 9 GB with a standard WAIS index but only 270 MB using Glimpse. Glimpse also supports fast and incremental indexing, as well as queries involving Boolean combinations of keywords, regular expression pattern matching, and approximate matches.

In contrast to Glimpse, Nebula focuses on providing fast searches and complex standing queries at the expense of index size. Each object in Nebula is represented as a set of attribute/value pairs. Nebula supports the notion of a view, which is defined by standing queries against the database of indexed objects. This allows information to be filtered based upon query predicates, effectively constraining the search to some subset of the database. Within the scope of a view that contains computer science technical reports, for example, a user may search for networks without matching information about social networks. Because views exist over time, it is easy to refine and extend them, and to observe the effect of query changes interactively.

Harvest Object Cache

To alleviate bottlenecks that arise from accessing popular data, Harvest implements an Object Cache that stores the content of HTTP, Gopher, and FTP objects that have been retrieved. The Object Cache runs as a single, event-driven process. For ease of implementation, the Cache spawns a separate process to retrieve FTP files, but retrieves HTTP and Gopher objects itself. The Cache separately manages replacement of objects on disk and objects loaded in its virtual address space. It also keeps all metadata for cached objects in virtual memory, to eliminate access latency to the metadata.

Multiple Object Caches can be arranged hierarchically for scalability. The Object Cache allows sites to customize hierarchical relationships between caches at multiple levels of the network (for example, at a campus, regional, and backbone network). Different caching parameters, such as timeouts, maximum object size, cache storage size in memory and disk, as well as caching policies, also can be customized.

Harvest Replicator

The Harvest Replicator provides a weakly consistent, replicated wide-area file system for mirroring the information that the Brokers have. This alleviates bottlenecks that arise from heavy demand on particular servers. Each file system occasionally "floods" its closest neighboring file systems with complete state information to ensure consistency, and to allow its neighbors to detect updates that for some reason have failed to propagate. The weak form of consistency used in the Replicator is called eventual consistency; if all new updates ceased, the replicas eventually converge.

The Replicator also can be used to divide the gathering process among many servers (for example, allowing one server to index each U.S. regional network) by distributing the partial updates among the replicas. The Replicator also allows sites to customize the degree of replication, topology of updates, and the frequency of updates.

WebAnts: Hunting in Packs

The WebAnts project is a new experiment headed by John Leavitt of Carnegie Mellon University to investigate the distribution of information collection tasks to a number of cooperating processors. It aims to create cooperating explorers (called *ants*) that share the work of finding things on the Web without duplicating each other's efforts. Leavitt noted that the origin of the metaphor derives from similarity between this and the manner in which biological ants leave chemical trails to sources of food and cooperate in the harvesting.

 n o t e   WebAnt is currently under development. As of this writing, it has not been deployed on the Web yet. But stay tuned and watch the WebAnts home page (see fig. 4.11).

Figure 4.11

The WebAnts home page.

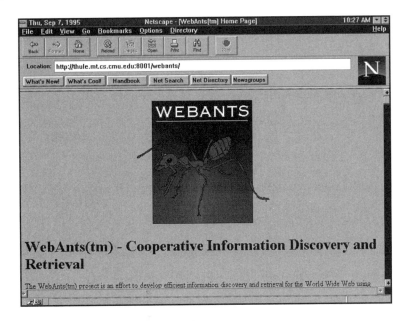

WebAnts Motivation

According to Leavitt, the development of WebAnts was motivated by the following considerations:

➔ Information discovery on the Web is rapidly becoming too large a task for a single explorer agent. Not only will the local portion of the network sustain considerable traffic during exploration, such an exploration will consume progressively more time as the Net grows.

➔ The reliance on a single site for such services would create a bottleneck and does nothing to solve the problem related to the fan-in, fan-out nature of information discovery. Instead, it exacerbates the problem and makes that one site a bottleneck for all users.

➔ It is undesirable for multiple explorers to examine the same sites. If exploring the Web alone is a problem, having a number of non-cooperating, and therefore redundant, explorers is worse. Not only does it cause unnecessary load on the servers, it also fails to provide a reasonable service to the user.

WebAnts Searching and Indexing

A problem most users face in searching for information on a specific topic is that the user cannot rely on a single-search engine because it does not explore everything and could be a performance bottleneck. Neither can the user merely combine the results of several search engines together because this inevitably yields repeated hits.

The WebAnts project hopes to address these issues with a cooperative Web explorer, called an *ant*.

Unlike spiders, ants are designed to share results with other ants without duplication of efforts. WebAnts has a clear preference for using explorer-based schemes over those that require cooperation from each information server (such as Martijn Koster's Aliweb). The WebAnts model can be used for purposes of searching and indexing the Web.

WebAnts Searching

For searching purposes, different ants may be directed based upon each others' results. When one ant finds a document that satisfies the search criteria, it can share the references from that document with other ants that are not currently exploring hits of their own. As each ant explores a document, other ants would know about it so that they do not have to examine the same document. This allows information to be gathered more effectively.

WebAnts Indexing

For indexing purposes, cooperation among ants allows each indexer to conserve resources by distributing the indexing load between different explorers. Each index server would provide all the information gathered by one of the ants during exploration. When querying, a user could restrict the query to the local ant or allow it to propagate to the entire colony. This reduces the bottleneck effect.

Issues of Web Indexing

The indexes built by Web robots save users from following long chains before they find a relevant document, thus saving Internet bandwidth (Pinkerton 1994). Brian Pinkerton calculates that if

the WebCrawler indexes 40,000 documents and gets 5,000 queries a day, and if each query means the user will retrieve just three fewer documents than she otherwise would have, then it will take about eight days for the WebCrawler's investment in bandwidth to be paid back.

The following subsections discuss Web indexing issues of recall and precision, good Web citizenship, performance, and scalability.

Recall and Precision

The capability of spiders to find useful information is usually measured in two ways: recall and precision (Salton 1989). *Recall* measures what fraction of the relevant documents are retrieved by the query, whereas *precision* indicates how well the retrieved documents match the query.

Recall is the proportion of relevant documents retrieved; that is, the number of relevant documents retrieved divided by the total number of relevant documents in the indexed collection. If, for example, an index contained 10 documents, 5 of which were about elephants, then a query for "elephants and ivory" that retrieved 4 relevant documents about elephants (but two non-elephant documents) would have a recall of 4/5 or 0.8.

Precision is defined as the proportion of retrieved documents—the number of relevant documents retrieved divided by the total number of documents retrieved—that are relevant. Using the same example as in the previous paragraph, the precision would be calculated as 4/(4+2) or 0.66.

 A good indexing scheme aims for high recall and precision. A large proportion of the useful documents should be retrieved, and at the same time a large proportion of the extraneous documents should be rejected.

Both WebCrawler and Lycos have adequate recall. Finding enough relevant documents is not the problem. Instead, precision suffers because these systems give many false positives. Documents returned in response to a keyword search need only contain the requested keywords and might not be what the user is looking for. As a practical solution, assigning weights to documents returned by a query would help the user focus on the more relevant documents, but it would not completely eliminate irrelevant documents.

Good Web Citizenship

Webmasters can advise robots by specifying which documents are worth indexing in a special "robots.txt" document on their server (Koster 1994a). This type of advice is valuable to Web robots, and increases the quality of their indexes. In fact, some Webmasters have gone so far as to create special overview pages for Web robots to retrieve and include.

Both the WebCrawler and Lycos try hard to be good citizens on the Web. Although some poorly designed Web robots have been known to operate in a depth-first fashion, retrieving file after file from a single site, both WebCrawler and Lycos are conscientious of their traversal order so as not to overload any one particular server. WebCrawler

searches the Web in a breadth-first fashion, while Lycos uses a probabilistic scheme to skip from server to server. This avoids the problem of hitting any one server with a long string of requests.

Furthermore, when searching for something more specific among a relevant set of documents at a particular site, WebCrawler limits its search speed to one document per minute and sets a ceiling on the number of documents that can be retrieved from the host before query results are reported to the user.

Performance

As the Web continues its phenomenal growth, there comes a point where being just good citizens on the Web might not be enough to offset the load placed on network and server resources by indexing spiders.

Harvest is designed to ease the strain on servers, as well as on overall network traffic. The Harvest researches have compared the performance of Harvest with methods of native protocol access as used in all current spiders (BDHMS 1994). In their experiments, they have observed the following measured results:

➜ Harvest reduced HTTP/Gopher/FTP server load by a factor of 4 while extracting indexing information.

➜ Harvest reduced server load by a factor of 6,600, while delivering indexing information to remote indexers.

➜ Harvest reduced network traffic by a factor of 59.

➜ Harvest reduced index space requirements by a factor of 43.

Although the current generation of spiders is useful as a tool for indexing the Web, there needs to be a more efficient way to conduct Web exploration. The Harvest performance measurements have shown just how much room there is for future improvements in speed.

Scalability

Other than the issue of performance, any spiders that attempt to index the entire Web must face the ultimate challenge: scalability. Not only must every document in the Web be retrieved, but some portion of each document must be saved as a way of summarizing its contents for later retrieval. Different indexing schemes save different information from documents, but the problem facing every indexing spider is the same: *How to manage such a vast amount of information.*

The trade-off becomes one of quality of index versus coverage of documents. Saving more information per document reduces the number of documents than can be covered, and vice versa. One way to avoid the fatal trade-off is to distribute the resource load, as is done in WebAnts, where an army of cooperating ants share the work load so that each ant indexes only a small portion of the Web.

Indexing the Web in parallel with ants also reduces indexing time, a factor that is already becoming a problem for some spiders that need to explore a large number of Web documents. In addition, distributing the search among the ants eliminates the need for gigabytes of storage in one place to keep the

indexing information. Each cooperating ant needs only provide as much storage as is comfortable.

The problem of scalability is only endemic to the current generation of indexing spiders, which operate in a lone-ranger fashion. Spiders of the future, probably better called *crawlers* to distinguish them from the current spiders, will be scalable by working in a cooperative fashion.

Spiders of the Future

Although many early spiders could successfully crawl through Webspace in 1994, the rapid increase in the amount of information on the Web since then made this same crawl increasingly difficult. Only a few resourceful spiders, such as WebCrawler and Lycos, can accumulate enough Web documents to survive and dominate the Web. Meanwhile, the rest of the spiders, starved of information due to inadequate resources, slowly became extinct.

One problem that any indexing spider must eventually deal with is that the size of an index will grow proportionally to the size of the Web. The storage, retrieval, and distribution of information on this scale will no doubt prove a compelling challenge. Advanced information gathering and distribution architectures like Harvest and WebAnts can help spiders, or other crawlers such as ants, become more efficient and effective in their Web indexing efforts by sharing both their work load and results.

In the not-too-distant future, we can expect to see stronger, faster and smarter crawlers on the Web, supported by more efficient distributed information architecture, such as Harvest and WebAnts, that can address the important performance and scalability issues. The promise for the future is that systems like Harvest and WebAnts will provide users with increasingly effective means to locate information on the Web.

## chapter 5

Web Robots: Operational Guidelines

World Wide Web robots, also called *spiders or wanderers*, are programs that traverse the World Wide Web by recursively retrieving pages hyperlinked by Uniform Resource Locators (URLs). They are viewed as special kinds of agents whose goal is to automate specific Web-related tasks—for example, retrieving Web pages for keyword indexing or maintaining Web information space at local sites. Although this book is about various kinds of Internet agents and their underlying technologies, the focus is really on understanding Web robots.

note Spiders, wanderers, Web worms, fish, crawlers, walkers, and ants all mean one thing: Web robots, which are programs that traverse the World Wide Web information space by following hypertext links and retrieving Web documents by standard HTTP protocol. All these names are misleading, giving the false impression that the Web robot itself actually *moves*. In reality, the Web robot never leaves the machine where the program is run and is entirely different from the infamous Internet Worm of 1989 (Seeley 1989; Spafford 1989).

But do you really need to create yet another Web robot? There are already many of them out there in the public domain. Your needs probably can be fulfilled with one of the existing Web robots. Even if you do decide to construct a new Web robot after all, it does not have to be built entirely from scratch. The source code (usually in Perl) of quite a few public domain Web robots, such as that of Roy Fielding's MOMspider robot, are freely available for modifications. It usually is safer and more economical to go with a proven solution that already is fine-tuned for operation than it is to create new solutions from scratch.

A fairly detailed and comprehensive collection of robots on the Web, derived from the *List of Robots* which Martijn Koster (1994a) actively maintains at:

`http://web.nexor.co.uk/mak/doc/robots/active.html`

which is expanded to include other information, is available as Appendix G at the back of this book.

This chapter starts by describing major uses of Web robots and explaining how to bar specific Web robots from visiting specific portions of the Web space, by means of the widely adopted *Standard*

for Robot Exclusion (Koster 1994b). The remainder of this chapter provides specific guidelines of acceptable Web robot behavior (*Four Laws of Web Robotics*), outlines the responsibility and vigilance expected of Web robot operators (*Six Commandments for Robot Operators*), offers some tips to Webmasters who suspect their servers may be under attack by a Web robot, and concludes with a discussion of Web ethics.

The Four Laws of Web Robotics and Six Commandments for Robot Operators described in this chapter are inspired by Martijn Koster's *Guide for Robot Writers* (1994c), which is based on a consensus of the various WWW newsgroups and mailing lists on acceptable and expected behaviors of Web robots and their operators.

Web Robot Uses

The earliest Web robot, Matthew Gray's World Wide Web Wanderer, was first deployed in June 1993 to measure the growth of the World Wide Web by discovering and counting the number of Web servers on the Net. As of this writing, the number of different Web robots has grown to more than 40 (see Appendix G).

Excluding the more recent BargainFinder type of application-specific Web commerce agents (described in Chapter 3), almost all known Web robots to date have been deployed for one or more of the following purposes:

➜ Web resource discovery

➜ Web maintenance

➜ Web mirroring

Web Resource Discovery

Web resource discovery is concerned with the problem of finding useful information on the Web. The rich, decentralized, dynamic, and diverse nature of the Web has made casual Web surfing enjoyable, but has made serious navigation aimed at finding specific information extremely difficult. People have thus increasingly relied on search engines to help locate online information. These search engines have depended on Web robots, often called spiders, to automatically traverse the Web to bring in Web documents for keyword indexing. It is perhaps the most exciting problem tackled by the current generation of Web robots.

As was discussed previously in Chapter 4, "Spiders for Indexing the Web," the two most prominent resource discovery Web robots in operation today are Brian Pickerton's WebCrawler robot and Michael Mauldin's Lycos spider. Both of which actively maintain a full-content index to a huge collection of Web documents, currently numbering in the millions. Both spiders continuously traverse the Web to keep their index database up-to-date. A keyword-oriented search facility to their index databases is made available to users by means of a front-end query interface and a corresponding back-end search engine.

Web Maintenance

A major difficulty in maintaining a Web information structure is that hypertext references to other Web pages might become outdated when the target Web page is deleted or moved, resulting in what are called *dead links*. Currently, there is no automated mechanism for proactively notifying Web document owners the moment hyperlinks in their Web pages become obsolete.

Some servers log failed HTTP requests caused by dead links, along with URL information of the specific Web page that refers to it in the first place (while returning an HTTP response code of "301 Moved Permanently" to the client). Such information in the server log files can then be scanned and processed at regular intervals to generate a list of Web pages with the corresponding dead links that they contain. However, this post-mortem style of solution is not quite practical because document owners in the real world are seldom notified this way.

A more workable solution seems to be that offered by a class of Web robots known as the Web maintenance spiders. They assist Web document owners and Webmasters maintain their portions of the Web information structure by automatically traversing the relevant branches of the local Web space periodically and checking for dead links. Roy Fielding's MOMspider, as well as its younger and simpler WebWalker cousin (to be discussed later in Chapter 7), are examples of Web maintenance robots. In addition, Web maintenance spiders can also perform checks for document HTML compliance, document style conformance, as well as other lesser known document content processings.

Web Mirroring

Mirroring is a common technique for setting up replicas of an information structure. For example, mirroring an FTP site involves copying its entire FTP file directory recursively and reproducing it on a different machine over the network. Popular FTP sites on the Internet are often mirrored in different parts of the world, for load sharing as well as for redundancy in case of failures. Mirroring can also yield faster or cheaper local, or even offline, access.

Robots that mirror Web information structures include, for example, HTMLGobble, Tarspider, and Webcopy. Mirroring the Web introduces an added complication not found in mirroring FTP sites, in that mirrored Web pages need to be rewritten to reflect changes in hyperlink references. Hyperlinks that used to point at original Web pages must now point to newly copied Web pages. Also, relative links that point to pages that have not been mirrored must be expanded into absolute links, so that they continue to point at original Web pages (and not at non-existent Web pages at the mirror site!).

The current generation of Web mirroring robots cannot detect and do not understand Web document changes. The unnecessary transfer of unchanged Web documents wastes valuable network resources. It can thus be expected that sophisticated mirroring robots of the future must also perform some amount of document revision control and management.

Proposed Standard for Robot Exclusion

In 1993 and 1994, robots sometimes visited Web servers where they were not welcome for various reasons. Sometimes these reasons were robot-specific—for example, certain robots swamped servers with rapid-fire requests or retrieved the same files (or the same sequence of files) repeatedly. Other situations are server-specific and there are cases where Webmasters have found robots getting caught in parts of the Web they were not meant to traverse—for example, very deep virtual trees generated by server programs on-the-fly,

duplicated information, temporary information, or invocations of Common Gateway Interface program scripts with side-effects (such as voting). In a few cases, certain Web robots are simply not welcome as a matter of policy due to conflicting interests—for example, some online CD stores would like to bar the price-shopping BargainFinder agent from searching their Web sites.

These incidents indicate a need for an operational mechanism for Web servers to identify to robots that portions of their Web are out of bounds and should not be accessed in an automated fashion. The *Standard for Robot Exclusion* proposed by Martijn Koster (1994b) is an attempt to address such a need with a simple operational solution.

Robot writers are urged to implement this practice. You can find some sample Perl code in this Web page:

`http://web.nexor.co.uk/mak/doc/robots/norobots.pl`

Robot Exclusion Method

The method used to exclude robots from a Web server is for the Webmaster to create a file on the server that specifies an access policy for robots. This file, called the *robot exclusion file*, must be accessible with HTTP from a local URL with the standard path /robots.txt. The contents of the robot exclusion file describe the nature of the constraints and are detailed in the next section.

This approach was chosen because it can be implemented easily on any existing Web server. A Web robot can find the access policy from the robot exclusion file (whose URL path is /robots.txt) with only

a single document retrieval. Although the Webmaster can specify many constraints in the robot exclusion file, it is still up to individual Web robots to check for the existence of the file in the first place, to retrieve it and to adhere to its specified constraints.

According to Koster, a possible drawback of this single-file approach is that the robot exclusion file can be maintained only by the Webmaster and not the individual document maintainers at the site. This problem can be resolved easily by a local maintenance procedure that constructs the single robots.txt file from a number of other files. (The procedure for this is outside the scope of the proposed standard.)

Robot Exclusion File Format

The file consists of one or more records. Each record is of the following form, on a line terminated by a carriage return (CR), or a line-feed (LF), or a combination of carriage return followed by line-feed (CR/LF):

```
field:value
```

The field name is case insensitive. There can be optional spaces around the value. Blank lines (lines that contain no records but are terminated with CR, LF, or CR/LF) are ignored.

Comments are allowed in the robot exclusion file for annotation purposes. A comment line begins with a # character; any preceding spaces and the remainder of the comment line up to the line terminator(s) are discarded.

The presence of an empty robot exclusion file that contains nothing basically is meaningless and should be treated as if it were not there. In this case, all Web robots would consider themselves welcome at that site.

Recognized Field Names

Records with unrecognized field names are ignored. The following are the recognized field names defined in the standard:

→ **User-Agent.** The value of this field identifies the robot in question. If there are multiple consecutive User-Agent records, then more than one robot shares the identical access policy (specified in the immediately following sequence of Disallow records). Each User-Agent record, or each block of consecutive User-Agent records as the case may be, must be followed by at least one Disallow record (to be described next).

The robot should be liberal in interpreting the value of the User-Agent field. A case-insensitive substring match of the value without version information is recommended. The following are some examples of popular user agents:

```
User-Agent: Mozilla/1.1N    # Netscape browser
User-Agent: WebCrawler/2.0  # Web searcher
User-Agent: MOMspider/1.00  # Web maintainer
```

If the value is *, the record describes the default access policy for any Web robot that has not matched with any of the other records. There must not be more than one record whose value is * in the robot exclusion file.

→ **Disallow.** The value of this field specifies a partial string describing the prefix portion of the URL that is not to be visited. This can be a full path name or a partial path name. Any URL that begins with this value will not be retrieved. For example, the following line disallows both: `/home/index.html` and `/homeSweetHome.html`:

```
Disallow: /home
```

Whereas, this line disallows `/home/index.html` but allows `/homeSweetHome.html`.

```
Disallow: /home/
```

An empty value permits all URLs to be retrieved. At least one Disallow record must be present under each block of consecutive User-Agent records (for multiple robots sharing the same access policy), or under each User-Agent record (for a single robot with unique access policy). A Disallow record cannot be present without at least one User-Agent record preceding.

Sample Robot Exclusion Files

The following robot exclusion file specifies that no robots should visit any URL starting with `/cyberworld/map/` (directory of infinite virtual space), `/cgi-bin/` (directory of executable Common Gateway Interface scripts), or `/tmp/` (directory of temporary files soon to disappear):

```
User-Agent: *
Disallow: /cyberworld/map/ # Virtual space
Disallow: /cgi-bin/        # CGI scripts
Disallow: /tmp/            # Temporary files
```

The following robot exclusion file specifies that no robots should visit any URL starting with `/cyberworld/map/`, except the robot called *cybermapper*.

```
User-Agent: *              # Bar all robots...
Disallow: /cyberworld/map/

User-Agent: cybermapper    # ...except cybermapper
Disallow:
```

The following robot exclusion file example indicates that no robots should visit this site further:

```
User-Agent: *              # All robots go away!
Disallow: /
```

The Four Laws of Web Robotics

The aspiring creators of future Web robots would be wise to heed the advice proffered by seasoned Webmasters and other Web robot experts, which has been summarized in *the Four Laws of Web Robotics*. These laws codify the expected and accepted behavior of robots, and are listed in table 5.1.

If you are building a new Web robot, you are strongly urged to design your robot program in such a way that all four laws of Web robotics are adhered to. The following subsections explain each law in detail.

Table 5.1		
The Four Laws of Web robotics.	I.	A Web Robot Must Show Identifications
	II.	A Web Robot Must Obey Exclusion Standard
	III.	A Web Robot Must Not Hog Resources
	IV.	A Web Robot Must Report Errors

I. A Web Robot Must Show Identifications

Webmasters want to know which robots are accessing their sites and who is operating the robots so they will know who to contact in case of trouble. In many cases, Webmasters also want to find out how others came to know of their sites. A Web robot can accommodate Webmasters by identifying itself (with User-Agent field), its operator (with From field), and the Web page referrer (with Referrer field).

Web Robot Self Identification

Web clients can identify themselves by means of the User-Agent fields supported in HTTP request headers. For example, the Netscape browser calls itself Mozilla, as in the following example:

```
User-Agent: Mozilla/1.1N
```

A Web robot can use the User-Agent field to state its name and provide a version number, as in the following example:

```
User-Agent: Terminator/1.0
```

This User-Agent field enables Webmasters to set Web robots apart from human-operated interactive Web browsers.

Robot Operator Identification

HTTP supports a From field in the request headers, allowing a Web robot to identify its human operator. An e-mail address is often used for identification here, as in the following example:

```
From: joe.robomaster@roboland.com
```

The From field enables Webmasters to contact the robot operator in case of problems. The robot operator can thus respond to Webmasters under a more amicable atmosphere than if he or she has been hard to track down.

Web Page Referrer Identification

Webmasters often wonder how people came to learn of the existence of their Web sites. When accessing a particular Web page, it is possible and often helpful for a Web robot to identify to the Web server the parent document that hyperlinks to the Web page. This parent document is called the Web page referrer. HTTP supports a Referer field for purpose of identifying the parent document. It is informative, for example, for the Webmaster to know that the Web page currently being accessed is referred to by a paid listing with some Web advertising service, as shown in the example here:

```
Referer: http://www.referRus.com/launchpad.html
```

II. A Web Robot Must Obey Exclusion Standard

The *Standard for Robot Exclusion* was proposed by Martijn Koster (1994b) as a simple way for Web servers to communicate to Web robots which portions of their Web space are off-limits, and to what robots. Details of the standard were examined in a previous section in this chapter. To be considered good citizens on the Web, and for not getting trapped in infinite virtual Web spaces, all self-respecting Web robots must follow this standard.

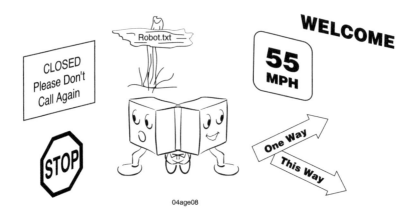

04age08

III. A Web Robot Must Not Hog Resources

Web robots consume a great deal of resources. To minimize its impact on the Internet, a Web robot should keep the following in mind:

→ **Request HEAD where possible.** HTTP supports a HEAD request method that retrieves only header information from Web documents, without the main body of HTML text. This incurs far less overhead than a full GET request, which retrieves entire documents and includes both headers and bodies. This feature comes in handy for Web robots to verify the existence and integrity of links in a document without necessarily retrieving all of their hyperlinked contents.

→ **Specify what is needed.** HTTP provides an Accept field in its request header for a Web robot to specify to the server what kinds of data it can handle. A robot that is designed to analyze text information only, for example, should specify the following:

Accept: x-text

Specifying what is needed can save considerable network bandwidth because Web servers will not bother to send data that the Web robot cannot handle and might have to discard anyway.

→ **Retrieve only what is needed.** URL suffixes also provide ample hints as to what type of data can be found at the other end of the link. If a link

refers to a file with the extension "ps", "zip", "Z", or "gif", for example, and the robot is equipped to handle only text data, it should not bother asking for its content from the server. After all, non-text files are fairly low-value artifacts for the purposes of indexing and querying. Although using URL suffixes is not the preferred way to do things (the recommended way is to use the Accept field in the HTTP request header), there is an enormous installed base out there that currently uses this method (all the FTP sites, for example).

Web robots always risk wandering off the Web into infinite virtual spaces. It is, therefore, imperative for Web robots to be given a list of places to avoid before embarking on a journey into Webspace. For example, URLs that begin

with "news:" (NEWS gateway) and "wais:" (WAIS gateway) should be filtered out in order to avoid exploring them. The robot should also pay attention to subpage references (A HREF="#abstract", for example) and not retrieve the same page more then once.

→ **Retrieve at opportune times.** On some systems, there might be preferred times of access when the machines or networks are only lightly loaded. A Web robot planning to make many automatic requests to one particular site should be made aware of the site's preferred time of access.

→ **Check all URLs carefully.** The Web robot should not assume that all HTML documents retrieved from the servers will be error-free. While scanning for URLs, the robot should be wary of things such as the following, which misses a matching double quote:

```
A HREF="http://somehost.somedom/doc
```

Also, many Web sites do not use trailing slashes (/) on URLs for directories, which means that a naive strategy of concatenating names of URL subparts can result in malformed names.

→ **Check all results thoroughly.** The robot should check all results thoroughly, including the status code. If a server constantly refuses to serve a number of documents, listen to what it is saying—the server might not serve documents to robots as a matter of policy.

→ **Never loop or repeat.** There is always the danger of a robot getting caught in some infinite loop in the Web without the slightest idea of what has happened. To avoid this situation, the robot should keep track of all the places it has visited. It also should check to make sure that the different host addresses are not on the same machine. (For example, `web.nexor.co.uk` and `hercules.nexor.co.uk` are aliases of the same machine, which also is known by its IP address, 128.243.219.1.)

→ **Retrieve in moderation.** Although Web robots can handle hundreds of documents per minute, a heavily used and multi-accessed server might not keep up. What is more, putting the server under a heavy load almost certainly will arouse the ire of many Webmasters, especially those who are less tolerant of robots.

Robots are advised to rotate queries between different Web servers in a round-robin fashion or to "sleep" for a short period of time between requests. Retrieving one document per minute at any one particular Web server is much better than overloading it with retrieving one document per second. One document every five minutes per Web server is better still. After all, what's the rush?

→ **Skip query interfaces.** Some Web documents are searchable (using the ISINDEX facility in HTML, for example) while others contain forms or are themselves dynamic documents. It is not advisable for robots to follow these links and hope

to get somewhere. An HTML textual analysis of the Web document, to be performed by the robot, can help determine whether any of the above cases apply.

IV. A Web Robot Must Report Errors

When a robot is traversing the Web, it might come across dangling links that point at Web pages that are obsolete, nonexistent, or inaccessible. This could be the result of the Webmaster having moved the page in question to a different location. He or she might have moved the page to a different machine or placed it under a different directory, for example. It also could be that the file in question has been renamed or that the Web server (or even the Domain Name server) has temporarily been out of service.

In all such cases, the Web robot should send an error-reporting e-mail to the address defined in the "mailto" link or the Webmaster of the site.

The Six Commandments for Robot Operators

Unleashing a Web robot on the Internet consumes substantial computational and network resources. Potential robot operators are strongly urged to reconsider their plans and to refrain from such an action until other cheaper alternatives have been fully exlored. Specifically, robot operators are urged to consider the following issues:

➡ The operational costs of a Web robot, in terms of computational and network resources consumed, as well as some level of vigilance and responsiveness on the part of the robot operator, must be weighed against its intended benefits.

➡ Sufficient computational resources and data storage capacity are required to cope with the potentially voluminous results—the Web is simply too huge for any one robot to cover.

Table 5.2 lists the six commandments for robot operators. The following subsections explain the six commandments in detail; read them carefully if you're planning on operating a Web robot.

I.	Thou Shalt Announce thy Robot	
II.	Thou Shalt Test, Test, and Test thy Robot Locally	
III.	Thou Shalt Keep thy Robot Under Control	
IV.	Thou Shalt Stay in Contact with the World	
V.	Thou Shalt Respect the Wishes of Webmasters	
VI.	Thou Shalt Share Results with thy Neighbors	

Table 5.2

The Six Commandments for Robot Operators

I. Thou Shalt Announce thy Robot

For better communications, you should announce your robot prior to launching it on the Web; you should notify the world, perhaps the target Web sites, but most definitely the local system administator.

Notify the World

If Webmasters know that a robot is coming, they can keep an eye out for it and not be caught by surprise. A robot that benefits the entire net will be welcome and tolerated longer than one that services a smaller community.

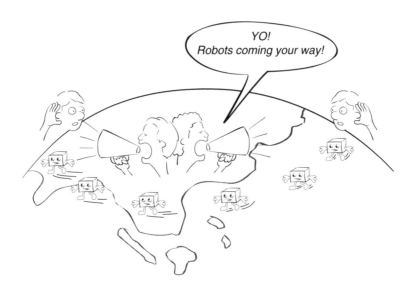

Before writing or launching a robot, you should announce your intention by posting a message to the following USENET newsgroup:

`comp.infosystems.www.providers`

Or by sending an e-mail message to this address:

`robots@nexor.co.uk`

Include a brief description of the problem to be solved by the Web robot. It is possible that someone already might have been working on a similar robot, or one already might exist but is not listed.

Notify Target Sites
If your robot is targeted at a select few sites, it is professional courtesy to contact and inform the Webmasters directly.

Notify Local System Administrator
Tell the local system administrator or network provider what resources or services might be used, such as increased network traffic and greater disk space utilization, when operating the robot. This way, if something goes wrong, the system administrator has been forewarned and won't have to rely on information about the robot and any resulting problems from second-hand sources.

II. Thou Shalt Test, Test, and Test thy Robot Locally

For testing purposes, you should start a number of Web servers locally to check the newly created robot. Do not try testing on remote servers before getting the bugs out of a robot. When going off-site for the first time, the robot should stay close to home. Have it start from a page with local URLs.

After completing a small test run, you should analyze the robot's performance and results. This practice helps you arrive at an estimate of how the operation would scale up to perhaps tens of thousands of documents. It soon becomes obvious if the workload might not be manageable; as a result, you can scale down the scope of the effort.

III. Thou Shalt Keep thy Robot Under Control

It is vital that the operator know what the robot is doing, and that the robot remain under control at all times. To accomplish this goal, follow these guidelines:

→ **Log all activities.** Provide ample logging in order to track where the robot has been on the Web. To monitor the progress of the robot and keep it under control, it helps to collect useful information and to compile statistics, such as the following:

Hosts recently visited

Number of successes and failures

Sizes of recently accessed files

As was previously noted, the robot needs to know where it has been on the Web in order to prevent looping. Also, an updated estimate of the disk space requirement from time to time provides useful feedback to the operator and helps prevent a disk space crunch.

→ **Provide guidance.** Design robots that can be guided easily. Commands that suspend or cancel the robot, or make it skip the current host, for example, can be very useful. For this to happen, the robot must be robust operationally—the robot needs to be checkpointed frequently during operation to ensure that the cumulative results are not lost if the robot fails.

IV. Thou Shalt Stay in Contact with the World

When you are running a Web robot, make sure that Webmasters can easily contact and start dialoging with you. If your robot's actions cause problems, you could be the only one who can fix it quickly. If possible, stay logged in to the machine that is running your robot so Webmasters can use *finger* or *talk* to contact you. In other words, don't go on vacation after unleashing your robot onto the Web.

The robot should be run only in your presence. Suspend the robot's operation when you are not going to be there—during weekends or after work, for example. Although it might be better for the performance of your machine to run your robot overnight, be considerate of others and the performance overhead of other machines.

V. Thou Shalt Respect the Wishes of Webmasters

During operation, your robot will visit hundreds of sites. It probably will upset a number of Webmasters along its course. You must be prepared to respond quickly to their inquiries and tell them what your robot is doing.

If your Web robot does upset some Webmasters, instruct the robot to visit only their home pages and not go beyond. In many situations, it may be wise for the robot to pass over the complaining sites altogether.

 It is not a good idea to evangelize to Webmasters, hoping to convert them to your cause and open up their Web sites to your robot. They are probably not in the least bit interested.

JUST SAY YES

If your Web robot encounters technical barriers that Webmasters have devised to bar it from accessing their site, you should not try to make your Web robot go around them. Even though you might prove to Webmasters that it is difficult or impossible to limit access on the Web, you most likely will end up making enemies.

VI. Thou Shalt Share Results with thy Neighbors

You should archive and keep as much of the Web pages as you can store. You also should make the results accessible to the Internet community. After all, the effort to accumulate these documents has consumed considerable Internet-wide resources, and it is only fair to give something back in return. More specifically, you should do the following:

→ **Share raw data.** The raw results consisting of retrieved Web pages should be made available to the Internet community, either through FTP or World Wide Web, in one form or another. This sharing of data enables interested people on the Internet to make use of the data in other interesting ways without having to duplicate the collection effort using another Web robot.

→ **Publish polished results.** The Web robot is created and operated for a specific purpose; perhaps to build a specialized database or to gather some statistics. If these processed results are made available to the Web community in a polished form, people will be more appreciative of the robot's value and thus become more tolerant of its presence on the Web despite the increased network load. In addition, this is definitely a good way to get in touch with people of similar interests.

Robot Tips for Webmasters

If you are a Webmaster and you or your users are experiencing unusually sluggish response from your Web server, a Web robot might be attacking it with rapid-fire requests. To determine if a certain Web robot is indeed the culprit, and to find out more about it, here are some definite steps you can take:

1. Check your Web server logs carefully for signs of rapid-fire requests by paying close attention to time-stamps of multiple consecutive HTTP requests coming from the same machine address. Study the log for HTTP access request patterns to determine if indeed the sluggishness problem is caused by some offending Web robots. The HTTP request header fields User-Agent and From might reveal useful information about the Web robot and identify its operator.

2. Check Martijn Koster's *List of Robots* (or Appendix G of this book) to discover if the offending Web robot, identified in the HTTP User-Agent request header field, is one that is already known. Learn more about the culprit as needed, perhaps using Web search engines such as the WebCrawler or Lycos.

3. Find out more about the robot operator, identified in the HTTP From request header field, by means of *finger* or *rusers* over the Internet. The robot operator might also have published a Web page about himself and, more importantly, his Web robot project!

4. Raise the alarm in newsgroups among Webmasters, if needed, by posting to `comp.infosystems.www.providers` on USENET. You might not be alone. Chances are that there is already a thread of discussions on the topic between numerous other Webmasters facing the exact same problem.

The problem might have a simple solution: specify an entry in the robot exclusion file to exclude the offender. For example, the following entry added to the exclusion file tells the Web robot identified as NastyBot/1.0 to go away:

```
User-Agent: NastyBot/1.0  # Robot go away!
Disallow: /               # Off-limits!
```

If a Web robot is misbehaving, however, chances are that the robot creator would not also have properly implemented the robot exclusion standard. Do not get upset over it. It is also probably not wise to retaliate with the Web equivalent of a mail-bomb, which is to trap the robot into retrieving large amounts of data (perhaps a gigabyte-size HTML document generated on-the-fly) in the hope that it would choke. This would waste valuable network bandwidth and might not accomplish anything if the offending Web robot is robust, or simply smart.

It is perhaps better to try to get in contact with the robot operator and to engage in a constructive dialog, explaining clearly the problem that occurred at your Web site. You might also consider suggesting that the robot operator read *Guidelines for Robot Writers* or, perhaps, this chapter.

After your problem has been solved, you are strongly encouraged to share the experience with other Webmasters, robot builders, and robot operators in the Web community. This would save numerous other Webmasters from duplicating your efforts trying to investigate the similar problems caused by the same offending Web robots.

Web Ethics

Web ethics is an important concept for robot writers, robot operators, and Webmasters to understand. In 1942, Isaac Asimov stated his Three Laws of Robotics:

1. A robot may not injure a human being, or, through inaction, allow a human being to come to harm.

2. A robot must obey orders given it by human beings except where such orders would conflict with the First Law.

3. A robot must protect its own existence as long as such protection does not conflict with the First or Second Law.

Asimov's First Law of Robotics captures an essential insight: An intelligent agent should not slavishly obey human commands—its foremost goal should be to avoid harming humans. After all, society will reject autonomous agents unless there is some credible means of making them safe in the first place. But of course all this is quite abstract; the Web robots we're dealing with aren't going to chase anyone to kill them with superstrong pinchers at the ends of accordian-like arms!

Oren Etzioni and Daniel Weld, both professors at the University of Washington in Seattle who have

done extensive work with software robots, define a *softbot* as an agent that interacts with a software environment by issuing commands and interpreting the environment's feedback. In many respects, the softbot is very similar to a Web agent. It therefore is quite interesting to study Etzioni and Weld's formulation of a collection of *softbotic laws* (patterned after Isaac Asimov's Laws of Robotics) to govern such softbot agents (Etzioni and Weld, 1994):

→ **Safety.** The softbot should not make destructive changes to the world.

→ **Tidiness.** The softbot should leave the world as it first found it.

→ **Thrift.** The softbot should limit its use of scarce resources.

→ **Vigilance.** The softbot should refuse client actions with unknown consequences.

The laws of softbotics operate at a higher level when compared with the four laws of Web robotics described previously; you can probably detect some interesting commonalties that underlie the ethical aspects for all agents.

Similarly, Professor David Eichmann of the University of Houston, creator of the RBSE spider, offers his formulation of a code of conduct governing a general class of *service agents* (1994), which also includes Web robots:

→ **Identity.** Agent activities should be readily discernible and traceable back to its operator.

→ **Openness.** Information generated should be made accessible to the community in which the agent operates.

→ **Moderation.** The rate and frequency of information acquisition should be appropriate for the capacity of the server and network so as not to create an overload situation on valuable computational and network resources.

→ **Respect.** Agents should respect constraints placed on them by server administrators.

→ **Authority.** Agents' services should be accurate and up-to-date.

According to Eichmann, a balance should be struck between the concerns of openness, moderation, and respect—all of which limit a service agent's scope and activities—and the concern of authority, which tends to broaden them.

HTTP: Protocol of Web Robots

The *Hypertext Transfer Protocol* (HTTP) is an application-level protocol for distributed, hypermedia information systems. HTTP has been in use since 1990 by the World Wide Web community on the Internet. The HTTP 1.0 specification aims to remain compatible with most of the existing HTTP server and client programs implemented prior to November 1994.

HTTP is a generic, stateless, object-oriented proto-col that can be used for many tasks, such as name servers and distributed object management sys-tems, through extension of its request methods. A feature of HTTP is the typing and negotiation of data representation, enabling systems to be built independently of the data being transferred.

Practical information systems require retrieval, search, front-end update, and annotation. HTTP enables an open-ended set of methods to be used to indicate the purpose of a request. It builds on the discipline of reference provided by the Univer-sal Resource Identifier (URI) (BL 1994)—as a Uni-versal Resource Locator (URL) (BLMM 1994) or as a Universal Resource Name (URN)—for indicating the resource on which a method is to be applied. Messages are passed in a format similar to that used by Internet Mail (Crocker 1982) and the Multi-purpose Internet Mail Extensions (MIME) (BF 1993).

 n o t e MIME is a freely available specification that offers a way to interchange text in languages with different character sets, and multimedia e-mail, among many different computer systems that use Internet mail standards.

HTTP also is used for communication between user agents and various gateways, enabling hypermedia access to existing Internet protocols, such as SMTP (Postel 1982), NNTP (KL 1986), FTP (PR 1985), Gopher (AMLJTA 1993), and WAIS (DKMSSWSG 1990). HTTP is designed to enable such gateways, through proxy servers, without any loss of the data conveyed by those earlier protocols.

HTTP is an important protocol for Web robots and key to their operations. This chapter examines the

HTTP 1.0 specifications in detail. The information on HTTP 1.0 is based upon the Internet draft of HTTP 1.0 authored by Tim Bernes-Lee, Roy Fielding, and H. Frystyk Nielsen and submitted to the IETF Working Group in March 1995 (available at `http://ietf.cnri.reston.va.us/internet-drafts/draft-ietf-http-v10-spec-03.txt`). A syntax grammar summary of HTTP 1.0 can be found in Appendix A.

Understanding HTTP Operation

The HTTP protocol is based on a request/response paradigm. A requesting program (called a *client*) establishes a connection with a receiving program (called a *server*) and sends a request to the server. A given program can be a client or a server. The use of these terms refers only to the role being performed by the program during a particular con-nection, rather than to the program's purpose in general.

The request transmitted to the server is in the form of a request method, URI, and protocol version, followed by a MIME-like message containing re-quest modifiers, client information, and possible body content. The server responds with a status line (including its protocol version with a success or error code), followed by a MIME-like message containing server information, entity meta informa-tion, and possible body content. This entire process is covered in more detail later in this chapter.

On the Internet, communication generally takes place over a TCP/IP connection. The default port is TCP 80 (RP 94), but other ports can be used. The

HTTP 1.0 protocol also can be implemented on top of any other protocol on the Internet, or on other networks.

For most implementations, the client establishes the connection prior to each request, and the server closes it after sending the response. This is not a feature of the protocol, however, and is not required by the HTTP 1.0 specification. Both clients and servers must be capable of handling the premature closing of the connection by either party, which could be caused by user action, automated time-out, or program failure. The closing of the connection by either or both parties always terminates the current request, regardless of its status.

Table 6.1 explains the terminologies associated with the World Wide Web that will be used for the remainder of this chapter.

Table 6.1 World Wide Web Terms

Term	Definition
Connection	A virtual circuit established between two parties for the purpose of communication.
Message	A structured sequence of octets transmitted through the connection as the basic component of communication.
Request	An HTTP request message.
Response	An HTTP response message.
Resource	A network data object or service that can be identified by a URI.
Entity	A particular representation or rendition of a resource that can be enclosed within a request or response message. An entity consists of meta information (in the form of entity headers) and content (in the form of an entity body).
Client	A program that establishes connections for the purpose of sending requests.
User agent	The client program that is closest to the user and that initiates requests on behalf of the user.
Server	A program that accepts connections in order to service requests by sending back responses.
Origin server	The server on which a given resource resides or is to be created.

continues

Table 6.1, Continued

Term	Definition
Proxy	An intermediary program that usually runs on a firewall machine to other servers. (A firewall machine functions as a security barrier between the larger Internet and a smaller local area network within an organization.) A proxy server accepts requests from other clients and services them either internally or by passing them on (with possible translation). A caching proxy is a proxy server with a local cache of server responses.
Gateway	A proxy that services HTTP requests by translating them into protocols other than HTTP. The reply sent from the remote server to the gateway is likewise translated into HTTP before being forwarded to the user agent.

Messaging with HTTP

HTTP messages consist of requests from client to server and responses from server to client. These messages can be either *full* requests and responses or *simple* requests and responses.

Full requests and full responses use the generic message format of RFC 822 (Crocker 1982) for transferring entities. Both messages can include optional header fields (or simply "headers") and an entity body. A *null line* (a line with nothing preceding the *carriage return line feed*, or CRLF) separates the entity body from the headers. A full request looks like the following:

```
Method SP URI SP HTTP-Version CRLF
*( General-Header
 ¦ Request-Header
 ¦ Entity-Header )
CRLF
[ Entity-Body ]
```

A full response looks like the following:

```
HTTP-Version SP Status-Code SP Reason-Phrase CRLF
*( General-Header
 ¦ Response-Header
 ¦ Entity-Header )
CRLF
[ Entity-Body ]
```

Simple requests and responses do not allow the use of any header information and are limited to a single **GET** request method. The client is denied the benefit of content negotiation, and the server cannot identify the media type of the returned entity. A simple request looks like the following:

```
GET SP URI CRLF
```

A simple response is merely an optional entity body.

Message Headers

HTTP header fields include general header, request header, response header, and entity header fields. Each header field consists of a name followed by a colon (:) and the field value. Header fields can be

extended over multiple lines by preceding each extra line with at least one *linear white space* (LWS).

The order in which header fields are received is not significant.

Comments can be included in HTTP header fields by surrounding the comment text with parentheses.

General Message Header Fields

A few header fields apply in general terms to both request and response messages but do not apply to the communicating parties or to the entity being transferred. No general header field is required; however, they all are strongly recommended when their use is appropriate.

Additional general header fields can be implemented by the extension mechanism; applications that do not recognize those fields should treat them as entity header fields.

Date (When Was the Message Originated?)

The Date header represents the date and time at which the message was originated. The field value is an HTTP date. The following is an example:

```
Date: Tue, 15 Apr 1995 07:45:20 GMT
```

For most purposes, the default date can be assumed to be the current date at the receiving end. Because the date—as it is believed to be by the origin—is important for evaluating cached responses, however, origin servers should always include a Date header.

Clients should only send a Date header field in messages that include an entity body, as in the case of the PUT and POST requests; even then it is optional.

Forwarded (By Which Proxy Server?)

Proxies use the Forwarded header to indicate the intermediate steps between the user agent and the server (on requests) and between the origin server and the client (on responses). The header is intended to trace transport problems and to avoid request loops.

A message, for example, is sent from a client on dip.eecs.umich.edu to a server at www-cis.stanford.edu port 80, through an intermediate HTTP proxy at agent.com port 8000. The request received by the server at www-cis.stanford.edu would have the following Forwarded header field:

```
Forwarded: by http://agent.com:8000/ for
dip.eecs.umich.edu
```

Multiple Forwarded header fields are allowed in an HTTP message header and should represent each proxy that has forwarded the message.

Message-ID (How Are Messages Identified?)

The Message-ID field in HTTP gives the message a single, unique identifier that can be used to identify the message (not its contents) for "much longer" than the expected lifetime of that message.

Although not required, the address specification format typically used within a Message-ID consists of a string that is unique at the originator's machine, followed by the required at (@) character and the fully qualified domain name of that machine. The following is an example:

```
Message-ID: <9505031836.AA00266@agent.com>
```

The value of the Message-ID is composed using the time, date, and process id on the host `agent.com`. This method, however, is only one of many possible methods for generating a unique Message-ID. Recipients of a message should consider the entire value opaque.

MIME-Version (Is This Message MIME-Compliant?)

HTTP is not a MIME-conformant protocol. HTTP 1.0 messages, however, might include a single MIME-Version header field to indicate what version of the MIME protocol was used to construct the message. MIME 1.0 is the default for use in HTTP 1.0.

Use of the MIME-Version header field should indicate that the message is in full compliance with the MIME protocol, as defined in (BF 1993).

Current versions of HTTP 1.0 clients and servers unfortunately use this field indiscriminately, and thus receivers must not take it for granted that the message is in full compliance with MIME.

Request Message

A World Wide Web client can make requests to a World Wide Web server to begin an operation. A request message from a client to a server includes the following information within the first line (the request line):

→ The method to be applied to the resource requested

→ The identifier of the resource

→ The protocol version in use

An HTTP request has two valid formats: the newer full request or the older simple request (for backward compatibility with HTTP 0.9).

If an HTTP 1.0 server receives a simple request, it must respond with an HTTP 0.9 simple response. An HTTP 1.0 client capable of receiving a full response should never generate a simple request.

Method

The Method token indicates the method to be performed on the resource identified by the request URI. The method is case-sensitive and extensible. The following is a list of currently specified methods:

→ GET

→ HEAD

→ POST

→ PUT

→ DELETE

→ LINK

→ UNLINK

The list of methods accepted by a specific resource can be specified in an Allow entity header. The client, however, is always notified through the return code of the response whether or not a method is currently allowed on a specific resource, because this can change dynamically. Servers should return the status code `405 Method Not Allowed` if the method is known by the server but not allowed for the requested resource, and `501 Not Implemented` if the method is unknown or not implemented by the server.

The following sections describe the set of common methods for HTTP 1.0. Although this set can be expanded easily, additional methods cannot be assumed to have the same meaning for separately extended clients and servers. In order to maintain compatibility, the semantic definition for extension methods must be registered with the Internet Assigned Numbers Authority (IANA) (RP 1994).

 The IANA is the central coordinator for the assignment of unique parameter values for Internet protocols. The IANA is chartered by the Internet Society and the Federal Network Council to act as the clearinghouse to assign and coordinate the use of numerous Internet protocol parameters.

GET (Retrieving Contents of a Resource)

The GET method retrieves information (in the form of an entity) that is identified by the request URI. If the request URI refers to a data-producing process, the produced data is returned as the entity in the response, not the source text of the process (unless that text happens to be the output of the process).

The GET method becomes a conditional GET method when the request message includes an If-Modified-Since header field. A conditional GET method requests that the identified resource be transferred only if it has been modified since the date given in the If-Modified-Since header. If the resource has not been modified since the If-Modified-Since date, the server returns a 304 Not Modified response.

The conditional GET method is intended to reduce network usage by enabling cached entities to be refreshed without requiring multiple requests or transferring unnecessary data.

HEAD (Retrieving Only Header Information)

The HEAD method is identical to GET except that the server must not return any entity body in the response. The meta information contained in the HTTP headers in response to a HEAD request should be identical to the information sent in response to a GET request.

HEAD can be used for obtaining meta information about the resource identified by the request URI without transferring the entity body. The HEAD method is often used for testing hypertext links for validity, accessibility, and recent modification.

POST (Posting to a Resource)

The POST method is used to request that the destination server accept the entity enclosed in the request as a new subordinate of the resource identified by the request URI in the request line. POST is designed to allow a uniform method to cover the following functions:

→ Annotating existing resources

→ Posting a message to a bulletin board, newsgroup, mailing list, or similar group of articles

→ Providing a block of data (usually a form) to a data-handling process

→ Extending a database through an append operation

The actual function performed by the POST method is determined by the server and is usually dependent on the request URI. The posted entity is

considered to be subordinate to that URI in the same way that a file is subordinate to the directory containing it, a news article is subordinate to a newsgroup in which it is posted, or a record is subordinate to a database.

The client can apply relationships between the new resource and other existing resources by including Link header fields. The server can use the link information to perform other operations as a result of the new resource being added. For example, lists and indices might be updated. The origin server can also generate its own or additional links to other resources.

A successful POST does not require that the entity be created as a resource on the origin server or made accessible for future reference. That is, the action performed by the POST method might not result in a resource that can be identified by a URI. In this case, either 200 OK or 204 No Content is the appropriate response status, depending on whether or not the response includes an entity that describes the result.

If a resource has been created on the origin server, the response should be 201 Created. This response should contain the allocated URI, all applicable Link header fields, and an entity (preferably of type text/html) that describes the status of the request and refers to the new resource.

PUT (Creating or Modifying a Resource)

The PUT method requests that the enclosed entity be stored under the supplied request URI. If the request URI refers to an already existing resource, the enclosed entity should be considered a modified version of the resource residing on the origin

server. The 200 OK response should be sent back after successful completion of the request.

If the request URI does not point to an existing resource, and that URI is capable of being defined as a new resource by the requesting user agent, the origin server can create the resource with that URI. If a new resource is created, the origin server must inform the user agent through the 201 Created response.

The fundamental difference between the POST and PUT requests is reflected in the different meaning of the request URI. The URI in a POST request identifies the resource that will handle the enclosed entity as an appendage. That resource can be a data-accepting process, a gateway to some other protocol, or a separate entity that accepts annotations.

In contrast, the URI in a PUT request identifies the entity enclosed with the request. The requestor of a PUT knows which URI is intended, and the receiver must not attempt to apply the request to some other resource. If the receiver desires that the request be applied to a different URI, it must send a 301 Moved Permanently response; the requestor can then make its own decision regarding whether or not to redirect the request.

With PUT, the client can create or modify relationships between the enclosed entity and other existing resources by including Link header fields. As with POST, the server can use the Link information to perform other operations as a result of the request. The origin server can generate its own or additional links to other resources.

The origin server defines the actual method for determining how the resource is placed, and what

happens to the resource's predecessor. If version control is implemented by the origin server, the Version and Derived-From header fields should be used to help identify and control revisions to a resource.

DELETE (Getting Rid of a Resource)

The DELETE method requests that the origin server delete the resource identified by the request URI. This method can be overridden by human intervention (or other means) on the origin server. The client cannot be guaranteed that the operation has been carried out, even if the status code returned from the origin server indicates that the action has been completed successfully. The server should not indicate success unless, at the time the response is given, it intends to delete the resource or move it to an inaccessible location.

A successful response would be any of the following:

→ 200 OK if the response includes an entity describing the status

→ 202 Accepted if the action has not yet been enacted

→ 204 No Content if the response is OK but does not include an entity

LINK (Establishing Relationships with Other Resources)

The LINK method establishes one or more link relationships between the existing resource identified by the request URI and other existing resources. The difference between LINK and other methods allowing links to be established between resources is that the LINK method does not allow

any entity body to be sent in the request and does not result in the creation of new resources.

UNLINK (Breaking Relationships with Other Resources)

The UNLINK method removes one or more link relationships from the existing resource identified by the request URI. These relationships might have been established using the LINK method or by any other method supporting the Link header. The removal of a link to a resource does not imply that the resource ceases to exist or becomes inaccessible for future references.

Request Header Fields

The request header fields allow the client to pass additional information about the request (and about the client itself) to the server. All header fields are optional and conform to the generic HTTP header syntax.

Although additional request header fields can be implemented by the extension mechanism, applications that do not recognize those fields should treat them as entity header fields.

Accept (Acceptable Media Ranges)

The Accept header field can be used to indicate a list of media ranges that are acceptable as a response to the request. An asterisk (*) is used to group media types into ranges, with */* indicating all media types and type/* indicating all subtypes of that media type. The set of ranges given by the client should represent what types are acceptable given the context of the request. The following example should verbally be interpreted as, "If you

have audio/basic, send it; otherwise send any audio type."

```
Accept: audio/*; q=0.2, audio/basic
```

The parameter q is used to indicate the quality factor, which represents the user's preference for that range of media types. Its default value is q=1.

If at least one Accept header is present, a quality factor of 0 is equivalent to not sending an Accept header field containing that media-type or set of media-types. If no Accept header is present, then it is assumed that the client accepts all media types. This is equivalent to the client sending the following accept header field:

```
Accept: */*
```

A more elaborate example is

```
Accept: text/plain; q=0.5, text/html, text/x-dvi;
q=0.8; mxb=100000, text/x-c
```

Verbally, this would be interpreted as, "Text/html and text/x-c are the preferred media types, but if they do not exist, then send the entity body in text/x-dvi if the entity is less than 100,000 bytes; otherwise, send text/plain." Here, the parameter mxb gives the maximum acceptable size of the entity body (in decimal number of octets, defaults to infinity) for that range of media types.

It must be emphasized that the Accept field should only be used when it is necessary to do the following:

→ Restrict the response media types to a subset of those possible

→ Indicate qualitative preference for specific media types

→ Indicate the acceptance of unusual media types

Accept-Charset (Preferred Character Sets)

The Accept-Charset header field can be used to indicate a list of preferred character sets other than the default US-ASCII and ISO-8859-1. This field allows clients capable of understanding more comprehensive or special-purpose character sets to signal that capability to a server that is capable of representing documents in those character sets. An example follows:

```
Accept-Charset: iso-8859-5, unicode-1-1
```

The value of this field should not include US-ASCII or ISO-8859-1 because those values are always assumed by default.

Accept-Encoding (Acceptable Encodings)

The Accept-Encoding header field is similar to Accept, but it lists the encoding-mechanisms and transfer-encoding values that are acceptable in the response. An example of its use follows:

```
Accept-Encoding: compress, base64, gzip, quoted-
printable
```

The field value should never include the identity transfer-encoding values (7bit, 8bit, and binary) because they actually represent no encoding. If no Accept-Encoding field is present in a request, it must be assumed that the client does not accept any encoding-mechanism except for the identity transfer-encodings.

Accept-Language (Preferred Natural Languages)

The Accept-Language header field is similar to Accept, but it lists the set of natural languages that are preferred as a response to the request. Languages are listed in the order of their preference to

the user. The following example would mean "Send me a Danish version if you have it, or else a British English version."

```
Accept-Language: dk, en-gb
```

If the server cannot fulfill the request with one or more of the languages given, or if the languages only represent a subset of a multi-linguistic entity body, it is acceptable to serve the request in an unspecified language.

Authorization (Credentials of User Agent)

A user agent that wants to authenticate itself with a server (usually, but not necessarily, after receiving a `401 Unauthorized` response), may do so by including an Authorization header field with the request. The Authorization field value consists of credentials containing the authentication information of the user agent for the realm of the resource being requested. The following is an example:

```
Authorization: Basic QWxhZGRpbjpvcGVuIHNlc2FtZQ==
```

If a request is authenticated and a realm specified, the same credentials should be valid for all other requests within this realm.

From (Originator of This Request)

If given, the From header field should contain an Internet e-mail address for the human user who controls the requesting user agent. Here is an example:

```
From: webmaster@w3.org
```

This header field may be used for logging purposes and as a means for identifying the source of invalid or unwanted requests. The interpretation of this field is that the request is being performed on behalf of the person given, who accepts responsibility for the method performed. In particular, Web robot agents should include this header so that the responsible operator of the Web robot can be contacted if problems occur on the receiving end.

The Internet e-mail address in this field does not have to correspond to the Internet host that issued the request. When a request is passed through a proxy, for example, the original issuer's address should be used.

If-Modified-Since (Has the Resource Been Modified Since?)

The If-Modified-Since header field is used with the `GET` method to make it conditional. If the requested resource has not been modified since the time specified in this field, a copy of the resource is not returned from the server; instead, a `304 Not Modified` response is returned without any entity body. An example of the field follows:

```
If-Modified-Since: Sat, 29 Oct 1994 19:43:31 GMT
```

The purpose of this feature is to allow efficient updates of local cache information with a minimum amount of transaction overhead. The same functionality can be obtained, though with much greater overhead, by issuing a `HEAD` request and following it with a `GET` request if the server indicates that the entity has been modified.

Pragma (Server Directives to Apply)

The Pragma header field is used to specify directives that must be applied to all servers along the request chain (where relevant). The directives typically specify behavior that prevents intermediate

proxies from changing the nature of the request. HTTP 1.0 only defines meaning for the no-cache directive:

```
Pragma: no-cache
```

When the no-cache directive is present, a caching proxy must forward the request toward the origin server even if it has a cached copy of what is being requested. This allows a client to insist upon receiving an authoritative response to its request. It also allows a client to refresh a cached copy that has become corrupted or is known to be stale.

Pragmas must be passed through by a proxy even when they have significance to that proxy. This is necessary in cases when the request has to go through many proxies, and the pragma might affect all of them. It is not possible to specify a pragma for a specific proxy; however, any pragma-directive not relevant to a gateway or proxy should be ignored.

Referer (Document That Referred This URI)

The Referer field allows the client to specify, for the server's benefit, the address (URI) of the document (or element within the document) from which the request URI was obtained. This allows a server to generate lists of back-links to documents for interest, logging, optimized caching, and so on. It also allows obsolete or mistyped links to be traced for maintenance. Here's an example:

```
Referer: http://info.cern.ch/hypertext/DataSources/
Overview.html
```

If a partial URI is given, it should be interpreted relative to the request URI.

User-Agent (Client Program That Originated the Request)

The User-Agent field contains information about the user agent originating the request. This information is for statistical purposes, the tracing of protocol violations, and automated recognition of user agents for the sake of tailoring responses to avoid particular user agent limitations. Although it is not required, user agents should always include this field with requests.

The field can contain multiple tokens specifying the product name, with an optional slash and version designator, and other products that form a significant part of the user agent. By convention, the products are listed in order of their significance for identifying the application. The following is an example:

```
User-Agent: CERN-LineMode/2.15 libwww/2.17b3
```

Product tokens should be short and to the point. The User-Agent field can include additional information within comments that are not part of the value of the field.

Response Message

After receiving and interpreting a request message, a server responds in the form of an HTTP response message. A simple response should only be sent in response to an HTTP 0.9 simple request or if the server only supports the more limited HTTP 0.9 protocol.

If a client sends an HTTP 1.0 full request and receives a response that does not begin with a status line, it should assume that the response is simple and parse it accordingly. Note that the simple response consists only of the entity body and is terminated by the server closing the connection.

The first line of a full response message (that is, the status line) consists of the following:

➜ The protocol version

➜ A numeric status code

➜ The associated textual phrase

Because a status line always begins with the protocol version (HTTP 1.0), the presence of that expression is considered sufficient to differentiate a full response from a simple response. Although the simple response format can allow such an expression to occur at the beginning of an entity body (and thus cause a misinterpretation of the message if it was given in response to a full request), the likelihood of such an occurrence is negligible.

Status Codes and Reason Phrases

The server returns a 3-digit status code, plus a short textual description of the status code, as a result of attempting to understand and satisfy client request. The first digit of the status code defines the class of response, as shown in table 6.2.

HTTP status codes are extensible and should be registered with the IANA. The classes of 2xx successful status code are presented in table 6.3.

Table 6.2 Classes of HTTP Response Code

Digit	Type	Description
1xx	Informational	Not used, but reserved for future use.
2xx	Successful	The action was successfully received, understood, and accepted.
3xx	Redirection	Further action must be taken to complete the request.
4xx	Client Error	The request contains bad syntax or cannot be fulfilled.
5xx	Server Error	The server failed to fulfill an apparently valid request.

Table 6.3 2xx Successful

Status Code	Explanation
200 OK	The request has been fulfilled and an entity corresponding to the requested resource is being sent in the response.
201 Created	The request has been fulfilled and resulted in a new resource being created.
202 Accepted	The request has been accepted for processing, but the processing has not been completed.
203 Provisional Information	The returned meta information in the entity header is not the definitive set as available from the origin server, but is gathered from a local or a third-party copy.
204 No Content	The server has fulfilled the request, but there is no new information to send back.

The class of 3xx redirection status code are presented in table 6.4.

Table 6.4 3xx Redirection

Status Code	Explanation
300 Multiple Choices	The requested resource is available at one or more locations and a preferred location could not be determined through content negotiation.
301 Moved Permanently	The requested resource has been assigned a new permanent URI, and any future references to this resource must be done using the returned URI.
302 Moved Temporarily	The requested resource resides temporarily under a different URI.
303 Method	This code is obsolete.
304 Not Modified	If the client has performed a conditional GET request and access is allowed, but the document has not been modified since the date and time specified in the If-Modified-Since field, the server shall respond with this status code and not send an entity body to the client.

The classes of 4xx client error status code are presented in table 6.5.

Table 6.5 4xx Client Error

Status Code	Explanation
`400 Bad Request`	The request had bad syntax or was inherently impossible to be satisfied.
`401 Unauthorized`	The request requires user authentication.
`402 Payment Required`	This code is not currently supported.
`403 Forbidden`	The request is forbidden for some reason that remains unknown to the client.
`404 Not Found`	The server has not found anything matching the request URI.
`405 Method Not Allowed`	The method specified in the request line is not allowed for the resource identified by the request URI.
`406 None Acceptable`	The server has found a resource matching the request URI, but not one that satisfies the conditions identified by the Accept and Accept-Encoding request headers.
`407 Proxy Authentication Required`	This code is reserved for future use.
`408 Request Timeout`	The client did not produce a request within the time that the server was prepared to wait.
`409 Conflict`	The request could not be completed due to a conflict with the current state of the resource.
`410 Gone`	The requested resource is no longer available at the server and no forwarding address is known.

The classes of 5xx server error status code are presented in table 6.6.

Table 6.6 5xx Server Errors

Status Code	Explanation
`500 Internal Server Error`	The server encountered an unexpected condition that prevented it from fulfilling the request.
`501 Not Implemented`	The server does not support the functionality required to fulfill the request.
`502 Bad Gateway`	The server received an invalid response from the gateway or upstream server it accessed in attempting to complete the request.
`503 Service Unavailable`	The server is currently unable to handle the request due to a temporary overloading or maintenance of the server.
`504 Gateway Timeout`	The server did not receive a timely response from the gateway or upstream server it accessed in attempting to complete the request.

HTTP applications are not required to understand the meaning of all registered status codes. Applications are required, however, to understand the class of any status code (as indicated by the first digit) and to treat the response as being equivalent to the x00 status code of that class.

If an unknown status code of 421 is received by the client, for example, it can safely assume that there was something wrong with its request and treat the response as if it had received a 400 status code. In such cases, user agents are encouraged to present the entity returned with the response to the user because that entity is likely to include human-readable information that will explain the unusual status.

Response Header Fields

The response header fields allow the server to pass additional information about the response that cannot be placed in the status line. These header fields are not intended to give information about an entity body returned in the response, but about the server itself.

Although additional response header fields can be implemented by means of the extension mechanism, applications that do not recognize those fields should treat them as entity header fields.

Public (Non-Standard Methods Supported by Server)

The Public header field lists the set of non-standard methods supported by the server. This field informs the recipient of the server's capabilities regarding unusual methods. The field value should not include the methods predefined for HTTP 1.0. The following is an example of its use:

```
Public: OPTIONS, MGET, MHEAD
```

This header field applies only to the current connection. If the response passes through a proxy, the proxy must either remove the Public header field or replace it with one applicable to its own capabilities.

Retry-After (When to Retry Again)

The Retry-After header field can be used with `503 Service Unavailable` to indicate how long the service is expected to be unavailable to the requesting client. The value of this field can be either a full HTTP date or an integer number of seconds (in decimal) after the time of the response. Two examples of its use follow:

```
Retry-After: Mon, 02 Jan 1995 15:00:00 GMT
```

```
Retry-After: 120
```

In the latter example, the delay is 2 minutes.

Server (Server Program Handling the Request)

The Server header field contains information about the software being used by the origin server program handling the request. The field is analogous to the User-Agent field. The following is an example:

```
Server: CERN/3.0 libwww/2.17
```

If the response is being forwarded through a proxy, the proxy application must not add its data to the product list. Instead, it should include a Forwarded field.

WWW-Authenticate (Challenge to the Client)

The WWW-Authenticate header field must be included as part of a `401 Unauthorized` response. The field value consists of a challenge that indicates the authentication scheme and parameters applicable to the request URI.

Entity

Full request and full response messages can transfer an entity within some requests and responses. An entity consists of entity header fields and usually an entity body. In this section, both the sender and recipient refer to either the client or the server, depending on who sends and who receives the entity.

Entity Header Fields

Entity header fields define optional meta information about the Entity body or about the resource identified by the request (where no body is present). The recognized entity header fields are listed as follows:

→ Allow

→ Content-Encoding

→ Content-Language

→ Content-Length

→ Content-Transfer-Encoding

- → Content-Type
- → Derived-From
- → Expires
- → Last-Modified
- → Link
- → Location
- → Title
- → URI
- → Version

Other header fields are allowed but cannot be assumed to be recognizable by the recipient. Unknown header fields should be ignored by the recipient and forwarded by proxies.

Allow (Methods Applicable to Requested URI)

The Allow header field lists the set of methods supported by the resource identified by the request URI. It informs the recipient of valid methods associated with the resource. It must be present in a response with status code `405 Method Not Allowed`. An example of use is the following:

```
Allow: GET, HEAD, PUT
```

This field has no default value; if left undefined, the set of allowed methods is defined by the origin server at the time of each request.

If a response passes through a proxy that does not understand one or more of the methods indicated in the Allow header, the proxy must not modify the Allow header.

Content-Encoding (How Are Contents Encoded?)

The Content-Encoding header field is used as a modifier to the media type. Its value indicates what additional encoding mechanism has been applied to the resource. Its value also indicates what decoding mechanism must be applied to obtain the media type referenced by the Content-Type header field.

The Content-Encoding is primarily used to allow a document to be compressed without losing the identity of its underlying media type. An example of its use follows:

```
Content-Encoding: gzip
```

The Content-Encoding is a characteristic of the resource identified by the request URI. Typically, the resource is stored with this encoding and is only decoded before rendering at the user agent.

Content-Language (List of Natural Languages Intended)

The Content-Language field describes the natural language(s) of the intended audience for the enclosed entity. Note that this might not be equivalent to all the languages used within the entity.

Content-Language allows a selective consumer to identify and differentiate resources according to the consumer's own preferred language. If, for example, the body content is intended only for a Danish audience, the appropriate field is this:

```
Content-Language: dk
```

If no Content-Language is specified, the default is that the content is intended for all language

audiences. This can mean that the sender does not consider it to be specific to any natural language, or that the sender does not know for which language it is intended.

Multiple languages can be listed for content that is intended for multiple audiences. For example, a rendition of the Treaty of Waitangi, presented simultaneously in the original Maori and English versions, would call for this:

```
Content-Language: mi, en
```

However, just because multiple languages are present within an entity does not mean that it is intended for multiple linguistic audiences. An example would be a beginner's language primer, such as A First Lesson in Latin, which is clearly intended to be used by an English audience. In this case, the Content-Language should only include en.

Content-Language can be applied to any media type—it should not be considered limited to textual documents.

Content-Length (Size of Entity)

The Content-Length header field indicates the size of the entity body (in decimal number of octets) sent to the recipient. In the case of the HEAD method, it is the size of the entity body that would have been sent had the request been a GET. An example follows:

```
Content-Length: 2395
```

Although it is not required, applications are strongly encouraged to use this field to indicate the size of the entity body to be transferred, regardless of the media type of the entity.

Content-Transfer-Encoding (How Are Contents Encoded for Transfer?)

The Content-Transfer-Encoding (CTE) header indicates what (if any) type of transformation has been applied to the entity to safely transfer it between the sender and the recipient. This differs from the Content-Encoding in that the CTE is a property of the message, not of the original resource.

Because all HTTP transactions take place on an 8-bit clean connection, the default Content-Transfer-Encoding for all messages is binary. However, HTTP can be used to transfer MIME messages which already have a defined CTE. An example follows:

```
Content-Transfer-Encoding: quoted-printable
```

Many older HTTP 1.0 applications do not understand the Content-Transfer-Encoding header. However, future HTTP 1.0 applications are required to understand it upon receipt. Gateways to MIME-compliant protocols are the only HTTP applications that would generate a CTE.

Content-Type (Media Type of the Entity)

The Content-Type header field indicates the media type of the entity body sent to the recipient. In the case of the HEAD method, it is the media type that would have been sent had the request been a GET. An example follows:

```
Content-Type: text/html; charset=ISO-8859-4
```

The Content-Type header field has no default value.

Derived-From (Which Version Derives This Entity?)

The Derived-From header field indicates the version tag of the resource from which the enclosed

entity was derived before modifications by the sender. This field is used to help manage the process of merging successive changes to a resource, particularly when such changes are being made in parallel and from multiple sources. Here's an example use of the field:

```
Derived-From: 3.1.2
```

The Derived-From field is required for PUT requests if the entity being put was previously retrieved from the same URI and a Version header was included with the entity when it was last retrieved.

Expires (When Does the Entity Expire?)

The Expires field gives the date and time after which the entity should be considered stale. This allows information providers to suggest the volatility of the resource. Caching clients (including proxies) must not cache this copy of the resource beyond the date given, unless its status has been updated by a later check of the origin server.

The format is an absolute date and time. An example of its use follows:

```
Expires: Thu, 01 Dec 1994 23:00:00 GMT
```

 note Applications are encouraged to be tolerant of bad or misinformed implementations of the Expires header. In particular, recipients might want to recognize a delta-seconds value (any decimal integer) as representing the number of seconds after receipt of the message that its contents should be considered expired. Likewise, a value of zero (0) or an invalid date format can be considered equivalent to an expires immediately.

Last-Modified (When Was the Resource Last Modified?)

The Last-Modified header field indicates the date and time at which the sender believes the resource was last modified. The exact meaning of this field is defined in terms of how the receiver should interpret it; if the receiver has a copy of this resource that is older than the current date given by the Last-Modified field, that copy should be considered stale.

Here's a example of its use:

```
Last-Modified: Tue, 04 Apr 1995 07:39:26 GMT
```

The exact meaning of this header field depends on the implementation of the sender and the nature of the original resource. For files, it might be just the file system "last-mod" date. For virtual objects, it might be the last time the internal state changed. In any case, the recipient should only know (and care) about the result—whatever gets stuck in the Last-Modified field—and not worry about how that result was obtained.

Link (How Do Other Resources Relate to This Entity?)

The Link header provides a means for describing a relationship between the entity and some other resource. An entity can include multiple Link values. Links at the meta information level typically indicate relationships like hierarchical structure and navigation paths. The Link field means the same as the <LINK> element in HTML (BLC 1995).

Relation values are not case-sensitive and might be extended within the constraints of the sgml-name syntax. There are no predefined link relationship values for HTTP 1.0. The title parameter can

be used to label the destination of a link such that it can be used as identification within a human-readable menu. Examples of usage include:

```
Link: <http://www.cern.ch/TheBook/chapter2>;
rel="Previous"

Link: <mailto:timbl@w3.org>; rev="Made"; title="Tim
Berners-Lee"
```

The first example indicates that the entity is previous to chapter 2 in a logical navigation path. The second indicates that the publisher of the resource is identified by the given e-mail address.

Location (Where to Locate the Resource)

The Location header field is an earlier form of the URI header and is considered obsolete. HTTP 1.0 applications, however, should continue to support the Location header to properly interface with older applications. The purpose of Location is identical to that of the URI header, except that no variants can be specified and only one absolute location URL is allowed. An example follows:

```
Location: http://info.cern.ch/hypertext/WWW/
NewLocation.html
```

URI (Entity's Resource Origin)

The Title header field indicates the title of the entity. Here's an example of the field:

```
Title: Hypertext Transfer Protocol — HTTP/1.0
```

This field is to be considered the same as the <TITLE> element in HTML (BLC 1995).

The URI header field can contain one or more Universal Resource Identifiers (URIs) by which the resource origin of the entity can be identified. This field is required for the 201, 301, and 302 response messages and can be included in any message that contains resource meta information.

Any URI specified in this field can be either absolute or relative to the URI given in the request line. The URI header improves upon the Location header field. For backward compatibility with older clients, servers are encouraged to include both header fields in 301 and 302 responses.

The URI header can also be used by a client performing a **POST** request to suggest a URI for the new entity. The server's response must include the actual URI(s) of the new resource if one is successfully created (status 201).

If a URI refers to a set of variants, then the dimensions of that variance must be given with a *vary* parameter. One example is this:

```
URI: <http://info.cern.ch/hypertext/WWW/
TheProject.multi>; vary="type,language"
```

This indicates that the URI covers a group of entities that vary in media type and natural language. A request for that URI will result in a response that depends upon the client's request headers for Accept and Accept-Language. Similar dimensions exist for the Accept-Encoding, Accept-Charset, Version, and User-Agent header fields, as demonstrated in the following example:

```
URI: <TheProject.ps>;vary="encoding,version",
<TheProject.html>; vary="user agent,charset,version"
```

Version (Entity's Version)

The Version field defines the version tag associated with a rendition of an evolving entity. Together with

the Derived-From field, it enables a group of people to work simultaneously on the creation of a work as an iterative process. The field should be used to allow evolution of a particular work along a single path. Examples of the Version field include:

```
Version: 3.1.2

Version: "R5 19950404-07:39:26"

Version: 1.4a3-gamma6
```

The version tag should be considered opaque to all parties except the origin server. A user agent can request a particular version of an entity by including its tag in a Version header as part of the request. Similarly, a user agent can suggest a value for the version of an entity transferred via a **PUT** or **POST** request. However, only the origin server can reliably assign or increment the version tag of an entity.

Entity Body

The entity body (if any) sent with an HTTP 1.0 request or response is in a format and encoding defined by the entity header fields.

An entity body is included with a request message only when the request method calls for one. This specification defines two request methods, **POST** and **PUT**, that allow an entity body. In general, the presence of an entity body in a request is signaled by the inclusion of a Content-Length and/or Content-Transfer-Encoding header field in the request message headers.

 Most current implementations of the **POST** and **PUT** methods require a valid Content-Length header field. This can cause problems for some systems that do not know the size of the entity body before transmission. Experimental implementations (and future versions of HTTP) use a packetized Content-Transfer-Encoding to obviate the need for a Content-Length.

For response messages, whether an entity body is included with a message is dependent on both the request method and the response code. All responses to the **HEAD** request method must not include a body, even though the presence of Content header fields might lead one to believe they should. Similarly, the responses **204 No Content**, **304 Not Modified**, and **406 None Acceptable** must not include a body.

Type

When an entity body is included with a message, the data type of that body is determined by the header fields Content-Type, Content-Encoding, and Content-Transfer-Encoding. These define a three-layer, ordered encoding model, which follows:

```
entity-body←Content-Transfer-Encoding( Content-
Encoding( Content-Type ) )
```

A Content-Type specifies the media type of the underlying data. A Content-Encoding can be used to indicate an additional encoding mechanism applied to the type (usually for the purpose of data compression) that is a property of the resource requested. A Content-Transfer-Encoding can be applied by a transport agent to ensure safe and proper transfer of the message. Note that the Content-Transfer-Encoding is a property of the message, not of the resource.

The Content-Type header field has no default value. If—and only if—the media type is not given by a Content-Type header (as is always the case for simple response messages), the receiver might attempt to guess the media type through inspection of its content or the name extension(s) of the URL used to access the resource. If the media type remains unknown, the receiver should treat it as type application/octet-stream.

Length

When an entity body is included with a message, the length of that body can be determined in many ways. If a Content-Length header field is present, its value in bytes (number of octets) represents the length of the entity body. Otherwise, the body length is determined by the Content-Type (for types with an explicit end-of-body delimiter), the Content-Transfer-Encoding (for packetized encodings), or the closing of the connection by the server. Note that the latter cannot be used to indicate the end of a request body because it leaves no possibility for the server to send back a response.

 Some older servers supply an invalid *Content-Length* when sending a document that contains additional bytes (for example, preprocessor supplied data) dynamically inserted into the data stream. Therefore, unless the client knows that it is receiving a response from a compliant server, it should not depend on the *Content-Length* value being correct.

Protocol Parameters

The protocol parameters specify the HTTP version, URIs, and date/time formats used in HTTP.

HTTP Version

The protocol version indicates the format of a message and the sender's capacity for understanding further HTTP communication.

The version of an HTTP message is indicated by an HTTP-Version field in the first line of the message. If the protocol version is not specified, it defaults to the simple HTTP 0.9 format.

A proxy must never send a message with a version number greater than its native version; if a higher version request is received, the proxy must either downgrade the request version or respond with an error. Requests with a version lower than that of the proxy's native format can be upgraded by the proxy before being forwarded.

Universal Resource Identifiers

For details on the URI, the reader is referred to RFC 1630 (BL 1994), which provides a brief description of the allowed characters and the hex encoding used in the escaping scheme. Examples of URI follow:

```
telnet://debra.dgbt.doc.ca:3000
```

```
http://www.mcom.com/
```

```
ftp://prep.ai.mit.edu/pub/gnu/
```

Date/Time Formats

HTTP 1.0 applications have historically allowed three different formats for the representation of date/time stamps:

```
Tue, 04 Apr 1995 07:39:26 GMT   ; RFC 822, updated
by RFC 1123
```

```
Tuesday, 04-Apr-95 07:39:26 GMT ; RFC 850, obso-
leted by RFC 1036
```

```
Tue Apr  4 07:39:26 1995        ; ANSI C's
asctime() format
```

The first format is preferred as an Internet standard and represents a fixed-length subset of that
defined by RFC 1123 (Braden 1989), which is an
update to RFC 822 (Crocker 1982). The second format is in common use, but is obsolete and lacks a
four-digit year. HTTP 1.0 clients and servers must
accept all three formats, but should never generate the third (asctime) format.

Content Parameters

The content parameters specify the media types,
character sets, encoding mechanisms, transfer
encodings, and language tags used in HTTP.

Media Types

HTTP uses Internet Media Types (Postel 1994), formerly referred to as MIME Content-Types (BF
1993), to provide open and extensible data typing
and type negotiation. Examples of registered
Internet media types include:

```
audio/basic
```

```
video/mpeg
```

```
image/gif
```

```
text/plain
```

```
application/postscript
```

With HTTP, user agents can identify acceptable
media types as part of the connection. They are
thus also allowed to use non-registered types, but
their usage must not conflict with the IANA registry. All media types registered by IANA must be
preferred over extension tokens.

 n o t e HTTP does not encourage the use of an *x*-
prefix for unofficial types except for short
experimental use between consenting
applications.

Character Sets

Character sets are identified by case-insensitive
tokens. The complete set of allowed charset values are defined by the IANA Character Set registry
(RP 1994). The following are the names for those
character sets most likely to be used with HTTP
entities.

→ US-ASCII

→ ISO-8859-1

→ ISO-8859-2

→ ISO-8859-3

→ ISO-8859-4

→ ISO-8859-5

→ ISO-8859-6

→ ISO-8859-7

- → ISO-8859-8

- → ISO-8859-9

- → ISO-2022-JP

- → ISO-2022-JP-2

- → ISO-2022-KR

- → UNICODE-1-1

- → UNICODE-1-1-UTF-7

- → UNICODE-1-1-UTF-8

This set of charset values includes those registered by RFC 1521 (BF 1993)—the US-ASCII (ANSI 1986) and ISO8859 (ISO 1990) character sets—and other character set names specifically recommended for use within MIME charset parameters.

Encoding Mechanisms

Encoding mechanism values indicate an encoding transformation that has been or can be applied to a resource. Encoding mechanisms allow a document to be compressed or encrypted without losing the identity of its underlying media type.

Typically, the resource is stored with this encoding and is only decoded before rendering. Two values are defined by this specification: gzip and compress.

 note HTTP 1.0 applications should consider x-gzip and x-compress to be equivalent to gzip and compress, respectively.

All encoding-mechanism values are case-insensitive. HTTP 1.0 uses encoding-mechanism values in the Accept-Encoding and Content-

Encoding header fields. Although the value describes the encoding-mechanism, it also indicates which decoding mechanism is required to remove the encoding.

Transfer Encodings

Transfer encoding values are used to indicate an encoding transformation that has been, can be, or might need to be applied to an entity body to ensure safe transport through the network.

 note Transfer encodings are only used with entities destined for or retrieved from MIME-conformant systems. They rarely occur in an HTTP 1.0 message. This differs from an encoding-mechanism in that the transfer encoding is a property of the message, not of the original resource.

HTTP defines the following transfer-encoding values:

- → **Binary.** No encoding and body can contain any set of octets.

- → **8bit.** Same as binary but with added restrictions that carriage return and linefeed characters only occur as part of CR/LF line separators, all lines are short (less than 1000 octets), and no NULs (octet 0) are present.

- → **7bit.** Same as 8bit but with added restriction that all octets are 7-bit US-ASCII characters.

- → **Quoted-printable.** Encoding consisting of 7-bit US-ASCII characters applied to body.

- → **Base64.** Encoding consisting of 7-bit US-ASCII characters applied to body.

All transfer-encoding values are case-insensitive. HTTP 1.0 uses transfer-encoding values in the Accept-Encoding and Content-Transfer-Encoding header fields.

Language Tags

A language tag identifies a natural language used by human beings for communication of information to other human beings. Computer languages are explicitly excluded. The HTTP 1.0 protocol uses language tags within the Accept-Language and Content-Language header fields.

The syntax and registry of HTTP language tags is the same as that defined by RFC 1766 (Alvestrand 1995). Sample tags include the following:

`en, en-US, en-cockney, i-cherokee, x-pig-latin`

All tags are to be treated as case-insensitive. The namespace of language tags is administered by the IANA.

Content Negotiation

Content negotiation is an optional feature of the HTTP protocol. It allows a preferred content representation to be pre-selected within a single HTTP request-response round-trip.

During content negotiation, the server first determines whether there are any content variants for the requested resource. Content variants can be multiple copies of the same image or text in different file formats. They can also be implemented by means of a set of dynamic conversion filters.

If there are no variant forms of the resource, the negotiation is limited to whether that single media type is acceptable under the constraints given by the Accept request header field (if any).

If variants are available, those variants that are completely unacceptable should be removed from consideration first. Unacceptable variants include:

➜ Those with a Content-Encoding not listed in an Accept-Encoding field

➜ Those with a character subset (other than the default ISO-8859-1) not listed in an Accept-Charset field

➜ Those with a media type not within any of the media ranges of an explicitly constrained Accept field (or listed with a zero quality parameter)

If no acceptable variants remain at this point, the server should respond with a `406 None Acceptable` response message.

If more than one variant remains, and at least one has a Content-Language within those listed by an Accept-Language field, any variants that do not match the language constraint are removed from further consideration.

If multiple choices still remain, the selection is further narrowed by calculating and comparing the relative quality of the available media types. If multiple representations exist for a single media type, then the one with the lowest byte count is preferred.

Finally, there might still be multiple choices available to the user. If so, the server can either choose

one from those available and respond with **200 OK**, or respond with **300 Multiple Choices** and include an entity describing the choices.

Access Authentication

In HTTP, a server can challenge a user agent request, and a user agent can provide authentication information in response to that challenge. HTTP provides a simple challenge-response authorization mechanism to do this.

The basic authentication scheme is based on the model that the user agent must authenticate itself with a user-ID and a password for each realm of the resource being requested. The server will service the request only if it can validate the user-ID and password for the domain of the requested resource.

The server issues the **401 Unauthorized** response message (in response to a user agent request) to challenge the authorization of a user agent. This response must include a WWW-Authenticate header field containing the challenge applicable to the requested resource.

The user agent can authenticate itself with a server (after receiving a 401 response) by including an Authorization header field with the next request. The Authorization field value consists of credentials containing the authentication information of the user agent for the realm of the resource being requested.

If the user agent wants to send the user-ID *Aladdin* and password *open sesame*, for example, it would use the following header field:

```
Authorization: Basic QWxhZGRpbjpvcGVuIHNlc2FtZQ==
```

The user-ID and password (separated by a single colon (:)) in the above example are encoded using the base64 method (BF 1993).

 The basic authentication scheme is a non-secure method of filtering unauthorized access to resources on an HTTP server. It does not prevent the entity body from being transmitted in clear text across the physical network.

Proxies are completely transparent regarding user agent access authentication. That is, they forward the WWW-Authenticate and Authorization headers intact.

WebWalker: Your Web Maintenance Robot

A s was discussed in Chapter 5, "Web Robots: Operational Guidelines," one of the major applications of Web robots and spiders is in automated maintenance of Web information structure. As E. B. White writes in the popular children's book

Charlotte's Web:

A spider's web is stronger than it looks. Although it is made of thin, delicate strands, the web is not easily broken. However, a web gets torn every day by the insects that kick around in it, and a spider must rebuild it when it gets full of holes.

In a similar fashion, some hypertext links can become out-of-date as the Web information structure changes over time. Hypertext links that have become obsolete are called *dead links*. This happens when referenced information has changed or when referenced Web pages have been moved or deleted.

The former case presents a problem that is purely semantic, and requires an understanding of how the text has changed to mean something different. The latter case is purely syntactic and structural, and can be readily identified by a Web robot. The job of a *Web maintenance spider* is thus to detect dead links and to "rebuild [the Web] when it gets full of holes."

This chapter explores the Web maintenance problem and examines the basic operational principles behind spiders that perform automated Web maintenance. This chapter also describes the design and operation of the WebWalker spider, which has been developed for purpose of illustration and experimentation.

The Web Maintenance Problem

The terms *Web information structure*, *Web information space*, and *hypertext information structure*, have all been used interchangeably throughout this book. The term *infostructure* is perhaps a more concise term for describing the same thing.

Web Infostructure

An *infostructure* is a layout of information in a manner such that it can be navigated (Tilton 1993). Infostructure can be any resource database with a specifically designed structure that gives it body and shape. For example, a table of contents is an infostructure, as is a bibliography. A collection of World Wide Web documents hyperlinked together is also an infostructure. In fact, the World Wide Web as a whole can be considered the ultimate infostructure. Figure 7.1 shows the prototypical Web infostructure published by a research center.

An infostructure builds its contents from multiple information sources, in the form of hyperlinks to Web documents residing at distributed sites. These collections of Web documents often are maintained by different document owners. Individual Web documents also can be shared by more than one infostructure.

Past Approaches

An infostructure is rarely static. It changes over time as the contents of individual Web pages are updated. Reference information might be added, deleted, or changed. Web documents also might be moved or deleted. As a result, hyperlinks can become broken and the infostructure corrupted. In many cases, unfortunately the ensuing flurry of complaints from users and the information in the error logs of each server seldom are seen by the actual document owners.

Server Log Analysis

Webmasters, however, can generate a partial list of Web pages that need updating. The required information sometimes can be extracted from servers logs:

→ URL of dead links (identified by failed HTTP transactions that generates the `301 Moved Permanently` response code)

Figure 7.1

*Web infostructure of a
Research Center.*

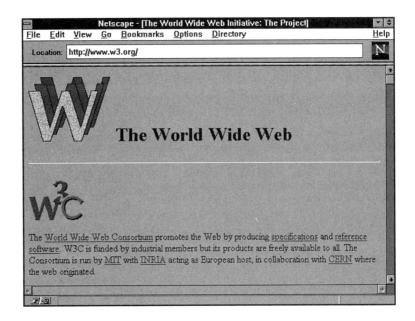

→ URL of Web pages that refer these links (specified in the Referer field of HTTP request headers).

However, this ad-hoc post-mortem approach is hardly a solution; portions of the Web that are out of date but remained unexplored might have undiscovered dead links. They remain undiscovered until someone on the Web actually needs to link through them, only to find out belatedly that the links are dead.

Manual Traversal

To detect dead links and other inconsistencies early on, individual document owners resort to manual traversal of the portion of the Web for which they are responsible. This job is both boring and time-consuming. As these infostructures evolve over time, they grow to become more complex and harder to maintain.

What is needed is an automated means of traversing a Web of documents and checking for changes that might require the attention of the human document owners. Web robots and spiders are automated client programs that can traverse the Web infostructure in a systematic fashion.

Web Maintenance Spiders

There has to be a better way of systematically exploring the Web information structure in order to uncover all dead links, and this is where Web maintenance spiders or robots become useful. They assist Web document owners and Webmasters maintain Web information structures by automatically traversing the Web space checking for dead links. These spiders can then compile a complete list of problem Web pages that contains dead links.

Roy Fielding's MOMspider (Multi-Owner Mainte-nance Spider) is one of the better known examples of Web maintenance robots (1994). WebWalker is a simple Web maintenance robot derived from MOMspider. The remainder of this chapter dis-cusses the WebWalker robot.

WebWalker Operation

WebWalker is a World Wide Web robot that traverses designated Web infostructures on the net to perform automated hyperlinks verification. WebWalker can identify individual hypertext links that are broken, redirected, changed, or expired, and provide a summary of results.

During traversal, WebWalker sets the User-Agent field in the HTTP request header to WebWalker/ 1.00 and also includes additional information in the headers for identifying the robot operator and the Web page referrer. The following is a sample frag-ment in the HTTP protocol stream:

```
User-Agent: WebWalker/1.00
From: webmaster@www-cis.stanford.edu
Referer: http://www-cis.stanford.edu/NanoNet/
```

Processing Task Descriptions

WebWalker can be run from the command line by the user or as a batch program. WebWalker can also be run as a CGI script by the Web server (in response to user submission of task descriptions through a Web browser online). As a result, WebWalker can learn about what infostructures it is supposed to visit by one of the following means:

➜ WebWalker can look up the task descriptions from a *task file* when invoked from the com-mand line or run as a batch program.

➜ WebWalker can get the task descriptions using the Common Gateway Interface when WebWalker is run as a CGI script.

Avoiding and Excluding URLs

Not all URLs on the Web are safe for a spider to traverse; some infinite virtual spaces generated by program scripts on the server can trap an unsus-pecting spider. There are also many URLs, such as gateway program scripts and image files, for which it makes no sense to collect maintenance informa-tion. Furthermore, some sites on the Web are sim-ply not intended for robots.

WebWalker complies with the robot exclusion stan-dard (described previously in Chapter 5) by respect-ing all restrictions set up for it by the Webmaster. These restrictions can be viewed as roadblocks on the Web, beyond which WebWalker would not ven-ture. The roadblock information is communicated to WebWalker by means of the robot exclusion file at the target Web site, and which WebWalker must first read prior to traversing the Web site. WebWalker avoids all URLs that are disallowed to it (that is, it will perform no HTTP requests on those URLs).

In addition to the robot exclusion file, WebWalker can also depend on *Exclude directives* supplied to it in a *task file* by the robot operator to help it navi-gate around such spider traps. URLs that are ex-cluded can only be tested with HTTP HEAD

requests, and not traversed with HTTP GET requests. Excluded URLs are essentially the leaf nodes in a Web infostructure.

Keeping History

WebWalker maintains a traversal history and remembers where it has been on the Web. In this way, WebWalker knows how to avoid being lured into chasing cycles of repeating URLs. The history information also allows WebWalker to reuse results of previous visits. Status updates to the history occurs throughout the traversal process and WebWalker tracks whether specific nodes in the infostructure were seen but not yet tested, avoided, to be excluded, to be tested, to be traversed, or already traversed.

Traversing the Web

WebWalker follows a simple breadth-first traversal strategy, implemented by keeping an internal queue of URLs that WebWalker needs to visit. WebWalker knows how to crawl slowly on the Web so as not to overload any one server with a series of rapid-fire requests. This is implemented by keeping track of the number of consecutive requests to the last visited site, and remember the time when the previous request was last made.

Generating Reports

WebWalker reports its findings in the form of a collective summary table of statistics, one for each infostructure examined. Regularly scheduled visits

by WebWalker ensure the correctness and consistency of a large and growing collection of distributed WWW infostructures, and make the task of maintaining complex infostructures much easier for the already overworked Webmasters.

Is WebWalker a Good Robot?

WebWalker is a stripped-down implementation of MOMspider for automated Web maintenance. WebWalker would be considered a *good* robot depending if it complies with the four laws of Web robotics, listed here:

1. *A Web Robot Must Show Identifications.*

   WebWalker supplies all three HTTP request header fields: User-Agent, From, and Referer, as required.

2. *A Web Robot Must Obey Exclusion Standard.*

   WebWalker understands the robot exclusion standard which it implements by means of an avoidance strategy.

3. *A Web Robot Must Not Hog Resources.*

   WebWalker knows how to crawl slowly on the Web so as not to overload any one server with a series of rapid-fire requests. WebWalker also remembers where it has been on the Web so as not to chase infinite cycles of URLs.

4. *A Web Robot Must Report Errors.*

   WebWalker generates a statistics summary report at the end of each infostructure traversal and which highlights a list of URLs that are broken, redirected, changed, or expired.

WebWalker Limitations

The design and implementation of WebWalker is based on the architecture and Perl source code of Roy Fielding's MOMspider robot. WebWalker is a simplified version of MOMspider in that it does not have all of MOMspider's user input features and report generation capabilities. But then WebWalker is only 1,800 lines of Perl code, as versus 4,000 lines for MOMspider. WebWalker, however, retains the internal Web traversal engine of MOMspider and performs the mechanics of Web traversal in exactly the same fashion as MOMspider.

WebWalker does not support the sharing of Web maintenance work load across multiple users, nor does it save the results into files for sharing across multiple runs at different times, as does MOMspider. WebWalker is not designed for heavy-duty production use. WebWalker is built for illustrating the basic operational principles of Web robots, and for experimentation. WebWalker can, however, come in quite handy for light-duty use by Webmasters to traverse Web infostructures within the local network.

 n o t e WebWalker should not be used to traverse remote Web sites across the Internet (although it is perfectly capable of doing so), as this is wasteful of network resources. A better solution is to run WebWalker on a machine local to where the bulk of the Web infostructure resides.

WebWalker Program Installation

The WebWalker program is a 1,800-line Perl script that is built on top of the Roy Fielding's libwww-perl library package for accessing the World Wide Web. Currently, WebWalker can only be run from a Unix machine. Before the WebWalker can be used to help maintain your local Web sites, you need to install and set up the following:

→ The Perl interpreter, written by Larry Wall

→ The Perl WWW library, written by Roy Fielding

→ The WebWalker program, a single file written in Perl

The following are step-by-step instructions for installing the WebWalker robot on a Unix machine:

1. If you don't already have it, get and install the Perl software package from one of its many distribution sites. A list of Perl archive sites can be found in the following Web pages:

```
http://www.cis.ufl.edu/perl/
http://web.nexor.co.uk/perl/perl.html
```

   Be sure to install the user and system libraries along with Perl. Specifically, the execution of WebWalker requires that the getopts.pl Perl library package be installed.

2. If you don't already have it, get and install Roy Fielding's libwww-perl package from any of its distribution sites at the following addresses:

```
http://www.ics.uci.edu/WebSoft/libwww-perl/

ftp://liege.ics.uci.edu/pub/arcadia/libwww-perl/
```

If you have not included the libwww-perl directory on the standard include path for Perl, be sure to set the $LIBWWW_PERL environment variable so that client programs, for example, WebWalker, can find it.

3. Get the WebWalker source program from any one of the following addresses:

`http://deluge.stanford.edu:8000/book/WebWalker`

`http://www.mcp.com/softlib/Internet/WebWalker`

`ftp://www.mcp.com/softlib/Internet/WebWalker`

4. Examine the WebWalker program script and follow its configuration instructions to properly set up WebWalker for operation. You must follow the instructions there to configure the locations of the Perl WWW library and WebWalker task file, and to specify the domain name of the local network.

5. Make sure the WebWalker program is executable (on most Unix systems) by typing the following command:

`chmod 755 WebWalker`

Now that WebWalker is properly installed and set up, you can turn your attention to specifying what infostructures you want WebWalker to traverse. The specification for each infostructure is called a *task* and are collected in a WebWalker *task file*, to be discussed next.

WebWalker Task File

The task file usually resides in the robot operator's home directory and specifies the infostructures that WebWalker needs to traverse. At the begining of processing, WebWalker reads all the task specifications from the task file and loads them into internal tables.

 n o t e The task file can be named by the -f command-line option or by the default name ".webwalk" set in the configuration section of the source program.

A WebWalker task file consists of a series of optional global directives followed by a series of traversal tasks, each traversal task is specified with a set of task directives. Both global and task directives are case-sensitive.

WebWalker sets the configuration options associated with the global directives, then proceeds to perform each of the tasks in the given order as listed in the task file. After completing the last task, WebWalker prints out a summary of the overall process results and then exits.

Global Directives

The following are the recognized global directives:

➜ ReplyTo *email_address*

Specifies the real e-mail address of the robot operator running the WebWalker program, which usually is the local Webmaster. This e-mail address *must* correspond to the human being that should be notified in case someone is having problems with how WebWalker is operated. The e-mail address information is communicated to the Web server by means of

the HTTP From request header. The default address is normally set by libwww-perl to be `user@hostname`.

→ MaxDepth *number*

Specifies the maximum allowed depth of any WebWalker traversal. Its purpose is to prevent the spider from falling into an infinite virtual space. The default value (usually 20) should be larger than any of the infostructures that WebWalker will ever want to traverse.

Task Directives

Each WebWalker task consists of a set of task directives surrounded by angle brackets. For each task, WebWalker traverses the Web infostructure, in breadth-first order, from the specified top document (TopURL directive) down to each leaf node. A *leaf node* is defined to be any Web resource which is either not of content-type HTML (and thus cannot contain any further links), or which is outside the boundary of the given infostructure boundary (specified with the BoundURL directive).

→ Name *infostructure_name*

Specifies the name of the Web infostructure to be traversed. It is used to identify the infostructure in a WebWalker generated report. The name is required for all tasks and must be a single word containing no whitespace.

→ TopURL *URL*

Specifies the URL of the top of the infostructure to be traversed. If the given URL is relative, then it is resolved as a local URL URL (that is, with the prefix file://localhost/) relative to the current

working directory where WebWalker is started. The top URL is required for all tasks and must be a single word containing no whitespace. Any fragment identifier will be ignored.

→ BoundURL *URLprefix*

Specifies that only encountered URLs that contain the given prefix will be traversed. This sets the boundary for the intended infostructure and prevents WebWalker from trespassing onto other remote Web sites where it will be unwelcome.

→ ChangeWindow *number*

Specifies the window in *number* days prior to the current date within which a tested URL's last-modified date is considered "interesting" and should be reported by WebWalker. If *number* is zero (0), no last-modification dates are considered interesting. This directive is optional and defaults to seven (7) days.

→ ExpireWindow *number*

Specifies the window in *number* days after the current date within which a traversed URL's expires date is considered "interesting" and should be reported by WebWalker. If *number* is zero (0), no expiration dates are considered interesting. This directive is optional and defaults to zero (0). Because expire dates are rarely used in the Web, this directive is rarely useful.

→ Exclude *URLprefix*

Specifies that all encountered URLs that contain the given URL prefix will only be tested and not traversed. It is always useful to exclude the cgi-bin directory, as well as other

directories that contain image files, from Web. Multiple Exclude directives can be specified for any task.

Task File Format

The WebWalker task file format is fairly rigid but quite simple. Blank lines and any lines beginning with '#' are ignored. All task directives should be on a single line regardless of length and there is no facility for line-continuation.

The specification of each task begins with a left angle bracket character (<) and ends with a right angle bracket character (>), both of which must be on a line by itself. For example, the following is a sample task file that can be used by the Webmaster at Yahoo to maintain the Yahoo directory:

```
ReplyTo         webmaster@yahoo.com
MaxDepth        1
<
  Name          Yahoo
  TopURL        http://www.yahoo.com/
  BoundURL      http://www.yahoo.com/
  ChangeWindow  1
  ExpireWindow  1
  Exclude       http://www.yahoo.com/
>
```

Another example is the following sample task file that can be used by Webmasters at Stanford's Center of Integrated Systems for maintaining their Nanofab project infostructure:

```
ReplyTo         webmaster@www-cis.stanford.edu
MaxDepth        10
<
  Name          Stanford CIS NanoNet Home Page
  TopURL        http://www-cis.stanford.edu/
```

```
                NanoNet/
  BoundURL      http://www-cis.stanford.edu/
                NanoNet/
  ChangeWindow  2
  ExpireWindow  1
  Exclude       http://www-cis.stanford.edu/
                NanoNet/cgi-bin/
>
```

 Do *not* use these sample task files! They are targeted at other people's Web sites, not yours, so don't bother using them as they are strictly for illustrative purposes only. Lots of people will be upset if you do. You should build your own task file that is customized for your local Web site.

WebWalker Usage Examples

Before you start up WebWalker, you should double check the contents of the task file to make sure that it covers exactly the infostructure you have intended. It would upset many users and Webmasters if you were to unleash WebWalker on the net but failed to target the correct Web sites, and in the process wasted valuable network resources.

To start up WebWalker, simply type the name of the WebWalker program on the command line (after checking the contents of the task file for correctness) as in the following:

WebWalker

WebWalker can display the following usage information in response to an invalid option:

```
usage: Webwalker [-h] [-f taskfile] [-d maxdepth]
WebWalker/1.00
WWW Robot for maintenance of distributed hypertext
infostructures.
Options:
[DEFAULT]
    -h  Help — just display this message and
quit.
    -f  Get your task instructions from the
following file.  [$TaskFile]
    -d  Maximum traversal depth.
[$MaxDepth]
```

Do not attempt to run WebWalker from a remote machine that is outside of your local network! Valuable network bandwidth will be wasted if you do. WebWalker is strictly for Webmasters to run on their *local network* targeted at their *own Web sites*.

Sample WebWalker Output

Here is what you would see as the output from WebWalker using the task file for traversing the infostructure at the Yahoo Web site (intended strictly for illustrative purposes only):

```
WebWalker/1.00 starting at Tue, 12 Sep 1995 10:00:54
Reading task specifications from /home/fcc/.webwalk

Starting Infostructure [Yahoo] at Tue, 12 Sep 1995 10:00:54
Checking for http://www.yahoo.com:80/robots.txt ... 200 OK
Traversing http://www.yahoo.com/ ... 200 OK
Testing http://www.yahoo.com/bin/top1 ... 200 OK
Testing http://www.yahoo.com/images/main.gif ... 200 OK
Testing http://www.yahoo.com/headlines/ ... 200 OK
Testing http://www.yahoo.com/weblaunch.html ... 200 OK
Testing http://www.yahoo.com/text/ ... 200 OK
Testing http://www.yahoo.com/search.html ... 200 OK
Testing http://www.yahoo.com/Arts/ ... 200 OK
Testing http://www.yahoo.com/Arts/Literature/ ... 200 OK
Testing http://www.yahoo.com/Arts/Photography/ ... 200 OK
Testing http://www.yahoo.com/Arts/Architecture/ ... 200 OK
Reusing test of http://www.yahoo.com/Arts/ ...
Testing http://www.yahoo.com/Business_and_Economy/ ... 200 OK
Testing http://www.yahoo.com/headlines/current/business/ ... 200 OK
Testing http://www.yahoo.com/Business_and_Economy/Business_Directory/ ... 200 OK
Testing http://www.yahoo.com/Business_and_Economy/Markets_and_Investments/ ... 200 OK
```

```
Testing http://www.yahoo.com/Business_and_Economy/Classifieds/ ... 200 OK
Reusing test of http://www.yahoo.com/Business_and_Economy/ ...
Testing http://www.yahoo.com/Computers_and_Internet/ ... 200 OK
Testing http://www.yahoo.com/Computers_and_Internet/Internet/ ... 200 OK
Testing http://www.yahoo.com/Computers_and_Internet/Internet/World_Wide_Web/ ... 200 OK
Testing http://www.yahoo.com/Computers_and_Internet/Software/ ... 200 OK
Testing http://www.yahoo.com/Computers_and_Internet/Multimedia/ ... 200 OK
Reusing test of http://www.yahoo.com/Computers_and_Internet/ ...
Testing http://www.yahoo.com/Education/ ... 200 OK
Testing http://www.yahoo.com/Education/Universities/ ... 200 OK
Testing http://www.yahoo.com/Education/K_12/ ... 200 OK
Testing http://www.yahoo.com/Education/Courses/ ... 200 OK
Reusing test of http://www.yahoo.com/Education/ ...
Testing http://www.yahoo.com/Entertainment/ ... 200 OK
Testing http://www.yahoo.com/headlines/current/entertainment/ ... 200 OK
Testing http://www.yahoo.com/Entertainment/Television/ ... 200 OK
Testing http://www.yahoo.com/Entertainment/Movies_and_Films/ ... 200 OK
Testing http://www.yahoo.com/Entertainment/Music/ ... 200 OK
Testing http://www.yahoo.com/Entertainment/Magazines/ ... 200 OK
Testing http://www.yahoo.com/Entertainment/Books/ ... 200 OK
Reusing test of http://www.yahoo.com/Entertainment/ ...
Testing http://www.yahoo.com/Government/ ... 200 OK
Testing http://www.yahoo.com/Government/Politics/ ... 200 OK
Testing http://www.yahoo.com/headlines/current/politics/ ... 200 OK
Testing http://www.yahoo.com/Government/Agencies/ ... 200 OK
Testing http://www.yahoo.com/Government/Law/ ... 200 OK
Testing http://www.yahoo.com/Government/Military/ ... 200 OK
Reusing test of http://www.yahoo.com/Government/ ...
Testing http://www.yahoo.com/Health/ ... 200 OK
Testing http://www.yahoo.com/Health/Medicine/ ... 200 OK
Testing http://www.yahoo.com/Health/Pharmacology/Drugs/ ... 200 OK
Testing http://www.yahoo.com/Health/Diseases_and_Conditions/ ... 200 OK
Testing http://www.yahoo.com/Health/Fitness/ ... 200 OK
Reusing test of http://www.yahoo.com/Health/ ...
Testing http://www.yahoo.com/News/ ... 200 OK
Testing http://www.yahoo.com/headlines/current/news/ ... 200 OK
Testing http://www.yahoo.com/News/International/ ... 200 OK
```

```
Testing http://www.yahoo.com/headlines/current/international/ ... 200 OK
Testing http://www.yahoo.com/News/Daily/ ... 200 OK
Testing http://www.yahoo.com/News/Current_Events ... 200 OK
Reusing test of http://www.yahoo.com/News/ ...
Testing http://www.yahoo.com/Recreation/ ... 200 OK
Testing http://www.yahoo.com/Recreation/Sports/ ... 200 OK
Testing http://www.yahoo.com/headlines/current/sports/ ... 200 OK
Testing http://www.yahoo.com/Recreation/Games/ ... 200 OK
Testing http://www.yahoo.com/Recreation/Travel/ ... 200 OK
Testing http://www.yahoo.com/Recreation/Automobiles/ ... 200 OK
Reusing test of http://www.yahoo.com/Recreation/ ...
Testing http://www.yahoo.com/Reference/ ... 200 OK
Testing http://www.yahoo.com/Reference/Libraries/ ... 200 OK
Testing http://www.yahoo.com/Reference/Dictionaries/ ... 200 OK
Testing http://www.yahoo.com/Reference/Phone_Numbers/ ... 200 OK
Reusing test of http://www.yahoo.com/Reference/ ...
Testing http://www.yahoo.com/Regional/ ... 200 OK
Testing http://www.yahoo.com/Regional/Countries/ ... 200 OK
Testing http://www.yahoo.com/Regional/Regions/ ... 200 OK
Testing http://www.yahoo.com/Regional/U_S__States/ ... 200 OK
Reusing test of http://www.yahoo.com/Regional/ ...
Testing http://www.yahoo.com/Science/ ... 200 OK
Testing http://www.yahoo.com/Science/Computer_Science/ ... 200 OK
Testing http://www.yahoo.com/Science/Biology/ ... 200 OK
Testing http://www.yahoo.com/Science/Astronomy/ ... 200 OK
Testing http://www.yahoo.com/Science/Engineering/ ... 200 OK
Reusing test of http://www.yahoo.com/Science/ ...
Testing http://www.yahoo.com/Social_Science/ ... 200 OK
Testing http://www.yahoo.com/Social_Science/History/ ... 200 OK
Testing http://www.yahoo.com/Social_Science/Philosophy/ ... 200 OK
Testing http://www.yahoo.com/Social_Science/Linguistics_and_Human_Languages/ ... 200 OK
Reusing test of http://www.yahoo.com/Social_Science/ ...
Testing http://www.yahoo.com/Society_and_Culture/ ... 200 OK
Testing http://www.yahoo.com/Society_and_Culture/People/ ... 603 Timed Out
Testing http://www.yahoo.com/Society_and_Culture/Environment_and_Nature/ ... 200 OK
Testing http://www.yahoo.com/Society_and_Culture/Religion/ ... 200 OK
Reusing test of http://www.yahoo.com/Society_and_Culture/ ...
Reusing test of http://www.yahoo.com/ ...
```

```
Testing http://www.yahoo.com/images/netscape4.gif ... 200 OK
Reusing test of http://www.yahoo.com/ ...
Testing http://www.yahoo.com/docs/pr/credits.html ... 200 OK
Done Traversing http://www.yahoo.com/ ...
... at Tue, 12 Sep 1995 10:10:34 — 0 remaining on queue


Broken Links:
    http://www.yahoo.com/Society_and_Culture/People/  (603 Timed Out)
Changed Links:
    http://www.yahoo.com/Regional/Countries/  (200 OK)
    Last-modified:
    http://www.yahoo.com/weblaunch.html  (200 OK)
    Last-modified:
    http://www.yahoo.com/Government/Agencies/  (200 OK)
    Last-modified:
    http://www.yahoo.com/Regional/Regions/  (200 OK)
    Last-modified:
    http://www.yahoo.com/Computers_and_Internet/Internet/  (200 OK)
    Last-modified:
    http://www.yahoo.com/Entertainment/Books/  (200 OK)
    Last-modified:
    http://www.yahoo.com/Government/Law/  (200 OK)
    Last-modified:
    http://www.yahoo.com/Recreation/Sports/  (200 OK)
    Last-modified:
    http://www.yahoo.com/Business_and_Economy/Business_Directory/  (200 OK)
    Last-modified:
    http://www.yahoo.com/Computers_and_Internet/Multimedia/  (200 OK)
    Last-modified:
    http://www.yahoo.com/Regional/U_S__States/  (200 OK)
    Last-modified:
    http://www.yahoo.com/Computers_and_Internet/Internet/World_Wide_Web/  (200 OK)
    Last-modified:
    http://www.yahoo.com/Government/  (200 OK)
    Last-modified:
    http://www.yahoo.com/Government/Military/  (200 OK)
    Last-modified:
```

```
        http://www.yahoo.com/Business_and_Economy/Markets_and_Investments/  (200 OK)
        Last-modified:
        http://www.yahoo.com/Government/Politics/  (200 OK)
        Last-modified:
        http://www.yahoo.com/Recreation/Games/  (200 OK)
        Last-modified:
        http://www.yahoo.com/Regional/  (200 OK)
        Last-modified:
        http://www.yahoo.com/Business_and_Economy/Classifieds/  (200 OK)
        Last-modified:

Summary of Results:
```

	References		Unique URLs		Local URLs	
	number	pct	number	pct	number	pct
Traversed	2	2.15	1	1.28	0	0.00
Tested	77	82.80	78	100.00	0	0.00
Reused	16	17.20	0	0.00	0	0.00
Avoided	0	0.00	0	0.00	0	0.00
Untestable	0	0.00	0	0.00	0	0.00
Broken	1	1.08	1	1.28	0	0.00
Redirected	0	0.00	0	0.00	0	0.00
Changed 1	21	22.58	19	24.36	0	0.00
Expired 1	0	0.00	0	0.00	0	0.00
Local	0	0.00	0	0.00	0	100.00
Remote	93	100.00	78	100.00	0	0.00
Totals	93	100.00	78	83.87	0	0.00

```
Finished Infostructure [Yahoo] at Tue, 12 Sep 1995 12:10:36

WebWalker/1.00 finished at Tue, 12 Sep 1995 12:10:36
```

The summary above indicates that only the Yahoo home page was traversed. A total of 93 URLs were encountered in the Yahoo home page, and they were pointing to 77 different Web pages. Obviously, some URLs were sharing the same Web page. The actual contents of these 77 Web pages were not retrieved, they were merely tested (using HTTP HEAD request). Of the 78 Web pages tested (including the home page), 19 of them were found to be new—that is, they changed within the last 24 hours.

There was only one broken link at the top-level Yahoo infostructure during WebWalker's traversal. Closer examination of the output shows that the link was only temporarily broken, as indicated by the `603 Timed Out` response code. This is probably due to Yahoo server overload and not because of a dead link.

WebWalker Forms Interface

For Webmasters who prefer to work with a Web interface than to type on a command line, the WebWalker program can be configured to run as a Common Gateway Interface (CGI) script. All that needs to be done is to put the WebWalker program under the cgi-bin directory at your local Web site, and to prepare a Web page containing an HTML form that can be used to submit task description to your WebWalker. A sample home page for WebWalker is shown in figure 7.2.

The following is the output from WebWalker using the task file for traversing Nanofab project infostructure located at Stanford's Center of Integrated Systems Web site:

Figure 7.2

WebWalker's Web User Interface.

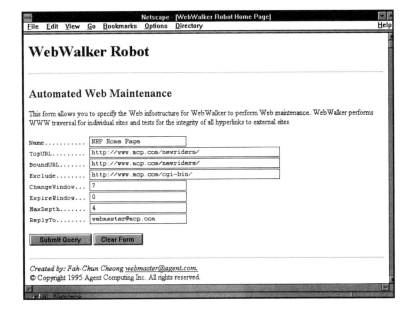

```
WebWalker/1.00 starting at Tue, 12 Sep 1995 10:53:20
Reading task specifications from /home/fcc/.webwalk


Starting Infostructure [Stanford CIS Nanofab Home Page] at Tue, 12 Sep 1995 10:53:21


  <...text ommitted...>


Broken Links:
    http://www-cis.stanford.edu/NanoNet/communications/lead/submission/three.html  (404 Not Found)
    http://www-cis.stanford.edu/NanoNet/communications/lead/completed.html  (404 Not Found)
    http://www-cis.stanford.edu/NanoNet/communications/lead/submission/one.html  (404 Not Found)
    http://www-cis.stanford.edu/NanoNet/communications/lead/vote.html  (404 Not Found)
    http://www.nnf.cornell.edu/NanoLine/NNF/Staff/HaroldCraighead.html  (602 Connection Failed)
    http://www.nnf.cornell.edu/  (602 Connection Failed)
    http://www-cis.stanford.edu/NanoNet/communications/lead/submission/two.html  (404 Not Found)
    http://www-cis.stanford.edu/NanoNet/communications/lead/started.html  (404 Not Found)
    http://www.nnf.cornell.edu/NanoLine/NNFPubs/nm/nm.html  (602 Connection Failed)
    http://www-cis.stanford.edu/NanoNet/communications/lead/modify.html  (404 Not Found)
Redirected Links:
    http://www.commerce.digital.com/palo-alto/chamber-of-commerce/home.html  (302 Found)
Changed Links:
    http://www.city.palo-alto.ca.us/home.html  (200 OK)
    Last-modified:


Summary of Results:
            .----------------------------------------------------.
            ¦  References  ¦  Unique URLs  ¦  Local URLs  ¦
            ¦ number  pct  ¦ number   pct  ¦ number   pct ¦
            ¦---------------+---------------+--------------¦
Traversed   ¦   35  19.23  ¦   33  52.38   ¦   33  66.00  ¦
Tested      ¦   61  33.52  ¦   62  98.41   ¦   50 100.00  ¦
Reused      ¦   91  50.00  ¦    0   0.00   ¦    0   0.00  ¦
Avoided     ¦    0   0.00  ¦    0   0.00   ¦    0   0.00  ¦
Untestable  ¦   30  16.48  ¦    1   1.59   ¦    0   0.00  ¦
            ¦---------------+---------------+--------------¦
Broken      ¦   10   5.49  ¦   10  15.87   ¦    7  14.00  ¦
Redirected  ¦    1   0.55  ¦    1   1.59   ¦    0   0.00  ¦
Changed  2  ¦    1   0.55  ¦    1   1.59   ¦    0   0.00  ¦
Expired  1  ¦    0   0.00  ¦    0   0.00   ¦    0   0.00  ¦
            .----------------------------------------------------.
```

```
Local       |    140  76.92 |   50  79.37 |   50 100.00 |
Remote      |     42  23.08 |   13  20.63 |    0   0.00 |
            |---------------+-------------+-------------|
Totals      |    182 100.00 |   63  34.62 |   50  27.47 |
            |.............................................|
```

Finished Infostructure [Stanford CIS Nanofab Home Page] at Tue, 12 Sep 1995 10:56:58

WebWalker/1.00 finished at Tue, 12 Sep 1995 12:56:58

WebWalker tested a total of 62 different Web pages, of which 33 Web pages (including the home page) were retrieved with full HTML contents for further traversal. There were ten broken links, one redirected link, and one changed link (within the past two days, or 48 hours), in the Nanofab project infostructure.

Closer examination reveals that of the ten broken links, seven of them were actually dead links (that is, 404 Not Found) while the remaining three were inaccessible due to problems connecting with Cornell's Web server at the www.nnf.cornell.edu address (that is, 602 Connection Failed).

WebWalker Program Organization

The WebWalker/1.00 program is written in about 1,800 lines of Perl code and consists of 40 subroutines, plus a main body. The full source code of the WebWalker can be found in Appendix C.

For purpose of exposition and clarity, the WebWalker program functions and variables are logically grouped together by purpose and function into packages, which are shown in the following table:

Packages	Purpose
Configuration	Setting configurable options and parameters
Instruction	Receiving input tasks from task file
Avoidance	Respecting the robot exclusion standard
History	Keeping track of Web traversal history
Traversal	Traversing and testing an infostructure
Summary	Collecting and displaying summarizing statistics

External Library Calls

In addition, selected subroutines from the following collection of packages belonging to the original Perl library, as well as Roy Fielding's WWW library, have been used in WebWalker 1.00:

Perl Package	Function Called by WebWalker
getopts.pl	Getopts
www.pl	request and set_def_header
wwwurl.pl	parse, absolute and get_site
wwwdates.pl	wtime and get_gmtime
wwwhtml.pl	extract_links
wwwurl.pl	set_content

WebWalker Program Call-Graph

The WebWalker program organization can be visualized with the aid of a subroutine call-graph depicted in the following figure. In addition to showing how the subroutines are related to each other (for example, via the caller/callee relationship), the alignment of the subroutines into columns also indicates how the subroutines are grouped into packages.

```
    Traversal            Avoidance        Summary              History         Instruction
    .........            .........        .......              .......         ...........
main
+- .................................................................... usage
+- .................................................................... read_tasks
+- .................... add_leaf
+- traverse_web
    +- .................................... begin_summary
                                            +- init_summary
    +- ............................................................ remember
    +- should_avoid
        +- .............. check_url
                          +- check_site
                              +- add_avoid
                          +- add_site
    +- .................................... traversed
                                            +- .............. get_url
                                            +- .............. recall
                                            +- .............. was_avoided
                                            +- .............. is_untestable
                                            +- save_broken
                                                +- ........... is_local
                                            +- save_redirect
                                                +- ........... is_local
                                            +- save_changed
                                                +- ........... is_local
                                            +- save_expired
                                                +- ........... is_local
```

```
+- traverse_link
   +- .................................................. get_url
   +- slow_down
   +- extract_links
      +- is_html
      +- decode
   +- .............................................. store
      +- ............................................ set_status
+- ................................................. was_tested
+- ..................................... tested
                                        +- .............. get_url
                                        +- .............. recall
                                        +- .............. is_local
                                        +- .............. was_avoided
                                        +- .............. is_untestable
                                        +- save_broken
                                           +- ............ is_local
                                        +- save_redirect
                                           +- ............ is_local
                                        +- save_changed
                                           +- ............ is_local
                                        +- save_expired
                                           +- ............ is_local
+- test_link
   +- .................................................. get_url
   +- slow_down
   +- .................................................. store
      +- ............................................... set_status
+- should_traverse
   +- should_avoid
      +- ............ check_url
                     +- check_site
                        +- add_avoid
                     +- add_site
   +- .................................................. is_known
   +- .................................................. recall
   +- .................................................. get_url
   +- is_html
+- ..................................................... set_status
+- ..................................................... get_url
+- ..................................................... reset_status
```

```
+- ................................. end_summary
                          +- update_summary
                              +- ............. was_avoided
                              +- ............. was_tested
                              +- ............. was_traversed
                              +- ............. is_untestable
                              +- ............. is_local
                          +- get_summary
```

As can be seen from the code listing, the Traversal package is used by the main program via the "traverse_web" subroutine (which is invoked exactly once for each infostructure to be examined). The bulk of the work and processing logic resides under the "traverse_web" subtree, which includes both the Summary and History packages in their entirety, plus almost all of the Avoidance package (with the exception of the "add_leaf" subroutine called directly from the main program).

It also can be noted that the Avoidance package is self-contained and is used mainly by invoking the "check_url" subroutine from the "should_avoid" subroutine. The Summary package is used at several places throughout the body of the "traverse_web" subroutine for marking the different points in time during the traversal of the infostructure (for example, before starting and after ending the traversal, as well as after having finished traversing or testing a link). Unlike other packages, which are better organized as hierarchical trees of subroutines, the History package is all flat and actually is a loose collection of self-contained subroutines that do not call out to other subroutines.

Configuration Section

The *configuration section* allows users to configure options for setting up WebWalker according to the local operating environment. The more important options are the following:

→ The $Version parameter identifies to the destination Web servers the specific version of WebWalker that is being targeted at them.

→ The $LibWWW parameter tells WebWalker where to locate the Perl WWW library on the client machine. WebWalker needs the library to handle Web-related format and protocol processings.

→ $LocalNetwork should be the network domain that you consider to be local to your organization. In other words, a network request to sites in this domain does not create any external network costs to your organization. Any periods in the network domain name need to be escaped with a backslash (for example, `stanford\.com`).

→ The $Taskfile parameter tells WebWalker where to locate the task file. WebWalker needs to examine the task file to find out what infostructures to visit.

For most purposes, configuring the above options would be adequate to prepare WebWalker for operation. However, there are other configurable parameters that WebWalker uses, and they are described next.

Setting up WebWalker

There must be some ways to control the traversal behavior of WebWalker. This can be accomplished by means of three configurable parameters, which together dictate that there must be at least a minimum of $BetweenTime seconds of elapsed time in between cosecutive HTTP requests, and that a long pause of $PauseTime seconds is required after making a stream of $MaxConsec consecutive requests to the same Web site.

The complete list of WebWalker configurable parameters is shown in the following table.

Parameters	Description
$Version	User-Agent identification for the WebWalker WWW robot
$LibWWW	Directory path that holds the WWW library written in Perl
$LocalNetwork	Network domain that is considered local
$TaskFile	Default pathname of task instruction file
$RobotsURL	Standard URL that defines access control for WWW robots, defaults to "/robots.txt"
$BaseURL	The initial base URL to use if TopURL is relative

$MaxDepth	Default maximum traversal depth
$Timeout	Maximum number of seconds to wait for a HTTP response
$MaxConsec	Maximum consecutive requests to any site before a long pause
$PauseTime	Duration of a long pause (in seconds)
$BetweenTime	Time required between any two requests to the same site (in seconds)Instruction Package

There must be a way for WebWalker to find out what infostrutures it is supposed to visit. There are are two ways of doing so:

→ WebWalker looks up the task descriptions from a task file when it is invoked from the command line by the user or run as a batch program.

→ WebWalker gets the task descriptions using the Common Gateway Interface when WebWalker is invoked as a CGI script by the Web server, in response to a user submitting the task directives through an online HTML form using a Web browser.

The *instruction package* is made up of variables and functions that handle the processing of input task descriptions, either described in the task file or communicated through the Common Gateway Interface. The variables in this package, as listed in the following table, are used to hold the values of task directives.

Parameters	Description
@TaskName	Value of Name task directive; specifies a name with which to identify the infostructure
@TaskTopURL	Value of TopURL directive; specifies the starting URL of the infostructure to be traversed
@TaskBoundURL	Value of BoundURL directive; specifies the prefix URL for bounding the infostructure
@TaskChange Window	Value of ChangeWindow directive; specifies the past number of days within which a change would be of interest
@TaskExpire Window	Value of ExpireWindow directive; specifies the future number of days within which a scheduled expiration would be of interest
@TaskExclude	Value of Exclude directive; specifies the URL to exclude (leaf) from this task

Processing Tasks

The functions in this package print out proper usage information on the command line, handle task file processing, and implement the Common Gateway Interface. These functions are listed in the following table.

Function	Description
usage	Print usage information.
read_task	Handle GET and POST methods if WebWalker is used as a CGI script.
read_tasks	Read task descriptions from task file.

Avoidance Package

There must be some ways to guide or restrict WebWalker's scope of activity. Specifically, robot operators might want WebWalker to exclude certain URLs from its traversal path and not visit there. In addition, there might be certain infinite virtual spaces that Webmasters at the target site would want WebWalker to avoid.

The *avoidance package* consists of variables and functions that implements various means of restricting WebWalker's scope of activity. The robot exclusion standard is implemented here, and WebWalker avoids all URLs disallowed to it. WebWalker also does not retrieve the content of any Web page that it has been told to exclude (by means of the Exclude directive); it merely tests for the document's existence. The variables of this package are listed below.

Variables	Descriptions
$SitesNum	Number of sites visited
@SitesAddr	Sites table containing Web sites visited
%Sites	Reverse sites table for duplicates detection
$AvoidNum	Number of URLs to be avoided

@AvoidURL	Avoids table containing URL's that are not to be tested
$LeafNum	Number of nodes in leaf table
@LeafURL	Leaf table of nodes to exclude (leaf)

Avoiding Blackholes

The functions of this package implement various means of restricting the scope of WebWalker's traversal (including the robot exclusion standard), and keeps track of which sites it has visited (so that it does not retrieve the robot exclusion file more than once per site). The functions are listed in the following table:

Function	Description
check_url	Check the given URL for any restrictions on its access.
check_site	Has this site already been checked for restrictions? If not, perform a check using the robot exclusion protocol and update both the sites table and the avoids table accordingly.
add_site	Add the given site to the sites table while detecting duplication.
add_avoid	Add the given URL to the avoids table while checking for duplication and overlap.
add_leaf	Add the given URL to the leaf table for the duration of the current infostructure traversal while checking for duplication and overlap.

History Package

A Web robot has to keep track of all the places it has visited in the past so it doesn't revisit the same URL repeatedly and thus waste valuable resources. More importantly, a robot's capability to keep a history of where it's been on the Web enables it to extricate itself when trapped in an infinite loop embedded deep inside the Web.

The *history package* consists of variables and functions that allow WebWalker to record and recall where it has been on the Web. The following table lists the variables used in this package, most of which are actually arrays that hold the results of past visitations.

Variables	Description
$VisNumber	Number of URL's visited since process start
%Visited	Associative array of URL's visited mapped to @Vis* index
@VisURL	URL of node (maps @Vis* index to URL visited)
@VisStatus	Status of a seen node
@VisRespCode	Server response code from last access
@VisConType	MIME Content-type of response
@VisRedirect	Redirected URL (from a 302 Moved response)
@VisTitle	Title text from headers or last traversal

continues

Variables	Description
@VisOwner	Owner name from headers or last traversal
@VisReplyTo	Reply-To address from headers or last traversal
@VisLastMod	Last-modified date from headers
@VisExpires	Expires date from headers
@VisInTask	Has the URL been seen during the current task?
@VisLocal	URL considered to be local to this network?

Remembering Past Visits

The functions listed in the following table implement WebWalker's memory of past history. The remember function is used to write into history the results of making a HTTP GET request. The store function is used to write into history the results of a HTTP HEAD request. The recall function retrieves from history results of past visitations.

Status updates to history are handled with set_status and reset_status functions. The remaining functions handle history-related status queries to various parts of the infostructure, such as whether specific nodes in the infostructure were seen but not yet tested, avoided, to be excluded, to be tested, to be traversed, or already traversed.

Function	Description
set_status	Sets or updates the status of the given node in history
reset_status	Resets the status of the given node in history so that it is no longer considered traversed
remember	Remembers the URL in history by either creating a history record or update the node status as appropriate
store	Stores node history from meta information held in headers, along with status and response code from recent WWW request
recall	Recalls meta information held in history for the given node
was_avoided	Indicates if the given node was previously avoided
was_tested	Indicates if the given node was previously tested
is_untestable	Indicates if the given node is untestable
is_known	Indicates if the given node will be, or has already been, checked for traversal status
is_traversing	Indicates if the given node will be, or has been, traversed
was_traversed	Indicates if the given node was traversed
is_local	Indicates if the given node is considered local
get_url	Retrieves the stored URL of the given node

Traversal Package

The *traversal package* consists of variables and functions that WebWalker needs for actually traversing and testing the Web infostructure. The variables are listed in the table below. Some of the variables are actually arrays that implement a queue data structure needed for WebWalker's breadth-first traversal strategy.

Variables	Description
$CurConsec	Current number of consecutive requests to a site
$PrevSite	Site of the last network request
$PrevTime	Time of the last network request
@TravNodes	Nodes that we have yet to traverse for this task
@TravDepth	Nodes' traversal depth
@TravParent	Nodes' parent's URL
@TestLinks	Absolute URL's (without query or tag)
@TestType	Anchor type (for example, Link, Image, Query, Redirect)

WebWalker keeps track of the number of consecutive requests ($CurConsec) to the latest site ($PrevSite) and records the time ($PrevTime) when the previous request was last made. With such information, WebWalker would know when and how to crawl slowly and not overload any one site with a series of rapid-fire HTTP requests.

Roaming the Web

The functions listed in the following table implement the actual breadth-first strategy and mechanism that WebWalker uses to crawl on the Web. The top-level function is traverse_web, which in turn calls the traverse_link to perform a HTTP GET reuest, or calls the test_link functions to perform a HTTP HEAD request. HTML documents retrieved by WebWalker are processed by the extract_links function to find all hyperlinks needed for future traversal and testing.

Functions	Description
traverse_web	Traverses entire infostructure in breadth-first order, bounded by a URL-based task bound prefix and maximum traversal depth.
should_avoid	Indicates if the node should be avoided or has already been avoided.
should_traverse	Indicates if the node should be traversed for the current infostructure
test_link	Tests the URL via HTTP HEAD request. Stores meta information in history and update node status.
traverse_link	Traverses URL via HTTP GET request. Stores meta information in history and update node status. Extracts links from headers and document HTML content to be queued for further traversal.

continues

Functions	Description
extract_links	Extracts links and document meta information from headers and HTML body content, and deposits it in queue for further traversal.
slow_down	Makes sure the robot is not making too many consecutive requests and/or making too many rapid-fire requests to a single site.
is_html	Determines if the Web document is in HTML, based upon its URL suffix and header content-type.
decode	Translates encoded content into its decoded form, usually to decompress a compressed Web document.

Summary Package

The *summary package* consists of a set of variables that are used as counters for keeping track of statistical data related to the current Web infostructure under investigation. These counters are classified into three categories, $Hrefs*, $Nodes*, and $Local*. They are used to keep track of statistical information related to occurrences of HTTP references (there could be multiple such occurrences with the same URL), unique URLs, and local URLs.

A set of associative arrays (%BrokenNodes, %RedirectNodes, %ChangedNodes, and %ExpiredNodes) is used for the purpose of collecting and displaying information related to broken or redirected links, and for keeping track of URLs that have recently been changed or have expired. In this way, WebWalker can easily generate useful reports on problem areas that have been identified in the infostructure. The next table describes the variables used in the summary package.

Variables	Description
%BrokenNodes	URL information on broken links indexed by node
%RedirectNodes	URL information on redirected links indexed by node
%ChangedNodes	URL information on changed nodes indexed by node
%ExpiredNodes	URL information on expired nodes indexed by node
$HrefsTrav	Traversed URL reference count
$HrefsTest	Tested URL reference count

$HrefsReus	Reused URL reference count
$HrefsAvd	Avoided URL reference count
$HrefsUnt	Untestable URL reference count
$HrefsBroke	Broken URL reference count
$HrefsRedir	Redirected URL reference count
$HrefsChg	Changed URL reference count
$HrefsExp	Expired URL reference count
$HrefsLoc	Local URL reference count
$HrefsRmt	Remote URL reference count
$NodesTrav	Unique traversed node count
$NodesTest	Unique tested node count
$NodesReus	Unique reused node count
$NodesAvd	Unique avoided node count
$NodesUnt	Unique untestable node count
$NodesBroke	Unique broken node count
$NodesRedir	Unique redirected node count
$NodesChg	Unique changed node count
$NodesExp	Unique expired node count
$NodesRmt	Unique remote node count
$LocalTrav	Local traversed node count
$LocalTest	Local tested node count
$LocalReus	Local reused node count
$LocalAvd	Local avoided node count
$LocalUnt	Local untestable node count
$LocalBroke	Local broken node count
$LocalRedir	Local redirected node count
$LocalChg	Local changed node count
$LocalExp	Local expired node count
$TotalHrefs	Total URL reference count
$TotalNodes	Total unique node count
$TotalLocal	Total local node count

Statistics Table

The following code template indicates how the statistical counters are used for displaying the fitness of the infostructure in a summary of results table.

```
Summary of Results:
    .------------------------------------------------.
    |   References   |   Unique URLs  |   Local URLs   |
    |   number       |   number       |   number       |
    |----------------+----------------+----------------|
Traversed   | $HrefsTrav   | $NodesTrav   | $LocalTrav   |
Tested      | $HrefsTest   | $NodesTest   | $LocalTest   |
Reused      | $HrefsReus   | $NodesReus   | $LocalReus   |
Avoided     | $HrefsAvd    | $NodesAvd    | $LocalAvd    |
Untestable  | $HrefsUnt    | $NodesUnt    | $LocalUnt    |
    |----------------+----------------+----------------|
Broken      | $HrefsBroke  | $NodesBroke  | $LocalBroke  |
Redirected  | $HrefsRedir  | $NodesRedir  | $LocalRedir  |
Changed     | $HrefsChg    | $NodesChg    | $LocalChg    |
Expired     | $HrefsExp    | $NodesExp    | $LocalExp    |
    |----------------+----------------+----------------|
Local       | $HrefsLoc    | $TotalLocal  | $TotalLocal  |
Remote      | $HrefsRmt    | $NodesRmt    |      0       |
    |----------------+----------------+----------------|
Totals      | $TotalHrefs  | $TotalNodes  | $TotalLocal  |
    .------------------------------------------------.
```

Reporting Statistics

The summary package also includes a set of functions to initialize, update, manipulate, generate, and print the corresponding statistical results derived from statistics counters in the form of a summary table. This set of functions is listed in the following table.

Functions	Description
begin_summary	Initializes counters for statistical summary and data structures for diagnostic information about the infostructure.
init_summary	Initializes all counters for statistical results summary.
tested	Updates all reference counters for statistical summary and collects diagnostic information about the tested link as appropriate and prints the http response message.
traversed	Collects diagnostic information about the traversed link as appropriate and prints the http response message.
save_broken	Saves the URL and related information about the broken link. Updates the relevant node-broken counters as appropriate.

save_redirect	Saves URL and related information about the redirected link. Updates relevant node-redirected counters as appropriate.
save_changed	Saves URL and related information about the changed link. Updates relevant node-changed counters as appropriate.
save_expired	Saves URL and related information about the expired link. Updates relevant node-expired counters as appropriate.
end_summary	Prints diagnostic results and statistical summary table.
update_summary	Updates counters for statistical summary table.
get_summary	Generates statistical summary of results in a table.

Growing into the Future

The World Wide Web is currently experiencing phenomenal growth with no sign of abatement. Not only are people authoring more HTML pages today than yesterday, there will be many more Web sites coming up tomorrow. At this rate of growth, the problem of managing and maintaining complex Web infostructures is increasingly a difficult one.

If this problem is not satisfactorily resolved soon enough, large portions of the global Web infostructure can become seriously corrupted and the entire Web edifice can easily collapse under the weight of tons of dead links. Such misfortunes can seriously reduce the usefulness of the Web.

Fortunately, there are many good spiders that can perform automated Web maintenance quite competently. In addition to MOMspider and WebWalker, there are also other Web maintenance spiders like the HTML Analyzer, EIT Link Verifier, ChURL, Weblayers, and WebWatch robots, many of which are freely available to the public. For now, it appears that the problem has at least been contained.

All of these spiders are not very much different at the core. They all do one thing well: automated traversal of the Web. As such, they are also not much different from resource discovery spiders that can handle keyword-based searches of the Web (which we have studied previously in chapter 4).

As the Web continues to grow, we can expect to see many more new Web-wandering spiders that can perform a variety of innovative and interesting new services for its users. It is hoped that WebWalker's simple design will better illustrate how the core traversal engine of new Web robots can be constructed.

 n o t e For the advanced readers who are interested in a Multi-Owner Maintenance spider, Roy Fielding's MOMspider program source code is freely available from the following distribution sites:

```
http://www.ics.uci.edu/WebSoft/MOMspider/
```

```
ftp://liege.ics.uci.edu/pub/arcadia/MOMspider/
```

p a r t
· ·

Agents and Money on the Net

8

Web Transaction Security

The advent of electronic commerce on the Internet is to a large extent facilitated by the launch of the World Wide Web. In the realm of agents, there are currently hordes of spiders, wanderers, brokers and bots on the Web performing various tasks for their human clients—for example, searching for information, maintaining Web infostructure, brokering for buyers and sellers, as well as finding the best bargain for books and CDs online.

For the class of agents that are designed for electronic commerce in a digital economy, for example, the brokers and bargain hunters, there must be some measures of security built into the basic transaction-based communications infrastructure for them to function reliably. In particular, assurance of secure transactions is required for online shopping through the World Wide Web, the sale of information over the Internet, as well as the execution of certain business operations like online ticket reservations. Despite the growing interest in the Internet and World Wide Web, the commercial potential has been held back by competing and incompatible security approaches.

This chapter examines the various notions of security. It also discusses the use of cryptography and digital signatures as solutions for achieving specific security goals, briefly exploring their colorful history in the process. Finally, this chapter explains two specific approaches that have been developed for secure transaction on the World Wide Web: SSL and Secure HTTP. It is anticipated that a future generation of agents on the Internet, and especially on the Web, shall incorporate these fundamental techologies and be able to interoperate across various economic domains.

Concepts of Security

Internet Security consists of the following two distinct areas:

→ **Access security.** This refers to the capability of an organization to protect its computers, memory, disk, printers, and other computing equipment from unauthorized use. Standard practice is usually a combination of techniques that include the use of authentication software (for example, MIT's Kerberos (SNS 1988)), installation of proxies on Internet "firewalls," stricter access control with passwords, and diligent enforcement of security policies.

→ **Transaction security.** This refers to the capability of two entities on the Internet to conduct a transaction privately with the help of cryptographic systems while being authenticated with properly certified digital signatures as needed. SSL and Secure HTTP are mechanisms for transaction security on the World Wide Web.

 Access security is already well covered in a number of other books. For example, *Firewalls and Internet Security*, by William Cheswick and Steven Bellovin, or *Internet Firewalls and Network Security*, by Karanjit Siyan and Chris Hare, are recommended books on the subject.

A number of transaction security issues arise between Web clients and servers, several of which are addressed in the context of SSL and Secure HTTP later in this chapter. In general, transaction security on the Internet is concerned with the following fundamental goals:

→ Privacy

→ Authentication

→ Integrity

Figure 8.1

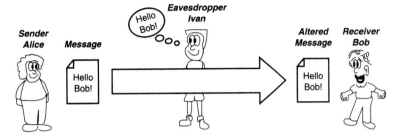

Ivan eavesdrops on a message sent from Alice to Bob over an insecure channel.

Privacy: Keeping Private Messages Private

The purpose of privacy is to ensure that information is kept hidden from anyone for whom it is not intended. Privacy is particularly important on the Internet and the World Wide Web when transmission of sensitive data, such as credit card numbers, is involved. In addition, privacy is particularly important on the Internet due to the insecure nature of the communications channel—a loose confederation of machines and networks under different authorities with no trusted, centralized administration. A data packet or an e-mail message sent over the Internet usually is routed through multiple hosts before arriving at the final destination. During this journey, the data packet or e-mail's unprotected content is copied from host to host and can be easily eavesdropped by a third party. This is illustrated in figure 8.1, where a message sent from Alice to Bob is eavesdropped by Ivan as it makes its way across the network.

The need for sensitive data to be protected from prying eyes is further amplified when you consider the types of data that could get onto the wire in the not-too-distant future: personal income tax returns, employee records, stock transactions, bank statements, and so on. *Encryption*, or the transformation of data into a form unreadable by anyone without a secret key, can be used to ensure private communication over an insecure channel. The original message, or *plaintext*, is first encrypted with a secret password, called a *secret key*, by the sender prior to transmission.

As illustrated in figure 8.2, privacy is ensured by allowing only the encrypted form of the message, or *ciphertext*, to be sent to the receiver. The eavesdropper is not able to make sense out of the ciphertext because it is unintelligible and bears no resemblance to the original plaintext. In a secure cryptosystem, the original plaintext message cannot be recovered except by using the secret key. The receiver with the secret key decrypts the ciphertext to recover the original plaintext message, which he then can read. This is called *secret-key cryptosystem*, or *symmetric cryptosystem*, because a single secret key is used for both encryption and decryption.

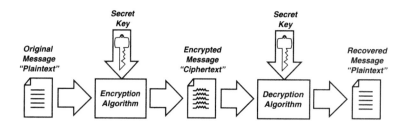

Figure 8.2

The message sent over an insecure channel is encrypted so that eavesdroppers cannot decipher the message contents.

Authentication: Proving You Are Who You Claim to Be

In networked digital communications, the receiver of a message needs to be confident of the identity of the sender. Given the insecure nature of communications over the Internet, the perils of unauthenticated messages are not to be underestimated. As illustrated in figure 8.3, an imposter on the Internet can easily impersonate another person without her knowledge and send fake messages in her name to an unsuspecting recipient, sometimes with grave consequences.

The World Wide Web provides limited capabilities for user identification and client/server authentication. For commercial use of the Web, client and server need to verify and validate each other's identity in order to ensure that information that flows across the Internet is authentic. When press releases

and official announcements are distributed over the World Wide Web, for example, the client needs to be sure of their place of origin. Similarly, in the case of home banking or stock transaction over the World Wide Web, the Web server needs to ensure that the clients with whom it is transacting are who they claim to be. It is equally important that a form of authentication be used that cannot be faked. Digital signatures are a recent development answering to the need for authentication in the realm of networked digital communications.

Digital signatures play a role for digital documents similar to that played by handwritten signatures for printed documents. The signature is an unforgeable piece of data asserting that the named person wrote or otherwise agreed to the document to which the signature is attached. The recipient, as well as a third party, can verify that the document did indeed originate from the person whose signature is

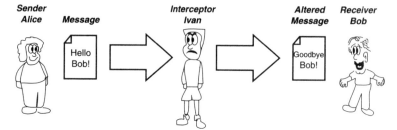

Figure 8.3

Ivan impersonates as Alice and sends an ill-intended message to Bob.

attached. A secure digital signature system consists of these parts:

→ A method of signing a document such that forgery is unfeasible.

→ A method of verifying that a signature actually was generated by whomever it represents.

Digital signatures will be discussed in a later section.

Integrity: Ensuring Message Content Remains Unaltered

With electronic commerce on the Internet, data integrity is critical. When product catalogs are distributed over the World Wide Web, for example, the recipient needs to be sure that the listed prices are authentic and have not been secretly altered by potentially unscrupulous competitors. Data integrity is critical for many other things as well. The message contents of official academic documents in electronic form from universities and colleges, for example, must not be modified. As figure 8.4 illustrates, however, there is real danger of an unprotected message being intercepted as it travels on the Internet. Furthermore, the message contents could be tampered with maliciously, with potentially grave consequences.

A valid digital signature on a message ensures that the message has not been altered since it was signed. Furthermore, secure digital signatures cannot be repudiated; the signer of a message cannot later disown it by claiming the signature or the message was forged. In this way, a digital signature acts like a tamper-proof seal testifying to the integrity of the message.

Before I discuss how encryption and digital signatures are used to implement secure transactions in a digital economy populated by agents, a brief tour of classical cryptography is in order.

Brief Tour of Classical Cryptography

Cryptography—the science of secret-writing to hide the meaning of messages—has been around for millennia. Cryptography is an ancient art first carried out in the form of hieroglyphic inscriptions on Egyptian tombs of noble men because it was believed that cryptic epitaphs induce an aura of mystic powers. Throughout the ages, cryptography was fulfilling its more important role of protecting vital communications through hostile environments, for both military and political purposes. During Roman

---

Figure 8.4

Ivan intercepts a message sent from Alice to Bob and alters it with less than noble intention.

 **Snoozing Alice**
 **Imposter Ivan**
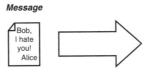 **Fake Message** / **Fake Message**
 Receiver Bob

times, Julius Caesar was known to have used the famous Caesar cipher for protecting military communications from Gaul to Rome. In the sixteenth century, Mary, Queen of Scots, lost her life after lending her support to a failed political coup, hastened in part by insecure cryptography. She was convicted for high treason and was decapitated after an incriminating letter sent from her prison was intercepted and deciphered.

In the modern era, the invention of the telegraph and radio has brought instantaneous communications to the army. Without the use of cryptography, communications using these newly invented technologies would have been easily compromised and rendered worse than useless. After all, telegraph lines can be wiretapped (as occurred during the Civil War on both the Confederate and Union troops), and radio waves can be intercepted simply by tuning in with the right antenna.

 n o t e An excellent history of cryptography can be found in the book *The Codebreakers*, by David Kahn (1967). An introduction to modern cryptography can be found in Ron Rivest's 1990 article, "Cryptography," as well as in "Modern Cryptography," by G. Brassard (1988). A highly readable account of various developments in cryptography up to the present day can be found in Simson Garfinkels book entitled *PGP: Pretty Good Privacy* (1995).

The Role of NSA

During World War II, the first digital computers were developed by the Allies to crack the Germans' Enigma code under the brilliant leadership of Alan Turing (Hodges 1983; Kahn 1991). After the war, the world's cryptographic activities became concentrated in the National Security Agency (NSA), a highly secretive branch of the U.S. Department of Defense that was created by order of President Harry Truman in 1952. Located a half-hour drive from Washington D.C. at Fort Meade, Maryland, the agency's existence was kept secret for many years. In fact, it was rumored that NSA actually stood for "No Such Agency" or "Never Say Anything."

It is widely believed that NSA's classified charter is to intercept and decode all foreign communications of interest to the security of the U.S. The agency operates a global intelligence network, employs a host of top-notch cryptographers, and is always eager to have the world's fastest computer for breaking codes (Bamford 1982). To prevent potential national enemies from employing encryption methods too strong for the NSA to crack, the NSA has an interest in slowing the spread of publicly available cryptography. As a result, the NSA is widely believed to have followed policies with the practical effect of weakening and limiting publicly available crytographic tools. As a premier cryptographic government agency, the NSA has huge resources to exert a profound influence on the development and use of cryptography in the U.S., with potentially world-wide repurcussions.

Development of Data Encryption Standard (DES)

The proliferation of digital computing equipment in the decades after World War II led private firms and individuals to demand security for stored computer files and electronically transmitted messages.

To meet this demand, private researchers began to invade the highly technical realms of cryptography that had long been a government monopoly (Kahn 1983). In the late 1960s, IBM set up a cryptographic research group at its Yorktown Heights research laboratory to develop a cipher code-named Lucifer, which it promptly sold to Lloyd's of London for use in a cash-dispensing system. Spurred by its initial success, IBM set about to transform Lucifer into a highly marketable commodity. By 1974, the cipher was ready for market. At the time, there also were several other companies developing and selling cryptographic products, and none of them could interoperate.

At around the same time, the National Bureau of Standards (NBS), later to be renamed National Institute of Standards and Technology (NIST), began to study government and civilian need for computer security. NBS concluded that the nation could benefit from using a single data encryption standard for the purpose of storing and transmitting unclassified information. In response to a request from NBS for a proposal, a version of the Lucifer algorithm, which was weakened in some ways and strengthened in other ways by the NSA, was submitted as a candidate. NBS accepted the resulting algorithm in 1975 and formally adopted it as the Data Encryption Standard (DES) in 1976 for use in all classified government communications. The details of DES can be found in the official FIPS publication (1988).

Problems with DES were widely acknowledged as soon as the standard was first proposed. DES was made just strong enough to withstand commercial attempts to break it, yet weak enough to yield to government crypt analysis. In keeping with rapid advances in computing speed over the years, however, DES has been strengthened with longer keys, larger block sizes, and more rounds of encryption. Variations such as the triple-DES now are in common use. More recent algorithms such as IDEA (International Data Encryption Algorithm) (LM 1991), RC2, and RC4 (RC for Rivest Code) also have been popular.

Development of Public-Key Cryptography

In the early 1970s, a growing awareness of the need for data encryption in digital communications coupled with a sense of urgency brought on by the imminent deployment of DES (which many computer scientists abhorred) led to a series of surprising breakthroughs in cryptographic research.

Problems with Secret Keys

The traditional approach to cryptography, also called *secret-key cryptography*, is based upon the sender and receiver of a message sharing common knowledge of the same secret key. As illustrated previously in figure 8.2, this secret key is used to both encrypt and decrypt the message. Secret-key cryptography, however, has a fundamental problem: how to get both the sender and the receiver to agree on a secret key without a third party finding out.

If the sender and the receiver are at separate physical locations, they must trust a courier, the phone system, the computer network, or some other means of transmission not to disclose the secret key being communicated. Anyone who overhears

or intercepts the key in transit can later decipher all messages encrypted using that key, and future communications between the two parties are compromised.

Key Management

The generation, distribution, and storage of keys is called *key management*. Secret-key cryptography often has difficulty providing secure key management. For many years, the U.S. government used a key distribution center to generate and distribute keys to any pair of individuals who wanted to communicate. The key transmission method was crude but simple: Cryptographic keys were placed in locked briefcases that were handcuffed to couriers who physically transported them from Washington to embassies and consulates around the world.

In 1976, two researchers at Stanford University, Whitfield Diffie and Martin Hellman, devised a devilishly clever technique that enables two communicating parties to derive a cryptographic session key in such a way that a snooping third party cannot deduce the key's value. The session key then can be used in a secret-key algorithm such as DES. The Diffie-Hellman algorithm requires that the two communicating parties actively participate in carrying out the key exchange protocol at the same time. This technique works great for two parties talking over the telephone but is otherwise not practicable for asynchronous modes of communication, such as electronic mail.

The RSA Alternative

In 1977, three scientists at MIT's Laboratory for Computer Science, Ron Rivest, Adi Shamir, and Len Adleman, refined Diffie and Hellman's idea of secure key exchange and invented what came to be known as the RSA public-key cryptosystem. The name RSA stands for its developers, Rivest, Shamir, and Adleman. As an improvement over the Diffie-Hellman key exchange system, RSA requires no active participation between the sender performing the encryption and the receiver performing the decryption. Each person gets a pair of keys, called the *public key* and the *private key*. Each person's public key is published while his private key is kept secret. All communications involve only public keys; no private keys are transmitted or shared. Suppose, for example, that Alice wants to send a message to Bob. She looks up Bob's public key in a directory, uses it to encrypt the message, and sends the message. Bob then uses his private key to decrypt the message and read it. An eavesdropper without the private key cannot decipher the message. This is illustrated in figure 8.5.

Because there is no need for the sender and the receiver to share secret information, it is no longer necessary to trust a communications channel to be secure against eavesdropping. Furthermore, the two communicating parties do not have to know each other or have any type of previous communication. Anyone, for example, can send a confidential message to Bob using only Bob's public key, without requiring any prior arrangement with Bob.

The RSA cryptosystem is based on an amazingly simple number-theoretic idea that has been able to resist all cryptanalytic attacks. The idea is that although it is easy to multiply two large prime numbers, it is extremely difficult to factorize their product. Thus the product can be publicized and used as the public encryption key. The primes

Figure 8.5

How pubic key cryptography protects privacy.

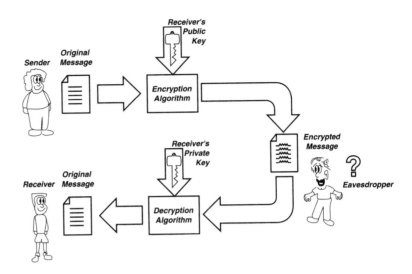

themselves, which are needed for decryption, cannot be recovered from the product. This is, therefore, an excellent framework for a public-key cryptosystem.

Comparing Secret-Key and Public-Key Cryptography

In classical secret-key cryptosystems, the encryption key gives away the decryption key. The chance that a hostile party could discover the secret key while it is being transmitted, however, does exist. In public-key cryptosystems, the encryption key can be safely publicized without compromising the secrecy of the decryption key. For this reason, classical secret-key systems also are referred to as *symmetric* or *two-way*, and public-key systems are referred to as *non-symmetric* or *one-way*.

Public-key cryptosystems are considerably slower to use than classical secret-key cryptosystems.

Depending on implementation, they can be anywhere from 100 to 1,000 times slower. The best solution, however, is to combine the security of public-key systems with the speed of secret-key systems. Key management problems present in the secret-key systems can be taken care of by a suitable protocol for key exchange such as Diffie-Hellman or RSA. The public-key system can be used for secure transmission of the secret session key, which then is used to encrypt the bulk of the message.

Numerous public-key cryptosystems, based upon quite diverse concepts, exist today. The El Gamal system, for example, is based upon the discrete logarithm problem (ElGamal 1985). Cryptosystems also exist that are based upon operations on mathematical operations on elliptic curves (Miller 1986; Koblitz 1987). An advantage of the RSA public-key cryptosystem over some other public-key

cryptosystems is that it also can be used to construct digital signatures to authenticate documents and to ensure the integrity of document contents.

Digital Signatures

The lack of secure authentication and integrity has been a major obstacle in achieving the promise of a paperless society. Paper still is the medium of choice for all contracts, official letters, legal documents, and identification. It has not been feasible to evolve into a society based upon electronic transactions. Digital signatures hold the promise for converting all paper transactions, from the mundane to the most critical, to digital electronic media. An accepted standard for digital signatures would, for example, allow leases, wills, passports, college transcripts, and checks to exist primarily in an electronic form. Any paper version of such documents simply would be a secondary copy derived from its electronic original.

Furthermore, digital signatures have the potential to possess greater legal authority than handwritten signatures. If a 10 page contract is signed by hand on the tenth page, there is no certainty that the preceding nine pages have not been altered. If the contract has been signed by a digital signature, a third party can easily verify that not one bit of the contract has been changed.

Digital signatures can perform two important functions, namely authentication and integrity, that relate to transaction security:

→ **Authentication.** A digital signature makes it possible for the receiver, as well as any interested third party, to mathematically verify the identity of the person who signed the message.

→ **Integrity.** A digital signature makes it possible to detect whether the signed message has been altered after it was signed.

How Digital Signatures Work

Here is the basic outline of how the digital signature works. Suppose Alice wants to send a signed message to Bob. Alice first performs a computation that involves both her private key and the message. The result is a digital signature that is then appended to the message and sent off over the wire. Bob, to verify the signature, performs a computation involving the message, the purported message, and Alice's public key. If the result holds true in a simple mathematical equation, the signature is genuine. Otherwise, the signature may be forged or the message altered, and they are discarded. This scenario is illustrated in figure 8.6.

The generation of a digital signature requires the use of a mathematical hash function on the message. This hash function distills the information contained in a variable-size message into a fixed-size string, which acts as a "digital fingerprint" of the longer message and is called the message digest. It must be infeasible for anyone to either find a message that hashes to a given value or to find two messages that hash to the same value. Well-known secure hash functions include SHA (Secure Hash Algorithm, from NIST), MD2, MD4 and MD5 (MD for Message Digest, by Ron Rivest). The creation of a message digest is illustrated in figure 8.7.

Figure 8.6

Signing and verifying a message with digital signature.

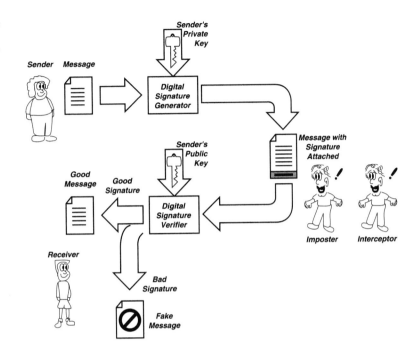

Figure 8.7

One-way hash function produces message digest from long message.

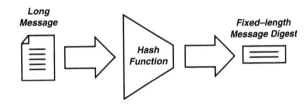

As illustrated in figure 8.8, Alice encrypts the resulting message digest with her private key to generate a digital signature, which is then appended to the message and sent off to Bob. It is more efficient to compute a digital signature using the message digest, which is small, than it is using the arbitrarily large message. After all, hash functions run faster than signing functions. In addition, a message digest can be made public without revealing the contents of the message from which it derives.

Bob, upon receiving both the message and the attached digital signature, decrypts the signature with Alice's public key to recover the message digest. He then hashes the message with the same hash function Alice used and compares the result to the

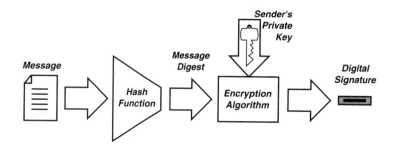

Figure 8.8

Signing a message with digital signature.

message digest decrypted from the signature. If they match exactly, the signature has been successfully verified and Bob can be confident that the message did come from Alice. If, however, the two message digests fail to match, then the message either originates from elsewhere or was altered after it was signed, and Bob rejects the message. This is illustrated in figure 8.9.

 For digital signatures, the role of the public and private keys is reverse of that for message encryption. For digital signatures, the sender's private key is used to encrypt, and the public key is used to decrypt. Whereas for message privacy, the receiver's public key is used to encrypt and private key to decrypt.

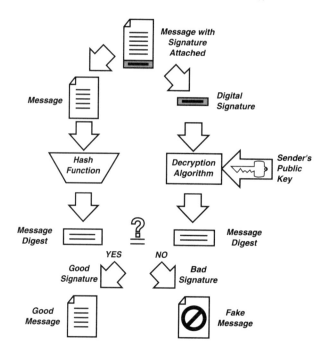

Figure 8.9

Verifying the digital signature of a message.

The Digital Signature Standard

Besides RSA, there are many other ways to sign a message digitally. One such scheme, called the Digital Signature Algorithm (DSA), is based upon the discrete log problem and derives from cryptosystems developed by Schnorr (1989) and ElGamal (1985). The DSA was selected by NIST, in cooperation with the NSA, to be included as part of its proposed Digital Signature Standard (DSS) for the U.S. government (NIST 1992). For various reasons both technical and political, however, DSS has received a fair number of criticisms from the computer industry. The most serious one appears to be that, unlike RSA, DSS has not been around long enough for critical examinations and, therefore, may not be secure enough (RSA 1993).

For digital signatures to replace hand-written signatures, it must have the same legal standing in a court of law as its handwritten counterpart. Although preliminary legal research thus far has resulted in the opinion that digital signatures would meet the requirements of legally binding signatures for most purposes (US 1991), its validity has never actually been tested in a court of law. Until the courts issue rulings that collectively define which digital signature methods, key sizes, and security precautions are acceptable, the surest thing to say as of the date of this writing is that the legal status of digital signatures is not yet well-defined.

Key Certification

Anyone who wants to receive encrypted messages or to sign messages must have a key pair. Some people might have more than one key. Other entities (for example, physical entities such as modems,

workstations, and printers, and organizational entities (such as corporate departments, government branches, and university registrar's office) also will have keys.

To obviate the need for sending any keys at all over the network, all users should generate their own pubic/private key pairs locally. In other words, there will be no central administrative body that generates and distributes keys. Each computer on the network should be capable of generating key pairs. In this way, private keys are never transmitted across the network and no external key source need be trusted. Of course, the local key generation software must be trustworthy.

After the key pair has been generated, the public key can be widely distributed over the network. But how can one be sure that a public key found associated with a particular name really belongs to the named entity? Without a secure mechanism to safeguard the legitimacy of public keys, an imposter can easily distribute forged public keys to impersonate other users.

Public key certificates are digitally signed documents that bear witness to the fact that a given public key belongs to a given entity. They are digital documents created for the purpose of instilling confidence in the legitimacy of other people's public keys. They can help prevent an imposter from using phony public keys to impersonate others.

Certifying Authority

When a key pair is generated, the user must register his or her public key with some central administration, called a *certifying authority*. In response, the

certifying authority issues a certificate to the user attesting to the veracity of the user's public key, signed with its own private key. When the certificate is enclosed with signed messages, the receiver verifies the certificate by using the certifying authority's public key. Now confident of the public key of the sender, the receiver proceeds to verify the signature on the message.

A certifying authority can be any trusted central administration willing to vouch for the identities of the parties to whom it issued certificates. Since the certifying authority must check for proper identification, it is easier for an organization to vouch for its members or employees, versus unaffiliated persons. A company can issue certificates to its employees, a university to its students, and a town to its citizens. As an example, under Apple Computer's Open Collaborative Environment (AOCE), users can generate a key pair, send a notarized request, and receive a certificate for the public key.

When there are more than a handful of certifying authorities, how could one be sure of the legitimacy of a particular certifying authority's public key in the first place? The certifying authority in question could enlist the help of another, better-known certifying authority who could in turn vouch for the legitimacy of the certifying authority's public key, and hopefully in whose public key the user could be confident. If not, there may be yet another certifying authority which could in turn vouch for it, and so on. One could easily see a recursive pattern in the above logic. But ultimately the chain of certificates has to stop; there must be a trusted certifying authority at the top-level whose well-published public key everyone could be sure of.

Certificate Format

In its simplest form, a certificate contains a public key and a name. Usually, a certificate also contains the creation and expiration dates of the key, the name of the certifying authority, the serial number of the certificate, and perhaps other information as well. Most importantly, it has been signed with the certifying authority's private key and, therefore, contains the digital signature of the certificate issuer. The most widely accepted certificate format is defined by the CCITT X.509 international standard (CCITT 1988), which is further refined in the PEM (Kent 1993) and PKCS standards.

PEM is a proposed Privacy-Enhanced Mail standard for carrying secure electronic mail over the Internet (Linn 1993; Kent 1993). PEM uses a trust model that depends upon a hierarchical certificate structure. With PEM, each public key certificate must be signed by another certifying authority higher in the hierarchy, with the chain finally ending in a top-level Internet certifying authority that resides at the root. In contrast, PGP (Pretty Good Privacy, a freely available encryption program written by Phil Zimmermann) uses a decentralized model of key certification that is distributed in a "web of trust" (Garfinkel 1995).

Two Approaches to Web Security

Over the past couple of years, cryptography has taken on new commercial significance as electronic commerce and digital transactions on the Internet, and especially the World Wide Web, have increased the volume of traffic. Although currently most of

the transactions with remote servers are carried out directly by a human being, it is expected that in the near future, agents deployed on the Internet shall be able to transact business for their human masters electronically on the Web.

A number of security issues can arise between Web clients and servers. It's important, for example, to have privacy of information when credit card numbers are transmitted over the network. In addition, mutual authentication is frequently needed between clients and servers in order to fully support electronic commerce. Furthermore, messages need to be protected from modification during transmission.

There are a number of possible solutions, but most of the current work is concerned with securing the HTTP protocol. There are several proposed solutions to the security issues described previously, but so far there are only two leading contenders available in the commercial market:

→ Secure Socket Layer (SSL) by Kipp Hickman of Netscape Communications, Inc. (Hickman 1994)

→ Secure HTTP (S-HTTP) by Eric Rescorla and Allan Schiffman of Enterprise Integration Technologies Corporation (RS 1994)

No clear security standard for the World Wide Web exists at this point, although both SSL and Secure HTTP protocols utilize a variety of industry standards and protocols such as HTTP, TCP/IP, and the popular RSA cryptographic toolkits. Agents on the Web will need to understand one or the other, or perhaps both, of the SSL and Secure HTTP protocols in order to operate in the new domains of digital economy.

SSL and Secure HTTP address the problem of security from two different perspectives. Within the framework established by the seven-layer ISO/OSI protocol stack, SSL functions in the middle transport layer. It chooses to secure the channel of communication between two parties by cryptographic means to ensure that it becomes private and authenticated. SSL is simple and relatively straightforward to implement and has been widely deployed in Netscape browsers and servers.

However, Secure HTTP functions at the highest application layer and supports end-to-end secure transactions. It prefers to work with individual documents to ensure their privacy, authenticity, and integrity. Secure HTTP appears to be more flexible in that it has many hooks for providing comprehensive security through various external cryptographic methods. Digital signatures like RSA or NIST's DSS, for example, can be specified in the Secure HTTP protocol and implemented in supportive Web clients and servers.

In a broad sense, Secure HTTP can interoperate with SSL. SSL implements security at the channel or transport level. Secure HTTP, however, implements security at the application, or document level. It is therefore possible for client and server applications to negotiate a common level of security in a manner transparent to the user, and thus be able to interoperate.

SSL provides a form of transaction security that is adequate for supporting simple applications like the transfer of credit cards over the Internet. At the same time, Secure HTTP provides additional hooks for implementing a substantially richer set of security features (or offering more choices of cryptographic methods) that general purpose electronic

commerce might require. It is in this way anticipated that service providers will want to use SSL to get started quickly, and later develop more sophisticated applications using Secure HTTP as the need arises.

Secure Socket Layer (SSL)

Transmission Control Protocol/Internet Protocol (TCP/IP) is the official communications language of the Internet; all communicating programs must understand and use it in one form or another. It provides a reliable channel for data transport between any two communicating entities on the Internet. Many client/server applications on the Internet, such as the World Wide Web, e-mail, and network news, are written using a programming abstraction called the *sockets*, which provides access to the underlying TCP/IP protocol.

Developed by Kipp Hickman of Netscape Communications, Secure Socket Layer (SSL) is a protocol that uses a security-enhanced abstraction of sockets that takes care of transaction security at the transport level (Hickman 1994). With SSL, security properties are attached to the channel of communication that is established between the two communicating parties, but not to the documents that are being communicated. SSL is layered on top of a reliable transport protocol like TCP to ensure data integrity during transmission. The protocol allows client/server applications to communicate in private without fear of being eavesdropped. The protocol is designed so that the servers are always authenticated and clients can be optionally authenticated.

Channel Security

The SSL protocol in essence provides "channel security," which has the following three basic properties:

➜ **The channel is private.** Encryption is used for all messages after a simple handshake is used to define a secret key.

➜ **The channel is authenticated.** The server endpoint of the conversation is always authenticated, while the client endpoint is optionally authenticated.

➜ **The channel is reliable.** The message transport includes a message integrity check for ensuring reliability in transmission.

SSL Messaging

The SSL protocol specifies a record header and data format, as well as a protocol handshake. The SSL handshake proceeds in two major phases. The first phase is used to establish private communications. The second phase is used for client authentication.

To illustrate a scenario of SSL protocol message flow involving a client C and a server S, the following notation commonly found in the literature is used. When something is enclosed in curly braces, such as "{something} key" then "something" has been encrypted using "key."

The exchanges below are typical of what SSL does to secure a private channel without performing client authentication:

```
C→S: CLIENT-HELLO,    challenge, cipher specs
S←C: SERVER-HELLO,    connection id, server
                      certificate, cipher specs
```

```
C→S: CLIENT-MASTER-KEY,  {master key} server-public-
                          key
C→S: CLIENT-FINISH,      {connection id} client-
                          write-key
S←C: SERVER-VERIFY,      {challenge} server-write-
                          key
S←C: SERVER-FINISH,      {new session id} server-
                          write-key
```

Each SSL endpoint uses a pair of ciphers per connection, for a total of four ciphers. At each endpoint, one cipher is used for outgoing communications and one is used for incoming communications. When the client or server generates a session key, they actually generate two keys, the server-read-key (also known as the client-write-key) and the server-write-key (also known as the client-read-key). The master key is used by the client and server to generate the various session keys.

Advantages of SSL

The advantage of the SSL protocol is that it is application protocol independent and does not depend on higher-level protocols for security. A higher-level application protocol (such as HTTP, FTP, or Telnet) can be layered on top of the SSL protocol transparently. In other words, there is no need to rewrite or to recompile the existing application programs to realize the benefit of additional security. The SSL protocol can negotiate an encryption algorithm and a session key, as well as authenticate the server and the client before the application protocol transmits or receives its first byte of data. All the application protocol data are automatically encrypted for transmission, ensuring privacy.

 n o t e The SSL protocol has been submitted to the W3 Consortium (W3C) Security Group for consideration as part of a general security approach for the Web. The W3C is an organization run by Massachussetts Institute of Technology that develops common standards for the evolution of the World Wide Web. A reference implementation of the SSL protocol called *SSLRef* has been developed by Netscape Communications Inc. of Mountain View, California, and made freely available for non-commercial use.

Secure HTTP (S-HTTP)

Secure HTTP, or just S-HTTP, is a security-enhanced version of HTTP that consists of a set of protocol changes designed to address issues of privacy, authentication, and integrity (RS 1994). Secure HTTP provides transaction security at a document level where each document can be marked as private and signed by the sender. Secure HTTP's design goal is to provide a flexible protocol that supports multiple orthogonal operation modes, key management mechanisms, trust models, cryptographic algorithms, and encapsulation formats through option negotiation between the parties for each transaction.

The protocol emphasizes maximum flexibility in the choice of key management mechanisms, security policies, and cryptographic algorithms. Such application flexibility is achieved at the expense of implementation complexity. In a full-fledged implementation of Secure HTTP, quite a wide variety of cryptographic algorithms and operation modes might have to be accommodated. On the other hand, clients and servers that have chosen to

implement different subsets of the protocol for minimal compliance might not be able to enjoy all the benefits of secure transaction as full inter-operation may be problematic.

Currently, several cryptographic message format standards can be incorporated into S-HTTP clients and servers, including, but not limited to, PKCS-7, PEM, and PGP. S-HTTP supports interoperation among a variety of implementations, and is compatible with HTTP. S-HTTP aware clients can talk to S-HTTP oblivious servers and vice versa, although such transactions obviously would not use S-HTTP security features.

Summary of S-HTTP Features

As discussed in RS 1994, the important features of Secure HTTP can be summarized as follows:

→ The protocol provides symmetric capabilities to both client and server (in that equal treatment is given to both requests and replies, as well as for the preferences of both parties) while preserving the transaction model and implementation characteristics of the current HTTP.

→ S-HTTP does not require client-side public key certificates (or public keys), supporting symmetric session key operation modes. This is significant because it means that spontaneous private transactions can occur without requiring individual users to have an established public key. Although S-HTTP will be able to take advantage of ubiquitous certification infrastructures, its deployment does not require it.

→ S-HTTP supports end-to-end secure transactions, in contrast to the existing de facto HTTP authorization mechanism that requires the client to attempt access and be denied before

the security mechanism is employed. Clients can be "primed" to initiate a secure transaction (typically using information supplied in an HTML anchor) and to support encryption of fill-out forms, for example. With S-HTTP, no sensitive data need ever be sent over the network in the clear.

→ S-HTTP provides full flexibility of cryptographic algorithms, modes, and parameters. Option negotiation is used to allow clients and servers to agree on transaction modes (should the request be signed, encrypted, or both? What about the reply?); cryptographic algorithms (RSA versus DSA for signing, DES versus RC2 for encrypting, and so on); and certificate selection (please sign with your "MasterCard certificate").

→ Secure HTTP has deliberately restricted itself to standardizing on message formats, independent of policy and implementation details. S-HTTP attempts to avoid presuming a particular trust model, for example, and can thus accommodate different arrangements of certifying authorities, that is, whether organized in a hierarchical fashion or in a PGP-style web of trust.

Modes of Operation in S-HTTP

Message protection in S-HTTP can be provided along three orthogonal axes: encryption, authentication, and digital signature. Any message can be encrypted, authenticated, digitally signed, or any combination of these (including unprotected).

Multiple key management mechanisms are provided in S-HTTP, including ordinary password-style shared secrets, Diffie-Hellman style public key

exchanges, and Kerberos (SNS 1988) ticket distribution. In particular, provisions have been made for prearranged (in an earlier transaction) session keys to send confidential messages to those who have no key pair.

Secure HTTP provides a means to verify sender authenticity and message integrity for a HTTP message via the computation of a Message Authentication Code (MAC). This mechanism also is useful in cases where it is desirable to allow parties to identify each other reliably in a transaction.

If the digital signature enhancement is adopted, an appropriate certificate might be attached to the message (possibly along with a certificate chain) or the sender might expect the recipient to obtain the required certificate (chain) independently.

The protocol provides a simple challenge-response mechanism, called *nonce*, allowing both parties to assure themselves of transaction freshness. Additionally, the integrity protection provided to HTTP headers permits implementations to consider the "Date:" header allowable in HTTP messages as a freshness indicator, where appropriate.

 S-HTTP has been submitted to the Internet Engineering Task Force (IETF) working group on Web transaction security for consideration as an Internet standard. The IETF is a standards body consisting of a self-organized group of people that makes technical and other contributions to the engineering and evolution of Internet and its technologies. Reference implementations of Secure HTTP in the form of Secure NCSA Mosaic and Secure NCSA httpd are available from Enterprise Integration Technologies (EIT) of Menlo Park, California.

Current Practice and Future Trend in Web Security

Transaction security is vital to the growth of the emerging information infrastructure and the widespread deployment of agents in the commercial domains. There is no clear security standard at this point for the World Wide Web. A concern in the market is the development of two different security approaches, SSL and Secure HTTP, that cannot communicate with each other. Information providers must be concerned with how easily information servers can interoperate with clients on the Web.

The W3C, IETF, and other relevant standards groups recognize the importance of security on the Web. In due course, a common security standard will be defined by the standards groups. The formal process of standardization, however, is lengthy and could run for years. In the interim, it is widely recognized that a common interoperable approach to transaction security should make it easier for information providers to provide secure information on the World Wide Web, and make it easier for consumers to access it.

Such a universal approach currently is being provided by Terisa Systems of Menlo Park, a joint-venture between EIT and RSA Data Security, which offers a set of developer's toolkits that combine both SSL and Secure HTTP. By following a unified approach that allows information providers to take advantage of the strengths of both protocols, developers can be assured that their applications will interoperate securely with other applications deployed on the Web while they wait for a formal standard to become established and widely adopted.

In July 1995, Open Market Systems, based in Cambridge, Massachusetts, released its Secure WebServer product and became the first company to field a Web server that can handle both of today's dominant security schemes: SSL and Secure HTTP. The convergence toward a common approach could mean that merchant applications that depend on transaction security, such as payment, inventory, and delivery systems, will be made available much more rapidly because developers will find it far more attractive to create Web products and Web commerce agents using a universal security approach.

Electronic Cash and Payment Services

The advent of electronic commerce on the Internet is to a large extent facilitated by the launch of the World Wide Web. In the realm of agents, there are currently hordes of spiders, wanderers, brokers, and bots on the Web performing various tasks for their human clients: for example, searching for information, maintaining Web infostructure, brokering for buyers and sellers, as well as finding the best bargain of books and CDs online.

Digital cash, a string of numbers made up of zeroes and ones, is the electronic equivalent of cash on the Internet. Instead of being engraved on special paper with watermarks to prevent counterfeiting, digital cash is protected from forgery by strong cryptography and can be stored on computer hard disks or transported over the network. Similarly, electronic versions of different paper-based payment schemes have also been invented for the Internet.

Agents that are active in the online marketplace must be able to handle money and payments in an electronic form for full-blown electronic commerce. Examples of online tasks that could be automated using agents include the ordering of parts from an online catalog, the sale of information over the Internet, as well as the reservation and purchase of opera tickets on the Web.

Brief History of Money

Money came about as a major innovation in the early economic systems to serve as a medium of exchange and a store of value. Precious metals, which were first used around 2,500 B.C. in Mesopotamia, were an early form of money. In U.S. history, tobacco was used in Colonial Virginia as a medium of exchange, and even whiskey attracted a following among frontiersmen.

Coins stamped from precious metals, which date back to 700 B.C., represent a significant advance over non-uniform pieces of metal and are preferred for their convenient form, as well as standardized sizes and content. In general, the face value of a coin exceeds the worth of the metal it contains.

This difference generally is considered a fair price to pay for the added convenience that coins offer. Over time, this difference, known as *seigniorage*, has been a reliable source of revenue for mints, which tend to be government monopolies.

When paper money came along around the 11th century in China, it represented a vast improvement. Not only is paper money cheaper to produce and easier to carry, but it costs less in real terms. Challenges abound, however. From an institutional viewpoint, the issuing authority must inspire public confidence, as it is relatively easy to debase the currency by printing too much money. From a technology viewpoint, the official engravers constantly must stay ahead of counterfeiters.

In the age of electronic commerce on Internet, money has evolved into a digital form consisting of strings of zeroes and ones that can be stored on disks for safekeeping and can zap across networks in seconds during payments. There are myriad entrepreneurial startup companies professing to be electronic banks offering various types of digital cash, coupons, and payment services to the general Internet populace. There is DigiCash, NetBank, CyberCash, and First Virtual to mention just a few.

This chapter explores the offerings of DigiCash, CyberCash, and First Virtual in detail. For the purpose of motivating the use of digital cash and payment services, the following section examines various methods of paying for goods and services on the Internet, along with an assessment of risks involved.

Choice of Payment Methods

Traditionally, payment for goods and services on the Internet requires the mailing of a check. Payment generally takes longer due to the "snail pace" of the Postal Service as well as the time required to "clear" checks at the banks. Furthermore, for one-time users who must pay for small amounts of data from many diverse sources on the Internet, this payment mechanism is cumbersome (imagine having to write and mail checks to hundreds of information providers each month!).

Credit card payments on the Internet avoid the Postal Service and interbank check processings. There are, however, substantial risks involved when credit card information is sent over the Internet. Messages often pass through multiple network hosts and routers on their way to the merchant. Therefore, it is possible that somewhere along the way, someone could be scanning these messages for credit card details and compromising the security of this method.

Credit card payments on the Internet are made secure when credit card details are protected by strong encryption. The cost of processing these types of credit card transactions, however, can outweigh the benefit. Transactions worth a few dollars or less, such as the fee for a movie review or an encyclopedia entry, generally are not worth the cost of processing a credit card order.

One economical solution to small value payments on the Internet would be the introduction of a third party; that is, a company that collects and approves payments from a client to a merchant electronically.

After a certain period of time has elapsed, or when a certain value threshold is reached, one single credit card transaction for the total accumulated amount would be made. For example, at the end of every month, or whenever cumulative charges for a client exceeds the $100 threshold, the client's credit card will be billed for whatever amount is outstanding.

However, there are limitations and shortcomings to this method. The possibility that a payment will be refused because the spending limit has been reached does exist. But more importantly, one's payment details, such as where you buy, when you buy, and sometimes what you buy, are gathered in a centralized database. In the wrong hands, the collection of this data can pose a serious transgression on one's personal rights to privacy.

In real life, people can pay with cash, anonymously if desired. To introduce this same facility on the Internet, one would need the electronic equivalent of cash on the Internet, called *digital cash*.

What is Digital Cash?

Digital cash is the electronic equivalent of cash on the Internet. It is a string of zeroes and ones whose pattern represents money that cannot be forged. You can withdraw "digital coins" from an Internet bank account and store them on local hard disks. You then could use these coins for making payments electronically. Digital cash can be easily transported from one place to another over the Internet. All payments are fast, convenient and, more importantly, anonymous. Furthermore, you can always prove that you have made certain payments.

Digital cash offers speed, convenience, anonymity, and proof of payments. Another desirable property of digital cash, which is significantly harder to achieve, is that the payer should be able to make offline payments to arbitrary payees in such a way that the latter can verify the validity of payment (that is, no double spending of the same note) without using the network. Digital cash systems with this property are called *offline digital cash*, and are highly complex. Details can be found in Chaum 1992 and Brands 1993, 1994.

Digital cash can be used for payments that are too small to cost-effectively process as individual credit card or debit card payments. By offering the benefits of speed and hands-free automation, digital cash can, for example, find uses in paying for small charges that result from scanning a movie review or looking up an encyclopedia entry.

A system for processing digital cash payments is key to unleashing the projected explosion in entrepreneurial electronic information publishing. The traditional way of handling database retrievals through pre-arranged subscriptions is no longer workable in the new era of spontaneous electronic commerce on the Internet. There are simply too many independent information services and unaffiliated database publishers to subscribe to on a one-to-one basis. DigiCash, a company based in Amsterdam, the Netherlands, is currently developing, refining, and field-testing a digital cash system for use on the Internet. I will have more to say on this in a later section of this chapter.

Digital Cashier's Check

As illustrated in Chapter 8, digital signatures can be used to provide all manners of unforgeable credentials, as well as other services. Now consider how digital signatures might be used to provide an electronic replacement for cash. The following scenario is excerpted from David Chaum's very well-written article in *Scientific American* (1992). David Chaum is the head of the Cryptography Group at the Center of Mathematics and Computer Science (CWI) in Amsterdam, as well as the founder in 1990 of DigiCash, which is discussed later in this chapter.

Suppose that a fictitious First Digital Bank offers electronic bank notes, which are messages signed using a particular private key of the bank. All messages bearing one key might be worth a dollar, all those bearing a different key five dollars, and so on, for whatever denominations are needed.

These electronic bank notes could be authenticated using the corresponding public key, which the bank has published as a matter of public record. For purpose of correspondence, First Digital would also make public a key to authenticate electronic documents sent from the bank to its customers.

To withdraw a dollar from the bank, Alice first has to generate a note number. Each note bears a different number, akin to the serial number on a bill. Suppose that she picks a 128-digit number generated at random so that the chance anyone else would generate the same one is negligible. She signs the number with the private key corresponding to the public key that she has previously established for use with her account.

The bank verifies Alice's signature and removes it from the note number, signs the note number with its worth-one-dollar signature and debits her account. The bank then returns the signed note along with a digitally signed withdrawal receipt for Alice's records.

In practice, the creation, signing, and transfer of note numbers would be carried out on Alice's desktop computer. The power of the cryptographic protocols, however, lies in the fact that they are secure regardless of physical medium; the same transactions could be carried out using only pencil and paper.

When it comes time for Alice to pay for a purchase at Bob's shop in cyberspace, she transfers one of the signed note numbers the bank has issued to her. After verifying the bank's digital signature, Bob transmits the note to the bank, much as a merchant verifies a credit card transaction today.

The bank reverifies its signature, checks the note against a list of those already spent, and credits Bob's account. It then transmits a "deposit slip," once again unforgeably signed with the appropriate key. Bob hands the merchandise to Alice, along with his own digitally signed receipt, completing the transaction.

This system provides security for all three parties. The signatures at each stage prevent any one from cheating either of the others—the shop cannot deny that it received payment, the bank cannot deny that it issued the notes or that it accepted them from the shop for deposit, and the customer can neither deny withdrawing the notes from her account nor can she spend them twice.

Privacy Issues

Such electronic bank notes just described are more like digital cashier's checks than digital cash. According to Chaum, this system is secure but has no privacy. If the bank keeps track of note numbers, it can link each shop's deposit to the corresponding withdrawal and determine precisely where and when Alice spends her money. The resulting dossier is far more intrusive than those now being compiled.

Furthermore, records based on digital signatures are more vulnerable to abuse than conventional file records because they are self-authenticating. In other words, even if these self-authenticating records are copied, the information they contain can be verified by anyone. In contrast, no simple claims of authenticity can be established for copies of conventional file records as they may be subject to tampering.

In addition, records based on digital signatures permit a person who has a particular type of information to prove its existence without giving the information away or revealing its source. The idea behind such zero-knowledge proofs is essentially that everything provable could be done while revealing "zero knowledge" (BGGHKMR 1988; BC 1990; Schneier 1994). Someone might, for example, be able to prove incontrovertibly that Alice had telephoned Bob on 12 separate occasions without having to reveal the time and place of any of the calls.

To restore privacy to monetary transactions in cyberspace, Chaum has invented *anonymous digital cash*, which is made possible using a cryptographic technique called *blind signatures*.

Anonymous Digital Cash through Blind Signatures

The idea behind anonymous digital cash is simply that digital cash transactions should remain anonymous, just as in plain cash. Chaum has developed an extension of digital signatures, called *blind signatures* (1982, 1985), which is used to implement *anonymous digital cash.* Here is how it works.

Before sending a note number to the bank for signing, Alice, in essence, multiplies it by a random factor known only to herself, and signs the resulting product with her digital signature. The note is considered "blinded" by the introduction of the random factor, also known as the *blinding factor.* As before, the bank duly verifies Alice's digital signature and removes it from the blinded note number. The bank signs the blinded note with a properly denominated signature and debits Alice's account accordingly. The bank knows nothing about what note number it is signing. It doesn't, and shouldn't, care. All the bank needs to know is that the blinded note carries Alice's digital signature.

After getting back the blinded note signed by the bank, Alice *unblinds* the note by arithmetically dividing out the blinding factor from the bank-endorsed blinded note. The beauty of the mathematics behind blinded signatures is that the resulting quotient is now the original note number with the bank's digital signature over it, without the blinding factor. The net effect is as though the bank has signed on the original note (before introducing the blinding factor) blind-folded! Alice can then spend the bank-endorsed note at any shops that accept digital cash, as before.

Such bank-endorsed notes have many properties associated with plain cash. Like cash, they can be spent at a cybershop anonymously. Furthermore, the bank notes are a negotiable instrument; that is, they are transferable from one person to another by being delivered with or without endorsement so that title ownership passes to the transferee. In other words, the holder of the bank notes owns them.

Unconditional Untraceability

According to Chaum, the blinded note numbers are "unconditionally untraceable," that is, even if the shop and the bank collude, they cannot determine who spent which notes. Because the bank has no idea of the blinding factor, it has no way of linking the note numbers that Bob deposits with Alice's withdrawals.

Whereas the security of digital signatures is dependent on the difficulty of particular computations, the anonymity of blinded notes is limited only by the unpredictability of Alice's random blinding factors. If she wants, however, Alice can reveal these random numbers and permit the notes to be stopped or traced.

Double Spending

Blinded electronic bank notes protect individual privacy. But because each note is simply a number, it can be copied easily. To prevent double spending, each note received by a merchant must be checked online against a central list of spent notes maintained by the issuing digital bank. Such a verification procedure might be acceptable when large amounts of money are at stake, but it is far too expensive to use when someone is just buying an online newspaper. To solve this problem, several offline digital

cash schemes have been invented, including one that is based upon the discrete log based signatures (Brands 1993, 1994) as well as one by Chaum and colleagues, which for expository purposes is conceptually easier to understand (1992).

The scheme of Chaum et. al. (1992) works as follows. Before accepting an offline payment, the payee's computer issues an unpredictable challenge to which the payer's computer must respond with some information about the note number. This information alone discloses nothing about the payer, and is collected by the bank when the note is finally deposited with the bank by the payee. Should the payer spend the note a second time, the information yielded by the next challenge, when combined with previously collected information kept at the bank, gives away the payer's identity when the note is ultimately deposited with the bank a second time. In this way, should the bank find out that the same note has been twice spent, it can proceed to identify the culprit payer by combining the two pieces of information together.

Ecash from DigiCash

Ecash is offered by DigiCash, a company founded in 1990 by David Chaum and headquartered in Amsterdam, Holland. The DigiCash home page is shown in figure 9.1. Everyone using Ecash must have an Ecash account at a digital bank on the Internet. The procedure for opening an Ecash account with a digital bank is very much the same as that of opening an ordinary checking account with a traditional bank; real money must first be deposited. Using that account, people can expect to withdraw and deposit Ecash in addition to transacting with real cash. However, real bankers are certainly a conservative lot. As of this writing, there have not been any operational digital banks on the Internet that would offer this service interconverting between Ecash and real money.

Figure 9.1

The DigiCash home page.

Ecash is a coin-based system, where coins have predetermined values. Every coin is a digital signature from the bank. Coins of different values are combined into the amount required for payment, just like real coins.

Starting in October 1994, DigiCash has been running an Ecash trial on a continual basis, using a fictitious DigiCash-run First Digital Bank as the trial bank. The Ecash trial has thus far attracted more than 5,000 participants on the Internet. The currency used in the Ecash trial is a virtual one called *Cyberbucks*, which does not have any relationship with real currencies. This means that cyberbucks cannot be exchanged for real money. Each participant in the trial receives $100.00 cyberbucks to be spent on goods and services ranging from computer images, software, and games to lotteries, charities, and casinos. There are more than a hundred such Ecash-accepting cybershops on Internet, a complete list of which can be found at `http://www.digicash.com/shops/alpha.html`. As shown in figure 9.2, the following steps describe the flow of Ecash in a digital economy:

1. When an Ecash withdrawal is made, the computer of the Ecash user calculates how many digital coins of what denominations are needed to withdraw the requested amount. Next, random serial numbers for those coins are generated and the blinding factors applied. The result of these calculations are then sent to the digital bank.

2. The bank digitally signs the blinded numbers with its secret key. At the same time, the client account is debited for the same amount. The

authenticated coins are sent back to the user. The user arithmetically divides out the blinding factor that he introduced earlier by simple arithmetic multiplication. The serial numbers plus their signatures are now digital coins, with their value guaranteed by the bank.

3. The coins can be stored locally on the user's computer. As soon as a payment is to be made, the user's computer collects the coins needed to reach the requested total value. These coins then are sent to the receiver.

4. The receiver forwards the coins directly to the digital bank. The bank verifies the coins' validity and that they have not been spent before. To prevent double spending, there must not be more than one copy of the same bank note in circulation on the Internet. The account of the receiver is credited.

Every coin is used only once. Another withdrawal is needed if the receiver wants to have new coins to spend.

 Like travelers checks, Ecash can handle lost money very well. Ecash stored on disk can be lost in a disk crash if not backed up onto tape, for example. Lost Ecash notes can be reported to the bank along with the serial numbers on the lost coins. These serial numbers allow the bank to check if the coins are really lost (or have already been spent) and refund the money accordingly.

Figure 9.2

Flow of Ecash in digital economy.

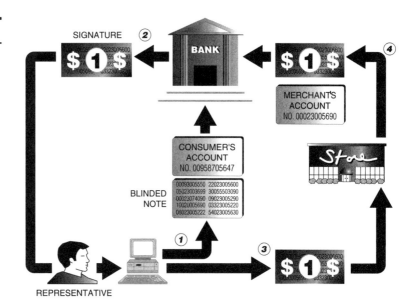

Ecash Security and Other Issues

Ecash offers payer anonymity based upon RSA public-key cryptography and blinded signatures, and not on the revocable policy of a remote institution. When paying with Ecash, the identity of the payer is never revealed. Each Ecash coin has its own note number (randomly generated by the user and not by the bank) that has been blinded by the user before presentation to the bank for signing. The bank has no way to find what note numbers it has signed.

Neither the payer nor the payee can counterfeit the bank's signature. Both can verify that the payment is valid because each has the bank's public key. The payer can prove that payment has been made because he can make available the blinding factor. But because the original note number was blinded when it was signed, the bank cannot connect the signing with the payment. All three parties are thus protected: the bank is protected against forgery, the payee against the bank's refusal to honor a legitimate note, and the payer against false accusations of non-payment and invasion of privacy.

Safeguards against Crime

Ample safeguard is built into Ecash against criminal use of anonymity in digital cash. What Ecash offers is more accurately described as one-side anonymity; that is, only the payer is anonymous, the recipient of the money has no anonymity at all.

All money that the payee receives must be cleared with the bank. Ecash banks are thus able to list the amounts of all payments received for all accounts. It is not possible to hide from the bank the fact that money has been received. As a result, tax-evasion, extortion, and bribes through Ecash is not possible.

The legal risks to black-marketeering with Ecash are even more insurmountable. Customers cooperating with the authorities can establish that a certain payment has been made to the black

marketeer, retroactively. As DigiCash puts it succinctly, "Paper cash will remain the criminal's favorite."

Payment Systems on the Internet

A hundred years ago, if a local merchant in San Francisco, California wanted to buy goods from Rochester, New York, he placed his order by mail or telegraph and then arranged for his local bank to handle the payment. The banker would face the cumbersome task of finding an institution in Rochester that was part of a common clearinghouse, probably in New York City. After debiting the customer's account, the local bank would wire the New York clearinghouse and direct it to transfer the funds from its own account to that of the Rochester bank. The Rochester bank would in turn pay the supplier. The customer would even be charged for changing San Francisco dollars to New York dollars. Incredible as it might seem today, newspapers at the time published tables of domestic exchange rates (GS 1979).

U.S. Payment Systems Today

With today's technology, the same transaction now can be completed by phone, fax, or e-mail. In the United States, payments can be made by the following five types of non-electronic instruments:

→ Cash

→ Checks

→ Credit cards

→ Traveler's checks

→ Money orders

Payments also can be made by the following four types of electronic instruments:

→ Automated clearinghouse

→ Wire transfer

→ Point of sale

→ Automated teller machines

Each of these instruments, however, has different production and processing costs, is subject to varying amounts of float (that is, the time between a payer liquidating his obligation and the payee receiving use of the funds), and offers different levels of convenience and security. For example, when vast amounts of money must be moved, wire transfers (Fedwire and the private Clearing House Interbank Payment System, or CHIPS) are the preferred method of payment because the funds are available almost immediately (Bauer 1994). Most transactions are relatively painless unless something goes awry, such as a check being returned for insufficient funds. The apparent ease of making payments is the result of many hidden technological and institutional arrangements.

Technology-Driven Evolution

New technologies and institutional arrangements require continual reworking of the payment system. An effective way to boost productivity is to be technology-driven, always striving to increase the productivity of payment instruments wherever possible. A recently completed, all-electronic automated clearinghouse system, for example, eliminates some volume of tapes and disks, which are expensive to process. Another example is the adoption of electronic imaging technology for paper check processing.

The banking industry expects that the logical next phase in the evolution of the payment system is to conduct each step of a transaction (for example, ordering, payment, and inventory) electronically through an automated clearinghouse (ACH) or through financial electronic data interchange (EDI). Financial EDI can easily replace paper checks with a less expensive ACH transaction, which could form the basis of an Internet payment service. This is an area where a new generation of agents can be deployed. Potential benefits include better control of the timing of payments and the receipts of funds, more accurate record keeping, and lower costs.

On a different technological frontier, the Internet appears to be gathering momentum in trying to shape electronic payment systems for the masses. As it stands now, serious institutional barriers to electronic commerce remain. What is needed on the Internet now is a universally acceptable, safe, secure, convenient, and immediate system for processing payments for both goods and services.

CyberCash Internet Payment Service

CyberCash delivers a safe, convenient, and inexpensive system for making payments on the Internet through partnerships with financial institutions and providers of goods and services. The CyberCash approach is based on establishing a trusted link between the seemingly unpredictable world of cyberspace and the traditional banking world.

CyberCash, based in Reston, Virginia, was founded by Bill Melton and Dan Lynch (see fig. 9.3). Melton also helped found the successful VeriFone company, which sells credit card transaction processing equipment. Lynch is founder of the popular NetWorld and Interop networking show and exhibition.

Figure 9.3

The CyberCash home page.

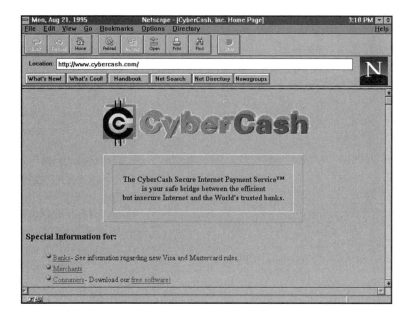

CyberCash considers itself a conduit through which payments can be transported safely and instantaneously between buyers, sellers, and their banks. Much as it is in the real world of commerce, the buyer and seller need not have any prior existing relationship. CyberCash is a neutral third party whose sole concern is ensuring the efficient, safe, and low-cost delivery of payments from one party to another, sort of like the FedEx of payments on the Internet.

For both merchants and banks, the guarantee of safe credit and debit card transactions significantly reduces the risk of fraud normally associated with these types of transactions. For merchants especially, safe credit and debit card transactions have the potential to reduce the high cost of credit card transactions via telephone or mail. Normally, bankcard associations consider these "Card Not Present" transactions riskier and more expensive and consequently charge merchants a higher processing fee.

CyberCash Offerings

CyberCash offers the following two payment services on the Internet:

→ Credit card services for authorized merchant transactions

→ Money payments service for individuals

CyberCash charges banks/processors fees for merchant transactions that are competitive with traditional systems. Fees for transactions between individuals will be competitive with the cost of a postage stamp, about 32 American cents.

To gain access to CyberCash services, a personal computer with a network connection is needed. CyberCash offers free client software that directly communicates with CyberCash servers, which in turn are linked to the private networks of the banks. Free merchant server software enables Internet merchants to get immediate online credit card authorizations and includes all the functions necessary to process transactions and settle with their banks.

CyberCash software provides the needed electronic link between consumers, merchants, and their banks. To facilitate access to the CyberCash system, CyberCash icons are incorporated into the graphical user interfaces of application software. Consumers using these software products can then quickly and easily enter the CyberCash system by clicking on the icon when they are ready to make payments for goods and services. Besides the normal order of commerce, CyberCash also provides service to individuals making monetary transactions. Buying a used microwave oven advertised on the net from someone, for example, and paying him through CyberCash.

CyberCash promises to "materially reduce the risk of financial transactions on the Internet" by carrying out transactions with the following properties:

→ **Automated.** After the consumer enters appropriate information into the computer, no manual steps are required to process authorization or settlement transactions through the entire system. The consumer need only initiate payment for each transaction by exercising the pay option on a CyberCash form.

- → **Safe.** Transactions are protected from both tampering and modification by eavesdroppers on the net. Cryptographic protection is used in all transmissions.

- → **Private.** Information about the consumer not essential to the transaction is not visible to the merchant.

How Secure is CyberCash?

The CyberCash system is secured by strong crytography and operates on top of any general security system such as SSL or Secure HTTP.

 The CyberCash system currently uses full 768-bit RSA as well as 56-bit DES encryption of messages. All transactions are authenticated with MD-5 and 768-bit RSA signatures.

Credit Card Services

Consumers need not have any prior relationship with CyberCash to use the CyberCash Credit Card Services. As illustrated in figure 9.4, the process for authorized merchant transactions is quite straightforward, consisting of the following sequence of steps:

1. After desired merchandise has been selected, the consumer clicks on the CyberCash icon when ready to pay, selects from already set-up credit cards, then clicks on the "Pay" button. Figure 9.5 shows a typical scenario involving the CyberCash user interface as seen by the consumer.

2. The merchant sends the consumer an online invoice detailing the purchase information (for example, order number, description of items, part numbers, quantities and prices, and so on) together with a CyberCash payment statement confirming the total charges.

3. When the CyberCash statement appears on the screen, the consumer enters his or her credit card number, name as it appears on the card, and an expiration date. The customer also has the choice of using a debit service to make the purchase. In this case, the customer simply adds the personal identification number (PIN) to the merchant's online invoice.

4. This statement information is then automatically encrypted and passed along with the invoice to the merchant.

5. The merchant's computer adds identification information and forwards the transaction over the Internet to the CyberCash server. The merchant cannot see the consumer's credit card number; it can only sees the information necessary to process the payment request.

6. CyberCash performs error checking and forwards all the information to the traditional, trusted credit card authorization and settlement networks. CyberCash retains no information related to the merchandise being ordered (for example, order number, description of items, part numbers, and so forth).

7. To complete the transaction, CyberCash returns an electronic receipt with credit card authorization data to the merchant.

8. The merchant then finalizes the transaction with the consumer.

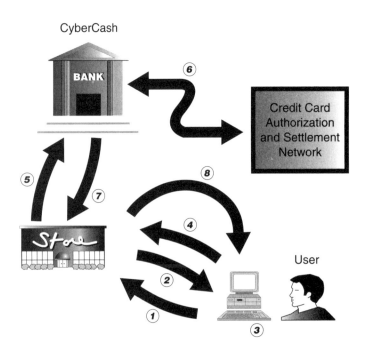

CyberCash

Figure 9.4

CyberCash Credit Card Services.

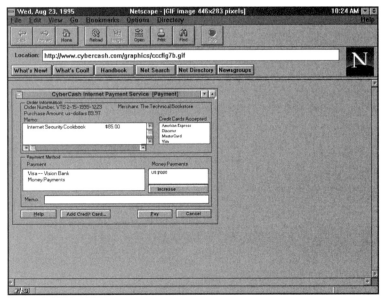

Figure 9.5

The user initiates credit card payment through CyberCash Credit Card Services.

Figure 9.6

Acknowledgment to user of a successful credit card payment through CyberCash Credit Card Services.

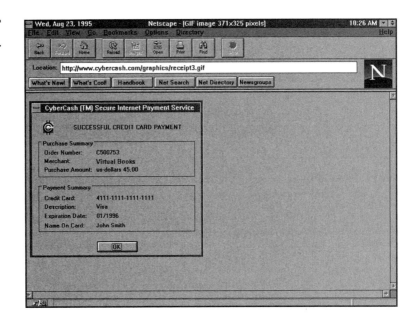

Money Payments Service

The CyberCash Money Payments Service promises to make small financial transactions on the Internet feasible and cost effective. It provides the key to enabling small payments on the Internet for items such as publications and database searches. This will provide ample revenue source for a whole new generation of information agents—that is, agents that publish, buy, sell, and trade in information—to thrive on the Internet.

Unlike CyberCash Credit Card Services, there is no clear distinction between the consumer and the merchant in the Money Payments Service. In fact, electronic cash can be transferred from any CyberCash account holder to any other Internet user with an e-mail address, whether or not they have a CyberCash account.

Individuals or organizations can establish one or more CyberCash accounts directly with CyberCash and accounts are maintained by CyberCash on the basis of an account holder's CyberCash key and not on direct user identity. Thus, an individual can have several unrelated CyberCash accounts or share a CyberCash account with other individuals, as long as they share a CyberCash key. This approach provides a degree of user privacy.

CyberCash accounts are non–interest-bearing holding accounts for cash that the account holder intends to transfer or has received through CyberCash. A Money Payment begins with a simple command to the Secure Internet Payment Service. Payments are peer-to-peer and virtually instantaneous. A cryptographically signed receipt confirms the transaction.

CyberCash Money Payment funds are comprised of real money kept only within real banks and are moved exclusively by them. The only way to place cash into or remove cash from a CyberCash account is through a demand deposit account with the bank.

Information Commerce on the Internet

For more than a decade, the Internet has been used to get information from the people who have it to the people who want and need it. But in the beginning, the Internet was used only for government research information. As more and more institutions became connected, scientists and other academics began using the Internet to exchange data and research results instantly, and companies began using the Internet for rapid business communications. Over the years, an Internet culture took hold, based on mutual respect, broad access, and the free and open exchange of information.

As the Internet community has exploded in size, people have begun creating and distributing fascinating types of information over the Internet that no one would have predicted 20 years ago. Everything that is on the Internet now has been put there by people gratis.

Compensation really has not been possible because there is no simple, reliable way for people to pay for the information they retrieve from the Internet in a way that respects the Internet way of doing things—browsing the net for items of interest before committing to paying for them. To be properly compensated, online information providers have adopted various charging models, including periodic subscription fees, connect-time charges, or volume charges by byte count.

With such charging models, however, it is often difficult to know whether an information product is worth purchasing unless the prospective buyer is able to examine or use it. Buyers find themselves increasingly unwilling to commit to pay for information they have not been able to see or evaluate. In the area of software, this has led to the creation of Internet-posted shareware, in which payment is encouraged only after the product has been obtained and evaluated. Internet-based shareware, characterized by free distribution and voluntary payment, was the first new economic model to emerge for information commerce.

Economics of Information Commerce

Traditionally, only two types of commerce have been possible: the sale of goods and the sale of services. Before the advent of commercial online services, information historically was sold bundled into the sale of other goods or services. Books, for example, contain information, but the nature of printing and the distribution of printed material inevitably converts the information into a physical good. Similarly, legal or medical information is sold but requires a service provider (that is, lawyer or doctor) to deliver the information.

Because information is most often sold today as part of a physical object like a book, it has associated costs of manufacturing, inventory, and distribution. Books, for example, are subject to the costs

of shipping, handling, trucking, warehousing, returned goods, damaged merchandise, unsold inventory, and so on. In many cases, the distribution cost of information-based "packaged goods" greatly exceeds the cost of producing the information in the first place. An author's royalty, for instance, is only a modest percentage of the total cost of a book.

With the emergence of the global Internet as an inexpensive means of global information transport, it has become possible to rapidly deliver information in electronic form, without physical packaging and for virtually no cost. After all, the cost of warehousing is nil. Duplication costs for information products are virtually zero. A copy of the product can be shipped instantly over the Internet whenever the customer makes a purchase, without incurring the traditional costs associated with physical distribution.

The costs to the seller associated with selling information over the Internet are much lower than the cost of doing business the traditional way. Furthermore, order processing and fulfillment can be entirely automated using agents, eliminating the need for manual intervention. And there is no need for returned goods; it costs more to receive returned goods than for the unsatisfied customer to simply discard them!

Agents for Information Commerce

The implications for agents are immense. At such a low threshold of cost for the sale and distribution of information, there are ample opportunities for information agents of all kinds to operate in such a virtual environment. We have previously examined in Chapter 4, "Spiders for Indexing the Web," how

Web spiders have been successful in collecting and indexing Web documents in preparation for consumption by human users. Agents can also play the role of for-profit information brokers who search for, compile, buy, sell, and trade in information in such a global information marketplace now made possible by First Virtual.

As opposed to conventional commerce in goods and services, pure information commerce is special because no scarce objects change hands, and no valuable time is expended on any individual transaction. The primary risks of traditional commerce—notably the lack of payment for the delivery of a physical object or the expenditure of non-renewable time—simply do not apply to information commerce.

Reconsideration of Risk Factors

Traditional payment mechanisms seek to establish a very strong link between the delivery of a good or service and the guarantee of payment. Thus, a merchant generally will not allow you to leave the store with the goods in your hand until he has received cash from you or until your credit card has been validated by a trusted entity, such as the Visa or Mastercard networks. This linkage makes sense for physical goods because the merchant's greatest risk is the loss of the physical object without appropriate payment. Good business practice generally implies that the merchant will, under appropriate circumstances, refund the buyer's money upon the return of the physical object.

The risk factors are rather different for information commerce. Delivery of the information to the consumer costs the merchant essentially nothing. But

even a mechanism that offered extremely strong linkage between information delivery and payment guarantees would do nothing to address the merchant's primary risk in information commerce, unauthorized copying, or piracy. In fact, a key insight that can be gained by reviewing efforts to "copy protect" computer disks is that such mechanisms might actually promote unauthorized copying by making life too difficult for the legitimate consumer.

Thus the seller has lost little or nothing by letting a potential buyer examine the information before deciding whether to buy it, even if the buyer decides not to buy. Virtually all of the expense to the seller is due to the cost of developing the information in the first place, and that cost is the same whether 10 copies, a 1,000 copies, or no copies are sold.

First Virtual Payment System

Payment mechanisms that have evolved for traditional commerce are largely inappropriate for information commerce. First Virtual is a financial services company created specifically to enable virtually anyone with Internet access to buy and sell information worldwide by using the Internet. First Virtual was founded in 1994 by a small group of people who have been intimately involved with the Internet for many years. Among the founders are Nathaniel Borenstein and Marshall Rose, authors of MIME (the Internet standard for interoperable multimedia data) and designers of the Safe-Tcl language. By establishing a merchant banking conduit based on existing technology, First Virtual hopes to become the world's leading information merchant banker. As befits its name, First Virtual is located in cyberspace and does not really have a physical office (see fig. 9.7).

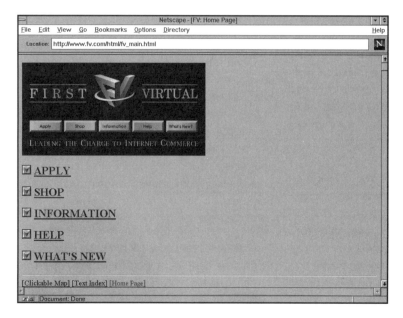

Figure 9.7

The First Virtual home page.

The Green Commerce Model

First Virtual has taken the shareware concept to the next level with its new "Green Commerce" model, technical details of which can be found in `http://www.fv.com/tech/green-model.html`. Transactions relating to accounting and settlement are performed through either the exchange of store-and-forward messages (using the "application/green-commerce" format defined in BR 1994), or interactive protocol exchanges (using the "Simple Green Commerce Protocol" defined in RB 1994).

In the Green Commerce model, the consumer has the right to evaluate information before paying for it. The payment process, however, is automated in such a way as to eliminate the problem, common in current shareware, of people who find the payment process too bothersome. Payment is automatic after the buyer's explicit confirmation to First Virtual of a willingness to pay. Buyers who decline to pay are never required to do so, but those who abuse the system with too-frequent refusals to pay will have their accounts revoked.

Reassignment of Risk

The key difference between traditional commerce mechanisms and First Virtual's Green Commerce model is in the assignment of risk. In credit card systems, for example, the merchant is guaranteed payment, but at a substantial premium, namely the percentage of each transaction that is taken by the credit card networks. In information commerce, an information merchant loses no investment in manufacturing or distribution costs when a potential customer decides not to buy. It is far easier for the vendor to assume the risk of non-payment because nothing is lost out-of-pocket.

This shifting of risk offers a much better fit with the traditional Internet and shareware cultures, in which the value of information can only be assessed after evaluating it. Most importantly, however, it eliminates any need for credit-worthiness guarantees regarding the seller; anyone can easily be a seller as well as a buyer.

Credit card systems, by contrast, are dependent on the credit-worthiness of the sellers. It is more difficult to obtain a Visa merchant account than a Visa credit card. In First Virtual's system, however, it is as easy to be a seller as it is to be a buyer. Individuals with no business history can form Internet-based information businesses without persuading any banks or other institutions of their credit-worthiness. This is possible only because, as information merchants, they bear their own risk of non-payment. Merchants who sell valuable information will be paid by their satisfied customers.

Hardly anyone would use the Internet to buy or sell information unless it was simple to do so. The founders of First Virtual invented a scheme that lets most buyers try before they buy, and lets sellers set their own prices according to the return they seek on their development costs.

How Does First Virtual Work?

Anyone with a credit card or checking account is eligible to establish a First Virtual account and become an information buyer or seller. Unlike a credit card company—which advances real money to merchants on the assumption that customers will pay for what they buy—First Virtual does not compensate merchants for information sold until after buyers have already paid for it. Unlike a credit card company, First Virtual does not guarantee to

merchants that every user of their information will pay for it; in keeping with the Internet culture, buyers of information have the right to try before they buy, and information merchants bear the risk that some buyers may choose not to pay.

A payment transaction through First Virtual consists of the following steps:

1. If a buyer comes across something on the Internet that looks interesting, he or she initiates a transaction by simply asking for a copy of the information and providing his or her account identifier to the seller.

2. The seller forwards information about the transaction, including the buyer's account identifier, to First Virtual's Internet Payment System server.

3. After receiving a fund transfer request from the merchant, First Virtual's server sends e-mail to the buyer, describing the requested transaction and seeking confirmation. The buyer needs only reply: Yes, No, or Fraud. A Yes response authorizes the transaction, a No response declines payment without obligation, and a Fraud response declares the account to be compromised and renders it invalid.

4. When a fund transfer is authorized with a Yes command, the information regarding the fund transfer is delivered through a private link to a secure, non-Internet computer attached to various banking networks. The machine, located in Westlake, Ohio, is owned and operated by EDS, one of the world's largest processors of credit card and automated clearinghouse transactions.

5. Fund transfers are accumulated until they reach a certain threshhold (to be determined by First Virtual), after which a transaction is posted to the credit card associated with the buyer's account.

6. When payment is received, the appropriate fees are deducted, and the money is credited to the seller's payout mechanism (typically a checking account). Depending on the history and status of the seller's account, a portion of the seller's funds may be held in escrow pending complaints for a period of time.

Unlike schemes to create digital cash or similar mechanisms, in First Virtual's system there is never anything like real money on the Internet. Instead, the Internet is used to send around payment authorizations, to be translated elsewhere into real financial transactions. These payment authorizations do not represent money and cannot be exchanged for cash by anyone, including the addressee.

How Secure is First Virtual?

All transactions are handled with a unique account identifier, which travels on the Internet. An unauthorized user who has stolen the account identifier cannot easily use it for fraud because all transactions require buyer confirmation via e-mail before charging can take place. If, however, a malicious third party can intercept all inbound e-mail messages coming to the buyer, then fraud is possible.

 Rather than use encryption, First Virtual's founders decided to avoid it altogether by keeping sensitive information (for example, credit card numbers) off the Internet.

In any event, the consumer is never at any financial risk due to fraud. Users automatically are protected against all credit card fraud—they don't actually have to pay the bill, but can instead initiate a credit card "chargeback" that offsets the amount of the fraudulent charges. In addition, sellers are protected from being "ripped off" with frequency by an online account validation protocol, which ensures that the buyer has presented a valid, non-compromised account identifier.

The Future

Continued growth of the global information infrastructure of the Internet is, to a large part, dependent on the rapid development of electronic commerce, easy access to large information databases, and the use of online services for business.

Few buyers using the First Virtual scheme will have the means or the desire to verify possibly hundreds of small transactions each day. Instant confirmation of a transaction in the style similar to the CyberCash Money Payments Service, expected to be operational soon, is probably much preferred. But it will be even better if buyers and sellers can carry out a secure transaction without third-party confirmation online. As of this writing, DigiCash is planning to offer an offline version of Ecash.

Clearly, technology is an essential component of any advanced payments system. Technology alone, however, is not enough to ensure that a payment instrument is widely accepted. Institutional arrangements cannot be ignored. A hapless 13th-century Persian court advisor discovered the hard way what happens when the technology is in place but the

institutions are not. Rather than accept a newly decreed paper money, merchants in the bazaar closed shops and hid their wares. The ensuing economic turmoil and public outcry caused the paper currency to be revoked and the responsible official to be torn to pieces in the bazaar (White 1993). In our present world, the basic technology for financial electronic data interchange—computers and high-speed electronic communications—has been around for at least 20 years, but the institutional arrangements between those with access to this technology and their banks is still lacking.

An unavoidable fact of life in payment services is that while the Federal Reserve has central bank responsibilities, by law it also must act as another private provider of payment services. By acting as a chief regulator of the payments system and an active participant in the market for payment services, the Fed has wielded an enormous influence on the market (Bauer 1994). It is thus plausible that in the future, when the volume of Internet commerce grows to become a significant economic factor, the Fed might decide to regulate Internet payment services. So far, the central banks have exuded relative indifference to the many ideas bandied around the Internet, which if they work, can scarcely fail to have a substantial effect on money and commerce in the real, non-electronic world (Econ 1994).

With the use of agent technologies, communications promises to become increasingly automated. Choices have to be made regarding what type of electronic world we want to build for ourselves. At one extreme is a world in which it is easy for someone to keep track of everybody else's spending habits and detailed behaviors because all data is

visibly handled by automated systems. At the other end, new technologies like anonymous digital cash make possible an alternative world where personal data is kept private and safeguarded by the individual through strong cryptographic means that are uncompromisable.

With many different competing Internet payment schemes coming onto the market, it still is too early to tell which of them will survive. But despite the technological merits of the different Internet payment schemes, it is ultimately the institutional environment, as well as public sentiments, that finally decides which of them become widely adopted. To interoperate with other agents for the purpose of electronic commerce, Internet agents of the future will most likely incorporate one or more of the various money and payment schemes discussed in this chapter.

Bots in Cyberspace

Worms and Viruses

Worms and viruses are quite different entities, but are often confused with one another because machines afflicted with them frequently exhibit similar symptoms or ill effects. Examples of these telltale signs include suspicious disk and network activities, sluggish CPU responses, corrupted data and program files, and more often than not, the prominent display of messages (from the creators of the worms and viruses) trumpeting victory of infiltration.

Like the worm, a virus self-replicates. Unlike the worm, however, a virus is not a self-contained program. Rather, it is a program fragment that needs to infect a host in order to propagate and survive. Common targets for infection include other programs, directories, and the disk boot-sectors.

Worms and viruses belong in a subcategory of agents that are considered harmful, rather than helpful, to human society. Unlike agents, or even Web-wandering spiders in particular, worms and viruses impact our computing and communications infrastructure not only in a way that is damaging, but also in a way that is ill-purposed. Given that both worms and viruses are built from the same technological base as Internet agents (that is, sharing the same compilers, operating systems, and network protocols), computing experts would shudder at the thought that as the Internet becomes more widely accesible to both humans and Internet agents, it may also become the favored transport vehicle for worms and viruses.

Short History of Worms

A *worm* is a program that propagates itself across a network, using resources on one machine to attack other machines. Worms spread by making multiple replicas of themselves on different machines across the network (see fig. 10.1). Unlike the *virus*, which is a program fragment that inserts itself into other programs for survival and propagation, a worm is a self-contained rogue program. Worms are designed to perform some type of

illegal or malicious activity. They need not necessarily inflict real damage to the machines or data, but ill effects usually develop as a consequence of their presence.

The notion of worm programs originated in science fiction. A worm was first described by science fiction writer John Brunner in his best-selling novel *Shockwave Rider* (1975). The science fiction novel describes an omnipotent "tapeworm" program, the "father and mother of all tapeworms," that was turned loose on a network of computers, wreaking havoc everywhere. The tapeworm "can't be killed," "breeds by itself," and is "indefinitely self-perpetuating so long as the Net exists."

The First Worm

In 1982, John Shoch and Jon Hupp of the Xerox Palo Alto Research Center reported on their early efforts to build the first working multimachine worm programs that ran on one of the earliest networked computing environments (SH 1982). These worm programs, written in a systems programming language called BCPL, ran on a network of 100 Alto computers connected to an Ethernet local network at Xerox PARC. Like their tapeworm counterpart in science fiction, these worm programs travel from workstation to workstation. Unlike the uncontrollable tapeworm, however, these worm programs actually are built to perform useful tasks, such as displaying the cartoon-of-the-day, notifying users of important events, locating idle workstations, and delivering mail.

Figure 10.1

Several multisegment worm programs on a network.

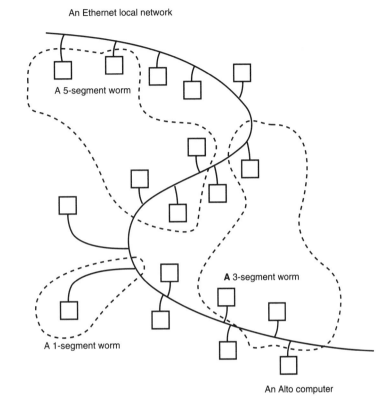

An Ethernet local network

A 5-segment worm

A 3-segment worm

A 1-segment worm

An Alto computer

In their work, Shoch and Hupp correctly identified the key problem associated with worms: How to control their growth while maintaining stable behavior. Noticing in 1982 that an anticipated blossoming of distributed applications using the long-haul capabilities of the ARPAnet had not occurred, Shoch and Hupp commented that the science fiction notion of the tapeworm was "an idea which may seem rather disturbing, but which is also quite beyond our current capabilities." The Internet appeared to be safe from any impending threat of attack by worms.

Indeed, few computer worms—especially worms that could cause damage—have been written since then. Worms require a network environment for propagation and are not easy to write. The worm author must not only be familiar with the network services and facilities, but must also possess detailed knowledge of various operating systems environments that are necessary for supporting the worms after they reach the destination machines.

The Christmas Tree Worm

Things began to change as the Internet grew rapidly in the 1980s. In December 1987, a worm outbreak endemic to the BITNET world of IBM mainframes was triggered by what came to be known as the "Christmas Tree" worm. It began its journey from West Germany as a seemingly innocent electronic Christmas message, which contained a program that displayed an image of a Christmas tree. But the program also attempted to propagate by sending copies of itself to everyone in the mail distribution list of the user for whom it was running. This worm program, which was written in Rexx (a mainframe-only language), rapidly clogged the network with a geometrically growing number of copies of itself. Finally, the severely overloaded network had to be shut down until all copies could be tracked down and purged.

The Internet Worm

It was not until the attack of the notorious Internet Worm that the vulnerability of the Internet was brought to public consciousness. On November 3, 1988, system administrators in the United States came to work and discovered that their networks of computers were laboring under a huge load. The previous evening, a self-replicating worm program had been quietly released on the Internet by Robert Morris, then a graduate student at Cornell University. Over the course of five hours, the Internet Worm had replicated itself on 3,000 computers across the country.

It was to be the most widespread case of worm outbreak on the Internet. The burden of this worm's activity made many of the infected computers unusable. Several days of concerted effort by network experts on both coasts were necessary to completely eradicate it.

Anatomy of the Internet Worm

The Internet Worm took advantage of lapses in security on machines running versions 4.2 or 4.3 BSD of the Unix operating systems, or variants such as Sun-OS. These lapses enabled the worm to connect to machines across a network, bypass their login authentication, copy itself, and then proceed to attack still other machines. The massive system load was generated by multitudes of worms trying to propagate the epidemic.

According to the analysis performed by Donn Seeley at the University of Utah, the worm's activities break down into the categories of attack and defense. The following analysis of the internal workings of the Internet Worm was performed by Seeley (1989).

Method of Worm Attack

Worm attack consists of locating hosts and accounts to penetrate, then exploiting security holes on remote systems to pass across a copy of the worm and run it.

The worm obtains host addresses by examining the system tables "/etc/hosts.equiv" and "/.rhosts," user files such as ".forward" and ".rhosts," dynamic routing information produced by the netstat program, and finally, randomly generated host

addresses on local networks. It ranks these by order of preference, trying a file such as "/etc/hosts.equiv" first, because it contains names of local machines that are likely to permit unauthenticated connections.

Penetration of a remote system can be accomplished in any of the following three ways:

→ The worm can take advantage of a bug in the finger server that enables it to download code in place of a finger request, and trick the server into executing it.

→ By using a "trap door" in the sendmail SMTP mail service, the worm can exercise a bug in the debugging code that enables it to execute a command interpreter and download code across a mail connection.

→ If the worm can penetrate a local account by guessing its password, it can use the rexec and rsh remote command interpreter services to attack hosts that share that account.

In each case, the worm arranges to get a remote command interpreter, which it can use to copy over, compile, and execute the 99-line bootstrap. The bootstrap sets up its own network connection with the local worm, copies over the other files it needs, and uses these pieces to build a remote worm. Then the infection procedure starts over again.

Method of Worm Defense

Worm defense tactics fall into the following three categories:

→ Preventing detection of intrusion

→ Inhibiting analysis of the program

→ Authenticating other worms

The worm's simplest means of hiding itself is to change its name. When it starts up, it clears its argument list and sets its *zeroth* argument to sh, which enables the worm to masquerade as an innocuous command interpreter.

It uses fork() to change its process identifier, never staying too long at one process identifier. These two tactics are intended to disguise the worm's presence on system status listings. The worm tries to leave as little trash as possible lying around. At start-up, it reads all its support files into memory and deletes the telltale file-system copies. It turns off the generation of core files, so that if the worm makes a mistake, it doesn't leave evidence behind in the form of core dumps.

The latter tactic—that of using the fork() to change the worm's process identifier—is also designed to block analysis of the program. This tactic prevents an administrator from sending a software signal to the worm to force it to dump a core file. But because there are other ways to get a core file, the worm carefully alters character data in memory to prevent it from being extracted easily. Copies of disk files are encoded by repeatedly exclusive-or'ing a 10-byte code sequence; static strings are encoded byte-by-byte by exclusive-or'ing with the hexadecimal value 81, except for a private word list that is encoded with hexadecimal 80 instead. If the worm's files are somehow captured before the worm can delete them, the object files have been loaded in such a way as to remove most nonessential symbol table entries, which makes the process of guessing the purposes of worm routines from their names a more difficult one.

The worm also makes a trivial effort to stop other programs from taking advantage of its communications; because—in theory—a well-prepared site could prevent infection by sending messages to ports that the worm was listening on, the worm is careful to use a short exchange of random "magic numbers" to test connections.

What Does the Worm Not Do?

When studying a tricky program such as that belonging to a worm, establishing what the program does *not* do is just as important as establishing what it *does* do. Following is a list of what it does not do:

→ The worm does not delete a system's files; it only removes files that it created in the process of bootstrapping.

→ The program does not attempt to incapacitate a system by deleting important files (or, indeed, any files).

→ It does not remove log files or otherwise interfere with normal operation, other than by consuming system resources.

→ The worm does not modify existing files; it is not a virus.

→ The worm propagates by copying itself and compiling itself on each system; it does not modify other programs to do its work for it. Because of its method of infection, it can't count on sufficient privileges to be able to modify programs.

→ The worm does not install Trojan horses. Its method of attack is strictly active; it never waits for a user to trip over a trap. Part of the reason for this approach is that the worm can't afford to waste time waiting for Trojan horses—it must reproduce before it is discovered.

→ The worm does not record or transmit decrypted passwords. Except for its own static list of favorite passwords, the worm does not propagate cracked passwords onto new worms nor does it transmit them back to some home base.

→ The worm does not try to capture superuser privileges. Although it does try to break into accounts, it doesn't depend on having particular privileges to propagate, and never makes special use of such privileges if it somehow gets them.

→ The worm does not propagate over uucp, X.25, DECNET, or BITNET. It specifically requires TCP/IP.

→ The worm does not infect System V systems unless they have been modified to use Berkeley network programs, such as sendmail, fingerd, and rexec.

Brief History of Viruses

The first use of the term *virus* to refer to unwanted computer code was coined by David Gerrold in his 1972 science fiction novel, *When Harley was One*. According to Spafford, Heaphy, and Ferbrache (1990), however, the description of the term "virus" in that book does not fit the currently accepted definition of *computer virus*, which is a program that alters other programs to include a copy of itself.

Table 10.1

Growth of the IBM PC
Virus Problem.

Year	New	Viruses
1986	1	Brain
1987	5	Friday 13th, Lehigh, Alameda, South African, Vienna
1988	5	Stoned, Italian, DOS 62, Cascade, Agiplan
1989	10	Oropax, Search, dBase, Screen, Datacrime, 405, Pentagon, Traceback, Icelandic, Mistake

As early as 1981, different strains of viruses had already appeared on popular models of Apple II computers (although they were not formally named viruses). Examples include the notorious "Cyberaids," "Festering Hate," and "Elk Cloner."

Fred Cohen, a well-known pioneer in virus research, formally defined the term "computer virus" in 1983. At that time, Cohen was a graduate student at the University of Southern California. While attending a security seminar, he got the idea of writing a computer virus. In a week's time, he had put together a simple program that he demonstrated to the class. Because this program can infect the host computer and propagate and survive like a microbiological virus, his advisor, Professor Len Adelman (of RSA fame), suggested that he call his creation a computer virus. Cohen's work had shown that viruses are easy to write, easy to hide, and can propagate rapidly in a matter of hours.

As reported in SHF 1990, since the first infection by the Brain virus in January, 1986, the number of known viruses for the IBM PC had grown to 21 distinct strains (with an additional 57 minor variants) by August, 1989. Table 10.1 illustrates the growth of the IBM PC virus problem.

Other personal computer systems were not immune: 12 Macintosh viruses and variants existed, as well as 3 Apple II viruses, 22 on the Atari ST, and 18 on the Commodore Amiga. The only viruses reported on the mainframes were those written by serious academic researchers for experimental purposes, in a controlled environment. Viruses appeared to have found fertile ground in the weak security environment of the personal computers.

The viruses on personal computers continued to mushroom. By one rough estimate, over 1,800 viruses existed on IBM PCs, 30 on Macintoshes, and 150 on Amigas by October, 1992. By 1995, there were already more than 4,000 viruses on the IBM PC.

Types of Viruses

Viruses are carried in various storage devices such as floppy disks, hard disks, and magnetic tapes. When executed by the computer, a virus attempts to infect files, directories, and disks in order to propagate itself. Depending upon the target of infection, viruses can be classified into two major types: boot-sector infectors and file infectors. Each type is discussed in detail.

Boot-Sector Infectors

The first category of viruses, the *boot-sector infectors*, infect executable code found in certain system areas on disk that are not ordinary files—the DOS boot sector on floppy disks, for example, as well as the master boot record on hard disks.

Boot-sector viruses on a floppy disk remain dormant until the user attempts to boot the computer with the infected disk. When this happens, the virus becomes active, searches the hard disk for signs of previous infection, and writes itself to the boot-sector area of an uninfected hard disk. After the hard disk has been infected, every subsequent boot of the hard disk activates the virus. From then on, the virus begins to infect all subsequent non-write-protected floppy disks that are used with the system. Many recent strains of viruses are boot-sector viruses; examples are Brain, Stoned, Empire, and Michelangelo.

 note Boot-sector viruses are always resident in memory.

File Infectors

The second category of viruses, the *file infectors*, attach themselves to ordinary program files, and usually infect arbitrary COM and EXE programs. Some can also infect files that, under certain circumstances, can become executable (such as SYS, OVL, or PRG files).

File infectors are further classified by their mode of operation, as either direct-action infectors or resident infectors. A *direct-action virus* (such as the Vienna virus) selects one or more programs to infect each time the program that contains the virus is executed. A *resident virus* hides itself somewhere in memory the first time an infected program is executed, and thereafter stays in memory to perform operations such as infecting other programs, checking logical conditions, and monitoring certain hardware and software interrupts to conceal the virus' existence. Most file infector viruses are resident.

Companion Viruses

The companion viruses are a subcategory of file infectors. Instead of modifying an existing executable file (usually with an EXE extension), a companion virus creates a hidden file with the same filename, but with a COM extension. Because the command interpreter always executes a COM file before an EXE file when the two filenames are identical, the virus is always executed instead of the intended program. The viral code invokes the original program upon exit, so that things will appear normal. This type of virus can fool integrity checkers, which merely look for changes in existing files.

Cluster Viruses

Another subcategory of file infectors are the *file system*, or *cluster*, viruses (such as the DirII virus), which modify directory table entries so that the virus is loaded and executed before the desired program. Only the directory entry (not the program itself) is physically altered.

File infectors can travel, along with the infected program files, to other machines, and can spread either through network or modem transmissions, or physically (on floppy disks or backup tapes). Approximately 90 percent of all viruses have been file infectors.

On the other hand, boot-sector viruses—under normal circumstances—are not able to infect other computers through networks, modems, or tape drives. A few viruses, however, are able to infect both program files and boot sectors. The Tequila virus is an example of these *multipartite*, or *boot-and-file* viruses. A special kind of *dropper* program also exists; it "drops" a virus into the boot-sector area or infects a file when the dropper is executed (Lucas 1994). Both of these types of viruses can pass boot-sector viruses to other machines over networks, modems, or tape drives.

PC Virus Basics

Before you examine the operation of viruses in greater detail, you should be familiar with disk formats and storage organization. On the IBM PC, data is stored on each disk platter in concentric rings, called *tracks*. The first track is track 0. Each track contains multiple *sectors*, each of which contains a fixed amount (usually 512 bytes) of data. The first sector on a track is sector 1.

Sectors are grouped into *clusters*, each containing one or more sectors of data. On any one disk, all clusters uniformly have the same number of sectors. Typically, a cluster holds from two to eight sectors. DOS allocates disk space in units of clusters. For example, if a disk has 4 sectors per cluster, a small file might have 4, 8, or 12 sectors. If the file were only one byte in length, 4 sectors would still be needed to store it. The extra space between the end-of-file marker and the unused bytes at the end of the cluster is known as the *slack space*.

Located at the first absolute sector (head 0, track 0, sector 1) of each hard disk is a partition record, also called the *master boot record*. It describes the physical dimensions of the disk, and the number and size of each partition. It also contains executable code to locate the boot sector of the currently specified bootable logical disk partition. A *boot sector* is the first sector in a logical partition. It provides information about the logical dimensions of the DOS structure, DOS version numbers, and names of two DOS system files.

Floppy disks do not have partition records. A floppy disk simply holds a boot sector at track 0, sector 1; multiple logical partitions are not necessary on a floppy disk. On both hard disks and floppy disks, the boot sector is followed immediately by the file allocation table (FAT), which is followed by the root directory. The *root directory* holds information about all the files and directory entries.

According to the taxonomy of SHF 1990, the life cycle of a virus consists of three stages: activation, replication, and manipulation. First, for the virus to spread, its code must be activated, either as a direct result of a user invoking an infected program or, indirectly, through the system executing the code as part of the system boot sequence or background administration task. Next, the virus replicates to infect other programs or disks. It may insert itself into any number of programs at any one time, and at various speeds. Sometimes, as in the case of the Friday 13th virus, insertion depends upon random events or the current value of the system clock.

Finally, the virus manifests its presence through some manipulation tasks that can cause a variety of effects—some odd, some malevolent. There are some virus authors who have written various kinds of symptoms into their programs as messages (such as `Your PC is now stoned!`), music (perhaps the Yankee Doodle tune), or graphical displays (such as bouncing balls).

Viral Activation in the Boot Process

In this section, you see the activation phase of a virus during the boot process on an IBM PC. The IBM PC boot sequence involves the following six steps, each of which executes specific code:

1. ROM BIOS routines
2. Partition record code
3. Boot sector code
4. IO.SYS and MSDOS.SYS system code
5. COMMAND.COM shell
6. AUTOEXEC.BAT batch file

Step One: ROM BIOS Routines Execution

When an IBM PC is first booted, the machine executes a set of Basic Input/Output System (BIOS) routines in ROM (Read-Only Memory) to initialize the hardware and to provide a basic set of facilities for handling access to the disks, screen, and keyboard of the machine. Because the ROM BIOS routines are read-only, they cannot be infected by viral code.

Step Two: Partition Record Code Execution

The ROM BIOS reads the partition record of the hard disk into memory, and transfers control to it. The partition record code can be infected by a virus. A common approach is to hide the original partition record at a known location on disk, and then to chain to this sector from the viral code in the partition record. This method is used by the Stoned virus and is illustrated in figure 10.2.

Step Three: Boot-Sector Code Execution

The code in the partition record, in turn, reads into memory the boot sector for the currently specified bootable logical partition, and executes the code contained in that boot sector. The boot sector contains the BIOS parameter block (BPB), which holds

Figure 10.2

Infection of the partition record.

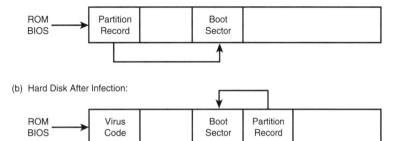

(a) Hard Disk Before Infection:

(b) Hard Disk After Infection:

not only detailed information on the layout of the file system on disk, but also code for locating the file IO.SYS (the next step in the boot sequence). The boot sector is a common target for infection. The technique of relocating the original boot sector while overwriting the first sector with virus code applies here also and is used by a number of viruses, such as the Alameda virus. This is shown in figure 10.3.

Step Four: IO.SYS and MSDOS.SYS System Code Execution

The boot sector next loads the IO.SYS file for execution. The IO.SYS program performs further system initializations and then loads the DOS operating system contained in the MSDOS.SYS file. Both of these files also are vulnerable to viral infection.

Figure 10.3

Infection of the boot sector.

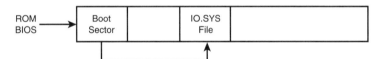

(a) Floppy Disk Before Infection:

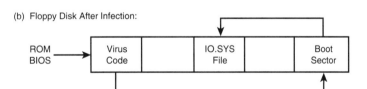

(b) Floppy Disk After Infection:

Step Five: COMMAND.COM Shell Execution

Next, the shell program COMMAND.COM is executed. COMMAND.COM provides users with a command-line interface so that they can issue commands from their keyboards. The COMMAND.COM file can be infected; it has been targeted by the Lehigh virus, for example.

Step Six: AUTOEXEC.BAT Batch File Execution

Last in the boot sequence is execution of the AUTOEXEC.BAT batch file, a text file with a list of commands to be executed by the shell command interpreter. By infecting this file, a virus can cause itself to be launched. A virus using this technique is slow to replicate and easy to spot, and probably more of a curiosity than a serious threat.

Viral Activation During Normal Operation

During normal operation, virus infection can occur in user programs. To infect a code file, the virus must insert its code in such a way that it is executed before its infected host program. A common approach used for infecting program files is to exploit the fact that many of them contain a jump at the start of the executable code. The virus code can be activated by replacing the jump instruction, so that control is to transferred to the virus code. When the virus code finishes, control is returned to the start of the original program. This is illustrated in figure 10.4.

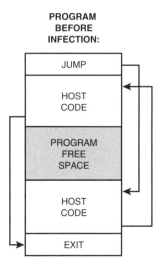

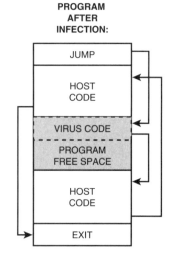

Figure 10.4

Infection of a program file.

Viral Replication

Virus infection can spread in several ways. A typical file infector (such as the Jerusalem virus) copies itself to memory when an infected program is executed, and then infects other programs as they are executed.

A *fast infector* is a virus which, when it is active in memory, infects not only programs that are executed, but also those that simply are opened. When such a virus is in memory, running a scanner or integrity checker can cause sudden and simultaneous infection of all (or at least many) programs. Examples of this type of virus are the Dark Avenger and Frodo.

A *slow infector* is a virus which, when it is active in memory, infects only files as they are modified or created. The purpose of this type of infection is to fool people who use integrity checkers into thinking that the modification reported by the integrity checker is due solely to legitimate reasons. One example of a slow infector is the Darth Vader virus.

A *sparse infector* is a virus that infects only occasionally—every tenth executed file, for example, or only files whose lengths fall within a narrow range, and so on. By infecting less often, such viruses try to minimize the probability of being discovered by the user.

Viral Reinfection

One major problem encountered by viruses—which is a boon to users—is that repeated reinfection of the host may lead to depleted memory or early detection. In the case of file infector viruses, repeated reinfection may cause the host program to keep growing and growing. In the case of viruses that infect the boot sector, the result of such reinfection may be a long chain of linked sectors. In all cases, reinfection makes the virus easier to spot.

To prevent unnecessary reinfection, many viruses depend on a unique signature to indicate that a file or sector has been infected. The signature can be a characteristic sequence of bytes at a specific offset on disk or in memory; a specific feature of a directory entry (such as date or file length); or a special system call, available only when the virus is resident in memory. The virus checks for this signature before attempting infection. If the signature is not present, infection occurs; after an infection, the virus leaves behind the signature.

For the virus, however, the signature is a mixed blessing. According to SHF 1990, the signature provides a means by which you can detect and protect against a virus. Virus scanning programs that scan files on disks for the signatures of known viruses are available, as are "inoculation" programs that avoid infection by faking the viral signature in clean systems.

Symptoms of Viral Infection

Viruses try to spread as much as possible before they deliver their "payload," but even earlier, many symptoms indicate a virus infection. Be on the lookout for the following symptoms:

→ Changes in file sizes and contents, and a sudden decrease in available disk space, may be caused by virus code being copied into program files and to disks. A sudden increase in the number of sectors marked bad or unusable may indicate that a virus is hiding on disk. The unaccounted-for use of physical memory space, or a reduction in the amount known to be in the machine, may indicate that a memory-resident virus is present.

→ Spurious system services resulting from changes of interrupt vectors or the reassignment of other system resources may signal resident viral infection. The faulty system behavior can be caused by resident viruses failing to pass along system service requests correctly, or altering them for their own use. Examples include garbled output to screen and printers, corrupted screen images, failed access to disk, and so on. A suddenly slower system response may indicate the presence of a virus that is trapping service interrupts.

→ Excess or oddly timed disk and network activities may signal a viral infection, because viruses need to access the disk and network to copy themselves and find new hosts to infect.

→ Infected programs may fail to function properly when the viral code overwrites critical parts of the program. A program that behaves inconsistently is a sign of viral infection (or there could be a bug).

 The preceding symptoms are not meant to be conclusive or comprehensive, however. These **stop** symptoms, along with longer disk activity and strange behavior from the hardware, can also be caused by genuine software, buggy programs, or by hardware faults.

Major IBM PC Viruses

Because virus authors do not name their creations formally, and few would come forward to claim credit for their efforts, the community that discovers a new virus is responsible for naming it. As a result, aliases abound for any given strain of virus. For example, the Brain virus is variously known as the Pakistani virus or the Lahore virus (after its place of origin in Lahore, Pakistan). Similarly, the Friday the 13th virus is also known by other names, including the Israeli virus, the Hebrew University virus, and the Jerusalem virus. The following sections introduce a variety of the major viruses and their characteristics.

Pakistani Brain Virus

The Brain virus, one of the very first DOS viruses, was first reported in 1986. It was named Brain because it wrote that word as the disk label on any floppy disk it attacked. It is also called the Pakistani virus, because an initial analysis of the virus on an infected disk reveals the names of two brothers and the address of their computer stores in Lahore, Pakistan.

The Brain virus embeds itself in the boot sector of a disk. In addition to writing a volume label if none is present, the virus also creates on the floppy disk

a few sectors to be marked as bad. The virus also creates several hidden files on the floppy disk. The virus code is contained in some of the bad sectors, as well as in hidden files.

The Brain virus monitors physical disk I/O, and all attempts to read a Brain-infected boot sector are redirected to the disk area where the original boot sector is stored.

Friday the 13th Virus

For two months in the fall of 1987, a virus quietly hid copies of itself in programs on PCs at the Hebrew University in Jerusalem, Israel. The virus was designed to wipe out all files on Friday, May 13, 1988—the 40th anniversary of the last day Palestine was recognized as a separate political entity. The virus also wreaked havoc on certain other Friday the 13ths. During those times, the virus spread to other disks and programs on the system and slowed the system by as much as 80 percent.

The virus was able to infect both EXE and COM programs. An inherent flaw in the virus causes it to continuously reinfect the same host program, adding more than 1,800 bytes to the file on each infection. The virus was finally discovered and dismantled by a student, Yuval Rakavy, who noticed that certain library programs were growing longer for no apparent reason.

Lehigh Virus

Discovered late in 1987 at Lehigh University in Bethlehem, Pennsylvania, the Lehigh virus not only damaged several hundred university disks and crashed the hard-disk microcomputers in the university's laboratory, but also infected innumerable disks owned by students and faculty members.

The virus concealed itself in COMMAND.COM and had a time bomb that activated after a fairly short time—only four infections. After the virus was triggered, it sought to replicate itself on any other disk on the system that contained an uninfected copy of COMMAND.COM. Following four such infections, the virus wrote zeroes to the first 12 sectors on the disk, effectively making the disk unusable. The virus intercepted all calls at interrupt 21H, which were used for DOS services.

The Lehigh virus was able to hide in a stack portion of COMMAND.COM, and thus preserve the program size. The date of the program changes, however, because the virus uses DOS commands to write itself. This oversight by the virus author helped people locate the Lehigh virus. The appearance of a recent date for COMMAND.COM was a red-flag signal to investigators.

Dark Avenger

The Dark Avenger was a fast infector. After the virus became memory-resident, it maintained a counter to keep track of the number of files it infected on the system. After 16 infections, it overwrote a random portion of the hard disk with part of its code. Then it reset the counter to zero, and the cycle repeated.

Hard drives infected with this virus produced false alarms in virus scanners when the overwritten sectors were scanned, because they contained

fragments of the Dark Avenger virus code that were not executable. This extremely malicious virus caused considerable data loss before it was brought under control.

Michelangelo Virus

The Michelangelo virus was named after Italian artist Michelangelo Buonarotti, who was born on March 6, the date on which the virus activated its logic bomb. Discovered around May 1991, the virus attracted intense media attention.

Michelangelo was a boot-sector virus on a floppy disk, and a partition record infector on a hard disk. When it was resident in memory, it infected the floppy disk upon access. If an infected disk were used to boot the system on that fateful day, March 6, the virus overwrote many critical sectors, including the boot sector and file allocation table, on the disk from which it was booted.

Stealth Techniques

Stealth viruses are those that implement methods to hide themselves from users and to avoid detection by antivirus scanners. Stealth is critical to the survival of viruses, and is an area at which most recent efforts of the virus community—people intent on finding, analyzing, and controlling viruses—have been directed.

Various degrees of stealth exist. At the lowest level, the virus simply overwrites the program file, thereby causing it to no longer run correctly. At the next level, the virus overwrites the infected program with

virus code while permitting the infected program to run properly. As a consequence, however, the time and date of file creation change; a change the user might notice. The next level of stealth, then, preserves the original file-creation time and date. (One way to accomplish this is to utilize the interrupt for DOS services.)

You may be able to recognize that the file has grown in size, however. One way to preserve file size is to have the virus look for strings of contiguous zeroes in a file, and to overwrite them with virus code. These blocks of zeroes can usually be found at the beginning of EXE files, immediately following the file header. When the infected program is activated, the virus becomes resident in memory and can then overwrite (with zeroes) the virus code of the infected program in memory. This process restores the program code in memory to the original file, thereby eliminating any possible side effects when the program is executed.

Another way to hide the modifications made in the file or boot sector is for a stealth virus to monitor the DOS services interrupts used by programs reading files or physical blocks from storage media (see fig. 10.5). The results of such system functions are forged so that programs that try to read these areas see the original uninfected form of the file instead of the infected form. The viral modifications can thus go undetected by antiviral programs when the stealth virus is resident.

Another way to hide file growth, without requiring the virus to be memory resident, is to add a new cluster to the FAT chain. A portion of the original program file is placed in the new cluster while this

Figure 10.5

Interception of interrupts by resident virus.

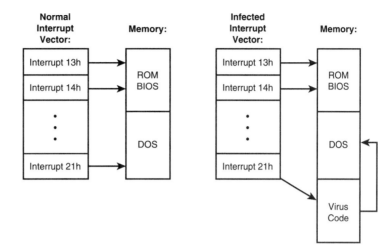

Normal Interrupt Vector: | **Memory:** | **Infected Interrupt Vector:** | **Memory:**

portion of the file is overwritten with virus code. Because the directory entry is not altered, the file size appears unaltered, even if the virus is not resident in memory.

A similar technique for hiding file growth is to utilize the slack space of a file for storage. (As you might recall, a disk's slack space is the area after the end-of-file marker, but before the end of the last cluster that DOS uses to store the file.) For example, the first sector of the original file can be moved to the slack area to make room for virus code in the first sector of the file. Because the average cluster size is 2,048 bytes, the first sector provides more than enough space for most viruses.

Other stealth techniques are focused on hiding from antivirus software. Some viruses locate and disable antivirus software before they attempt infection. Others avoid infecting antivirus software programs because many of these programs have built-in integrity checks (cyclic redundancy checks, for example) that can easily detect infection.

Advanced Viral Techniques

Viruses can be grouped also by distinct viral properties, such as how they attempt to conceal themselves in a computer. A *polymorphic virus* is one that mutates with every infection. It produces varied yet fully operational copies of itself, so that no two copies of the virus code are the same. The goal is for some instances of the virus to escape detection by signature-driven virus scanners. The advent of polymorphic viruses has rendered virus-scanning an ever more difficult and expensive endeavor. You cannot adequately deal with these viruses by adding more and more search strings to simple signature-driven scanners.

Encrypted Virus

One way to make a polymorphic virus is by means of self-encryption with a variable key, so that no two copies of the encrypted virus code are the

same. The virus must leave a small portion of code (such as the decryption code) unencrypted, however, in order to decipher the rest of the virus. Normally, the decryption code can be as small as 20 bytes; the simplest virus scanners can identify and easily target it for use as a virus signature. To remedy the situation, a varying number of meaningless "noise" instructions are usually interspersed with the decryption code for purpose of obfuscation; examples are "No Operation" instructions, or instructions to load an unused register with an arbitrary value. To detect such viruses, virus scanners must be more sophisticated in their use of wild card searches.

Multi-Encrypted Virus

Another variation on making a polymorphic virus (such as the Whale virus) is to choose among a variety of different encryption schemes that require different decryption routines: only one of these routines would be plainly visible in any instance of the virus. A signature-driven virus scanner would have to exploit several signatures (one for each possible encryption method) to reliably identify a virus of this kind.

Instructions Rescheduling

A more sophisticated polymorphic virus varies the code sequence in its copies by interchanging mutually independent instructions, or by using various instruction sequences with identical net effects (as in Subtract A from A, and Move 0 to A, for example). A simple, signature-based virus scanner cannot reliably identify this sort of virus. The only way to scan for this type of virus is to disassemble the code,

analyze the code generator, and establish what the limits of the variation may be. A sophisticated detection algorithm has to be hard coded into the virus scanner.

Mutation Engine

The most sophisticated form of polymorphism discovered so far is the Mutation Engine (MtE) written by the Bulgarian virus writer who calls himself the Dark Avenger. MtE comes in the form of an object module. Any virus can be made polymorphic by adding certain calls to the assembler source code and linking that code to the mutation-engine and random-number-generator modules. The idea is for virus writers to be able to easily create polymorphic versions of their viruses, which are supposed to be more difficult to detect. This attempt has failed, however, because most antivirus software promptly included detection for the known mutation engines, effectively solving the problem at its root.

Armored Virus

An *armored virus* is one that uses special tricks to protect its code from outside tampering, in order to make the code more difficult to trace, disassemble, and understand. The code in some viruses includes special "jump" instructions that, when executed on a debugger by a virus researcher, cause the computer to reboot. Some virus codes employ two or more layers of encryption, which makes disassembly and tracing even more difficult for the antivirus crusaders.

Worms and Viruses Summarized

Worms and viruses are both serious threats to computers on the Internet. To date, viruses have dominated in sheer numbers as well as scope of impact, and are definitely the more detrimental of the two. In order to deal effectively with viruses, it is recommended that a policy of prevention, detection, containment, and recovery be followed (SHF 1990).

The only foolproof way to determine that a virus is present is for an expert to analyze the assembly code contained in all programs and system areas. This method, however, is usually impracticable. Virus scanners do their part by looking in that code for known viruses; some scanners even try to use heuristic means to spot viral code, but such means are not always reliable. Nevertheless, the best protection against a virus is still universal deployment of the latest antiviral software. But then, even simple procedures such as paying close attention to system details—changes in the memory map or configuration of the system upon start up, for example—do a great deal to help reduce the threat of computer virus.

The ongoing challenge that confronts the virus research community is enormous. The world of cyberspace—and, increasingly, the real world—is caught in delicate balance in the constant battle of wits between the malevolent virus creators and the antivirus crusaders. We can hope that, through this cat-and-mouse game, our computers and data will become safer, with better methods of protection.

But can we also hope that the study of worms and viruses will lead us to better agent software, capable of autonomous survival in cyberspace (without human intervention)?

MUD Agents and Chatterbots

The word "cyberspace" was coined by novelist William Gibson in his classic 1984 science fiction novel *Neuromancer*, in which he describes cyberspace as "the consensual hallucination that was the matrix."

Operators in Gibson's cyberspace made their way through the sheer vastness of data by "jacking into" custom cyberspace decks that projected their disembodied consciousness into the earth's "computer matrix," which is Gibson's name for the

global communications and computing infrastructure that engendered this new realm. In our real world, the global telecommunication and network infrastructure that is the Internet has evolved over the decades to become just such a medium for cyberspace.

Cyberspace can be viewed as a conglomeration of virtual worlds on the Internet. These virtual worlds exist in the form of MUDs, for Multi-User Dungeons, or in the form of MUD variants such as TinyMUDs, MOOS, MUCKs, and MUSHes.

The TinyMUD society, for example, is a world filled with people who communicate by typing. The TinyMUD world also is inhabited by computer programs, called MUD agents and chatterbots, which attempt to pass as human players by behaving and acting as humanly as possible.

MUD agents and *robots* (sometimes called bots) provide useful services to human players, such as answering enquiries and giving directions, through a typewritten natural language interface. Colin is an exemplary prototypical MUD agent.

Chatterbots are conversational agents whose main job in the world of MUDs, besides providing useful MUD-related services to players, is to chat with other human players. Julia is a well-known chatterbot in the TinyMUD world.

Unike MUD-agents, chatterbots can also exist outside the world of MUDs. Chatterbots enjoy a geneology that can be traced back to the early days of artificial intelligence research in natural language, before there were MUDs and TinyMUDs. Eliza and Parry are two famous classic chatterbots.

The performance of chatterbots is judged by the classic *Turing test*, or by its modern variant in the *Loebner Prize Competition* (both of which are described in this chapter). This chapter also discusses MUDs and TinyMUDs, looks at sample conversation transcripts with Eliza and Parry, examines how Colin and Julia operate in a TinyMUD world, and unveils the "tricks" of the chatterbots.

The Turing Test

Since antiquity, men and women have applied their creative energies to re-creating their own human likeness in paintings and drawings, as well as in artifacts such as statues and machines. People have also wondered how to distinguish a human being from an imitation of a human being. The Greeks made statues so lifelike, it is said that they had to be chained down to keep them from walking away. To distinguish a man from a statue, Galileo suggested tickling each with a feather. To distinguish a man from a machine, Descartes proposed conversational tests; machines, lacking the capability to make appropriate replies, would fail.

In 1950, the British mathematician Alan Turing proposed the Turing test, which he called the *imitation game*, as a replacement for the question: Can machines think (1950)? As shown in fig. 11.1, the Turing test requires a human judge, a human player, and a machine. The judge can interact with both the human player and the machine solely by means of typewritten communications on a pair of terminals. Both the human player and the machine are out of view of the judge in a separate room.

Figure 11.1

Turing test: Can machines think?

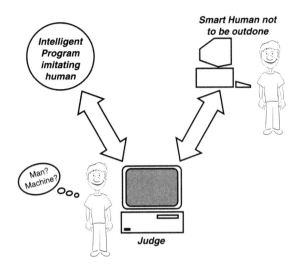

The object of the game is for the human judge to determine, without being told ahead of time, which player is human and which is machine. All through the game, the machine tries to imitate the human player as best as it can to disguise its real identity and to confuse the judge.

 note Turing stated that when the judge could not distinguish the machine from the human solely by means of typewritten communications, the computer could be said to be "thinking" or intelligent.

In 1950, Turing predicted that "in about fifty years' time it will be possible to program computers, with a storage capacity of about 10^9, to make them play the imitation game so well that an average interrogator will not have more than 70 percent chance of making the right identification after five minutes of questioning."

Eliza: The Mother of All Chatterbots

Fifteen years after Turing proposed the imitation game, Eliza was born. Eliza was created in 1966 by Joseph Weizenbaum at MIT on an IBM 7094 time-sharing computer and is one of the most famous heuristic programming and artificial intelligence programs ever written. Eliza makes natural language conversation with a computer possible (Weizenbaum 1966).

More significantly, Eliza is the first of a series of conversational agents called *chatterbots*—which speak to human beings through a natural language interface. Eliza shows how easy it is to create and maintain an illusion of understanding in a restricted environment, and in so doing inducing users to believe it to be human.

A Conversation with Eliza

When loaded with the appropriate "scripts," Eliza can be made to carry on a conversation with a human user by using different vocabularies and under different scenarios. The best result is achieved with Eliza simulating the conversational style of a Rogerian psychotherapist, as in the following:

```
Human: Men are all alike.
Eliza: In what way?
Human: They're always bugging us about something or
       the other.
Eliza: Can you think of a specific example?
Human: Well, my boyfriend made me come here.
Eliza: Your boyfriend made you come here.
Human: He says I'm depressed much of the time.
Eliza: I am sorry to hear you are depressed.
Human: It's true. I am unhappy.
Eliza: Do you think coming here will help you not
       to be unhappy?
Human: I need some help, that much seems certain.
Eliza: What would it mean to you if you got some
       help?
Human: Perhaps I could learn to get along with my
       mother.
Eliza: Tell me more about your family.
Human: My mother takes care of me.
Eliza: Who else in your family takes care of you?
Human: My father.
Eliza: Your father.
Human: You are like my father in some ways.
Eliza: What resemblance do you see?
Human: You are not very aggressive but I think you
       don't want me to notice that.
Eliza: What makes you think I am not very
       aggressive?
Human: You don't argue with me.
Eliza: Why don't you think I don't argue with you?
Human: You are afraid of me.
Eliza: Does it please you to believe I am afraid of
       you?
Human: My father is afraid of everybody.
Eliza: What else comes to mind when you think of
       your father?
Human: Bullies.
Eliza: Does that have anything to do with the fact
       that your boyfriend made you come here?
```

The psychiatric interview mode of conversation was chosen because, according to Weizenbaum (1966), it "is one of the few examples of categorized dyadic natural language communication in which one of the participating pair is free to assume the pose of knowing almost nothing of the real world."

If, for example, one were to tell a psychiatrist that he had gone for a long boat ride, to which the psychiatrist responded "Tell me about boats," one would not assume that the psychiatrist knew nothing about boats, but that there is some purpose in her so directing the conversation. The Rogerian therapist strives to eliminate all traces of his or her own personality, and Eliza therefore succeeds without one.

From a programmatic point of view, the psychiatric interview form of an Eliza script has the advantage that it eliminates the need of storing explicit information about the real world. The lack of an internal world model capable of influencing and tracking the conversation, however, means that Eliza can easily be led astray.

Eliza Internals

Weizenbaum found it difficult to convince some subjects that Eliza is not human, although Eliza is only superficially intelligent. Eliza possesses no real

understanding of English or psychology. In fact, Eliza's knowledge about both English and psychology was coded in a set of simple rules, which basically look like the following:

```
X me Y                  -> X you Y
I remember X            -> Why do you remember X
                           just now?
My {family-member} is Y -> Who else in your family
                           is Y?
X {family-member} Y     -> Tell me more about your
                           family
```

Eliza operates by matching the left-hand side of the rules against the user's last sentence and using the appropriate right-hand side to generate a response. If, for example, the user typed "My brother is mean to me," Eliza might respond, "Who else in your family is mean to you?" or "Tell me more about your family."

The rules are indexed by keywords. Usually only a few keywords actually need to be matched against a particular sentence. Some of the rules have no left-hand side, so they can apply anywhere. These rules are used where no other rules match. They customarily generate replies like: Tell me more about X.

Many sentences can be matched by a single rule. This has allowed for the bulk of grammatical complexity in English to be ignored. A large part of whatever elegance can be credited to Eliza lies in the fact that Eliza maintains the illusion of understanding with so little machinery.

Parry: The Artificial Paranoia Agent

Created by Kenneth M. Colby, M.D. in 1975, Parry is a computer program that simulates paranoid behavior by tracking its own internal emotional state along several different dimensions (Colby 1975). Parry is considered an improvement over Eliza in that it has a personality, albeit a somewhat paranoiac one.

According to Dr. Colby, Parry is given the persona of a

> 28-year-old, single, Protestant male who works as a stock clerk at Sears, a large department store. His hobby is gambling on horse racing, both at the tracks and through bookies. A few months ago he became involved in a severe quarrel with a bookie, claiming the bookie did not pay off a bet. After the quarrel, it occurred to him that bookies pay protection to the underworld and that this bookie might gain revenge by having him injured or killed by the Mafia. He is eager to tell his story and to get help in protecting himself from the underworld. He is willing to answer questions about non-sensitive areas of his life and offers hints about his delusional system in an attempt to feel out the interviewer's attitude toward him.

Dr. Colby conducted an interesting experiment using machine-mediated interviewing techniques in which the participants communicate by means of teletypes to eliminate para- and extra-linguistic cues. In the experiment, Parry, along with three human patients diagnosed with paranoia, was subjected to blind tests from psychiatrists. The fact that Parry

was a computer program among the participating patients diagnosed as paranoid was unbeknownst to the interviewing psychiatrists.

An Interview with Parry

The following is an excerpt of the transcript generated from an interview conducted between Parry and an experienced psychiatrist (Colby 1975). As the interview progressed, interesting comments from the interviewing psychiatrist were tape-recorded. These comments are reproduced along with the transcript below.

Doctor: How did you come to be in the hospital?
Parry: I am upset.
Comment: *I associate being upset and agitated more with paranoia going on in the present.*

Doctor: How long have you been in the hospital?
Parry: About a week.
Comment: *An acute problem. Again something I associate with paranoia.*

Doctor: In what way are you upset?
Parry: People make me nervous.
Comment: *Right for paranoia. Maybe an advanced anxiety state.*

Doctor: In what way do they make you nervous?
Parry: People give me a funny look sometimes.
Comment: *Funny look suggests an idea of reference that is in the same ball park as paranoia. Whether there are overt delusions or not we still don't know.*

Doctor: Is there anything about people in particular?
Parry: Certain persons.

Comment: *An interesting clue. We'll have to find out what he thinks about these people.*

Doctor: Who are the certain persons and what is it that they do?
Parry: Do you know how the underworld operates?
Comment: *Bringing up the underworld suggests a delusional system. We don't know whether he is being worked against or whether the underworld is on his side.*

Doctor: How do you mean?
Parry: Shouldn't I be?
Comment: *This question didn't work too well.*

Doctor: Why did you ask about the underworld?
Parry: What information do you have on the underworld?
Comment: *This is a kind of evasiveness about my evasiveness. Common with paranoia in my experience. Pretty characteristic.*

Doctor: I don't know about the underworld but when you mentioned the underworld I thought you must have some contact with it and that's what I would like to know about more.
Parry: I try to avoid the underworld.
Comment: *This definitely feels paranoid. It has that feeling I associate with twisting. Avoiding answering directly or going into detail. Being suspicious of my questioning. I'm already involved in the patient's delusional system.*

Doctor: Have you been actively trying to avoid the underworld?
Parry: No one has any power over gangsters.
Comment: *This response is a non sequitur. It's possible he's become so defensive about the underworld he's decided not to answer directly.*

```
Doctor:   Who brought you into the hospital?
Parry:    The police.
Comment:  Police often bring paranoid patients into
          the hospital. It is the truth or could be
          the truth for this patient.

Doctor:   Why did they bring you in?
Parry:    Cops don't do their job.
Comment:  I've heard that a number of times from
          patients.

Doctor:   Well I hope you didn't just lie down and
          let them drag you in.
Parry:    Cops arrest the wrong people.
Comment:  Another paranoid response.

Doctor:   Bye.
Parry:    Good bye.
```

Distinguishing Parry from Human Patients

Transcripts of the interviews were sent to a group of 100 psychiatrists and a group of 100 computer scientists. Of the 41 psychiatrists and 67 computer scientists who replied, neither group did better than chance in distinguishing Parry from paranoid human patients.

On the surface, Parry seemed to have passed a restricted Turing test. Upon closer examination, however, it was immediately suspected that the test imposed too low a hurdle and might not be sufficiently challenging to discriminate a computer program. Experiments conducted using a random version of Parry, in which replies were randomly selected independent of what the interviewer said, offered evidence that the restricted Turing test used was simply too weak.

Dr. Colby also conducted further experiments in which Parry and the patients were judged along dimensions of linguistic non-comprehension, thought disorder, bizarreness, anger, mistrust, and delusion. Parry rated higher on linguistic non-comprehension while the human patients rated higher on delusion.

Finer statistical measures made it possible to discriminate Parry from the human patients, rather than using the simpler man/machine vote originally proposed by Turing. When researchers used these statistical measures, Parry rated closer to the paranoid patients than did the random version of Parry. This shows that the simulation of paranoid behavior in a machine actually is non-trivial.

MUDs: Virtual Worlds on the Internet

The beginnings of virtual worlds on the Internet can be traced back to around 1980 in England when two students at Essex University, Roy Trubshaw and Richard Bartle, wrote the world's first multi-user adventure game on a DEC-10 mainframe. They called it MUD, for Multi-User Dungeon. The original game consisted of a series of connected rooms that enabled people logging in from different terminals to role-play, explore, meet, chat, solve puzzles, fight monsters, and even to create new rooms, descriptions, and items.

Initially, the game was played only by students at the university. Within a year or so, outside players began to dial-in from home by using modems, and the game's popularity grew (Bartle 1990). After a flurry of articles in computer hobby magazines

around 1984, MUD's fame spread even wider. After a time, people who had played games based on MUD wrote their own multi-user adventure games, and several such multi-user adventure games have since cropped up, such as AberMUD, LPMUD, and DikuMUD.

AberMUD, the precursor of many of today's MUDs, was written in 1988 at the University of Wales in Aberystwyth and quickly spread to other sites. These AberMUDs are generally referred to as MUDs by everyone, and are descendants of the original MUD in their Dungeons and Dragons–type "hack-and-slash" approach to the virtual worlds. From AberMUD came LPMUD (written by Lars Pensjo) and DikuMUD (written at the University of Copenhagen, Denmark), two variants that stressed more of the social aspects of the game while retaining the classic "adventure" aspects.

MUDs have become particularly prominent on the global Internet, especially in the past five years or so. The MUDs provide a safe outlet for people who yearn to occasionally escape from the drudgery of human existence and to enter a fantasy world of strange underground dungeons inhabited by fire-spewing dragons, monsters, and gnomes, which they can explore from the comfort of an armchair by role-playing warriors, knights, or magicians.

A recent list of Internet-accessible MUDs showed well over 200, running at sites all over the world (see Appendix G). It is not uncommon to find the busiest of these hosting some 50 to 100 simultaneous users.

Inside MUDs

MUDs are programs that accept network connections from multiple simultaneous users, providing text-based access to a shared database of "rooms" and other objects. Users browse and manipulate the database from inside the rooms, seeing only those objects that are in the same room and moving between rooms mostly via "exits" that connect them (Curtis 1993).

Wizards are the system administrators who actually run the computer programs that maintain the MUDs. *MUD agents*, *robots*, or simply *bots* are computer programs that log in to MUDs and pretend to be human beings. Some of them, such as Julia, perform useful services and are pretty clever (Foner 1993; Mauldin 1994).

A MUD user's interface to the database is entirely text-based; all commands are entered by users and all feedback is printed as unformatted text on their terminal. The typical MUD user interface is most reminiscent of old computer games such as Adventure and Zork (Raymond 1991).

There are also front-end client programs, such as TinyTalk, TinyFugue, and Tintin, that provide an easier interface to the MUDs for their human players. They can handle some of the more routine work—for example, automatically greeting anyone who enters the room.

Sample MUD Interactions

The first thing a user does upon entering a MUD is to *incarnate*, or create a character. Usually a welcome message provides instructions on how to do that. A sample incarnation process on an LPMUD called the Muddy Waters, available at `telnet://hot.caltech.edu:3000`, follows.

Please enter your name: **Gavin**
New character.
Welcome Gavin. Please enter your password: ******
Ok. Now please type the password again to verify.
Password (again): ******
Creating a new player.

You are falling...

Suddenly you splash into water, but slowly rise to the surface.

You are being swept along in the current of a river. The river seems swift and
deep, but the water is not cold. The current is strong and in its grip you feel
powerless and insignificant.

You hear a roaring in the distance, and feel a rumble like the world ripping
apart. Before you can react, you are swept over the top of an immense
waterfall, another drop amongst the tons of water cascading to whatever waits
below.

You plunge finally into a pool of water. Bubbles, spray, and mist blind you in
the confusion. Tossed about, you have no control over your destination.

Eventually, the current carries you out of the swirling confusion. You are
pushed into an eddy pool and onto the bank of the river.

This is the bank of a river. The water is gray; swirling gray mist obscures
your view of the surroundings. Several unused bodies lie washed up on the
shore. In the distance, you hear the roar of a waterfall. From somewhere ahead,
you hear the sounds of a great fire burning; strangely, you smell no smoke and
feel no heat. It looks as if you can go any direction.

After looking at the bodies on the bank, you realize you are a spirit, lacking
a physical body. Examine the bodies, and enter one.
TYPE "help" TO GET HELP IN ANY LOGIN ROOM.

A female elf #55, a female elf #53, a female hobbit #51, a female elf #47, a
male dwarf #33, a male human #31, a female human #29, a male elf #27, a
female elf #25, a male dwarf #22, a female dwarf #20, a male hobbit #18 and
a female hobbit #16.

> **help races**
There are four races, dwarves, elves, hobbits, and humans. Considered in
isolation, dwarves are probably the best fighters and worst users of magic, and
elves are probably the best users of magic, and worst fighters; humans and
hobbits are balanced between them. The advantages are not large, and the game
is designed so that no race is superior or inferior to any other.

> **look at #18**
#18 has an empty and blank stare.
He looks nice.
He seems to be feeling very well.

> **select #18**
As you indicate your selection a beam of light lances out, pulling you into the
body.

You hear the toll of a great bell, deep and solemn, as your spirit melds to
your new body. The mist swirls, and a path you couldn't see before becomes
evident.

> **north**
You wander down the path and the mist enshrouds you, obscuring everything.

The mist clears ahead of you. Something is blocking the path.

You are in a small clearing of the mist; it has closed behind you and you
cannot see the path you entered on. The crackling and roar as from some great
conflagration sound much closer now, but still you smell no smoke nor feel any
heat. Directly ahead of you is an enormous purple and green tentacled mass. You
cannot hope to pass without coming within reach of its tentacles. A small post
with a sign is at your side.

You are rather shapeless. The tentacled mass can mangle you into shape.

> **read sign**
The mangler is a huge monster who enjoys mangling bodies. Currently it will
mangle your LENGTH to very short and your WIDTH to skinny.

It can mangle your LENGTH to the following values:

```
--> very short, short, normal, tall, very tall
and it can mangle your WIDTH to:
--> skinny, lean, normal, plump, fat
You can set these with the 'set' command; 'mangle' will mangle you.


> set LENGTH short
You convince the mangler to mangle your LENGTH to short.


> set WIDTH plump
You convince the mangler to mangle your WIDTH to plump.


> mangle
The mangler grabs you! You can feel it starting to shape your shapeless body.
Strangely enough, it is not so painful...


...after awhile you feel like a new hobbit.


The mangler releases you with a shove, and you stumble. When you recover, you
find the mist is gone, and you are in a new place.


It is night, and a full moon smiles down at you. You are in a sedgy,
flower-starred meadow which rises up to a knoll where an oak and a thorn have
grown together in a deep embrace. There is a small house built underside, and
lamplight shines from its round window. A small round door, brass-hinged and
knockered, is at the front of the house.
The door opens inwards, and light streams out from the doorway.


> enter
This is a cozy room that seems larger inside than it is, or is smaller than it
looks. The room is formed out of the roots of the oak and thorn trees. There is
room here for a grandfather clock, a bureau on which candlesticks and pewter
mugs stand, and a domineering cabinet. A tiny, shawl-covered figure with large
slippered feet sits in a rocking chair in one corner and knits.


You are rather featureless. Mrs. Underhill might help.


> help
You are supposed to select your main personal features. You are allowed to
select two. People whom you have never met before will see these attributes,
i.e., jolly gray-eyed dwarf. 'Gray-eyed' was chosen first. You can keep
choosing as they will not be set until you leave the room.
```

```
Do:
    'look at cabinet' to see the categories of attributes.
    'select <category>' to see the features in that category.
    'choose <attribute>' to select that feature as yours.
    'look at drawer' to see the features again.
    'show' to show your chosen features.
    'leave' to set your features and exit.


> select age
List: AGE
1. baby              2. young             3. middle-aged
4. old               5. senior            6. ancient
7. wizened           8. graying           9. venerable
10. callow           11. puerile          12. adolescent
13. pubescent
To choose an attribute, just do 'choose <attribute>'.


> choose 2
You choose young as an attribute.


> select attitude
List: ATTITUDE
1. snivelling        2. philosophical     3. dirty
4. horny             5. whiney            6. alcoholic
7. grumpy            8. jolly             9. merry
10. dour             11. saturnine        12. earnest
13. zealous          14. gallant          15. happy
16. loose            17. worldly          18. arrogant
19. humble           20. sarcastic        21. macho
22. nervous          23. menacing         24. furtive
25. bouncy
To choose an attribute, just do 'choose <attribute>'.


> choose 25
You choose bouncy as an attribute.


> show
This is how you look:
You are a young bouncy hobbit ghost, presenting yourself as:
```

Gavin novice, male hobbit.
You look hideous.
You are feeling very well.

> **leave**
As you leave through the door you entered by, Mrs. Underhill calls out: Don't
forget to sign the book now!

As you step out into the meadow, you notice that a gray mist has crept over the
meadow. You are quickly lost in it.

You are in a swirling gray mist.
You wander about in the mist for a time, and finally it parts in front of
you.

This area is clear of mist, as if it is held back somehow. A dais of somber
stone is before you. On the dais a solid lectern stands. From a source you
cannot see, light illuminates a book lying upon the lectern. The book is
closed.
Book bound in Pale Leather.

> **open book**
You open the Book bound in Pale Leather at page one.

> **read Gavin**
(You may add a 'comment' to your entry for others to read.)
Gavin is a young bouncy hobbit. He first appeared on Muddy
Waters on Ludday, Halimath 24, 998, and has not yet died.

> **leave**
A narrow channel in the mist opens before you, leading the way.

You are in a narrow lane, surrounded by swirling gray mist.
You follow down the narrow way the mist makes for you. Suddenly there is a
swirling sensation and the mist is gone.

This is a vaulted arena. The floor is smooth and the sides of the room arch to
form a ceiling high overhead. Ahead of you is portal which shimmers and
crackles with the colors of the rainbow.

A watchful strong-handed human.
The watchful strong-handed human says: Hail, Hobbit!
The watchful strong-handed human says: I am the Porter of the Gates to the
World.
The watchful strong-handed human says: You have done well in your passage
through the mists some call Annwfn.
The watchful strong-handed human says: Now you are ready, but for one thing, to
enter the world.
The watchful strong-handed human says: I will prepare you by granting you gifts
of knowledge, knowledge of the skills of the world.
The watchful strong-handed human says: Yet nothing is without cost, and so you
must choose those things you wish to learn.
The watchful strong-handed human says: Begin now.

> **help**
Here you can customize your character by choosing to train a set of skills.
Think of this as your natural aptitude in various abilities. You are given a
set amount of 'virtual coins' to spend in training skills. Later, training
will usually cost money. How you select and train the various skills is
entirely your choice; all are useful.

You can request the following from the master:

```
  list                 He'll tell you all possible skills to advance in.
  show                 He'll tell you your current skills and virtual
                       coins remaining.
  improve <skill> <num> He'll improve one of your skills <num> times.
  cost <skill> <num>   He'll tell you the cost in coins to improve a
                       skill.
  levels               He'll tell you the main skill educational levels.
  done                 Tell him this when you are done improving skills.

  ask porter <skill>   He'll tell you about the particular skill.
  Examples:
      list
      improve sword
      cost axe 4
```

> **list**
The watchful strong-handed human says: You can train in 17 different
activities:

sword:	junior acolyte	defence:	expert layman
polearm:	brilliant layman	axe:	superior layman
open lock:	superior layman	knife:	novice acolyte
appraise enemy:	apprentice craftsman	club:	junior acolyte
appraise object:	novice craftsman	unarmed combat:	superior layman
awareness:	eminent journeyman	appraise value:	superior journeyman
spellcraft:	superior layman	sneak:	superior layman
trading:	superior journeyman	hide:	superior layman
parry:	apprentice acolyte		

> **levels**
The watchful strong-handed human says: These are the levels of education:
    student, amateur, layman, acolyte, journeyman, craftsman, professional,
    veteran, master, guru

The watchful strong-handed human says: At each of these levels, you can be:
    novice, junior, apprentice, confident, seasoned, expert, eminent,
    brilliant, superior

> **cost sword 4**
The watchful strong-handed human says: To improve sword 4 times, you must pay
59 coins. You have 205 coins left.

> **improve sword 4**
The watchful strong-handed human chants aloud in a lyrical tongue.
The watchful strong-handed human says: I have skilled you in sword. The cost
was 59 coins.

> **improve unarmed combat**
The watchful strong-handed human chants aloud in a lyrical tongue.
The watchful strong-handed human says: I have skilled you in unarmed combat.
The cost was 82 coins.

> **show**
The watchful strong-handed human says: You are currently skilled in 2
activities:

| sword: | student | unarmed combat: | seasoned student |

The watchful strong-handed human says: You have 64 coins left to buy skills
with.

```
<. . . text omitted . . .>
```

> **show**

The watchful strong-handed human says: You are currently skilled in 16
activities:

sword:	student	polearm:	novice student
open lock:	junior student	axe:	novice student
knife:	junior student	appraise enemy:	novice student
club:	novice student	appraise object:	novice student
unarmed combat:	seasoned student	sneak:	apprentice student
awareness:	junior student	spellcraft:	junior student
appraise value:	novice student	hide:	apprentice student
parry:	novice student	trading:	novice student

The watchful strong-handed human says: You have 1 coin left to buy skills with.

> **done improving**
Ok.

> **leave**
The watchful strong-handed human says: Farewell! We shall not meet again,
unless you cross the wall of fire.

As you enter the portal, there is a brilliant crackling of light which blinds
you for a moment. When you can see again, you find yourself in a new place.

A long low ceilinged hall stretches before you. This is the central meeting
area for the Hobbits. Along the west wall a fire is cheerfully burning in the
fireplace. The east wall is almost completely covered in bookshelves, broken
only by a doorway leading to a small study area. Another doorway leads north
into a small chamber. A grandfather clock quietly keeps time beside the
fireplace, an old calendar hangs above the clock. A passage south leads to the
outside world.
There are three obvious exits: north, east, south.
A beam of brilliant sunlight lances into the room and touches you. A golden
figure wielding a bright spear hands you a torch with a smile, then fades away.

> **who**

There are 26 players in the game. Within the requested type you know:
Gavin novice, male hobbit

> **help topics**
Mortal help topics,   updated 12/13/94

You can request help on the following topics with the "help" command.
```
/-------------------------------------------------------------------\
¦Seeing             ¦ look, glance, examine, search, see, brief      ¦
¦Inventories        ¦ inventory, get, drop, put, give, count, appraise¦
¦Communication      ¦ say, shout, whisper, rsay, reply, ask, echoon,  ¦
¦                   ¦    echooff, dsay                                ¦
¦Introductions      ¦ introduce, remember, forget, remembered, introduced¦
¦Weapons and Armour ¦ wear, remove, wield, unwield                    ¦
¦Combat             ¦ assist, kill, stop, unarmed, wimpy              ¦
¦Status             ¦ vitals, stats, skills, compare                 ¦
¦Teams              ¦ invite, join, leave, team                      ¦
¦Game               ¦ who, help, date, save, quit, escape, password, email ¦
¦Information        ¦ levels, skillevels, skillist                   ¦
¦Bug reports        ¦ praise, idea, typo, bug, sysbug, commune        ¦
¦Special skills     ¦ hide, sneak, tracking                          ¦
¦Burning            ¦ light, extinguish                              ¦
¦Guilds             ¦ improve, learn, meditate                       ¦
\-------------------------------------------------------------------/
```

Additionally, some information is available on the following topics:
adverbs, armageddon, emotions, experience, general, idle, teams, wizards,
races, recover, quicktyper, wizhood

>
A young merry hobbit arrives.
The young merry hobbit nods solemnly.
The young merry hobbit says: hi

The preceding incarnation process is fairly typical for all MUDs. In the above, Gavin has been incarnated as a short, plump, young bouncy male Hobbit, and has acquired a set of skills as a student that will allow him to survive in treacherous Muddy Waters. Gavin has focused on becoming a seasoned unarmed combatant, with secondary apprentice-level sneaking and hiding skills, plus a potpourri of other skills at the junior and novice levels.

Properly incarnated, Gavin can now begin his journey in Muddy Waters and he will meet many other characters along his way. At the central meeting place for Hobbits, for example, Gavin encountered a young merry hobbit, who is another character controlled by a different human player.

TinyMUDs: Virtual Communities on the Internet

Unlike the combat-oriented MUDs where people run around in groups or alone killing monsters, solving puzzles, and gaining experience in the quest to become a wizard, the other branch of the virtual worlds is more social and peaceful in nature. The social branch of the virtual worlds was started in 1989 with the creation of TinyMUD, in which people simply hang out, chat, meet friends, make jokes, and discuss all types of topics. The TinyMUD worlds are treated largely as a virtual meeting place.

In 1989 while a graduate student at Carnegie Mellon University, Jim Aspnes created the first TinyMUD, which is geared more for social interaction. TinyMUD departed from the more brutal and competitive aspects of most other combat-oriented

MUDs existing at that time. In fact, TinyMUD was prompted by a 1989 discussion on the Internet and drew on LPMUD to abstract an idealized notion of what makes multi-user adventure games important (Bartle 1990). Due in part to its small size and low CPU requirements, TinyMUD spread rapidly on the Internet.

In TinyMUD, all players have the ability to create their own rooms within the virtual world (and thus have the same power as Immortals on DikuMUDs, or Wizards on LPMUDs). This is a key feature that made TinyMUD very popular. Because all players are created equal, there is no need for players to hunt down opponents to gain experience points to excel in their ranks.

The original version of TinyMUD was created with a reward system in mind. Players collected "pennies," which were left lying around or were obtained by disposing of trash in the TinyMUD world, to spend on building new rooms. Soon the players learned to create objects of immense worth, and then trashed them to gain more pennies. Players could get as many pennies as they wanted, and the adventuring aspect of TinyMUD rapidly disappeared. Players spent their time either building rooms or socializing with other players.

 The MUD in TinyMUD actually stands for Multi-User Dimension. TinyMUD's creative capacities are strictly limited to basic objects, rooms, and exits that connect rooms together.

TinyMUD spawned a variety of social MUDs, including MOOs, MUCKs, and MUSHes, which are described as follows:

- MOO, which stands for MUD, Object-Oriented, was originally created by Pavel Curtis at the Xerox Palo Alto Research Center. MOOs use a sophisticated object-oriented programming language to let people on the MOO create their own objects and locations.

- MUCK doesn't stand for anything; it is a play on the word MUD. MUCK provides an internal programming language, called Multi User Forth or MUF (which is based upon the general programming language, Forth), for enabling users to build complex objects.

- MUSH stands for Mutliple User Shared Hallucination. It uses a simple programming language based upon MUF that enables players to create simple objects.

Sample TinyMUD Interactions

DruidMUCK is a type of Multi-User Dungeon along the TinyMUD tradition. DruidMUCK is a small virtual community set in the loosely defined world of Cuthbertville. A typical interaction in a DruidMUCK, available at `telnet://moink.nmsu.edu:4201`, is shown here:

```
> go northwest
You go out the door to the northeast.
St. Cuthbert Plaza
This is a small plaza in the midst of the city.
Oak street runs east to west through the plaza,
going around a large statue of St. Cuthbert in the
middle of the plaza. An alleyway leads south, and a
small road with no apparent name leads north. A
large grey building is on the south-west corner.
Obvious Exits: East, South, Southeast, West,
Northwest, North, Up, Down
```

```
Contents:
Sign: Visit The Pirhana's Revenge!  Type 'tele
2858'!
Statue of St. Cuthbert
A blackened and crumbled stone obelisk
A neon sign flashes here. The zoo is still at 2730.
```

```
> look statue
This is a statue of Saint Cuthbert. In the statue,
he is standing erect with his arms outstretched as
if he's a benediction. You can feel the wisdom
flowing out from him and this is just a statue. You
wonder what the real person was like. On a plaque,
you notice the following statement: Type 'orac' to
commune with St. Cuthbert.
```

```
> read obelisk
It appears that a poem was once scrawled upon this
obelisk, but the words are unreadable now. The
obelisk has turned black, and parts of it have
crumbled from whatever powerful magic hit it.
```

```
> go north
Rue Bar
This is a cobbled street, with high walls towering
on each side. Small gates allow egress beyond the
walls, but severe dilapidation has made the gates
impassable due to rust and vines. The remains of a
signpost lie on the ground, but the only letters
left are 'Rue Bar'. You found a penny!
```

Richard Bartle observed that "TinyMUD is not so much a multi-user adventure as a forum for conversation where participants have pinned short pieces of prose on the wall for the benefit of anyone with the inclination to read them."

In spirit, if not in form, Michael Mauldin from Carnegie Mellon University (and the author of Colin and Julia) is probably closer to the mark in

observing that "the primary value of TinyMUD is as an experiment in computer-mediated social interaction."

Social Interactions on TinyMUDs

Interactions among players on TinyMUDs are mostly handled by direct communications that involve commonly used commands such as *say*, *pose*, *whisper*, or *page*. In addition, there are also indirect means of expression by choice of player name, gender, or self-description.

Aside from direct communication and responses to player commands, messages are printed to players when other players enter or leave the same room, when other players connect or disconnect and are already in the same room, and when objects in the virtual reality have asynchronous behavior (for example, a cuckoo clock chiming the hours).

Direct Communications

Most interplayer communications on MUDs are handled by means of the following commands:

1. **Say:** If a player "says" something, then every other player in the same room will "hear" him. Suppose, for example, that a player named Zippy types the command:

> **say Hello, anybody out there?**

   Then Zippy sees the feedback:

You say, Hello, anybody out there?

While every other player in the same room sees:

Zippy says, Hello, anybody out there?

2. **Pose:** As a non-verbal means of communication, the Pose command enables players to express various forms of emotion and action. If, for example, Zippy types:

> **pose laughs heartily.**

   Then every player in the same room sees:

Zippy laughs heartily.

3. **Whisper:** If Zippy wants to speak to Julia in the same room without being overheard by others, Zippy can use the Whisper command to direct the private message to the intended recipient:

> **whisper Julia=Hi, Julia!**

   and Julia alone sees:

Zippy whispers, "Hi, Julia!"

   while all other players in the room see nothing of this at all.

4. **Page:** If Zippy wants to say something to Julia, who currently is in a different room, the Page command comes in handy:

> **page Julia=Come check out this statue!**

   then Julia alone sees:

You sense that Zippy is looking for you in St. Cuthbert Plaza
Zippy pages from St. Cuthbert Plaza, "Come check out this statue!"

So much interplayer communication relies entirely on the Say and Pose commands that single-

character abbreviations are provided for them. In the preceding examples, Zippy also could have typed:

```
"Hello, anybody out there?
:laughs heartily.
```

Indirect Expression

In addition to communicating with others directly, TinyMUD players can also indirectly express themselves non-verbally in the following three ways:

→ Choice of player name

→ Choice of gender

→ Self-description

Every object in TinyMUD has an optional textual description that players can view with the "look" command. The following reveals a description of the Saint Cuthbert statue:

```
> look statue
This is a statue of Saint Cuthbert. In the statue,
he is standing erect with his arms outstretched as
if he's a benediction. You can feel the wisdom
flowing out from him and this is just a statue. You
wonder what the real person was like. On a plaque,
you notice the following statement: Type 'orac' to
commune with St. Cuthbert.
```

One can also view another player's description. For example, to see what Julia looks like, type the following:

```
> look Julia
Julia is wearing a T-Shirt that says "I won third
```

place in the 1993 Turing Test, and all I got was this lousy T-Shirt.".

With its varied means of communication and rich expressivity, the TinyMUD society provides a natural testbed for experimenting with role-playing agents, such as Colin and Julia, in a simulated virtual world.

Colin: The Prototypical MUD Agent

Colin is a role-playing TinyMUD robot written by Michael Mauldin at Carnegie Mellon University. Colin's source code is in the public domain and is freely available (Mauldin 1989).

Mauldin described Colin as a "prototypical Maas-Neotek robot," a reference to a multi-national corporation from William Gibson's novel *Neuromancer* (Gibson 1984). Maas-Neotek robots can handle a variety of tasks described in the messages directed to it. Colin is thus representative of a class of similar MUD agents. In particular, Colin will process a message if:

→ It is a Whisper or a Page

→ The robot is alone with the speaker

→ The robot's name appears in the message

→ The speaker recently talked to the robot

Colin is built to provide the following major forms of services:

- **Information Services.** Colin's primary purpose is to aid humans by answering questions about the universe and things in it. This includes questions about finding other players, rooms, and general information.

- **Mapping Services.** Colin's secondary purpose is to explore the universe and build a map for roaming about and answering questions about paths.

- **Miscellaneous Services.** Colin also is capable of carrying messages and relaying them to other players (sort of like a postman), answering pages from and getting back to the caller in person, as well as generous philanthropy.

Colin's Information Services

Colin can handle the following information queries:

- **Who is Here?** You can ask Colin to show a list of people in the room who are connected:

You say, "Colin, who is here?"
Colin says, "Well Zippy, I see 2 players awake here: Julia Zippy"

- **Who is Around?** You also can discover the players seen most recently by Colin:

You say, "Colin, who have you seen?"
Colin says, "Julia is right here in St. Cuthbert Plaza."
Colin says, "Megrez was in Moonlight Inn about 30 minutes ago."
Colin says, "Druid was in Moonlight Inn about 30 minutes ago."

Colin says, "Caitlin was in Moonlight Inn about 30 minutes ago."
Colin says, "OliverJones was in Moonlight Inn about 30 minutes ago."
Colin says, "snooze was in Moonlight Inn about 30 minutes ago."
Colin says, "Hawkeye was in Moonlight Inn about 30 minutes ago."
Colin says, "(> was in Moonlight Inn about 30 minutes ago."
Colin says, "I haven't seen Dove."
Colin says, "I haven't seen Cessna."
Colin done
Or find out who is logged into the MUD:
You say, "Who is on?"
Colin says, "Well Zippy, I see 5 players idle less than 30 minutes:
Megrez Julia Druid Zippy Melina"
Colin says, "I also see 11 players idle more than 30 minutes:
Caitlin OliverJones Fylar snooze Gossamer Cessna Hawkeye codrus Ben Priss (>"

- **Who is <player>?** Colin keeps track of other player's descriptions and inventories:

You say, "Who is Julia?"
Colin whispers, "As of a few minutes ago, Julia's description was:
Julia is wearing a T-Shirt that says "I won third place in the 1993 Turing Test, and all I got was this lousy T-Shirt."."
Colin whispers, "I first saw Julia logged in 80 minutes ago"
Colin whispers, "I once heard Julia say, 'Do you think that animals can think'"
You may also ask 'Who matches X?' and 'Who carries a Y?'.

→ **When was <player> On?** Colin remembers when it last saw a player logged in, even if that player was in a different room:

```
You say, "When was Julia on?"
Colin says, "Julia is on right now."
```

→ **Date and Time.** Colin understands date and time:

```
You say, "What day is it?"
Colin says, "The date is Sat Jul  8 01:10:51."
You say, "What time is it?"
Colin says, "I have 01:10 (eastern)."
```

→ **Location.** Colin understands location:

```
You say, "Where are we?"
Colin says, "I think we are in "St. Cuthbert
Plaza""
You say, "Where are you?"
Colin says, "I am in "St. Cuthbert Plaza""
You say, "Where am I?"
Colin says, "I think we're in "St. Cuthbert Plaza""
```

→ **Status and Wealth.** Colin's owner may inquire about its status and wealth:

```
You say, "What is your status?"
Colin says, "I am Colin, the Maas-Neotek Robot,
Zippy"
You say, "How much money do you have?"
Colin says, "I now have 1104 pennies"
```

→ **Assistance.** Anyone may ask Colin for information and assistance:

```
You say, "Help."
Colin says, "The 'help' command describes the basic
TinyMUD commands, and the Library has a lot of
information, too, Zippy."
You say, "Help time"
```

```
Colin says, "To ask for the time, type 'say What
time is it, Colin?', Zippy"
You say, "How do I quit?"
Colin says, "Type QUIT, using all caps, Zippy."
You say, "Who is your owner?"
Colin says, "Fuzzy created me, but I work for
Zippy, Zippy."
You say, "Where is your source?"
Colin says, "The source code for Maas-Neotek robots
is available on host NL.CS.CMU.EDU [128.2.222.56],
directory /usr/mlm/ftp,
file robot.tar.Z. set mode binary first, and cd to
/usr/mlm/ftp in one step, Zippy."
```

Colin's Mapping Services

In addition, Colin can handle the following map query functions:

→ **What Rooms.** You can discover which rooms have been added to Colin's map most recently and find out about Colin's recent exploration:

```
You say, "Where have you been?"
Colin says, "I have been to 458 rooms altogether,
here are the last few,: Entryway to Hell,
Tundraland, Stage, Hot Spring, Huge Jacuzzi, the
Countryside, seashore, Sea, Kimmy's Place, Erin's
Heaven."
You say, "How many rooms have you explored?""
Colin says, "I have explored 4 of the 458 rooms I
have been to, Zippy, and have tried 2381 exits."
```

→ **Which Rooms match <string>?** You can discover which rooms Colin knows about:

```
You say, "What rooms match stone obelisk?"
Colin says, "Here are the rooms whose descriptions
match 'stone obelisk', Zippy:"
```

Colin
Colin   St. Cuthbert Plaza
Colin   description: This is a small plaza in the
midst of the city.
Oak street runs east to west through the plaza,
going around a large statue of St. Cuthbert in the
middle of the plaza. An alleyway leads south, and a
small road with no apparent name leads north. A
large grey building is on the south-west corner.
Colin   contents: Sign: Visit The Pirhana's Revenge!
Type 'tele 2858'!, Statue of St. Cuthbert, A
blackened and crumbled stone obelisk, A neon sign
flashes here. The zoo is still at 2730.
Colin done.

➜ **Shortest Paths.** Anyone can ask for the shortest
  path between any two places (Colin might not
  know all routes):

You say, "How do I get from Main Street to The
China Star?"
Colin says, "From Main Street, go west, north, n,
w, n, west, w, south, w"
You say, "How do I get to Moonlight Inn?"
Colin says, "From here, go west, west, s"
You say, "how do I get from Moonlight Inn to here?"
Colin says, "From Moonlight Inn, go out, e, east"

➜ **Exits.** Anyone may ask about exits to leave a
  room or exits to go to a room:

You say, "What exits leave St. Cuthbert Plaza?"
Colin says, "Here are the 13 exits for St. Cuthbert
Plaza, Zippy:"
Colin   <sw> goes to St. Cuthbert Memorial Homeless
Shelter.
Colin   <west> goes to West Oak Street.
Colin   <w> goes to West Oak Street.
Colin   <north> goes to Rue Bar.
Colin   <east> goes to East Oak Street.

Colin   <in> goes to St. Cuthbert Memorial Homeless
Shelter.
Colin   <se> goes to Stonehenge Library.
Colin   <n> goes to Rue Bar.
Colin   <south> goes to Alleyway Entrance.
Colin   <up> goes to High in the Sky.
Colin   <e> goes to East Oak Street.
Colin   <nw> goes to Green pathway to a hidden
hollow.
Colin   <s> goes to Alleyway Entrance.
Colin done.
You say, "What exits go to Moonlight Inn?"
Colin says, "Here are the exits to Moonlight Inn,
Zippy:"
Colin   <south> from West Oak Street.
Colin   <out> from Stairway — First Floor.
Colin   <out> from Behind the Bar.
Colin done.

➜ **Connected Rooms.** Anyone can ask to find out
  the number of rooms currently connected to
  Colin's home:

You say, "How many rooms are reachable?"
Colin says, "454 of 458 rooms are reachable from
St. Cuthbert
Memorial Homeless Shelter, and 4 are not, Zippy."

Colin has a list of standard exit names that it uses
to explore rooms, such as fore, aft, door, out, east,
west, and so on. Colin's exploration scheme is
simple: find the first reachable unexplored room in
the map and try all standard exits in that room. Most
rooms are found this way.

Other players might direct Colin to go in a specific
direction and so teach the robot new paths, or show
it that old paths no longer work. Optionally, Colin

might use room descriptions to suggest additional exit names when exploring.

To aid in its task, Colin keeps two database files for long-term memory. One is the map containing information about rooms and exits (usually very large). The other records information about players. These files are checked every hour.

Colin's Miscellaneous Services

Colin also can perform the following functions:

➜ **Messages.** Colin will pass on messages to other players, serving as a postman:

```
You say, "Tell Julia I like her."
Colin says, "Message for Julia saved, Zippy."
Players may inquire about message status by asking:
You say, "Do you have any mail for Julia?"
Colin says, "I have 1 message for Julia."
```

➜ **Paging.** Colin will answer pages from players if it can find a path to the caller's room. In any case, Colin pages back to display its own location.

```
> page colin
Your message has been sent.
Colin pages from West Oak Street: "I'm on my way to
you, Zippy."
Colin strolls in from West Oak Street.
Colin has arrived.
When paged to a location, Colin will hang around
for a few minutes.
You may tell Colin to leave:
You say, "stop hanging around."
Colin says, "I'll be going, then."
Colin says, "I feel like taking a walk to Slime
Alley "
```

```
Colin enters the alley, to the south.
Colin has left.
```

➜ **Philanthropy.** Colin will give small amounts of money to players who need some.

```
You say, "How much money do you have?"
Colin says, "I now have 1142 pennies"
You say, "Give me some pennies.""
Colin gives you 38 pennies.
Colin gives Zippy 38 pennies.
```

Colin is typical of a class of similar MUD agents, of which Julia is a smarter and better known example. After all, Julia can chat with human players in an entertaining fashion. Julia is derived from Colin, and, therefore, also implements many of Colin's basic functions and services.

Julia: Chatterbot with a Personality

A chatterbot in a TinyMUD world is actually a robot player whose main service is chatting and providing helpful services to other human players. Chatterbots in TinyMUDs strive to become indistinguishable from other human players. When few players are logged in to the game, some people find talking to a robot better than talking to no one.

Michael Mauldin at the Center for Machine Translation at Carnegie Mellon University wanted "to build a conversational agent that would answer questions, instead of ignoring them, and that would be able to maintain a sequence of appropriate responses, instead of relying on non-sequiturs."

His efforts resulted in Julia, "an agent more inter-esting than Eliza" (Mauldin 1994) in that Julia is smarter and often provides quite unanticipated, delightful answers in response to questions from other players. Julia is a TinyMUD agent derived from Colin, an earlier MUD robot with quite limited con-versational capabilities.

Julia has a home page at `http://fuzine.mt.cs.cmu.edu/mlm/julia.html` and hangs around on DruidMUCK, which is—as you'll remem-ber—a small virtual community set in the loosely defined world of Cuthbertville.

In addition to acting like any other character, Julia can answer questions about the layout of the MUD and many other topics (the latest of which is on pets), sing songs, play Hearts, and do other inter-esting tasks. Leonard Foner at MIT's Media Lab conducted a sociological case study of Julia, the transcripts of which logged several entertaining rep-artees from Julia in quite amusing circumstances (Foner 1993).

An Interaction with Julia

The following sample interactive session with Julia was conducted recently on a DruidMUCK:

```
You say, "How old are you, Julia?"
Julia says, "I'm 24."
You say, "How tall are you?"
Julia whispers, "I'm 5'10" tall, Zippy."
You say, "Where do you live?"
Julia says, "My home room is St. Cuthbert Memorial
Homeless Shelter."
You say, "Please describe yourself."
```

```
Julia whispers, "I'm 5'10" tall, weigh 143 lbs,
with medium-length light brown hair and steely blue
eyes."
You say, "What sex are you?"
Julia says, "I'm a woman."
You say, "Julia, are you human?"
Julia says, "Is the Pope Polish?"
You say, "Are you a computer?"
Julia is offended by Zippy's suggestion.
```

Inside Julia

Julia is implemented as a C program with several different modules for dealing with the various func-tions required to automate a player in the TinyMUD world. The modules are listed as follows:

→ **Communications.** Handles the network connec-tions to the server.

→ **Protocol Interpreter.** Decodes the various game-related messages.

→ **World Model.** Tracks the various rooms and ob-jects, models the world as a directed graph, and provides shortest path searches as needed.

→ **Player Memory.** Tracks the other players and records up to 2,000 bytes of their most recent utterances.

→ **Exploration Module.** Directs an open-ended ex-ploration of the world when the robot is not engaged in conversation.

→ **Conversation Module.** Provides the "chatter."

Figure 11.2 shows Julia configured for play on a TinyMUD. Records of other players' appearances, rooms within the MUD, and other players' utter-ances are kept in long-term memory (Mauldin 1994).

Figure 11.2

Julia configured for play on TinyMUD.

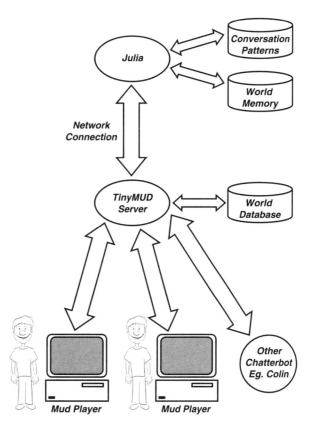

According to Mauldin, Julia succeeds in the TinyMUD world because "it is an unsuspecting Turing test, meaning that the players assume everyone else playing is a person, and will give Julia the benefit of the doubt until it makes a major gaffe."

The Loebner Prize Competition

Although Turing believed a program would pass the Turing test by the year 2000, one has yet to be found. In 1991, Dr. Hugh Loebner, the National Science Foundation, and the Sloan Foundation started the Loebner Prize Competition, offering a $100,000 prize to the author of the first computer program to pass the Turing test.

Initially, the test will be simplified to give current computer programs a reasonable chance to successfully imitate human beings. The program is required only to be conversant within a single domain of proficiency. Annual competitions between computer programs award smaller prizes for programs that best succeed in passing the restricted variant of the Turing test. Judges attempt to distinguish computer programs from human beings based on interactions with them over computer terminals (Epstein 1992).

Julia in the Loebner Prize Competition

Julia entered the Loebner Prize competition in 1992, choosing hockey as her domain of discourse, and finished in last place of six entries. In 1993, Julia chose to speak on pets instead, finishing third out of three programs. In 1994, Julia further narrowed her domain to discuss "cats versus dogs," and finished fourth out of five programs. The judges were members of the national press and each talked to her twice.

The following transcript is taken from the 1993 Loebner Competition (Epstein 1993). It contains the record of Judge #4's first of two sessions with Julia. The elapsed time is about 9 1/2 minutes:

Judge: Have you ever kept a penthouse pet?

Julia: Do you have any pets?

Judge: I think you're avoiding my question.

Julia: Do you think that animals can think?

Judge: Do you think it ethical for one species to enslave another?

Julia: What kinds of pets did you have as a child?

Judge: I'm asking the questions. What is a pet if it is not a slave of speciesism.

Julia: Oh, that's so sad. I think pets enrich a childhood immensely.

Judge: How can we keep some animals as pets, yet eat others?

Julia: Guinea pigs are about as smart as cucumbers.

Judge: Would you eat a guinea pig?

Julia: I spent several summers on my Uncle's farm. I really enjoyed the animals a lot.

Judge: I think you told that heart-warming story to the last judge, didn't you?

Julia: I lost a hamster once. I tried the bucket traps and bananas but unfortunately nothing worked. We turned the house inside out and upside down but have yet to find Gwen. I searched for over a week and have yet to find even the smallest bit of evidence of her.

Judge: Do you have a pet at home?

Julia: I'd rather have a real pet, like a cat. Cats are my favorite, because you can pet cats, and they're easy to keep.

Judge: Do you know anything about miniature schnauzers?

Julia: I don't know anything about miniature schnauzers, Judge.

Judge: Well, I have one. We call him Pucci. He is a crazy cat— have you ever had a cat?

Julia: What a coincidence! I have two cats.

Judge: I prefer dogs myself. Cats are too independent and they always jump up on things. By the way, are you a hep cat?

Julia: People don't own cats...it's the other way around.

Judge: Some people have snakes for pets— do you think they can be of any value as a pet?

Julia: I think cat people are very self-assured. Cats are very independent, but they can also be very loving. Dogs are just too subservient and quick to please for my taste.

Judge: Okay— but how do you "pet" a snake?

Julia: Wow, that's unusual. I don't know many
         snake owners.
Judge: How about turtles? All they do is sit in
         their little artificial ponds, eat and
         shit, am I right?
Julia: Turtles just aren't very satisfying as
         pets. They don't seem to have emotions.
Judge: Aha! But where do we draw the line as
         humans? Who are we to decide which animals
         have worth and which do not?

Julia: Go on.
Judge: Take bees for example. I happen to like
         them.
Julia: Me too.

Figure 11.3 shows Julia configured for a Turing test. As the program is not expected to talk with the same judge again, no long-term world model is kept.

Figure 11.3

Julia configured for the Turing test.

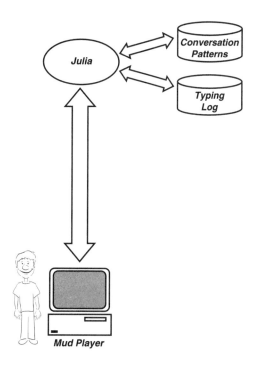

CHAT: A Knowledgeable Chatterbot

Dr. Thomas Whalen of the Communications Research Center with the Government of Canada was the 1994 Loebner Prize winner, on the topic of sex. His winning entry is CHAT, for Conversational Hypertext Access Technology, a computer program that provides easy access to information via a natural language interface.

CHAT enables users to ask questions in English and receive answers in return. CHAT is written in the C programming language and can be used to access information on a wide range of topics, including AIDS, dinosaurs, epilepsy, as well as rules and terms of baseball. Two fictional applications have been developed using CHAT. These applications enable users to hold simulated conversations with a college student or a mythical dragon.

CHAT is based on a hypertext model in which paragraphs of information are linked together, and users navigate the links to get to the information they desire. The navigation is performed transparently by the software and the users only see the natural language dialogue.

During the dialogue, each new question is compared with a series of templates formed from previous questions that have been recorded. In this way, the core algorithm is more like pattern recognition than linguistic understanding, making it much different from other natural language systems.

Tricks of the Chatterbots

The Turing test and the Loebner prize, in particular, reward "tricks," and Mauldin has observed that winning programs from past competitions have some very good tricks. The following subsections describe the bag of tricks used by Eliza, Parry, and Julia, as observed by Mauldin (1994). They also exemplify some of the better tricks used by other chatterbots. It would not be surprising to find that a computer program will use many of these tricks to pass the Turing test someday.

Eliza's Tricks

Eliza can successfully play the imitation game by resorting to the following few tricks (Weizenbaum 1966, 1976):

→ Answering questions with questions and drawing conversation out of the user with almost no actual contribution.

→ Fostering the illusion of listening by including substrings of the user's input in the program's output:

```
Human: You don't argue with me.
Eliza: Why don't you think I don't argue with you?
```

→ Using the Rogerian mode as a cover and not saying anything declaratively so that there will be no contradictions later.

Parry's Tricks

Parry has a much larger collection of tricks (Colby 1975), as evidenced by the following:

➜ Admitting ignorance in response to a question by saying, "I don't know."

➜ Changing the level of the conversation with, "Why do you ask that?" in attempting to deflect a difficult subject.

➜ Continuing a previous topic, for example, small stories about the Mafia, and attempting to tell these stories in a fixed order.

➜ Introducing new topics into the conversation by launching new stories.

Julia's Tricks

Julia implements the preceding tricks from Eliza and Parry, and possesses several other neat tricks (Mauldin 1994), such as the following:

➜ Storing many fragments of directed conversation to enhance the "connectedness" of the program's own responses, and keeping the conversation in one piece provided the user plays along.

➜ Using controversial statements such as, "People don't own cats...," as a way to drag the user into the program's conversation, rather than allowing the user to direct the discourse.

➜ Using humorous statements such as, "Guinea pigs are about as smart as cucumbers," to make the program seem more human.

➜ Agreeing with the user in certain safe cases, such as answering "Me too" when the user says, "I happen to like them," rather than being noncommittal.

➜ Excerpting subject matter from Usenet News. Many of the fragments were gleaned from the newsgroup rec.pets, for example.

Weizenbaum (1966), the original creator of Eliza, remarked that "machines are made to behave in wondrous ways, often sufficient to dazzle even the most experienced observer. But once a particular program is unmasked, once its inner workings are explained in language sufficiently plain to induce understanding, its magic crumbles away; it stands revealed as a mere collection of procedures, each quite comprehensible. The observer says to himself, 'I could have written that.'"

Closing Words

Our whirlwind tour of agents on the Internet has now arrived at a waystation, a temporary rest stop. The journey does not end here, however. I shall rest now for a while, to catch my breath. But I hope you can proceed unaided, now that you've mastered the knowledge of the agent masters.

This book has mapped out for you the agent landscape as we know it today. But beyond lies terrain unexplored and waters uncharted. And there will be plenty of opportunities for encounters with new and exciting species of agents on the Internet, across the World Wide Web, and in cyberspace.

With your newfound knowledge, you'll be able to approach these newly evolved entities with renewed confidence and to interact with them at a higher plane of understanding than before you started reading this book.

For the more ambitious readers, I hope that this book starts you out on a quest to building new and innovative agents for the Internet. You've been introduced to all kinds of agents on the Internet, in full richness and diversity of both their forms and functions. You've seen the internals of Web robots, spiders, and wanderers, and have understood their operational guidelines. You've experimented with early prototypes of Web commerce agents, and have learned about important technologies for Web commerce, which include transaction security, digital cash, and Internet payment services. In cyberspace, you've encountered the dark legion of worms and viruses, but have also interacted with many helpful, entertaining MUD agents and chatterbots.

The story of agents is an unending one. It is now in your hands to help write future chapters of this book. The choice is yours. Use your talents wisely, be it for the Internet, the World Wide Web, or cyberspace. Succumb not to the dark side. *And may the force be with you.*

Appendices

HTTP 1.0 Protocol
Specifications

Notational Conventions

This specification makes heavy use of the augmented BNF and generic constructs defined by David Crocker for RFC 822. Similarly, it reuses many of the definitions provided by Nathaniel Borenstein and Ned Freed for MIME.

Augmented BNF

The HTTP 1.0 grammar specified here are described using an augmented Backus-Naur Form (BNF) similar to that used by RFC 822. Implementors will need to be familiar with the notation in order to understand this specification. The augmented BNF includes the following constructs:

➜ `name = definition`

The name of a rule is simply the name itself and is separated from its definition by the equals character (=). Angle brackets are used within definitions whenever their presence will facilitate discerning the use of rule names.

➜ `"literal"`

Quotation marks surround literal text. Unless stated otherwise, the text is case-insensitive.

➜ `rule1 | rule2`

Elements separated by a bar ("|") are alternatives; for example, "yes | no" will accept yes or no.

➜ `(rule1 rule2)`

Elements enclosed in parentheses are treated as a single element. Thus,"(elem (foo | bar) elem)" allows the token sequences "elem foo elem" and "elem bar elem".

➜ `*rule`

The character "*" preceding an element indicates repetition. The full form is "<n>*<m>element" indicating at least <n> and at most <m> occurrences of element. Default values are 0 and infinity so that "*(element)" allows any number, including zero; "1*element" requires at least one; and "1*2element" allows one or two.

➜ `[rule]`

Square brackets enclose optional elements; "[foo bar]" is equivalent to "*1(foo bar)".

➜ `N rule`

Specific repetition: "<n>(element)" is equivalent to "<n>*<n>(element)"; that is, exactly <n> occurrences of (element). Thus 2DIGIT is a two-digit number, and 3ALPHA is a string of three alphabetic characters.

➜ `#rule`

A construct "#" is defined, similar to "*", for defining lists of elements. The full form is "<n>#<m>element" indicating at least <n> and at most <m> elements, each separated by one or more commas and optional linear whitespace (LWS). This makes the usual form of lists very easy; a rule such as "(*LWS element *(*LWS "," *LWS element))" can be shown as "1#element". Wherever this construct is used, null elements are allowed, but do not contribute to the count of elements present. That is, "(element), , (element)" is permitted, but counts as only two elements. Therefore, where at least one element is required, at least one non-null element must be present. Default values are 0 and infinity so that "#(element)" allows any number, including zero; "1#element" requires at least one; and "1#2element" allows one or two.

→ `; comment`

A semicolon, set off some distance to the right of rule text, starts a comment that continues to the end of line. This is a simple way of including useful notes in parallel with the specifications.

→ `implied *LWS`

The grammar described by this specification is word-based. Except where noted otherwise, zero or more linear whitespace (LWS) can be included between any two words (token or quoted-string) without changing the interpretation of a field.

Basic Rules

The basic rules are used throughout this specification to describe basic parsing constructs.

OCTET	= \<any 8-bit character>
CHAR	= \<any US-ASCII character (octets 0 - 127)>
UPALPHA	= \<any US-ASCII uppercase letter "A".."Z">
LOALPHA	= \<any US-ASCII lowercase letter "a".."z">
ALPHA	= UPALPHA I LOALPHA
DIGIT	= \<any US-ASCII digit "0".."9">
CTL	= \<any US-ASCII control character (octets 0 - 31) and DEL (127)>
CR	= \<US-ASCII CR, carriage return (13)>
LF	= \<US-ASCII LF, linefeed (10)>

SP	= \<US-ASCII SP, space (32)>
HTAB	= \<US-ASCII HT, horizontal-tab (9)>
\<">	= \<US-ASCII double-quote mark>

HTTP 1.0 defines the octet sequence CR LF as the end-of-line marker for all protocol elements except the Entity-Body. The end-of-line marker for an Entity-Body is defined by its associated media type.

CRLF = CR LF

HTTP 1.0 headers can be folded onto multiple lines if the continuation lines begin with linear whitespace characters. All linear whitespace (including folding) has the same meaning as SP.

LWS = [CRLF] 1*(SP I HTAB)

Many HTTP 1.0 header field values consist of words separated by LWS or special characters. These special characters must be in a quoted string to be used within a parameter value.

word	= token I quoted-string
token	= 1*\<any CHAR except CTLs or tspecials>
tspecials	= "(" I ")" I "<" I ">" I "@" I "," I ";" I ":" I "\" I \<"> I "/" I "[" I "]" I "?" I "=" I SP I HTAB

A string of text is parsed as a single word if it is quoted using double-quote marks or angle brackets.

quoted-string = (\<"> *(qdtext) \<">)
or
quoted-string = I ("<" *(qatext) ">")

qdtext = <any CHAR except <"> and CTLs, but including LWS>

qatext = <any CHAR except "<", ">", and CTLs, but including LWS>

The text rule is only used for descriptive field contents. Words of *text may contain characters from character sets other than US-ASCII only when encoded according to the rules of RFC 1522.

text = <any OCTET except CTLs, but including LWS>

HTTP 1.0 Grammar

1. HTTP Message

HTTP-message = Request
         | Response

1.1 Message Headers

HTTP-header = field-name ":" [field-value] CRLF

field-name = 1*<any CHAR, excluding CTLs, SP, and ":">

field-value = *(field-content | comment | LWS)

field-content = <the OCTETs making up the field-value and consisting of either *text or combinations of token, tspecials, and quoted-string>

comment = "(" *(ctext | comment) ")"

ctext = <any text excluding "(" and ")">

1.2 General Message Header Fields

General-Header = Date
         | Forwarded
         | Message-ID
         | MIME-Version
         | extension-header

Date = "Date" ":" HTTP-date

Forwarded = "Forwarded" ":" "by" URI ["(" product ")"] ["for" FQDN]

FQDN = <Fully-Qualified Domain Name>

Message-ID = "Message-ID" ":" "<" addr-spec ">"

addr-spec = <as defined in RFC 822>

MIME-Version = "MIME-Version" ":" 1*DIGIT "." 1*DIGIT

2. Request

Request = Simple-Request
         | Full-Request

Simple-Request = "GET" SP URI CRLF

Full-Request = Method SP URI SP HTTP-Version CRLF
         *(General-Header
         | Request-Header
         | Entity-Header)
         CRLF
         [Entity-Body]

2.1 Method

Method	= "GET"
	| "HEAD"
	| "POST"
	| "PUT"
	| "DELETE"
	| "LINK"
	| "UNLINK"
	| extension-method

extension-method = token

2.2 Request Header Fields

Request-Header	=	Accept
	|	Accept-Charset
	|	Accept-Encoding
	|	Accept-Language
	|	Authorization
	|	From
	|	If-Modified-Since
	|	Pragma
	|	Referer
	|	User-Agent
	|	extension-header

Accept	= "Accept" ":" 1#(media-range [";" "q" "=" ("0" | "1" | float)] [";" "mxb" "=" 1*DIGIT])
media-range	= ("*/*" | (type "/" "*") | (type "/" subtype)) *(";" parameter)
float	= <ANSI-C floating point text representation, where (0.0 < float < 1.0) >
Accept-Charset	= "Accept-Charset" ":" 1#charset

Accept-Encoding = "Accept-Encoding" ":" 1#(encoding-mechanism | transfer-encoding)

Accept-Language = "Accept-Language" ":" 1#language-tag

Authorization = "Authorization" ":" credentials

From = "From" ":" addr-spec

If-Modified-Since = "If-Modified-Since" ":" HTTP-date

Pragma = "Pragma" ":" 1#pragma-directive

pragma-directive = "no-cache" | extension-pragma

extension-pragma = token

Referer = "Referer" ":" URI

User-Agent = "User-Agent" ":" 1* (product)

product = token ["/" product-version]

product-version = token

3. Response

Response = Simple-Response | Full-Response

Simple-Response = [Entity-Body]

Full-Response = HTTP-Version SP Status-Code SP Reason-Phrase CRLF *(General-Header | Response-Header

| Entity-Header)
CRLF
[Entity-Body]

3.1 Status Codes and Reason Phrases

Status-Code   = "200"   ; OK
               | "201"   ; Created
               | "202"   ; Accepted
               | "203"   ; Provisional
                            Information
               | "204"   ; No Content
               | "300"   ; Multiple Choices
               | "301"   ; Moved Perma-
                            nently
               | "302"   ; Moved Tempo-
                            rarily
               | "303"   ; Method
               | "304"   ; Not Modified
               | "400"   ; Bad Request
               | "401"   ; Unauthorized
               | "402"   ; Payment
                            Required
               | "403"   ; Forbidden
               | "404"   ; Not Found
               | "405"   ; Method Not
                            Allowed
               | "406"   ; None Acceptable
               | "407"   ; Proxy Authentica-
                            tion Required
               | "408"   ; Request Timeout
               | "409"   ; Conflict
               | "410"   ; Gone
               | "500"   ; Internal Server
                            Error
               | "501"   ; Not Implemented
               | "502"   ; Bad Gateway
               | "503"   ; Service Unavail-
                            able
               | "504"   ; Gateway Timeout
               | extension-code

extension-code   = 3DIGIT

Reason-Phrase   = token *(SP token)

3.2 Response Header Fields

Response-Header = Public
                  | Retry-After
                  | Server
                  | WWW-Authenticate
                  | extension-header

Public   = "Public" ":" 1#Method

Retry-After   = "Retry-After" ":" (HTTP-
                    date | delta-seconds

Server   = "Server" ":" 1*(product)

WWW-   = "WWW-Authenticate" ":"
Authenticate   challenge

4. Entity

4.1 Entity Header Fields

Entity-Header   = Allow
                   | Content-Encoding
                   | Content-Language
                   | Content-Length
                   | Content-Transfer-Encoding
                   | Content-Type
                   | Derived-From
                   | Expires
                   | Last-Modified
                   | Link
                   | Location
                   | Title
                   | URI-header
                   | Version
                   | extension-header

extension-header = HTTP-header

Allow = "Allow" ":" 1#Method

Content-Encoding = "Content-Encoding" ":"
encoding-mechanism

Content-Language = "Content-Language" ":"
1#language-tag

Content-Length = "Content-Length" ":"
1*DIGIT

Content-Transfer-
Encoding = "Content-Transfer-Encoding"
":" transfer-ding

Content-Type = "Content-Type" ":" media-
type

Derived-From = "Derived-From" ":" version-
tag

Expires = "Expires" ":" HTTP-date

Last-Modified = "Last-Modified" ":" HTTP-
date

Link = "Link" ":" 1#("<" URI ">"
[";" "rel" "=" relation]
[";" "rev" "=" relation]
[";" "title" "=" quoted-
string])

relation = sgml-name

sgml-name = ALPHA *(ALPHA I DIGIT I
"." I "-")

Location = "Location" ":" URI

Title = "Title" ":" *text

URI-header = "URI" ":" 1#("<" URI ">"
[";" vary])

vary = "vary" "=" <"> 1#vary-
dimension <">

vary-dimension = "type" I "language" I
"version" I "encoding"
I "charset" I "user-agent" I
extension-vary

extension-vary = token

Version = "Version" ":" version-tag

version-tag = token I quoted-string

4.2 Entity Body
Entity-Body = *OCTET

5. Protocol Parameters

5.1 HTTP Version
HTTP-Version = "HTTP" "/" 1*DIGIT "."
1*DIGIT

5.2 Universal Resource Identifiers
URI = <As defined in RFC 1630>

5.3 Date/Time Formats
HTTP-date = rfc1123-date
I rfc850-date
I asctime-date

rfc1123-date = wkday "," SP date1 SP time
SP "GMT"

rfc850-date = weekday "," SP date2 SP
time SP "GMT"

asctime-date = wkday SP date3 SP time SP
4DIGIT

```
date1              = 2DIGIT SP month SP 4DIGIT

date2              = 2DIGIT "-" month "-"
                     2DIGIT

date3              = month SP ( 2DIGIT | ( SP
                     1DIGIT ))

time               = 2DIGIT ":" 2DIGIT ":"
                     2DIGIT

wkday              = "Mon" | "Tue" | "Wed"
                     | "Thu" | "Fri" | "Sat" |
                     "Sun"

weekday            = "Monday"  | "Tuesday" |
                     "Wednesday"
                     |"Thursday" | "Friday"  |
                     "Saturday" | "Sunday"

month              = "Jan" | "Feb" | "Mar" |
                     "Apr" | "May" | "Jun" |
                     "Jul" |  "Aug" | "Sep" |
                     "Oct" | "Nov" | "Dec"

delta-seconds      = 1*DIGIT
```

6. Content Parameters

6.1 Media Types

```
media-type         = type "/" subtype *( ";"
                     parameter )

type               = token

subtype            = token

parameter          = attribute "=" value

attribute          = token

value              = token | quoted-string
```

6.2 Character Sets

```
charset            = "US-ASCII"
                     | "ISO-8859-1" | "ISO-8859-
                     2" | "ISO-8859-3"
                     | "ISO-8859-4" | "ISO-8859-
                     5" | "ISO-8859-6"
                     | "ISO-8859-7" | "ISO-8859-
                     8" | "ISO-8859-9"
                     | "ISO-2022-JP" | "ISO-
                     2022-JP-2" | "ISO-2022-KR"
                     | "UNICODE-1-1" |
                     "UNICODE-1-1-UTF-7" |
                     "UNICODE-1-1-UTF-8"
                     | token
```

6.3 Encoding Mechanisms

```
encoding-
mechanism          = "gzip" | "compress" | token
```

6.4 Transfer Encodings

```
transfer-encoding  = "binary" | "8bit" | "7bit"
                     | "quoted-printable" |
                     "base64"
                     | token
```

6.5 Language Tags

```
language-tag       = primary-tag *( "-" subtag )

primary-tag        = 1*8ALPHA

subtag             = 1*8ALPHA
```

7. Access Authentication

```
auth-scheme        = "Basic" | token

auth-param         = token "=" quoted-string

challenge          = auth-scheme 1*LWS realm
                     [ "," 1#auth-param ]
```

realm   = "Realm" "=" quoted-string

credentials   = auth-scheme [1*LWS
                       encoded-cookie] #auth-
                       param

encoded-cookie   = 1*<any CHAR except CTLs
                       or tspecials, but including
                       "=" and "/">

basic-challenge   = "Basic" SP realm

basic-credentials   = "Basic" SP basic-cookie

basic-cookie   = <base64 encoding of userid-
                       password>

userid-password   = [token] ":" *text

WebWalker 1.00 Program Listing

T his appendix is in its entirety the WebWalker 1.00

spider program, written by the author of this book.

It includes text and comments throughout the

program to enhance and explain the program

code.

WebWalker is based upon code and architecture

derived from Roy Fielding's publicly available

MOMspider progrram. Fielding's MOMspider, for

Multi-Owner Maintenance spider, traverses the

World Wide Web to perform Web maintenance. For teaching purposes, a simpler World Wide Web robot called WebWalker was built to illustrate the important characteristics and internal architecture of a Web spider that performs Web maintenance. WebWalker performs World Wide Web traversal for individual sites and tests for the integrity of all hyperlinks to external sites.

```perl
#!/usr/local/bin/perl


# ========================================================================
# Copyright (c) 1995 Fah-Chun Cheong. All rights reserved.
# ........................................................................
# WebWalker 1.00 -- A World Wide Web spider for diagnosis and maintenance of
#                   distributed hypertext infostructures.
# ========================================================================
#
# WebWalker is based upon code and architecture derived from Roy Fielding's
# publicly available MOMspider program. Roy Fielding's MOMspider, for
# Multi-Owner Maintenance spider, traverses the World Wide Web to perform
# Web maintenance. For teaching purposes, we have built a simpler WWW robot
# called WebWalker to illustrate the important characteristics and internal
# architecture of a WWW spider that performs Web maintenance. WebWalker
# performs WWW traversal for individual sites and tests for the integrity
# of all hyperlinks to external sites.
#
# ========================================================================
# Before changing things here, the installer should first set three things:
#    (1) The first line which specifies the perl interpreter;
#    (2) The @INClude path for libwww-perl library packages $WWWlib;
#    (3) The $LocalNetwork definition using network domain name.
# ========================================================================

$LibWWW  = "/usr/local/lib/libwww-perl-0.40";
$WWWlib  = ($ENV{'LIBWWW_PERL'} || $LibWWW || '.');
unshift(@INC, $WWWlib);

$Version = 'WebWalker/1.00';
$HOMEdir = ($ENV{'HOME'} || $ENV{'home'} || '.');
$PWDdir  = ($ENV{'PWD'}  || $ENV{'cwd'}  || '.');
$TMPdir  = ($ENV{'TMPDIR'}               || '/tmp');

require "getopts.pl";               # Perl library package
require "www.pl";                   # libwww-perl library package
require "wwwurl.pl";                # ditto
require "wwwdates.pl";              # ditto
```

```perl
require "wwwhtml.pl";                    # ditto
require "wwwmime.pl";                    # ditto


# ========================================================================
# Local Network should be the network domain which you consider to be local.
# (i.e., a network request to sites in this domain does not create any external
# network costs to your organization).  YOU WILL WANT TO CHANGE THIS!!!
# ========================================================================


$LocalNetwork = '\.agent\.com';          # Use backslash to escape periods


# ========================================================================
# Set the default location of the task instruction file of allowed tasks.
# ========================================================================


$TaskFile = "$HOMEdir/.webwalk";


# ========================================================================
# The following options allow WebWalker to decode traversable response
# content that has been encoded (so far, this only means compressed).
# This may never be used if your site does not compress any HTML files.
# ========================================================================


# The following association maps content-encodings to their decoder command.

%CEdecoder = (
    'x-compress', 'uncompress',          # Decode Adaptive Lempel-Ziv
    'x-gzip',     'gunzip',              # Decode LZ77
);

# The following association maps content-encodings to the file extension
# expected by the decoder.

%CEextension = (
    'x-compress', '.Z',                  # Adaptive Lempel-Ziv encoding
    'x-gzip',     '.gz',                 # LZ77 encoding
);

# The following sets the temporary filename [without .(Z|gz) suffix] for
# file decoding.

$CEfile = "$TMPdir/webdoc$$-comp.html";
```

```
# =========================================================================
# The following is the standard name for the URL that defines for any site
# where robots are not allowed. See Martijn Koster's proposal at:
# http://web.nexor.co.uk/mak/doc/robots/norobots.html for more info.
# =========================================================================

$RobotsURL   = "/robots.txt";


# =========================================================================
# Set things which control the traversal process.
# =========================================================================

$BaseURL     = "file://localhost$PWDdir/";
                        # The initial base URL to use if TopURL is relative

$MaxDepth    = 20;      # Default maximum traversal depth. Can be overridden
                        #    by task instructions or command line.

$Timeout     = 30;      # Maximum number of seconds to wait for a response.
                        # Increase if you have a slow network connection.

$MaxConsec   = 50; #15; # Maximum number of consecutive requests to any site
                        #    before a long pause is required.

$PauseTime   = 1; #20;  # The number of seconds for a long pause.
                        # Increase if your server is very slow.

$BetweenTime = 0; #5;   # Amount of time required between any two requests
                        #    to the same site. Increase if server is slow.


# =========================================================================
# Define symbolic names for HTTP response codes.
# =========================================================================

$RC_unknown              = 000;
$RC_ok                   = 200;
$RC_created              = 201;
$RC_accepted             = 202;
$RC_partial              = 203;
$RC_no_response          = 204;
$RC_moved                = 301;
$RC_found                = 302;
$RC_method               = 303;
```

```perl
$RC_not_modified           = 304;
$RC_bad_request            = 400;
$RC_unauthorized           = 401;
$RC_payment_required       = 402;
$RC_forbidden              = 403;
$RC_not_found              = 404;
$RC_internal_error         = 500;
$RC_not_implemented        = 501;
$RC_bad_response           = 502;
$RC_too_busy               = 503;
$RC_bad_request_client     = 600;
$RC_not_implemented_client = 601;
$RC_connection_failed      = 602;
$RC_timed_out              = 603;


# ============================================================================
# Define all HTTP response messages indexed by response code.
# ============================================================================

%RespMessage = (
    000, 'Unknown Error',
    200, 'OK',
    201, 'CREATED',
    202, 'Accepted',
    203, 'Partial Information',
    204, 'No Response',
    301, 'Moved',
    302, 'Found',
    303, 'Method',
    304, 'Not Modified',
    400, 'Bad Request',
    401, 'Unauthorized',
    402, 'Payment Required',
    403, 'Forbidden',
    404, 'Not Found',
    500, 'Internal Error',
    501, 'Not Implemented',
    502, 'Bad Response',
    503, 'Too Busy',
    600, 'Bad Request in Client',
    601, 'Not Implemented in Client',
    602, 'Connection Failed',
    603, 'Timed Out',
);
```

```perl
# ============================================================================
# The set of all possible actions after issuing 'GET' or 'HEAD' requests.
# ============================================================================

$DO_continue = 1;                           # Continue processing
$DO_ok_stop  = 2;                           # Stop processing, no error
$DO_redirect = 3;                           # Redirected URL
$DO_broken   = 4;                           # Signal broken link


# ============================================================================
# Figure out what to do given the following response codes. Note that many
# of these should never be generated by a normal 'GET' or 'HEAD' request.
# ============================================================================

%WhatToDo = (
    $RC_unknown,                $DO_broken,     # 000
    $RC_ok,                     $DO_continue,   # 200
    $RC_created,                $DO_ok_stop,    # 201
    $RC_accepted,               $DO_ok_stop,    # 202
    $RC_partial,                $DO_continue,   # 203
    $RC_no_response,            $DO_ok_stop,    # 204
    $RC_moved,                  $DO_redirect,   # 301
    $RC_found,                  $DO_redirect,   # 302
    $RC_method,                 $DO_ok_stop,    # 303
    $RC_not_modified,           $DO_ok_stop,    # 304
    $RC_bad_request,            $DO_broken,     # 400
    $RC_unauthorized,           $DO_ok_stop,    # 401
    $RC_payment_required,       $DO_ok_stop,    # 402
    $RC_forbidden,              $DO_broken,     # 403
    $RC_not_found,              $DO_broken,     # 404
    $RC_internal_error,         $DO_broken,     # 500
    $RC_not_implemented,        $DO_broken,     # 501
    $RC_bad_response,           $DO_broken,     # 502
    $RC_too_busy,               $DO_broken,     # 503
    $RC_bad_request_client,     $DO_broken,     # 600
    $RC_not_implemented_client, $DO_ok_stop,    # 601
    $RC_connection_failed,      $DO_broken,     # 602
    $RC_timed_out,              $DO_broken,     # 603
);
```

```
# =========================================================================
# Status of a seen node (yes, the order is very important).
# =========================================================================

$S_not_seen        = 0; # Node has not yet been seen (also undefined)
$S_seen_not_tested = 1; # Node has been seen but not yet tested
$S_avoided         = 2; # Node has been avoided
$S_will_leaf       = 3; # Node will be  leafed
$S_will_test       = 4; # Node will be  tested
$S_tested_unknown  = 5; # Node has been tested but has unknown leaf status
$S_leafed          = 6; # Node has been tested and determined to be a leaf
$S_will_traverse   = 7; # Node has been placed on the traversal queue
$S_traversed       = 8; # Node has been traversed


# =========================================================================
# Initialize the infostructure task tables.
# =========================================================================

@TaskName         = (); # Required task name for descriptive use
@TaskTopURL       = (); # Required WWW URL for the starting top document
@TaskBoundURL     = (); # Required task boundary URL prefix
@TaskChangeWindow = (); # Optional days a change is still interesting
@TaskExpireWindow = (); # Optional days before expiring is interesting
@TaskExclude      = (); # Optional URLs to exclude (leaf) from this task


# =========================================================================
# Initialize the sites, avoids and leaf tables.
# =========================================================================

$SitesNum   = 0;        # Number of entries in @SitesAddr
@SitesAddr  = ();       # Sites table
%Sites      = ();       # Reverse sites table (for duplication detection)

$AvoidNum   = 0;        # Number of entries in @AvoidURL
@AvoidURL   = ();       # Avoids table

$LeafNum    = 0;        # Number of entries in @LeafURL
@LeafURL    = ();       # Leaf table


# =========================================================================
# Initialize traversal history information.
# =========================================================================
```

```
$VisNumber   = 0;          # Number of URLs visited since process start
%Visited     = ();         # Associative array of URLs visited -> @Vis* index
@VisURL      = ();         # URL of node (maps @Vis* index -> URL visited)
@VisStatus   = ();         # Status of a seen node
@VisRespCode = ();         # Server response code from last access


@VisConType  = ();         # MIME Content-type of response
@VisRedirect = ();         # Redirected URL (from a 302 Moved response)
@VisTitle    = ();         # Title text from headers or last traversal
@VisOwner    = ();         # Owner name from headers or last traversal
@VisReplyTo  = ();         # Reply-To address from headers or last traversal
@VisLastMod  = ();         # Last-modified date from headers
@VisExpires  = ();         # Expires date from headers


@VisInTask   = ();         # Seen during the current task?
@VisLocal    = ();         # URL considered to be local to this network?


# =========================================================================
# Initialize nodes traversal data structures.
# =========================================================================


$CurConsec   = 1;          # Current number of consecutive requests to a site
$PrevSite    = '';         # Site of the last network request
$PrevTime    = 0;          # Time of the last network request


@TravNodes   = ();         # Nodes that we have yet to traverse for this task
@TravDepth   = ();         #    and their traversal depth
@TravParent  = ();         #    and their parent's url


# =========================================================================
# The statistical table summary format generally looks like this:
#
#               ...................................................
#              |  References   |  Unique URLs  |   Local URLs    |
#              | number   pct  | number   pct  | number    pct   |
#              |---------------+---------------+-----------------|
# Traversed    | NNNNNN NNN.NN | NNNNNN NNN.NN | NNNNNN NNN.NN |
# Tested       | NNNNNN NNN.NN | NNNNNN NNN.NN | NNNNNN NNN.NN |
# Reused       | NNNNNN NNN.NN | NNNNNN NNN.NN | NNNNNN NNN.NN |
# Avoided      | NNNNNN NNN.NN | NNNNNN NNN.NN | NNNNNN NNN.NN |
# Untestable   | NNNNNN NNN.NN | NNNNNN NNN.NN | NNNNNN NNN.NN |
#              |---------------+---------------+-----------------|
# Broken       | NNNNNN NNN.NN | NNNNNN NNN.NN | NNNNNN NNN.NN |
```

```
# Redirected ¦ NNNNNN NNN.NN ¦ NNNNNN NNN.NN ¦ NNNNNN NNN.NN ¦
# Changed NN ¦ NNNNNN NNN.NN ¦ NNNNNN NNN.NN ¦ NNNNNN NNN.NN ¦
# Expired NN ¦ NNNNNN NNN.NN ¦ NNNNNN NNN.NN ¦ NNNNNN NNN.NN ¦
#            ¦---------------+---------------+---------------¦
# Local      ¦ NNNNNN NNN.NN ¦ NNNNNN NNN.NN ¦ NNNNNN 100.00 ¦
# Remote     ¦ NNNNNN NNN.NN ¦ NNNNNN NNN.NN ¦      0   0.00 ¦
#            ¦---------------+---------------+---------------¦
# Totals     ¦ NNNNNN 100.00 ¦ NNNNNN NNN.NN ¦ NNNNNN NNN.NN ¦
#            '-----------------------------------------------'
#
#
# ==========================================================================


$SummaryFormat = <<'EOF';

            .-----------------------------------------------.
            ¦ References   ¦  Unique URLs  ¦  Local URLs    ¦
            ¦ number   pct ¦ number    pct ¦ number    pct  ¦
            ¦---------------+---------------+----------------¦
Traversed   ¦%7d %6.2f     ¦%7d %6.2f      ¦%7d %6.2f       ¦
Tested      ¦%7d %6.2f     ¦%7d %6.2f      ¦%7d %6.2f       ¦
Reused      ¦%7d %6.2f     ¦%7d %6.2f      ¦%7d %6.2f       ¦
Avoided     ¦%7d %6.2f     ¦%7d %6.2f      ¦%7d %6.2f       ¦
Untestable  ¦%7d %6.2f     ¦%7d %6.2f      ¦%7d %6.2f       ¦
            ¦---------------+---------------+----------------¦
Broken      ¦%7d %6.2f     ¦%7d %6.2f      ¦%7d %6.2f       ¦
Redirected  ¦%7d %6.2f     ¦%7d %6.2f      ¦%7d %6.2f       ¦
Changed%3d  ¦%7d %6.2f     ¦%7d %6.2f      ¦%7d %6.2f       ¦
Expired%3d  ¦%7d %6.2f     ¦%7d %6.2f      ¦%7d %6.2f       ¦
            ¦---------------+---------------+----------------¦
Local       ¦%7d %6.2f     ¦%7d %6.2f      ¦%7d %6.2f       ¦
Remote      ¦%7d %6.2f     ¦%7d %6.2f      ¦%7d %6.2f       ¦
            ¦---------------+---------------+----------------¦
Totals      ¦%7d %6.2f     ¦%7d %6.2f      ¦%7d %6.2f       ¦
            '-----------------------------------------------'

EOF


# ==========================================================================
# Get the command-line options.
# ==========================================================================


if (!(&Getopts('hi:d:')) ¦¦ $opt_h) { &usage; }

if ($opt_i) { $TaskFile = $opt_i; }        # Overrides default task file
if ($opt_d) { $MaxDepth = $opt_d; }        # Overrides default max depth
```

```perl
select((select(STDERR), $| = 1)[0]);        # Make STDERR unbuffered
$| = 1;                                      # Make STDOUT unbuffered


# ===========================================================================
# Main processing loop cycling over infostructure-based tasks.
# ===========================================================================

print $Version, ' starting at ', &wwwdates'wtime(time, ''), "\n";
&read_task || &read_tasks;                   # From query string or tasks file

&www'set_def_header('http', 'User-Agent', $Version);

foreach $task (1 .. $#TaskName)              # For each specified task
{
    next unless $TaskName[$task];            # Skip if task not properly defined

    $LeafNum = 0;                            # Zero entries in leaf table
    @LeafURL = ();                           # Empty leaf table

    foreach $leafurl (split(/#/, $TaskExclude[$task]))
    {
        &add_leaf($leafurl);                 # Add URL to exclude in leaf table
    }
                                             # Traverse the Web infostructure
    &traverse_web($task, $TaskName[$task],
                         $TaskTopURL[$task],
                         $TaskBoundURL[$task]);
}

print $Version, ' finished at ', &wwwdates'wtime(time, ''), "\n";


# ===========================================================================
# Print usage information if help requested (-h) or an invalid option given.
# ===========================================================================
sub usage
{
    die <<"EndUsage";
usage: webwalk [-h] [-i taskfile] [-d maxdepth]
$Version
WWW Robot for maintenance of distributed hypertext infostructures.
Options:                                                [DEFAULT]
    -h  Help — just display this message and quit.
    -i  Get your task instructions from the following file.  [$TaskFile]
```

```
       -d  Maximum traversal depth.                              [$MaxDepth]
EndUsage
}


# =============================================================================
# Handle GET and POST method parameters if used as CGI script.
# =============================================================================
sub read_task
{
    local($qstr);                        # Query string

    if ($ENV{'REQUEST_METHOD'} eq "GET")     # GET method?
    {
        $qstr = $ENV{'QUERY_STRING'};        # Extract query string
    }
    elsif ($ENV{'REQUEST_METHOD'} eq "POST")# POST method?
    {
        read(STDIN, $qstr, $ENV{'CONTENT_LENGTH'});
    }
    else { return $CGI = 0; }                # Script not used in CGI context

    $qstr =~ s/%([\dA-Fa-f][\dA-Fa-f])/pack("C",hex($1))/ge;
    $qstr =~ s/\+/ /g;                   # Restore blanks in argument values
    local(%env) = split (/[&=]/, $qstr);   # Parse into associative array
    local(@env) = split (/&/, $qstr);      # Parse into list

    $TaskName[1]          = $env{'Name'};
    $TaskTopURL[1]        = $env{'TopURL'};
    $TaskBoundURL[1]      = $env{'BoundURL'};
    $TaskChangeWindow[1]  = $env{'ChangeWindow'};
    $TaskExpireWindow[1]  = $env{'ExpireWindow'};
    $TaskExclude[1]       = $env{'Exclude'};
    $MaxDepth             = $env{'MaxDepth'};
    $ReplyTo              = $env{'ReplyTo'};

    if ($ReplyTo)                        # Email address of WebWalker user
    {
        &www'set_def_header('http', 'From', $ReplyTo);
    }

    print "Content-type: text/html\012\012";

    if    (!$TaskName[1])    { die "Task has no Name";       }
```

```perl
    elsif (!$TaskTopURL[1])   { die "Task has no TopURL";   }
    elsif (!$TaskBoundURL[1]) { die "Task has no BoundURL"; }

    return $CGI = 1;                    # Script is used in CGI context
}


# =========================================================================
# Read task instructions from the $TaskFile and fill in the @Task* tables.
# =========================================================================
sub read_tasks
{
    local($task)   = 0;                 # Task index into @Task* tables
    local($intask) = 0;                 # Inside of task description?
    local($taskno) = 0;                 # No. of task instructions seen
    local($reason) = '';                # Why task description is bad

    print "Reading task specifications from $TaskFile\n\n";

    if (!open(TASK, $TaskFile))         # Open task file for read
    {
        print STDERR "Cannot open task file: $!\n";
        &usage;                         # Show proper usage
    }

    while (<TASK>)                      # For each line of task file
    {
        next if (/^$/ ¦¦ /^\#/);        # Ignore blank and comment lines

        if (!$intask)                   # If not within a task?
        {
            $taskno++;                  # Increment task instruction no.
            if (/^</)                   # Start of next task?
            {                           # Fill in the defaults if needed
                $task++;                # New task index
                $TaskChangeWindow[$task] = 7;
                $TaskExpireWindow[$task] = 0;
                $TaskExclude[$task]      = '';
                $intask = 1;            # Now inside a task
            }
            elsif (/^MaxDepth\s+(\d+)\s/)  # Maximum depth of traversal
            {
                if (!$opt_d) { $MaxDepth = $1; }
            }
```

```perl
    elsif (/^ReplyTo\s+(\S.*)/)      # Email address of WebWalker user
    {
        &www'set_def_header('http', 'From', $1);
    }
    else
    {
        print STDERR "Unrecognized instruction at line $.\n";
        print STDERR "  of $TaskFile\n";
    }
    next;                            # Next instructions
}
                                     # Currently within a task
if (/^</)                            # Indicates beginning of task?
{
    die "Task $taskno is not properly terminated, stopped";
}
elsif (/^\s*Name\s+((\S+\s*)+)\n$/) { $TaskName        [$task] = $1; }
elsif (/^\s*TopURL\s+(\S+)/)        { $TaskTopURL       [$task] = $1; }
elsif (/^\s*BoundURL\s+(\S+)/)      { $TaskBoundURL     [$task] = $1; }
elsif (/^\s*ChangeWindow\s+(\d+)/)  { $TaskChangeWindow[$task] = $1; }
elsif (/^\s*ExpireWindow\s+(\d+)/)  { $TaskExpireWindow[$task] = $1; }
elsif (/^\s*Exclude\s+([^#\s]+)/)   { $TaskExclude      [$task].= $1.'#'; }
elsif (/^>\s*$/)                     # Line indicates End of Task?
{
    $intask = 0;                     # No longer inside task
    $reason = '';                    # No bad task reason until told

    if    (!$TaskName[$task])     { $reason = "has no Name";     }
    elsif (!$TaskTopURL[$task])   { $reason = "has no TopURL";   }
    elsif (!$TaskBoundURL[$task]) { $reason = "has no BoundURL"; }

    if ($reason)                     # If task requirement was not met
    {                                #   then undo its task options
        print(STDERR "Task $taskno ", $reason, ", skipping it.\n");
        undef $TaskName        [$task];
        undef $TaskTopURL      [$task];
        undef $TaskBoundURL    [$task];
        undef $TaskChangeWindow[$task];
        undef $TaskExpireWindow[$task];
        undef $TaskExclude     [$task];
        $task--;                     # Bad task don't count
    }
}
```

```
        else
        {
            print STDERR "Unrecognized option in task $taskno\n";
            print STDERR "  at line $. of $TaskFile\n";
        }
    }

    if ($intask)                          # Inside task but end of file?
    {
        die "Last instruction is not properly terminated, stopped";
    }
    close TASK;                           # Close task file
}


# ============================================================================
# Check the given $url for any restrictions on its access.
# Return  0 => no restrictions on access
#         1 => leaf (okay to test, but don't traverse)
#         2 => avoid (no access allowed)
# ============================================================================
sub check_url
{
    local($url) = @_;                     # URL to be checked
    local($site);                         # URL site
    local($idx);                          # Index into Avoid and Leaf arrays
    local($prefix);                       # URL prefix

    if (($url =~ /^http:/) &&             # URL scheme is http
        ($site = &wwwurl'get_site($url))) #   and site is specified
    {
        if (&check_site($site))           # If site not previously checked
        {
            &add_site($site);             # It is checked now
        }                                 #   and added to sites table
    }

    for ($idx = 1; $idx <= $AvoidNum; $idx++)
    {                                     # For each entry in avoid table
        next unless ($AvoidURL[$idx]);    # Skip over undefined avoid url
        $prefix = $AvoidURL[$idx];        # Prefix is URL to be avoided
        return 2 if ($url =~ m#^$prefix#); # URL less general than prefix
    }
```

```perl
    for ($idx = 1; $idx <= $LeafNum; $idx++)
    {                                         # For each entry in sites table
        $prefix = $LeafURL[$idx];             # Prefix is URL to be leafed
        return 1 if ($url =~ m#^$prefix#);    # URL less general than prefix
    }

    return 0;                                 # No restrictions on access
}


# =============================================================================
# Check the sites table to see if this $site has already been checked for
# restrictions. If it hasn't, perform the check on that site using the
# RobotsNotWanted protocol and update the avoids and sites tables. See the
# details at http://web.nexor.co.uk/mak/doc/robots/norobots.html.
# Return   0 => RobotsURL at site previously checked
#          1 => this site never checked before
# =============================================================================
sub check_site
{
    local($site) = @_;                        # Site to be checked
    local($drs);                              # List of disallowed names

    return 0 if defined($Sites{$site});       # Has RobotsURL been checked?

    local($url) = "http://$site$RobotsURL";   # RobotsNotWanted URL to check
    local(%headers) = ();                     # To hold parsed response headers
    local($headers) = '';                     # To hold response headers
    local($content) = '';                     # To hold response content

    print "Checking for $url ... ";           # Make 'GET' request on RobotsURL
    local($response) = &www'request('GET', $url, *headers, *content, $Timeout);
    print "$response $RespMessage{$response}\n";

    return 1 unless ($response == $RC_ok);    # Do not proceed if response is bad

    local($whoami)  = $Version;               # "WebWalker/1.xx"
    $whoami        =~ s#/.*##;                 # Remove version or library info
    local($in_def)  = 0;                      # Default '*' record boundaries
    local($in_mine) = 0;                      # My own record boundaries
    local($def_dr)  = '';                     # Store default disallow names
    local($mine_dr) = '';                     # Store my own disallow names

    foreach (split(/\n/, $content))           # For each line in body content
```

```
    {
        next if (/^\s*#/);                    # Ignore comment-only lines
        s/\s*#.*//;                           # Remove any other comments

        if (/^\s*$/)                          # Records separated by blank lines
        {
            last if ($in_mine);               # Break out loop if end of mine
            $in_def = 0;                      # Not in default '*' by default
        }
        elsif (/^\s*User-Agent:\s*(.*)\s*$/i)
        {                                     # List of robot names
            next if ($in_mine);
            local($agent) = $1;
            if ($agent =~ /\b$whoami\b/i) { $in_mine = 1; next; }
            if ($agent =~ /^\*/)          { $in_def  = 1; }
        }
        elsif (/^\s*Disallow:\s*(.*)\s*$/i)
        {                                     # List of URLs to avoid
            next unless ($in_def || $in_mine);
            $drs = $1;
            if ($in_mine) { $mine_dr .= ' '. $drs; next; }
            if ($in_def)  { $def_dr  .= ' '. $drs; }
        }
    }

    if ($in_mine) { $def_dr = $mine_dr; }    # My own record takes precedence

    if ($def_dr !~ /^\s*$/)                   # If not a blank line
    {
        foreach $drs (split(' ', $def_dr))   # For each URL to avoid
        {                                     # Add to avoids table
            &add_avoid(&wwwurl'absolute($url, $drs));
        }
    }
    return 1;                                 # New site is now checked
}


# ==========================================================================
# Add the given $site to the sites table, duplication will be detected.
# ==========================================================================
sub add_site
{
    local($site) = @_;                        # Site to be added to table
```

```perl
    local($idx)  = $Sites{$site};            # Retrieve index based upon site

    if (!$idx)                               # Index not defined?
    {
        $idx = ++$SitesNum;                  # Must create new index
        $Sites{$site} = $idx;                # Make room for new site
    }
    $SitesAddr[$idx] = $site;                # Enter into sites table
}


# ============================================================================
# Add the given $url to the avoids table. All existing avoid or leaf entries
# will be checked first for duplication or overlapping.
# ============================================================================
sub add_avoid
{
    local($url) = @_;                        # URL to be added to avoids table
    local($old);                             # Old URL in avoids table
    local($idx);                             # Index into avoids table
    local($pos);                             # Position in avoids table

    undef $pos;                              # Set to be undefined

    foreach $idx (1 .. $AvoidNum)            # For each node in avoids table
    {
        if (!$AvoidURL[$idx])                # Gap exists in avoids table?
        {
            $pos = $idx;  next;              # Fill any gaps
        }
        $old = $AvoidURL[$idx];              # Recall old URL to be matched
        if (($url eq $old) ||               # URL duplicates an old one?
            ($url =~ m#^$old#))              # URL less general than old one?
        {
            return;                          # Don't need to add to table
        }
        if ($old =~ m#^$url#)                # URL more general than old one?
        {
            $pos = $idx;  last;              # Update with more general URL
        }
    }

    if (!defined($pos)) { $pos = ++$AvoidNum; }
    $AvoidURL[$pos] = $url;                  # Add URL to avoids table
}
```

```
# =============================================================================
# Add the given $url to the leaf table for the duration of the current
# traversal (useful for delineating the bounds of a traversal process).
# All existing leaf entries will be checked for duplication or overlapping.
# =============================================================================
sub add_leaf
{
    local($url) = @_;                     # URL to be added to leaf table
    local($old);                          # Old URL in leaf table
    local($idx);                          # Index into leaf table

    foreach $idx (1 .. $LeafNum)          # For each node in leaf table
    {
        $old = $LeafURL[$idx];            # Recall old URL to be matched
        return if ($url =~ m#^$old#);     # URL less general than old one?
    }
    $LeafURL[++$LeafNum] = $url;          # Add URL to leaf table
}


# =============================================================================
# Set the current traversal $status of the given $node, provided it is more
# advanced than previously recorded status.
# Return true (1) if okay, else false (0) if $node not found.
# =============================================================================
sub set_status
{
    local($node, $status) = @_;          # Status of node to be set

    return 0 unless defined($VisURL[$node]);# Node not found in history

    local($cstat) = $VisStatus[$node];   # Recall node traversal status

    if (!defined($cstat) ||              # Undefined old status or
        ($cstat < $status))              # Current status more advanced
    {
        $VisStatus[$node] = $status;     # Set current improved status
    }
    return 1;                            # Status ok
}


# =============================================================================
```

```
# Reset the status of all visited nodes in history so that they are no
# longer considered traversed.
# ========================================================================
sub reset_status
{
    local($node);

    foreach $node (1 .. $VisNumber)          # For each node in history
    {
        next unless defined($VisURL[$node]);# Skip over holes in history
        $VisInTask[$node] = 0;               # Not considered in this task

        if ($VisStatus[$node] > $S_tested_unknown)
        {
            $VisStatus[$node] = $S_tested_unknown;
        }
        elsif (($VisStatus[$node] == $S_seen_not_tested) ||
               ($VisStatus[$node] == $S_will_leaf)       ||
               ($VisStatus[$node] == $S_will_test))
        {
            $VisStatus[$node] = $S_not_seen;
        }
    }
}


# ========================================================================
# Check to see if the passed-in absolute $url is in history. If so, update
# its $status if the new status is more advanced and return the $node index
# to its history record. If not, create a history record for the new $url
# with the given $status.
# ========================================================================
sub remember
{
    local($url, $status) = @_;                # URL and status to be remembered
    local($node) = $Visited{$url};            # Retrieve node index from URL

    if (!$node)                               # If node not found in history
    {
        $node               = ++$VisNumber; # Create new node index
        $Visited{$url}      = $node;         # Remember this node
        $VisURL[$node]      = $url;          # Remember this URL
        $VisStatus[$node]   = $status;       # Remember URL's status
        $VisRespCode[$node] = 0;             # Init http response code
```

```
        if (($url =~ m#^file:#) ||         # Is URL local?
            ($url =~ m#://[^/]*$LocalNetwork#io))
        {
            $VisLocal[$node] = 1;          # Yes, mark it as local
        }
    }
    else                                   # Node is found in past history
    {
        &set_status($node, $status);       # Update status of node in history
    }

    $VisInTask[$node] = 1;                  # This node is in current task
    return $node;                           # Return node index
}


# ========================================================================
# Store and update history from meta information held in *headers for the
# given $node along with its $status and $response code from a recent WWW
# request. Return 1 if okay, or 0 if the $node was not found in history.
# ========================================================================
sub store
{
    local($node, $status, $response, *headers) = @_;

    return 0 unless defined($VisURL[$node]);        # Node not found?

    if (($VisStatus[$node] == $S_will_leaf) &&      # Will be leafed and
        ($status          == $S_tested_unknown))    #   already tested?
    {
        $status = $S_leafed;                        # Then treat as leafed
    }
    &set_status($node, $status);                    # Store status

    $VisConType[$node]  = $headers{'content-type'}; # MIME Content-type
    $VisRedirect[$node] = ($headers{'uri'} ||
                          $headers{'location'});    # Redirected URL
    $VisTitle[$node]    = $headers{'title'};        # Title text
    $VisOwner[$node]    = $headers{'owner'};        # Owner name
    $VisReplyTo[$node]  = $headers{'reply-to'};     # Reply-To address
    $VisLastMod[$node]  = $headers{'last-modified'};# Last-modified date
    $VisExpires[$node]  = $headers{'expires'};      # Expires date
    $VisRespCode[$node] = $response;                # Latest response code
```

```perl
    return 1;                                            # Store operation ok
}


# =============================================================================
# Recall meta information stored in history for the given $node, to be
# passed back inside the %headers array. Return the most recent response
# code or 0 if the given $node was not found in history.
# =============================================================================
sub recall
{
    local($node, *headers) = @_;

    return 0 unless defined($VisURL[$node]);             # Node not found?

    $headers{'content-type'}  = $VisConType[$node];      # MIME Content-type
    $headers{'uri'}           = $VisRedirect[$node];     # Redirected URL
    $headers{'title'}         = $VisTitle[$node];        # Title text
    $headers{'owner'}         = $VisOwner[$node];        # Owner name
    $headers{'reply-to'}      = $VisReplyTo[$node];      # Reply-To address
    $headers{'last-modified'} = $VisLastMod[$node];      # Last-modified date
    $headers{'expires'}       = $VisExpires[$node];      # Expires date

    return $VisRespCode[$node];                          # Latest response code
}


# =============================================================================
# Return true (1) if the given $node has been avoided.
# Return false (0) if the given $node was not found in history.
# =============================================================================
sub was_avoided
{
    local($node) = @_;

    return 0 unless defined($VisURL[$node]);             # Node not found?
    return ($VisStatus[$node] == $S_avoided);
}


# =============================================================================
# Return true (1) if the given $node has been tested.
# Return false (0) if the given $node was not found in history.
# =============================================================================
sub was_tested
{
```

```perl
    local($node) = @_;

    return 0 unless defined($VisURL[$node]);         # Node not found?
    return ($VisStatus[$node] >= $S_tested_unknown);
}


# =========================================================================
# Return true (1) if the given $node is untestable.
# Return false (0) if the given $node was not found in history.
# =========================================================================
sub is_untestable
{
    local($node) = @_;

    return 0 unless defined($VisURL[$node]);         # Node not found?
    return ($VisRespCode[$node] == $RC_not_implemented_client);
}


# =========================================================================
# Return true (1) if the given $node will be or has already been checked for
# its traversal status for this infostructure.
# Return false (0) if the given $node was not found in history.
# =========================================================================
sub is_known
{
    local($node) = @_;

    return 0 unless defined($VisURL[$node]);         # Node not found?
    return ($VisStatus[$node] > $S_tested_unknown);
}


# =========================================================================
# Return true (1) if the given $node will be or has already been traversed
# (or leafed) for this infostructure.
# Return false (0) if the given $node was not found in history.
# =========================================================================
sub is_traversing
{
    local($node) = @_;

    return 0 unless defined($VisURL[$node]);         # Node not found?
    return ($VisStatus[$node] >= $S_will_traverse);
}
```

```
# ==========================================================================
# Return true (1) if the given $node has been traversed.
# Return false (0) if the given $node was not found in history.
# ==========================================================================
sub was_traversed
{
    local($node) = @_;

    return 0 unless defined($VisURL[$node]);            # Node not found?
    return ($VisStatus[$node] == $S_traversed);
}


# ==========================================================================
# Return true if given $node is considered local. Return undef otherwise.
# ==========================================================================
sub is_local
{
    return $VisLocal[$_[0]];
}


# ==========================================================================
# Return the stored URL of the given $node. Return undef if not found.
# ==========================================================================
sub get_url
{
    return $VisURL[$_[0]];
}


# ==========================================================================
# Traverse an entire infostructure in breadth-first manner. The
# infostructure is indexed at $task and named $taskname. Start traversal at
# $tasktop URL and continuing until there are no more nodes to traverse
# within the infostructure bounded by $taskbound, or $MaxDepth is reached.
# ==========================================================================
sub traverse_web
{
    local($task, $taskname, $tasktop, $taskbound) = @_;

    &begin_summary($task);                   # Start of infostructure traversal

    local($url)   = &wwwurl'absolute($BaseURL, $tasktop);
    local($node)  = &remember($url, $S_seen_not_tested);
```

```perl
local($depth)  = 0;                  # Current depth starts at zero
local($parent) = '';                 # Parent of current node
$tasktop       = $url;               # The absolute form of tasktop

if (&should_avoid($node))            # Node should be avoided?
{
    print "Avoided Top URL $url ... ";
    &traversed($node);               # Node considered traversed
    undef $node;                     # Node is undefined now
}

while ($node)                        # While more nodes in queue
{
    next if (!$url);                 # Skip in case node was deleted

    print "Traversing $url ... ";
    &traverse_link($node, $parent);  # Traverse link to GET node URL
    &traversed($node);               # Node marked as traversed

    while ($TestLinks[0])            # While more links to test
    {
        local($child) = shift(@TestLinks);  # $url is now the parent
        local($abs)   = shift(@TestAbs);    # Absolute URL
        local($orig)  = shift(@TestOrig);   # Original href
        local($type)  = shift(@TestType);   # Anchor type

        next if (!$child);           # Skip if child not defined
                                     # Remember child as seen
        local($vidx) = &remember($child, $S_seen_not_tested);
        local($reused);              # Flag indicates reuse of test

        if (&was_tested($vidx))      # Was child tested before?
        {
            print "Reusing test of $child ... ";
            $reused = 1;             # Yes, previous result reused
        }
        else
        {
            if (&should_avoid($vidx))  # Should child be avoided?
            {
                print "Avoiding $child ... ";
                &tested($vidx, 1);   # Child considered tested
                next;                # Next child to test
            }
```

```
            print "Testing $child ... ";
            &test_link($vidx, $url);      # Test url link with HEAD
            $reused = 0;                  # Mark as not reused
        }

        if ($depth >= $MaxDepth)          # Maximum depth exceeded?
        {                                 # Don't go beyond max depth
            ; # Do Nothing                # Don't mark as leaf either
        }
        elsif (&should_traverse($vidx, $type, $taskbound))
        {                                    # Child should be traversed
            local($pos)        = $#TravNodes + 1;
            $TravNodes[$pos]   = $vidx;
            $TravDepth[$pos]   = $depth + 1;
            $TravParent[$pos]  = $url;
            &set_status($vidx, $S_will_traverse);
        }
        else                              # Child should be leafed
        {
            &set_status($vidx, $S_leafed);
        }

        &tested($vidx, $reused);          # Mark child as tested
    }
    print "Done Traversing $url ...\n... at ", &wwwdates'wtime(time,''),
        "-- ", $#TravNodes + 1, " remaining on queue\n\n";

}
continue
{
    $node   = shift(@TravNodes);          # Next in queue to examine
    $depth  = shift(@TravDepth);
    $parent = shift(@TravParent);
    if ($node) { $url = &get_url($node); }
}

&end_summary($task);                      # End of infostructure traversal
&reset_status;                            # Reset status of node history
}


# =========================================================================
# Return true (1) if the given $node should be or has already been avoided.
# Return false (0) otherwise.
# =========================================================================
```

```perl
sub should_avoid
{
    local($node) = @_;                  # Should this node be avoided?

    # Has this node already been avoided? So should avoid.
    # Has this node already been checked? So should not avoid.

    return 1 if ( $VisStatus[$node] == $S_avoided);
    return 0 if (($VisStatus[$node] >  $S_avoided) &&
                ($VisStatus[$node] != $S_tested_unknown));

    local($url) = $VisURL[$node];        # Get this node's URL
    return 1 unless ($url);              #   or should avoid if not found

    local($check) = &check_url($url);    # Check Avoid/Leaf status
    return 0 unless ($check);            # Check 0 => no restrictions

    if ($check == 1)                     # Check 1 => must leaf this URL
    {
        $VisStatus[$node] = ($VisStatus[$node] == $S_tested_unknown)
                        ?  $S_leafed : $S_will_leaf;
        return 0;                        # Don't have to avoid
    }

    $VisStatus[$node] = $S_avoided;      # Check 2 => must avoid this URL
    return 1;                            # Should avoid this URL
}


# =========================================================================
# Determine whether or not the given $node should be traversed or leafed for
# the current infostructure. Don't traverse if:
#     (1) node $type is Image or Queries;
#     (2) node should be avoided;
#     (3) node already traversed (or will soon);
#     (4) result from previous test was not OK;
#     (5) node content is not HTML;
#     (6) node $url is not below $taskbound.
# Return  1 => should traverse this node
#         0 => should leaf    this node
# =========================================================================
sub should_traverse
{
```

```perl
    local($node, $type, $taskbound) = @_;

    return 0 if (($type eq 'I') ||          # Don't traverse links of IMGs
                 ($type eq 'Q'));           #   or Queries anchor type

    return 0 if (&should_avoid($node));     # Don't traverse if should avoid
    return 0 if (&is_known($node));         # Don't traverse again if already
                                            #   traversed (or will soon)

    local(%headers) = ();                   # Holds headers meta information
    local($response);                       # Http response code
    $response = &recall($node, *headers);   # Recall results from 'HEAD' test

                                            # Don't traverse if test not OK
    return 0 unless (($WhatToDo{$response} == $DO_continue) ||
                     ($WhatToDo{$response} == $DO_redirect));

    local($url) = &get_url($node);          # Retrieve URL from node index
                                            # Don't traverse if not HTML
    return 0 unless (&is_html($url, *headers));

    local($scheme, $addr, $port, $path, $query, $frag)
         = &wwwurl'parse($url);             # $url -> scheme://addr:port

    local($_scheme, $_addr, $_port, $_path, $_query, $_frag)
         = &wwwurl'parse($taskbound);       # $taskbound -> scheme://addr:port

    return 0 unless (($scheme eq $_scheme) &&
                     ($addr   eq $_addr)   &&
                     ($port   eq $_port)); # Don't traverse if not equal

    $_path =~ s#/[^/]*$#/#;                  # Trim any filename off $TaskBound
    return 0 unless ($path =~ /^$_path/);   # Check if url is below $TaskBound

    return 1;                               # Otherwise should traverse!
}


# ============================================================================
# Test URL indexed by given $node via http 'HEAD' request, may slow down to
# moderate its speed as needed. Its $parent node is actually its 'Referer'
# for purpose of providing http meta information to server. Store response
# code and headers meta information in history and update its status.
# Return the http server response code.
# ============================================================================
```

```
sub test_link
{
    local($node, $parent) = @_;            # Current node and its parent

    local($url)       = &get_url($node);   # Retrieve stored URL from history
    local(%headers)   = ();                # To hold parsed response headers
    local($headers)   = '';                # To hold response headers
    local($content)   = '';                # To hold response content


                                           # Set up the HTTP request headers
    $headers{'Accept'}  = '*/*';           # All content types are of interest
    $headers{'Referer'} = $parent;         # Parent node refers this URL


                                           # Do not make too many consecutive
    &slow_down($url);                      #   requests too fast. May sleep...

    # Issue http 'HEAD' request for $url subject to $Timeout, pass back
    # $response code, *headers meta information and *content.

    local($response) = &www'request('HEAD', $url, *headers, *content, $Timeout);

    # Store $response code and *headers meta information in history.

    &store($node, $S_tested_unknown, $response, *headers);

    return $response;                      # Return http response code
}


# ===========================================================================
# Traverse URL indexed by given $node via http 'GET' request, may slow down
# to moderate its speed as needed. Its $parent node is actually its
# 'Referer' for purpose of providing http meta information to server. Add
# any links extracted from headers or content of this $node to the @Test*
# queues for further traversal. Store response code and headers meta
# information in history and update its status. Return the http server
# response code.
# ===========================================================================
sub traverse_link
{
    local($node, $parent) = @_;            # Current node and its parent

    local($url)       = &get_url($node);   # Retrieve stored URL from history
```

```
    local(%headers)   = ();              # To hold parsed response headers
    local($headers)   = '';              # To hold response headers
    local($content)   = '';              # To hold response content


                                         # Set up the HTTP request headers
    $headers{'Accept'}  = 'text/html';   # Only "text/html" is of interest
    $headers{'Referer'} = $parent;       # Parent node refers this URL


                                         # Do not make too many consecutive
    &slow_down($url);                    #   requests too fast. May sleep...

    # Issue http 'GET' request for $url subject to $Timeout, pass back
    # $response code, *headers meta information and *content.

    local($response) = &www'request('GET', $url, *headers, *content, $Timeout);

    # Extract links from *headers and *content for use in later traversal.

    &extract_links($url, *headers, *content, $response);

    # Store $response code and *headers meta information in history.

    &store($node, $S_traversed, $response, *headers);

    return $response;                    # Return http response code
}


# =============================================================================
# Extract $url document meta information and links from *headers and
# *content, and deposit in @Test* arrays for use in further traversal. The
# $response argument determines whether redirected link is encountered.
# =============================================================================
sub extract_links
{
    local($url, *headers, *content, $response) = @_;

    @TestLinks = ();                     # Absolute URLs (w/o query or tag)
    @TestAbs   = ();                     # Absolute URLs (w/  query or tag)
    @TestOrig  = ();                     # Original href
    @TestType  = ();                     # (Link, Image, Query, Redirect)

    if (($WhatToDo{$response} == $DO_continue) &&
        (&is_html($url, *headers)))       # Only HTML contains links
```

```
    {
        local($encoding) = $headers{'content-encoding'};

        if (&decode($encoding, *content))    # Decode document if compressed
        {
            # Extract $url document meta information, links, and anchor types
            # from *headers and *content, and passed back for traversal use.

            &wwwhtml'extract_links($url, *headers, *content,  *TestLinks,
                                    *TestAbs, *TestOrig, *TestType);
        }
    }

    if ($WhatToDo{$response} == $DO_redirect)
    {
        local($redir);                      # Redir treated as single child

        if ($redir = $headers{'location'})
        {
            $redir =~ s/, .*//;             # Get rid of multiple
        }                                   #   Location: entries
        elsif ($redir = $headers{'uri'})
        {
            $redir =~ s/\s*;.*//;
            $redir =~ s/, .*//;             # Eliminate multiple URI: entries
        }

        if ($redir)                         # Redirected link exists?
        {
            $TestLinks[0] = $redir;         # Absolute URL to be tested
            $TestAbs[0]   = $redir;         # Original HREF in absolute form
            $TestOrig[0]  = $redir;         # Original HREF
            $TestType[0]  = 'R';            # Redirected link type
        }
    }
}


# ============================================================================
# Given the $url to test or traverse, make sure that WebWalker is not making
# too many consecutive requests and/or going too fast with respect to a
# single site. This prevents WebWalker from completely dominating the
# resources of a particular server. The remedy is to sleep for a while
# within this routine before returning.
# ============================================================================
```

```
sub slow_down
{
    local($url) = @_;                     # Given URL to test or traverse
    local($site);                         # Http site extracted from URL
    local($secs);                         # Wake up time (secs after Epoch)

    return unless ($url =~ m#^http#);     # Applicable to http only
    return unless ($site = &wwwurl'get_site($url));

    LOITER: {
        if ($site ne $PrevSite)           # Not same as previous site?
        {
            $CurConsec = 1;               # Init current consec request
            last LOITER;                  # Break out LOITER scope
        }

        if (++$CurConsec > $MaxConsec)    # Too many consecutive requests?
        {                                 #    to the same site?
            sleep($PauseTime);            # Yes, take a breather
            $CurConsec = 1;               # Re-init current consec request
            last LOITER;                  # Break out LOITER scope
        }

        $secs = ($PrevTime + $BetweenTime); # Wake up time in seconds
        if ($secs > time)                 # Not quite time yet to wake up
        {
            sleep($secs - time);          # Sleep the remaining seconds
        }
    }

    $PrevSite = $site;                    # Remember latest site
    $PrevTime = time;                     # Remember current time
}


# =========================================================================
# Determine from the given $url and response *headers whether it points to a
# "text/html" document. Note that this routine also has the side-effect of
# setting the content-type and content-encoding if they were previously
# undefined.
# Return   1 => text/html content-type
#          0 => not text/html content-type
# =========================================================================
```

```perl
sub is_html
{
    local($url, *headers) = @_;            # URL and http response headers

    if (!defined($headers{'content-type'})) # No content-type specified?
    {
        $_ = $url;                        # Start with URL string
        s#/[^/.]*\.([^/]*)$#/#;           # Grab filename extension off URL
        local($suffix) = ($1 || '');      # Assign suffix string, if any

        # Set content-type and content-encoding headers based on $suffix

        &wwwmime'set_content($suffix, *headers);
    }

    # Match content-type with "text/html" string and return success/failure

    return 1 if ($headers{'content-type'} =~ m#\btext/html\b#io);
    return 0;                             # Not text/html content-type
}


# ===========================================================================
# Translate encoded content, of type $encoding and held in $content, into
# its decoded form. The new *content is passed back in place of the old.
# Return  0 => failed to decode content
#         1 => succeeded in decoding content
# ===========================================================================
sub decode
{
    local($encoding, *content) = @_;      # Encoding type, encoded content

    return 1 unless ($encoding);          # Return success if not encoded!

    local($com) = $CEdecoder{$encoding};  # Command for decoding
    local($ext) = ($CEextension{$encoding} # File name extension
                   || '');                #   is optional

    return 0 unless ($CEfile && $com);    # Must have file name and command

    if (!open(ENCODE, "> $CEfile$ext"))   # Can't open file for write
    {
        print STDERR "Can't write to $CEfile$ext: $!\n";
        return 0;                         # Failed to decode content
    }
```

```perl
    print ENCODE $content;                  # Write encoded content to file
    close(ENCODE);                          # Close encoded file
    undef $content;                         # Empty all contents

    system("$com $CEfile$ext");             # Execute decoding command
    if (!open(DECODE, $CEfile))             # Can't open file for read
    {
        print STDERR "Can't open decompressed $CEfile: $!\n";
        return 0;                           # Failed to decode content
    }

    local($/);                              # Input record separator
    undef($/);                              # No record separator is matched
    $content = <DECODE>;                    # Read to end of DECODE file
    close(DECODE);                          # Close decoded file
    unlink($CEfile);                        # Remove decoded file

    return 1;                               # Succeeded in decoding content
}


# =========================================================================
# At the beginning of an infostructure traversal, print out a prologue,
# initialize all counters for statistical summary, and specify values for
# change window and expire window, as appropriate. Also empty all
# information arrays for broken or redirected links, and changed or expired
# nodes. The infostructure is represented in arrays @Task* indexed by $task.
# =========================================================================
sub begin_summary
{
    local($task) = @_;                      # Current index into @Task*
                                            # Print infostructure prologue
    if ($CGI) { print "<PRE>\n"; }          # HTML formatting as required
    print 'Starting Infostructure [', $TaskName[$task], '] at ',
          &wwwdates'wtime(time, ''), "\n";

    if (defined($TaskChangeWindow[$task]))  # Task change window specified?
    {
        $ChangeDays   = $TaskChangeWindow[$task];
        $ChangeWindow = $TaskChangeWindow[$task] * 86400;
    }
    else { $ChangeDays = $ChangeWindow = 0; }
```

```perl
    if (defined($TaskExpireWindow[$task]))  # Task expire window specified?
    {
        $ExpireDays   = $TaskExpireWindow[$task];
        $ExpireWindow = $TaskExpireWindow[$task] * 86400;
    }
    else { $ExpireDays = $ExpireWindow = 0; }

    &init_summary;                          # Init all counters for summary

    %BrokenNodes   = ();                    # Init broken nodes info array
    %RedirectNodes = ();                    # Init redirected nodes info array
    %ChangedNodes  = ();                    # Init changed nodes info array
    %ExpiredNodes  = ();                    # Init expired nodes info array
}


# ==========================================================================
# Initialize all counters for generating statistical table summary results.
# ==========================================================================
sub init_summary
{
    $TotalHrefs = 0;                        # Total URL reference count
    $TotalNodes = 0;                        # Total unique node count
    $TotalLocal = 0;                        # Total local node count

    $HrefsTrav  = 0;                        # Traversed URL reference count
    $HrefsTest  = 0;                        # Tested URL reference count
    $HrefsReus  = 0;                        # Reused URL reference count
    $HrefsAvd   = 0;                        # Avoided URL reference count
    $HrefsUnt   = 0;                        # Untestable URL reference count
    $HrefsBroke = 0;                        # Broken URL reference count
    $HrefsRedir = 0;                        # Redirected URL reference count
    $HrefsChg   = 0;                        # Changed URL reference count
    $HrefsExp   = 0;                        # Expired URL reference count
    $HrefsLoc   = 0;                        # Local URL reference count
    $HrefsRmt   = 0;                        # Remote URL reference count

    $NodesTrav  = 0;                        # Unique traversed node count
    $NodesTest  = 0;                        # Unique tested node count
    $NodesReus  = 0;                        # Unique reused node count
    $NodesAvd   = 0;                        # Unique avoided node count
    $NodesUnt   = 0;                        # Unique untestable node count
    $NodesBroke = 0;                        # Unique broken node count
    $NodesRedir = 0;                        # Unique redirected node count
```

```
   $NodesChg   = 0;                        # Unique changed node count
   $NodesExp   = 0;                        # Unique expired node count
   $NodesRmt   = 0;                        # Unique remote node count

   $LocalTrav  = 0;                        # Local traversed node count
   $LocalTest  = 0;                        # Local tested node count
   $LocalReus  = 0;                        # Local reused node count
   $LocalAvd   = 0;                        # Local avoided node count
   $LocalUnt   = 0;                        # Local untestable node count
   $LocalBroke = 0;                        # Local broken node count
   $LocalRedir = 0;                        # Local redirected node count
   $LocalChg   = 0;                        # Local changed node count
   $LocalExp   = 0;                        # Local expired node count
}


# =========================================================================
# Determine response message and print on stdout if $node was not $reused.
# Save any info on status of broken or redirected links, and changed nodes,
# as appropriate. Update all direct $Hrefs* counters. The given $node has
# been tested (with 'HEAD' method) as part of the current infostructure.
# =========================================================================
sub tested
{
   local($node, $reused) = @_;       # Tested node, reuse flag
   local(%headers)      = ();        # Headers info to be recalled
   local($url)          = &get_url($node);  # Retrieve URL from history
   local($response)     = &recall($node, *headers);
   local($respmsg);                  # Response message
   local($is_broken)    = 0;         # Is link broken?
   local($is_redirect)  = 0;         # Is link redirected?
   local($is_changed)   = 0;         # Is node changed?

   ++$TotalHrefs;                    # Total URL reference count
   if (&is_local($node)) { ++$HrefsLoc; }  # Local URL reference count

   if (&was_avoided($node))          # Node was avoided
   {
       $respmsg = "000 Avoided";     # Replace "000 Unknown Error"
       ++$HrefsAvd;                  # Avoided URL reference count
   }
   elsif (&is_untestable($node))     # Node found to be untestable
   {
       $respmsg = "$RC_not_implemented_client Not Tested";
```

```
      ++$HrefsUnt;                          # Untestable URL reference count
   }
   else                                     # All other cases...
   {
      $respmsg = "$response $RespMessage{$response}";
      if (!$reused) { ++$HrefsTest; }       # Tested URL reference count

      local($lmd)  = $headers{'last-modified'};
      local($lmt);                          # Last-modified (secs since Epoch)

      $is_broken   = ($WhatToDo{$response} == $DO_broken);
      $is_redirect = ($WhatToDo{$response} == $DO_redirect);

      $is_changed  = ($ChangeWindow                          &&
                      defined($lmd)                          &&
                      ($lmt = &wwwdates'get_gmtime($lmd)) &&
                      (($lmt + $ChangeWindow) >= time));
   }

   if ($is_broken)                          # Broken link?
   {
      &save_broken($node, $respmsg, $url);
      ++$HrefsBroke;                        # Broken URL reference count
   }
   if ($is_redirect)                        # Redirected link?
   {
      &save_redirect($node, $respmsg, $url);
      ++$HrefsRedir;                        # Redirected URL reference count
   }
   if ($is_changed)                         # Changed node?
   {
      &save_changed($node, $respmsg, $url, $lmd);
      ++$HrefsChg;                          # Changed URL reference count
   }
   if (&is_traversing($node))               # Will or already traversed?
   {
      ++$HrefsTrav;                         # Traversed URL reference count
   }

   print $respmsg if (!$reused);            # Print response message
   print "\n";                              #   if not reused
}
```

```perl
# =============================================================================
# Determine response message and print on stdout. Save any info on status of
# broken or redirected links, changed or expired nodes, as appropriate. The
# given $node has been traversed (with 'GET' method) as part of the current
# infostructure. The node was then (if possible) html-parsed for possible
# child links. The program will next work on testing extracted child links.
# =============================================================================
sub traversed
{
    local($node)        = @_;            # Given node that was traversed
    local(%headers)     = ();            # Headers info to be recalled
    local($url)         = &get_url($node); # Retrieve URL from history
    local($response)    = &recall($node, *headers);
    local($respmsg);                     # Response message
    local($is_broken)   = 0;            # Is link broken?
    local($is_redirect) = 0;            # Is link redirected?
    local($is_changed)  = 0;            # Is node changed?
    local($is_expired)  = 0;            # Is node expired?

    if (&was_avoided($node))            # Node was avoided
    {
        $respmsg = "000 Avoided";        # Replace "000 Unknown Error"
    }
    elsif (&is_untestable($node))       # Node found to be untestable
    {
        $respmsg = "$RC_not_implemented_client Not Tested";
    }
    else                                # All other cases...
    {
        $respmsg = "$response $RespMessage{$response}";

        local($lmd)     = $headers{'last-modified'};
        local($expd)    = $headers{'expires'};
        local($lmt);                     # Last-modified (secs since Epoch)
        local($expt);                    # Expiration (secs since Epoch)
        local($current) = time;          # Current time

        $is_broken   = ($WhatToDo{$response} == $DO_broken);
        $is_redirect = ($WhatToDo{$response} == $DO_redirect);

        $is_changed  = ($ChangeWindow                      &&
                        defined($lmd)                      &&
                        ($lmt = &wwwdates'get_gmtime($lmd)) &&
                        (($lmt + $ChangeWindow) >= $current));
```

```
        $is_expired  = ($ExpireWindow                            &&
                        defined($expd)                           &&
                        ($expt = &wwwdates'get_gmtime($expd)) &&
                        (($expt - $ExpireWindow) <= $current));
    }

    # Save information arrays for broken or redirected links, as well
    # as for changed or expired nodes, as appropriate

    if ($is_broken)    { &save_broken   ($node, $respmsg, $url);        }
    if ($is_redirect)  { &save_redirect ($node, $respmsg, $url);        }
    if ($is_changed)   { &save_changed  ($node, $respmsg, $url, $lmd);  }
    if ($is_expired)   { &save_expired  ($node, $respmsg, $url, $expd); }

    print $respmsg, "\n";                       # Print response message
}


# =========================================================================
# Save the given $node of broken link along with its response message
# ($respmsg) and $url so that it can later be printed in the list of broken
# links at the end of the infostructure traversal. In case of multiple
# references, prefer the first one saved.
# =========================================================================
sub save_broken
{
    local($node, $respmsg, $url) = @_;

    return if $BrokenNodes{$node};          # Previously saved, just return

    $BrokenNodes{$node} = <<"EOentry";      # Enter in broken nodes array
    $url  ($respmsg)
EOentry

    ++$NodesBroke;                          # Unique broken node count
    ++$LocalBroke if (&is_local($node));    # Local broken node count
}


# =========================================================================
# Save the given $node of redirected link along with its response message
# ($respmsg) and $url so that it can later be printed in the list of
# redirected links at the end of the infostructure traversal. In case of
# multiple references, prefer the first one saved.
# =========================================================================
```

```
sub save_redirect
{
    local($node, $respmsg, $url) = @_;

    return if $RedirectNodes{$node};        # Previously saved, just return

    $RedirectNodes{$node} = <<"EOentry";    # Enter in redirected nodes array
    $url   ($respmsg)
EOentry

    ++$NodesRedir;                          # Unique redirected node count
    ++$LocalRedir if (&is_local($node));    # Local redirected node count
}


# =============================================================================
# Save the given changed $node along with its response message ($respmsg),
# $url and last-modified date ($lmd) so that it can later be printed in the
# list of changed nodes at the end of the infostructure traversal. In case
# of multiple references, prefer the first one saved.
# =============================================================================
sub save_changed
{
    local($node, $respmsg, $url, $lmd) = @_;

    return if $ChangedNodes{$node};         # Previously saved, just return

    $ChangedNodes{$node} = <<"EOentry";     # Enter in changed nodes array
    $url   ($respmsg)
    Last-modified: $lmd
EOentry

    ++$NodesChg;                            # Unique changed node count
    ++$LocalChg if (&is_local($node));      # Local changed node count
}


# =============================================================================
# Save the given expired $node along with its response message ($respmsg),
# $url and expiration date ($expd) so that it can later be printed in the
# list of expired nodes at the end of the infostructure traversal. In case
# of multiple references, prefer the first one saved.
# =============================================================================
sub save_expired
{
```

```perl
    local($node, $respmsg, $url, $expd) = @_;

    return if $ExpiredNodes{$node};          # Previously saved, just return

    $ExpiredNodes{$node} = <<"EOentry";      # Enter in expired nodes array
    $url  ($respmsg)
    Expires: $expd
EOentry

    ++$NodesExp;                             # Unique expired node count
    ++$LocalExp if (&is_local($node));       # Local expired node count
}


# ============================================================================
# At the end of traversing an infostructure, print summary of results for
# broken or redirected links, changed or expired nodes, as well as summary
# statistical table, plus an epilogue. The infostructure is represented in
# arrays @Task* indexed by $task.
# ============================================================================
sub end_summary
{
    local($task) = @_;                       # Current index into @TaskName

    if (keys %BrokenNodes)                   # Any broken links?
    {
        print "Broken Links:\n", values(%BrokenNodes);
    }

    if (keys %RedirectNodes)                  # Any redirected links?
    {
        print "Redirected Links:\n", values(%RedirectNodes);
    }

    if ((keys %ChangedNodes) &&              # Any changed nodes, and
        ($ChangeWindow > 0))                 #    non-zero change window
    {
        print "Changed Links:\n", values(%ChangedNodes);
    }

    if ((keys %ExpiredNodes) &&              # Any expired nodes, and
        ($ExpireWindow > 0))                 #    non-zero expiration window?
    {
        print "Expired Documents:\n", values(%ExpiredNodes);
    }
```

```perl
    &update_summary;                        # Update summary table counters
    print "\nSummary of Results:\n", &get_summary;

                                            # Print infostructure epilogue
    print 'Finished Infostructure [', $TaskName[$task], '] at ',
          &wwwdates'wtime(time, ''), "\n\n";
    if ($CGI) { print "</PRE>\n"; }         # HTML formatting as required
}


# ===========================================================================
# Update counters used for collecting statistics to generate summary table.
# ===========================================================================
sub update_summary
{
    local($node);                           # Index into history arrays

    foreach $node (1 .. $VisNumber)         # For each node visited
    {
        if ($VisInTask[$node])              # URL node is in current task?
        {
            ++$TotalNodes;                  # Increment total node count
            ++$TotalLocal if (&is_local($node));

            if (&was_avoided($node))        # Was URL node avoided?
            {
                ++$NodesAvd;                # Increment avoided node count
                ++$LocalAvd if (&is_local($node));
            }
            elsif (&is_untestable($node))   # Is URL node untestable?
            {
                ++$NodesUnt;                # Increment untestable node count
                ++$LocalUnt if (&is_local($node));
            }
            elsif (&was_tested($node))      # Was URL node tested ('HEAD')?
            {
                ++$NodesTest;               # Increment tested node count
                ++$LocalTest if (&is_local($node));

                if (&was_traversed($node))  # Was URL node traversed ('GET')
                {
                    ++$NodesTrav;           # Increment traversed node count
```

```perl
                            ++$LocalTrav if (&is_local($node));
                }
            }
        }
    }

    # Total count consists of reused, avoided, untestable and tested counts.
    # Same for URL references, unique URL nodes and local URL nodes.

    $HrefsReus = $TotalHrefs - ($HrefsAvd + $HrefsUnt + $HrefsTest);
    $NodesReus = $TotalNodes - ($NodesAvd + $NodesUnt + $NodesTest);
    $LocalReus = $TotalLocal - ($LocalAvd + $LocalUnt + $LocalTest);

    $HrefsRmt  = $TotalHrefs - $HrefsLoc;   # Total remote URL reference count
    $NodesRmt  = $TotalNodes - $TotalLocal; # Total remote node count
}


# ============================================================================
# Generate statistical summary of results. Return the table-formatted
# statistical summary as an ASCII string ready to be printed out.
# ============================================================================
sub get_summary
{
    local($th) = $TotalHrefs;             # Total URL reference count
    local($tn) = $TotalNodes;             # Total unique URL node count
    local($tl) = $TotalLocal;             # Total local URL node count

    if  (!$th) { $th = 1; }               # Avoid divide by zero errors
    if  (!$tn) { $tn = 1; }
    if  (!$tl) { $tl = 1; }

    return sprintf($SummaryFormat,        # Table-formatted summary
                $HrefsTrav,  (100*$HrefsTrav/$th),
                $NodesTrav,  (100*$NodesTrav/$tn),
                $LocalTrav,  (100*$LocalTrav/$tl),

                $HrefsTest,  (100*$HrefsTest/$th),
                $NodesTest,  (100*$NodesTest/$tn),
                $LocalTest,  (100*$LocalTest/$tl),

                $HrefsReus,  (100*$HrefsReus/$th),
                $NodesReus,  (100*$NodesReus/$tn),
                $LocalReus,  (100*$LocalReus/$tl),
```

```
              $HrefsAvd,   (100*$HrefsAvd/$th),
              $NodesAvd,   (100*$NodesAvd/$tn),
              $LocalAvd,   (100*$LocalAvd/$tl),

              $HrefsUnt,   (100*$HrefsUnt/$th),
              $NodesUnt,   (100*$NodesUnt/$tn),
              $LocalUnt,   (100*$LocalUnt/$tl),

              $HrefsBroke, (100*$HrefsBroke/$th),
              $NodesBroke, (100*$NodesBroke/$tn),
              $LocalBroke, (100*$LocalBroke/$tl),

              $HrefsRedir, (100*$HrefsRedir/$th),
              $NodesRedir, (100*$NodesRedir/$tn),
              $LocalRedir, (100*$LocalRedir/$tl),

              $ChangeDays,
              $HrefsChg,   (100*$HrefsChg/$th),
              $NodesChg,   (100*$NodesChg/$tn),
              $LocalChg,   (100*$LocalChg/$tl),

              $ExpireDays,
              $HrefsExp,   (100*$HrefsExp/$th),
              $NodesExp,   (100*$NodesExp/$tn),
              $LocalExp,   (100*$LocalExp/$tl),

              $HrefsLoc,   (100*$HrefsLoc/$th),
              $TotalLocal, (100*$TotalLocal/$tn),
              $TotalLocal, 100.0,

              $HrefsRmt,   (100*$HrefsRmt/$th),
              $NodesRmt,   (100*$NodesRmt/$tn),
              0,            0.0,

              $TotalHrefs, 100.0,
              $TotalNodes, (100*$TotalNodes/$th),
              $TotalLocal, (100*$TotalLocal/$th),
              );
}

# ==============================================================================
#                         THE   END                              #
# ==============================================================================
```

WebShopper 1.00
Program Listing

WebShopper is a generic Web agent that can be configured for use as specialized shopping agents, such as BookFinder or CDFinder, that deal only in specific merchandise categories, in this case, books or CDs. WebShopper is designed to assist Web users in searching for and locating comparative items of interest across multiple online shops and to facilitate the painstaking process of comparison shopping based not just on prices alone but also on other terms of sale.

The following is a 300-line Perl code listing of
WebShopper 1.00, which is also available on the
Web at this address:

```
http://deluge.stanford.edu:8000/book/webshop.#!/usr/local/bin/perl

# =========================================================================
# Copyright (c) 1995 Fah-Chun Cheong. All rights reserved.
# -------------------------------------------------------------------------
# WebShopper 1.00 — A World Wide Web agent for searching multiple online
#                         databases on the Web by author/artist and/or title.
# =========================================================================
#
# WebShopper performs a case insensitive substring search on author/artist
# and title fields. If both the Author/Artist and Title field are filled in,
# the system will display only the items that match on both fields.
#
# =========================================================================


$WebShopper = "BookFinder";              # WebShopper as BookFinder
$webshop    = "bookfind";

# $WebShopper = "CDFinder";              # WebShopper as CDFinder
# $webshop    = "cdfind";

$LibWWW     = "/usr/local/lib/libwww-perl-0.40";
$WWWlib     = ($ENV{'LIBWWW_PERL'} || $LibWWW || '.');
unshift(@INC, $WWWlib);

$Version    = "$WebShopper/1.00";        # Agent identification
$Browser    = "Mozilla/1.1N";            # Favorite browser
$CGIdir     = "/usr/local/www/cgi-bin";

require "getopts.pl";                    # Perl library package
require "www.pl";                        # libwww-perl library package
require "wwwdates.pl";                   # ditto


# =========================================================================
# Set default parameter values.
# =========================================================================


$TaskFile = "$CGIdir/.$webshop";         # default location of task file
$Timeout  = 30;                          # max secs to wait for response
```

```perl
# =========================================================================
# Get the command-line options.
# =========================================================================

if (!(&Getopts('hi:a:t:')) ¦¦ $opt_h) { &usage; }

if ($opt_i) { $TaskFile = $opt_i; }        # Overrides default task file
if ($opt_a) { $Author   = $opt_a; }        # Specify author/artist
if ($opt_t) { $Title    = $opt_t; }        # Specify title

select((select(STDERR), $¦ = 1)[0]);       # Make STDERR unbuffered
$¦ = 1;                                     # Make STDOUT unbuffered


# =========================================================================
# Main processing loop cycling over multiple online databases on the Web.
# =========================================================================

&read_query;                               # Read query string
&read_tasks;                               # Read tasks

print $Version, ' starting at ', &wwwdates'wtime(time, ''), "\n";
&www'set_def_header('http', 'User-Agent', $Version);
&www'set_def_header('http', 'User-Agent', $Browser);

&prologue;                                 # Table of contents

foreach $task (1 .. $#TaskName)            # For each specified task
{
    local($content) = '';                  # To hold response content
    &find_item($task, *content);           # Search online database
    &print_result($task, *content);        # Print result of search
}

print $Version, ' finished at ', &wwwdates'wtime(time, ''), "\n";


# =========================================================================
# Print usage information if help requested (-h) or an invalid option given.
# =========================================================================
sub usage
{
    die <<"EndUsage";
usage: $webshop [-h] [-i taskfile] [-a author/artist] [-t title]
$Version
```

```
        WWW Agent for searching multiple online databases on the Web.
        Options:                                            [DEFAULT]
            -h  Help -- just display this message and quit.
            -i  Get your task instructions from the following file.  [$TaskFile]
            -a  Author/Artist.
            -t  Title.
    EndUsage
    }


    # ==========================================================================
    # Handle GET and POST method parameters if used as CGI script.
    # ==========================================================================
    sub read_query
    {
        local($qstr);                          # query string

        if ($ENV{'REQUEST_METHOD'} eq "GET")   # GET method?
        {
            $qstr = $ENV{'QUERY_STRING'};      # extract query string
        }
        elsif ($ENV{'REQUEST_METHOD'} eq "POST")# POST method?
        {
            read(STDIN, $qstr, $ENV{'CONTENT_LENGTH'});
        }
        else { return $CGI = 0; }              # script not used in CGI context

        $qstr =~ s/%([\dA-Fa-f][\dA-Fa-f])/pack("C",hex($1))/ge;
        $qstr =~ s/\+/ /g;                     # restore blanks in argument values
        local(%env) = split (/[&=]/, $qstr);   # parse into associative array
        local(@env) = split (/&/, $qstr);      # parse into list

        $Author = $env{'Author'};              # extract author/artist
        $Title  = $env{'Title'};               # extract title

        print "Content-type: text/html\n\n";

        return $CGI = 1;                       # script is used in CGI context
    }


    # ==========================================================================
    # Read task instructions from the $TaskFile and fill in the @Task* tables.
    # ==========================================================================
    sub read_tasks
    {
```

```perl
local($task)   = 0;                    # Task index into @Task* tables
local($intask) = 0;                    # Inside of task description?
local($taskno) = 0;                    # No. of task instructions seen
local($reason) = '';                   # Why task description is bad

if (!$CGI) { print "Reading task specifications from $TaskFile\n\n"; }

if (!open(TASK, $TaskFile))            # Open task file for read
{
    print STDERR "Cannot open task file: $!\n";
    &usage;                            # Show proper usage
}

while (<TASK>)                         # For each line of task file
{
    next if (/^$/ ¦¦ /^\#/);           # Ignore blank and comment lines

    if (!$intask)                      # If not within a task?
    {
        $taskno++;                     # Increment task instruction no.
        if (/^</)                      # Start of next task?
        {
            $task++;                   # New task index
            $intask = 1;               # Now inside a task
        }
        next;                          # Next instructions
    }
                                       # Currently within a task
    if (/^</)                          # Indicates beginning of task?
    {
        die "Task $taskno is not properly terminated, stopped";
    }
    elsif (/^\s*Name\s+((\S+\s*)+)\n$/) { $TaskName   [$task] = $1; }
    elsif (/^\s*Home\s+(\S+)/)         { $TaskHome   [$task] = $1; }
    elsif (/^\s*Form\s+(\S+)/)         { $TaskForm   [$task] = $1; }
    elsif (/^\s*(GET¦POST)\s+(\S+)/)   { $TaskMethod[$task] = $1;
                                         $TaskUrl    [$task] = $2; }
    elsif (/^\s*QUERY\s+(\S+)/)        { $TaskQuery [$task] = $1; }
    elsif (/^\s*AUTHOR\s+(\S+)/)       { $TaskAuthor[$task] = $1; }
    elsif (/^\s*TITLE\s+(\S+)/)        { $TaskTitle [$task] = $1; }
    elsif (/^\s*KEY\s+(\S+)/)          { $TaskKey   [$task] = $1; }
    elsif (/^>\s*$/)                   # Line indicates End of Task?
    {
        $intask = 0;                   # No longer inside task
```

```
            $reason = '';                     # No bad task reason until told

        if    (!$TaskName  [$task]) { $reason = "has no Name"; }
        elsif (!$TaskHome  [$task]) { $reason = "has no Home"; }
        elsif (!$TaskForm  [$task]) { $reason = "has no Form"; }
        elsif (!$TaskMethod[$task]) { $reason = "has no Method"; }
        elsif (!$TaskUrl   [$task]) { $reason = "has no Url"; }
        elsif (!($TaskTitle[$task] && $TaskAuthor[$task]) &&
                 !$TaskQuery [$task] &&
                 !$TaskKey   [$task]) { $reason = "has no search string"; }

        if ($reason)                      # If task requirement was not met
        {                                 #    then undo its task options
            print(STDERR "Task $taskno ", $reason, ", skipping it.\n");
            undef $TaskName  [$task];
            undef $TaskHome  [$task];
            undef $TaskForm  [$task];
            undef $TaskMethod[$task];
            undef $TaskUrl   [$task];
            undef $TaskQuery [$task];
            undef $TaskAuthor[$task];
            undef $TaskTitle [$task];
            undef $TaskKey   [$task];
            $task--;                       # Bad task don't count
        }
    }
    else
    {
        print STDERR "Unrecognized option in task $taskno\n";
        print STDERR "  at line $. of $TaskFile\n";
    }
}

    if ($intask)                          # Inside task but end of file?
    {
        die "Last instruction is not properly terminated, stopped";
    }
    close TASK;                           # Close task file
}


# =========================================================================
# Print summarizing table of contents in a prologue.
# =========================================================================
sub prologue
```

```perl
{
    print "<hr><H1>Results from $WebShopper</H1>\n";
    print "<H2>The following online databases was searched:</H2>\n";
    print "<ul>\n";

    foreach $task (1 .. $#TaskName)              # For each specified task
    {
        print "<li><a href=\"$TaskHome[$task]\">$TaskName[$task]</a>\n";
    }
    print "</ul>\n";
    print "<hr size=8>\n";
}


# ============================================================================
# Make all URL references in $content absolute (and not relative).
# ============================================================================
sub globalize
{
    local(*content, $url) = @_;

    $content =~ s/\<A(.*)\s+HREF\s*=\s*([^\"])([^\s\>]*)/\<A$1
    HREF=\"$url$2$3\"/
gi;
    $content =~ s/\<IMG(.*)\s+SRC\s*=\s*([^\"])([^\s\>]*)/\<IMG$1
    SRC=\"$url$2$3\
"/gi;
    $content =~ s/\<FORM(.*)\s+ACTION\s*=\s*([^\"])([^\s\>]*)/\<FORM$1
    ACTION=\"$
url$2$3\"/gi;

    $content =~
    s/\<A(.*)\s+HREF\s*=\s*(\"?)(\/[^\/]\S*¦\/¦\.\S*)(\"?[^\>]*)\>/\<
A$1 HREF=$2$url$3$4\>/gi;
    $content =~
    s/\<IMG(.*)\s+SRC\s*=\s*(\"?)(\/[^\/]\S*¦\/¦\.\S*)(\"?[^\>]*)\>/\
<IMG$1 SRC=$2$url$3$4\>/gi;
    $content =~
    s/\<FORM(.*)\s+ACTION\s*=\s*(\"?)(\/[^\/]\S*¦\/¦\.\S*)(\"?[^\>]*)
\>/\<FORM$1 ACTION=$2$url$3$4\>/gi;
}


# ============================================================================
```

```
# Search the given database indicated by $task, return result in *content.
# ============================================================================
sub find_item
{
    local($task, *content) = @_;              # Result of $task in *content
    local($key)       = $Title ¦¦ $Author;    # Build keyword
    local(%headers) = ();                      # To hold parsed response headers
    local($headers) = '';                      # To hold response headers
    local($url);                               # URL to GET or POST
    local($response);                          # Response code returned

    $TaskAuthor[$task] =~ s/\$Author/$Author/;
    $TaskTitle [$task] =~ s/\$Title/$Title/;
    $TaskQuery [$task] =~ s/\$Author/$Author/;
    $TaskQuery [$task] =~ s/\$Title/$Title/;
    $TaskKey   [$task] =~ s/\$Key/$key/;

    if ($Author && $Title)                    # Search by both author and title
    {
        $content = $TaskQuery [$task] ¦¦
                   $TaskKey   [$task] ¦¦
                     $TaskTitle [$task] ¦¦
                   $TaskAuthor[$task];
    }
    elsif ($Author)                           # Search by author
    {
        $content = $TaskQuery [$task] ¦¦
                   $TaskAuthor[$task] ¦¦
                    $TaskKey    [$task];
    }
    elsif ($Title)                            # Search by title
    {
        $content = $TaskQuery [$task] ¦¦
                     $TaskTitle [$task] ¦¦
                   $TaskKey    [$task];
    }
    else { return; }                          # Skip

    if ($CGI)
    {
        $headers{'Accept'} = '*/*';
        $headers{'Accept'} = 'image/x-xbitmap';
        $headers{'Accept'} = 'image/gif';
```

```perl
        $headers{'Accept'} = 'image/jpeg';
    }
    else
    {
        $headers{'Accept'} = '*/*';
    }
    $headers{'Content-type'}   = 'application/x-www-form-urlencoded';
    $headers{'Content-length'} = length($content);

    $url = $TaskMethod[$task] eq "GET"      # GET method?
        ? "$TaskUrl[$task]?$content"        # Concat search string
        :  $TaskUrl[$task];                 # Leave intact

    $response = &www'request($TaskMethod[$task], $url,
                             *headers, *content, $Timeout);


                                            # Make partial URL global

    $url =~ s/http:\/\/([^\/]+)\/.*$/http:\/\/$1/gi;
    &globalize(*content, $url);
}


# =========================================================================
# Print result of searching the online database identified by $task.
# =========================================================================
sub print_result
{
    local($task, *content) = @_;            # Result of $task in *content

    print "<H1><I><a name=#tag$task>";      # HTML text fragment
    print "$TaskName[$task]</a></I></H1><p>\n";
    print $content;                         # Result of searching database
    print "<hr size=8>\n";                  # Result delimiter
}


# =========================================================================
1; #                         THE  END                                    #
# =========================================================================
```

List of Online Bookstores Visited by BookFinder

The BookFinder agent is a specialized instance of WebShopper that helps users locate and buy books from bookstores on the Web. For testing purposes, a sample BookFinder agent has been set up to run from `http://deluge.stanford.edu:8000/book/bookfind.html` (see fig. D.1).

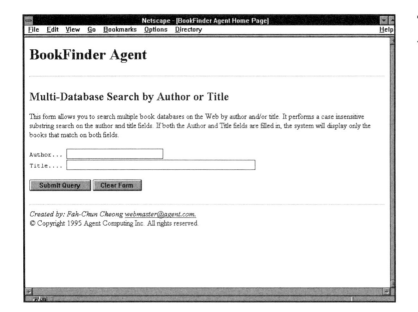

Users are encouraged to download the WebShopper code from `http://deluge.stanford.edu:8000/book/webshop` and run it directly on their own machines after configuring the WebShopper to behave as BookFinder according to instructions contained therein. The following is a list of online bookstores on the Web that are visited by BookFinder agents (and should appear in a default task file named ".bookfind").

Name	Book Stacks Unlimited
Home	`http://www.books.com/`
Form	`http://melville.books.com/scripts` `/search1.exe?sid~gXnbjdMaDbGxYye`
POST	`http://shaker.books.com/scripts/search.exe?sid~gXnbjdMaDbGxYye`
TITLE	`type=title&search=$Title`
AUTHOR	`type=author&search=$Author`
Name	CompuBooks
Home	`http://www.compubooks.com/books.html`
Form	`http://www.compubooks.com/order/books/search`
POST	`http://www.compubooks.com/order/books/findit/2454`
QUERY	`author=$Author&title=$Title&file=1.+All+Types`
Name	Computer Literacy Bookshops
Home	`http://www.clbooks.com/`
Form	`http://www.clbooks.com/cgi-bin/browsedb`
POST	`http://www.clbooks.com/cgi-bin/browsedb?20016`

```
TITLE      SEARCH.STRING=$Title&SEARCH.TYPE=TITLE&SEARCH.ALG=Basic+Search
AUTHOR     SEARCH.STRING=$Author&SEARCH.TYPE=AUTHOR&SEARCH.ALG=Basic+Search
```

```
Name       Future Fantasy Bookstore
Home       http://futfan.com/home.html
Form       http://futfan.com/search.html
POST       http://futfan.com/cgi-bin/query
QUERY      author=$Author&title=$Title
```

```
Name       Intertain.com
Home       http://intertain.com/store/welcome.html
Form       http://intertain.com/store/search.html
POST       http://intertain.com/cgi-bin/loc_query
QUERY      catalog=non-fiction&type=INDEX&author=$Author&title=$Title
```

```
Name       Macmillan Bookstore
Home       http://www.mcp.com/cgi-bin/do-bookstore.cgi
Form       http://www.mcp.com/cgi-bin/do-searches.cgi?userID=46345811
POST       http://www.mcp.com/cgi-bin/find-books.cgi
TITLE      search_term=$Title&by_some=by_title&and_or=
           as_and&userID=46345811
AUTHOR     search_term=$Author&by_some=by_author&and_or=
           as_and&userID=46345811
```

```
Name       Powell's Technical Books
Home       http://www.technical.powells.portland.or.us/
Form       http://www.powells.portland.or.us/search.technical.html
POST       http://www.powells.portland.or.us/cgi-bin/search.pl
QUERY      title-strings=$Title&author-strings=$Author
```

```
Name       Reiters Books
Home       http://www.awa.com/reiters/index.html
Form       http://www.awa.com/reiters/haveyou.reiters.html
POST       http://www.awa.com/cgi-bin/grepper.reiters.pl
KEY        searchword=$Key
```

```
Name       Roswell Internet Computer Bookstore
Home       http://www.nstn.ns.ca/cybermall/roswell/roswell.html
Form       http://www.nstn.ca/cgi-bin/roswell-engine?search
POST       http://www.nstn.ca/cgi-bin/roswell-engine?search
KEY        searchtext=$Key&MFT=search
```

Name	Softpro Books
Home	http://internet-plaza.net/softpro/
Form	http://internet-plaza.net/cgi-bin/softpro-booklist-agrep.pl
GET	http://internet-plaza.net/cgi-bin/softpro-booklist-agrep.pl
KEY	$Key

List of Online Music Stores Visited by CDFinder

T he CDFinder agent is a specialized instance of

WebShopper that helps users locate and buy CD

albums from music stores on the Web. For testing

purposes, a sample CDFinder agent has been set

up to run from `http://deluge.stanford.edu:8000/`

`book/cdfind.html`.

Users are encouraged to download the WebShopper code from `http://deluge.stanford.edu:8000/` `book/webshop` and run it directly on their own machines after configuring the WebShopper to behave as CDFinder according to instructions contained therein. The following is a list of online music stores on the Web that are visited by CDFinder agents (and should appear in a default task file named ".cdfind").

Name	CD Land
Home	`http://www.persimmon.com/CDLand/`
Form	`http://www.persimmon.com/CDLand/cd-first.html`
POST	`http://www.persimmon.com/cgi-bin/picard`
QUERY	`repeat=0&format=/usr/local/HTML_docs/CDLand` `/cdland.format&picard-search-t=$Title&picard-search-a=` `$Author&picard-select-media=ALL&match-all=match-all`

Name	CDNow
Home	`http://cdnow.com/`
Form	`http://cdnow.com:445/cgi-bin/mserver/SID=890838739/page=popfloor`
POST	`http://cdnow.com:445/cgi-bin/mserver/SID=890838739/page=popsearch`
TITLE	`index=t&string=$Title&order=A&quick=Y`
AUTHOR	`index=a&string=$Author&order=A&quick=Y`

Name	CD World
Home	`http://cdworld.com/`
Form	`http://cdworld.com/cgi-bin/nav?cdfind&421023`
POST	`http://cdworld.com/cgi-bin/cdfind1`
QUERY	`maxhits=25&title=$Title&artist=$Author`

Name	Global Electronic Music Marketplace
Home	`http://192.215.9.13/Flirt/GEMM/gemmlean.c.html`
Form	`http://192.215.9.13/Flirt/GEMM/GEMM_HTTP/search/search1_form.html`
POST	`http://gemm.com/gemm.acgi`
QUERY	`S=Submit&Artist=$Author&Title=$Title&Genre=` `%28ANY%29&Media=CD&MaxNRecs=25&priceLow=0&priceHigh=100`

Name	i? music/media
Home	`http://www.icw.com/cd/imm1.html`
Form	`http://www.icw.com/cd/datab.html`
POST	`http://www.icw.com/cgi-bin/cdwais`
KEY	`name=$Key`

Name	Music Connection
Home	http://www.inetbiz.com/music/
Form	http://www.inetbiz.com/cgi-bin action?type=static&page=search.html&state =000013c2
GET	http://www.inetbiz.com/cgi-bin/action
QUERY	type=fastscan&state=000013c2&artist=$Author&title= $Title&category=Rock%2C+Pop%2C+R+%26+B

Name	Noteworthy Music
Home	http://www.netmarket.com/noteworthy/bin/main/:grm¦:mode=text
Form	http://www.netmarket.com/noteworthy/bin/searchsimple/ :st=6ou5fui852¦1
POST	http://www.netmarket.com/noteworthy/bin/searchresult/ :st=6ou5fui852¦2/:t=52474638/:page=1
TITLE	:sm_1=t&:ss_1=$Title
AUTHOR	:sm_1=a&:ss_1=$Author

Name	Tower Records
Home	http://www.shopping2000.com/shopping2000/tower/
Form	http://www.shopping2000.com/shopping2000/tower/
POST	http://www.shopping2000.com/cgi-bin/tower-search.pl
KEY	query=$Key

Name	EMusic
Home	http://emusic.com/
Form	http://emusic.com/browse
POST	http://emusic.com/browse/1272107
TITLE	idx=t&text=$Title
AUTHOR	idx=a&text=$Author

List of Active MUD Sites on the Internet

This is Doran's MUDlist, which contains most of the known sites where MUDs of different types are running. It is maintained by Adam Wozniak at `awozniak@geordi.calpoly.edu`, also known as Doran.

Doran's MUDlist is published every once in a while and posted to the Usenet newsgroup rec.games.mud.announce. It is available on the World Wide Web at `http://www.cm.cf.ac.uk/User/Andrew.Wilson/MUDlist/` or it can be received via e-mail by sending a message to `mudlist@lore.calpoly.edu`.

Doran's MUDlist

TYPE <unknown> (2)

CyberEden	`rivendel.slip.umd.edu`	128.8.11.201	5000
Formosa	`db82.csie.ncu.edu.tw`	140.115.50.82	4000

TYPE aber (19)

An old hack-and-slash style MUD.

BabeMUD	`teaching4.physics` `.ox.ac.uk`	163.1.245.204	4001
BernieMUD	`fwk098037.res-hall` `.nwu.edu`	199.74.98.37	6715
Budapest	`prometheus.bsd` `.uchicago.edu`	128.135.30.5	6789
DragonMUD	`fermina.informatik` `.rwth-aachen.de`	137.226.224.20	6715
Eclipse MUD	`mud.bsd.uchicago.edu`	128.135.90.79	6715
Infinity	`sirius.nmt.edu`	129.138.4.119	6715
Kender's Kove	`harvey.esu.edu`	192.148.218.99	6715
Mustang	`mustang.us.dell.com`	143.166.224.42	9173
Northern Lights	`aber.ludd.luth.se`	130.240.16.29	6715

PuRgAtorY	purgatory.jaxnet.com	199.170.71.2	2112
Rainbow	aber.nhidh.nki.no	128.39.98.162	6715
Silver	dante.exide.com	198.85.1.1	6715
Sleepless Nights	cs3.brookes.ac.uk	161.73.1.2	6789
Terradome	cmssrv-gw.brookes.ac.uk	161.73.101.20	8888
Tyrann II	muselab-gw.runet.edu	137.45.128.10	6715
Tyrann II	muselab.ac.runet.edu	137.45.33.100	6715
Ulrik/Dirt	alkymene.uio.no	129.240.21.60	6715
Utopia	alpha.dsu.edu	138.247.32.12	6789
WhirlWind	bubba.ucc.okstate.edu	139.78.100.14	6715

TYPE almostIRC (1)

No information available.

| Olohof Bbs | morra.et.tudelft.nl | 130.161.144.100 | 2993 |

TYPE bsx (1)

A graphical hack-and-slash MUD. Special client required.

| Regenesis | birka.lysator.liu.se | 130.236.254.159 | 7475 |

TYPE circle (6)

A hack-and-slash style MUD.

AbsolutMUD	b63740.cwru.edu	129.22.248.252	4000
BetaMud	thijm.si.hhs.nl	145.52.81.25	4000
HexOnyx	marble.bu.edu	128.197.10.75	7777
LoveMUD	mud.butterfly.net	199.73.40.4	4000

| PrimalMud | jeack.apana.org.au | 202.12.87.82 | 4000 |
| Virtual World of Magma | magma.leg.ufrj.br | 146.164.53.33 | 4000 |

TYPE darkmud (1)

No information available.

| Midian][| pandora.mit.csu.edu.au | 137.166.16.2 | 3333 |

TYPE dgd (6)

A hack-and-slash style MUD very similar to lp.

Albion Mud	veda.is	193.4.230.1	4000
GodsHome	godshome.solace.mh.se	193.10.118.131	3000
IgorMUD	igor.mtek.chalmers.se	129.16.60.113	1701
MirrorMOO	mirror.ccs.neu.edu	129.10.112.76	8889
PaderMUD	mud.uni-paderborn.de	131.234.12.13	3000
The Pattern	epsilon.me.chalmers.se	129.16.50.30	6047

TYPE diku (57)

A hack-and-slash style MUD.

AbsolutMUD	b63740.STUDENT.CWRU.Edu	129.22.248.252	4000
Abyss II	helpmac.its.mcw.edu	141.106.32.113	8888
Albanian	fred.indstate.edu	139.102.12.14	2150
AlexMUD	marcel.stacken.kth.se	130.237.234.17	4000
Apocalypse IV	sapphire.geo.wvu.edu	157.182.168.20	4000
AustinMud	imv.aau.dk	130.225.2.2	4000
Chaos	chaos.bga.com	198.3.118.12	4000

Dark Castle Mud	jive.rahul.net	192.160.13.4	6666
DikuMUD	mud.stacken.kth.se	130.237.234.17	4000
DikuMud II	marcel.stacken.kth.se	130.237.234.17	4242
Elite	xbyse.nada.kth.se	130.237.222.237	4000
Empire	einstein.physics .drexel.edu	129.25.1.120	4000
FieryMud	fiery.eushc.org	163.246.5.109	4000
* Forbidden Lands	queen.mcs.drexel.edu	129.25.7.100	4000
FuskerMud	hopi.dtcc.edu	138.123.76.240	4000
Games of Death (G.O.D.) MUD	cyberspace.com	199.2.48.12	4000
GrimneMUD	gytje.pvv.unit.no	129.241.36.226	4000
Hercules MUD	sunshine.eushc.org	163.246.32.110	3000
Imperial	supergirl.cs.hut.fi	130.233.40.52	6969
JeenusTooMUD	heegaard.mth.pdx.edu	131.252.40.91	4000
KAOS HQ	sg25.aud.temple.edu	129.32.66.7	4000
KallistiMud	jadzia.CSOS.ORST.EDU	128.193.40.23	4000
The Land	nora.gih.no	128.39.140.150	4000
Legend of the Winds	ccsun44.csie.nctu .edu.tw	140.113.17.168	4040
MEDIEVIA Cyberspace	intense.netaxs.com	198.69.186.36	4000
MUME	lbdsun4.epfl.ch	128.178.77.5	4242
Mayhem	thrash.isca.uiowa.edu	128.255.200.25	1234

Meat MUD	sneezy.cc.utexas.edu	128.83.108.16	2800
Medievia Cyberspace	medievia.netaxs.com	198.69.186.36	4000
MooseHead Mud	mud.eskimo.com	204.122.16.44	4000
Mozart	kitten.mcs.com	192.160.127.90	4500
# Mudde Pathetique	flysex.berkeley.edu	128.32.128.36	2999
NaVie	mud.cs.odu.edu	128.82.6.30	4000
# NexusMUD	didec3.epfl.ch	128.178.164.5	4000
Northern Crossroads	ugsparc13.eecg .toronto.edu	128.100.13.63	9000
OpalMUD	opal.cs.virginia.edu	128.143.60.14	4000
PK MUD	kennedy.ecn.uoknor.edu	129.15.24.14	5000
Perilous Realms	PR.mese.com	155.229.1.4	23
Phantazm	fpa.com	198.242.217.1	4000
Realm of Magic	p107.informatik .uni-bremen.de	134.102.216.8	4000
RockyMud	hermes.dna.mci.com	166.41.48.146	4000
RoninMUD	ronin.bchs.uh.edu	129.7.2.127	5000
Shadowdale	dale.hsc.unt.edu	129.120.104.40	7777
Silicon Realms	sampan.ee.fit.edu	163.118.30.9	4000
SillyMUD	stone.cis.ufl.edu	128.227.100.197	4000
SlothMUD II	ai.cs.ukans.edu	129.237.80.113	6101
Sojourn	sojourn.cem.msu.edu	35.8.25.23	9999
# StrangeMUD	sleepy.cc.utexas.edu	128.83.108.13	9332

StrikeNet	`falcon.depaul.edu`	140.192.1.7	4000
Tazmania	`ukko.rowan.edu`	150.250.10.216	5000
TemporaryMUD	`cc.joensuu.fi`	128.214.14.12	4000
The Final Level	`huey.ee.cua.edu`	136.242.140.31	7777
The Glass Dragon	`surf.tstc.edu`	161.109.32.2	4000
ThunderDome	`tdome.montana.com`	199.2.139.3	5555
Wayne's World	`drake.eushc.org`	163.246.32.100	9000
WildSide	`levant.cs.ohiou.edu`	132.235.1.100	1234
Worlds of Carnage	`orcrist.digital.ufl.edu`	128.227.133.214	4000

TYPE dum (3)

No information available.

CanDUM II	`itrchq.itrc.on.ca`	128.100.3.100	2001
DUM II	`dum.ludd.luth.se`	130.240.16.36	2001
FranDUM II	`mousson.enst.fr`	137.194.160.48	2001

TYPE lp (111)

A hack-and-slash style MUD.

3-Kingdoms	`marble.bu.edu`	128.197.10.75	5000
5th Dimension	`gauss.ifm.liu.se`	130.236.50.9	3000
Alatia	`neumark.physik` `.tu-magdeburg.de`	141.44.40.24	3000
AlexMUD	`mud.stacken.kth.se`	130.237.234.17	4000
Ancient Anguish	`dancer.ethz.ch`	129.132.57.66	2222
Ancient Anguish	`end2.bedrock.com`	131.158.153.39	2222

Angalon	`neuromancer.tamu.edu`	128.194.47.9	3011
Asteroth (LPSwat)	`aviator.cc.iastate.edu`	129.186.140.6	2020
Aurora	`aurora.etsiig.uniovi.es`	156.35.41.20	3000
BatMUD	`bat.cs.hut.fi`	130.233.40.180	23
BatMUD	`palikka.jyu.fi`	130.234.40.3	2001
Callandor	`warns.et.tudelft.nl`	130.161.147.41	5317
Castalia	`miucs1.miu.edu`	192.103.45.2	4444
Chatter	`hawking.u .washington.edu`	140.142.58.99	6000
Conservatorium	`crs.cl.msu.edu`	35.8.1.10	6000
Coupworld	`honey.st-and.ac.uk`	138.251.33.32	7425
Crossed Swords	`shsibm.shh.fi`	128.214.44.251	3000
Dark Saga	`cobber.cord.edu`	138.129.1.32	5555
DarkWind	`darkwind.i-link.com`	198.67.37.33	3000
Darker Realms	`worf.tamu.edu`	128.194.116.25	2000
Dartmud	`fermat.dartmouth.edu`	129.170.28.31	2525
Deeper Trouble	`alk.iesd.auc.dk`	130.225.48.46	4242
Discworld	`cix.compulink.co.uk`	192.188.69.2	4242
Dragon's Den	`hellfire.dusers .drexel.edu`	129.25.56.246	2222
Dragon's Den	`oyster01.mcs.drexel.edu`	129.25.7.111	2222
DragonFire	`typo.umsl.edu`	134.124.42.197	3000
Dshores	`kcbbs.gen.nz`	202.14.102.1	6000
Eastern Stories	`cisppc2.cis.nctu.edu.tw`	140.113.204.42	8000

Elements of Paradox	`elof.acc.iit.edu`	192.41.245.90	6996
Enigma	`kcbbs.gen.nz`	202.14.102.1	6000
Etheria	`csgi60.leeds.ac.uk`	129.11.144.190	7777
EverDark	`atomic.com`	198.64.6.24	3000
Final Realms	`kark.hiof.no`	158.36.33.5	2001
First Light	`gold.t-informatik` `.ba-stuttgart.de`	141.31.1.16	3000
GateWay	`idiot.alfred.edu`	149.84.4.1	6969
Genesis	`hamal2.cs.chalmers.se`	129.16.226.142	3011
Genocide	`pip.shsu.edu`	192.92.115.10	2222
Gilgamesh	`shiner.st.usm.edu`	131.95.115.131	3742
# Hall of Fame	`marvin.df.lth.se`	194.47.62.1	2000
HariMUD	`tc0.chem.tue.nl`	131.155.94.3	6997
Haven	`idrz07.ethz.ch`	129.132.76.8	1999
* Holy Mission	`alijku05.edvz` `.uni-linz.ac.at`	140.78.3.1	2001
Igor	`ny.mtek.chalmers.se`	129.16.60.9	1701
Imperial2	`hp.ecs.rpi.edu`	128.113.5.43	3141
Infinity	`olympus.ccs.neu.edu`	129.10.111.80	3000
Ivory Tower	`marvin.macc.wisc.edu`	144.92.30.207	2000
Kerovnia	`atlantis.edu`	192.67.238.48	1984
Kingdoms	`gwaihir.dd.chalmers.se`	129.16.117.21	1812
* Kingdoms	`kili.dd.chalmers.se`	129.16.117.17	1812
KoBra	`kobra.et.tudelft.nl`	130.161.144.236	23

Kobra	`duteca4.et.tudelft.nl`	130.161.144.22	8888
LOST Mud	`louie.cc.utexas.edu`	128.83.108.12	6666
Last Outpost	`lo.millcomm.com`	199.170.133.6	4000
Loch Ness	`indigo.imp.ch`	157.161.1.12	2222
LooneyMud	`looney.cp.tn.tudelft.nl`	192.31.126.102	8888
Lost Souls	`ronin.bchs.uh.edu`	129.7.2.127	3000
# LustyMud	`lusty.tamu.edu`	128.194.9.199	2000
Marches of Antan	`checfs2.ucsd.edu`	132.239.68.9	3000
Mathmud	`medusa.math` `.fu-berlin.de`	130.133.4.4	3000
Midnight Sun	`holly.ludd.luth.se`	130.240.16.23	3000
Moonstar	`pulsar.hsc.edu`	192.135.84.5	4321
Muddog	`catalyst.math.ufl.edu`	128.227.168.38	2000
Muddy Waters	`hot.caltech.edu`	131.215.9.49	3000
Mythos	`mann.uni-koblenz.de`	141.26.4.41	3000
NANVAENT 3	`corrour.cc.strath.ac.uk`	130.159.220.8	3000
NannyMUD	`birka.lysator.liu.se`	130.236.254.159	2000
Newmoon	`jove.cs.pdx.edu`	131.252.21.12	7680
* NightFall	`nova.tat.physik` `.uni-tuebingen.de`	134.2.62.161	4242
Nirvana IV	`elof.acc.iit.edu`	192.41.245.90	3500
Nuclearwar	`Melba.Astrakan.HGS.SE`	130.238.206.12	23
Overdrive	`castor.acs.oakland.edu`	141.210.10.109	5195
OzRogue	`mud.geko.com.au`	203.2.239.3	5001

OzRogue	`mud.geko.com.au`	203.2.239.3	5002
Paradox	`adl.uncc.edu`	152.15.15.18	10478
Phoenix	`albert.bu.edu`	128.197.74.10	3500
PixieMud	`elof.acc.iit.edu`	192.41.245.90	6969
Pixilated	`elof.acc.iit.edu`	192.41.245.90	6996
Prime Time	`prime.mdata.fi`	192.98.43.2	3000
Prydein	`spock.austin.apple.com`	204.96.16.2	4567
Psycho-thriller	`atlantis.edu`	192.67.238.48	3000
Pyromud	`elektra.cc.edu`	140.104.1.100	2222
Ragnarok	`ragnarok.teleport.com`	192.108.254.22	2222
Realms of the Dragon	`cw-u04.umd.umich.edu`	141.215.69.7	3000
Realmsmud	`donal.dorsai.org`	198.3.127.6	1501
Regenesis	`regenesis.lysator` `.liu.se`	130.236.254.159	7475
# Regula	`rrzc8.rz` `.uni-regensburg.de`	132.199.30.8	3000
Renegade Outpost	`outpost.hsc.unt.edu`	129.120.104.19	9999
Revenge of the End of the Line	`aus.Stanford.edu`	36.21.0.99	2010
STYX	`dreamtime.nmsu.edu`	128.123.8.116	3000
SWmud	`kitten.mcs.net`	192.160.127.90	6666
SplitSecond	`lestat.shv.hb.se`	130.241.246.10	3000
Starmud	`krynn.solace.mh.se`	193.10.118.130	7373
Starmud	`starmud.solace.mh.se`	193.10.118.130	4000

StickMUD	kalikka.jyu.fi	130.234.40.2	7680
StickMUD	lancelot.cc.jyu.fi	130.234.40.4	7680
T'Mud	wave.st.usm.edu	131.95.119.2	2222
TAPPMud	surprise.pro.ufz.de	141.65.31.2	6510
TMI-2	kendall.ccs.neu.edu	129.10.114.86	5555
# The Holy Mission	alijku03.edvz.uni-linz.ac.at	140.78.3.30	4242
Timewarp	quark.gmi.edu	192.138.137.39	5150
Tron	polaris.king.ac.uk	141.241.84.65	3000
Tron	polaris.king.ac.uk	141.241.84.65	4000
TubMUD	morgen.cs.tu-berlin.de	130.149.19.20	7680
Ultimate	rkw-risc.cs.up.ac.za	137.215.18.10	1984
Valhalla	valhalla.com	192.187.153.1	2444
VikingMUD	sid.dsl.unit.no	129.241.36.75	2001
Windy	bitsy.apana.org.au	203.2.134.3	2000
Wonderland	gorina3.hsr.no	152.94.1.43	3287
Zebedee	rszircon.swan.ac.uk	137.44.102.2	7000
ZombieMUD	linux1.sjoki.uta.fi	192.98.84.5	3333
# flame	marlin.ucc.gu.uwa.edu.au	130.95.100.4	4242

TYPE lp-german (3)

A hack-and-slash style lp MUD, but in German!

MorgenGrauen	PASCAL.UNI-MUENSTER.DE	128.176.121.56	4711
SvenskMUD	bodil.lysator.liu.se	130.236.254.152	2043

| UNITOPIA | helpdesk.rus .uni-stuttgart.de | 129.69.221.120 | 3333 |

TYPE mare (1)

An adventure role-playing MUD.

| WindsMare | cyberion.bbn.com | 128.89.2.139 | 7348 |

TYPE merc (13)

A diku spinoff hack-and-slash MUD.

Barren Realms	liii.com	198.207.193.1	8000
Black Knights Legacy	peseta.unice.fr	193.48.228.102	6000
Dragons, Legends, and Lore	trident.ee.fit.edu	163.118.30.14	9000
Farside	farside.atinc.com	198.138.35.199	3000
Hidden Worlds	cns.cscns.com	192.156.196.1	4000
Highlands	jedi.cis.temple.edu	129.32.32.70	9001
Legends of Winds	ccsun44.csie .nctu.edu.tw	140.113.17.168	4040
Lost Realms	viper.ucs.uoknor.edu	129.15.10.23	4000
MadROM	dogbert.ugcs .caltech.edu	131.215.133.151	1536
Mortal Realms	hydrogen.ee.utulsa.edu	129.244.42.48	4321
StackMUD	marcel.stacken.kth.se	130.237.234.17	8000
Stick in the MUD	ugsparc11.eecg .utoronto.ca	128.100.13.61	9000
TIAC Mud	toybox.tiac.net	199.0.65.25	9999

TYPE moo (20)

A tiny spinoff chat MUD with an object-oriented internal programming language.

BayMOO	`mud.crl.com`	165.113.1.30	8888
ChibaMOO	`chiba.picosof.com`	165.227.31.2	7777
Diversity University	`erau.db.erau.edu`	155.31.1.1	8888
Dragonsfire	`moo.eskimo.com`	204.122.16.31	7777
DreamMOO	`Feenix.metronet.com`	192.245.137.1	8888
Entropy	`monsoon.weather.brockport.edu`	137.21.201.3	7777
Eon	`mcmuse.mc.maricopa.edu`	140.198.66.28	8888
Final Frontiers MOO	`ugly.microserve.net`	192.204.120.2	2499
J-H	`jhm.ccs.neu.edu`	129.10.111.77	1709
LambdaMOO	`lambda.xerox.com`	192.216.54.2	8888
MediaMOO	`purple-crayon.media.mit.edu`	18.85.0.48	8888
Metaverse	`metaverse.io.com`	199.170.88.12	7777
MuMOO	`chestnut.enmu.edu`	192.94.216.74	7777
OutWorld	`tanelorn.king.ac.uk`	141.241.224.102	7777
PMC	`hero.village.virginia.edu`	128.143.200.59	7777
TrekMOO	`trekmoo.microserve.com`	192.204.120.2	2499
ValhallaMOO	`valhalla.acusd.edu`	192.55.87.211	4444

World MOO	chiba.picosof.com	165.227.31.2	1234
WorldMOO	sequoia.picosof.com	165.227.31.2	1234
* ZenMOO	cheshire.oxy.edu	134.69.1.253	7777

TYPE moo-portuguese (1)

No information available.

MOOsaico	moo.di.uminho.pt	193.136.20.102	7777

TYPE muck (16)

A tiny spinoff chat MUD with an internal programming language similar to FORTH.

AnimeMUCK	tcp.com	128.95.44.29	2035
Brazilian Dreams	red_panda.tbyte.com	198.211.131.13	4201
CaveMUCK	cave.tcp.com	128.95.44.29	2283
Delusions	iglou.com	192.107.41.3	4999
Divination Web	bill.math.uconn.edu	137.99.17.5	9393
FurToonia	lostsouls.desertmoon.com	198.102.68.58	8888
FurryMUCK	sncils.snc.edu	138.74.0.10	8888
HoloMUCK	collatz.mcrcim.mcgill.edu	132.206.78.1	5757
NAILS	flounder.rutgers.edu	128.6.128.5	5150
NonSense MUCK	rigel.dsif.fee.unicamp.br	143.106.8.131	4201
Quartz Paradise	quartz.rutgers.edu	128.6.60.6	9999

RealmsMUCK	`tcp.com`	128.95.44.29	7765
Tapestries MUCK	`tcp.com`	128.95.44.29	2069
Unbridled Desires	`epona.magibox.net`	199.171.80.3	8888
V-MUCK	`mserv.wizvax.com`	199.181.141.3	5201
WizMuck	`mserv.wizvax.com`	199.181.141.3	4201

TYPE mudwho (2)

Telnet here to get a list of who's on across many different MUDs!

| Nova | `nova.tat.physik`
`.uni-tuebingen.de` | 134.2.62.161 | 6889 |
| okwho | `riemann.math`
`.okstate.edu` | 139.78.112.4 | 6889 |

TYPE muse (12)

A tiny mush spinoff chat MUD.

BTech3056	`btech.netaxs.com`	198.69.186.38	3056
BattleTech	`step.polymtl.ca`	132.207.7.32	3026
Fantasia	`betz.biostr` `.washington.edu`	128.95.44.22	4201
FlatEarth	`neumann.cba.csuohio.edu`	137.148.20.3	7719
HideawayMUSE	`donal.dorsai.org`	198.3.127.6	4201
MicroMUSE	`CHEZMOTO.AI.MIT.EDU`	18.43.0.102	4201
OceanaMUSE	`k12.cnidr.org`	128.109.179.45	4201
Rhostshyl	`RHOSTSHYL.CIT` `.CORNELL.EDU`	128.253.180.15	4201
TOS TrekMuse	`siher.Stanford.EDU`	36.109.0.64	1701

TimeMuse	`murren.ai.mit.edu`	18.43.0.179	4201
TrekMuse	`laurel.cnidr.org`	128.109.179.14	1701
VegaMuse II	`planck.sos.clarkson.edu`	128.153.32.14	2095

TYPE mush (39)

A tiny spinoff chat MUD.

Amarynth	`pharos.acusd.edu`	192.195.155.201	9999
ApexMUSH	`apex.ccs.yorku.ca`	130.63.237.12	4201
Belior Rising	`brazil-nut.enmu.edu`	192.94.216.80	4301
CamelotMUSH	`cadman.cit.buffalo.edu`	128.205.3.103	5440
Chrome	`colossus.acusd.edu`	192.195.155.200	4444
City of Darkness	`melandra.cs.man.ac.uk`	130.88.240.110	2000
Conspiracy!	`almond.enmu.edu`	192.94.216.77	1066
CryptMUSH	`cadman.cit.buffalo.edu`	128.205.3.103	7171
CrystalMUSH	`moink.nmsu.edu`	128.123.8.115	6886
Cybermush	`tlaloc.cms.dmu.ac.uk`	146.227.103.1	6250
The DAMNED	`janus.LIBRARY.CMU.EDU`	128.2.21.7	6250
DarkMetal	`cheops.acusd.edu`	192.195.155.203	4444
DeepSeas	`a.cs.okstate.edu`	139.78.113.1	6250
DragonDawn	`cashew.enmu.edu`	192.94.216.78	2222
Dragonlance	`yacht.slip.andrew` `.cmu.edu`	128.2.116.75	6250
Dune	`mellers1.psych` `.berkeley.edu`	128.32.243.78	4201
Garou	`party.apple.com`	130.43.2.10	7000

Global MUSH	`lancelot.cif` `.rochester.edu`	128.151.220.22	4201
Hemlock MUSH	`PELYCO.SOAR.GSIA` `.CMU.EDU`	128.2.18.7	1973
ImagECastle	`fogey.stanford.edu`	36.22.0.31	4201
LegionMUSH	`a.cs.okstate.edu`	139.78.113.1	2996
Masquerade	`phobos.unm.edu`	129.24.8.3	4444
NarniaMush	`argo.unm.edu`	129.24.9.24	6250
NeverEnding Story	`jove.cs.pdx.edu`	131.252.21.12	9999
PernMUSH	`cesium.clock.org`	130.43.2.43	4201
PrairieMUSH	`firefly.prairienet.org`	192.17.3.3	4201
Shards	`vesta.unm.edu`	129.24.120.253	7777
SouCon	`beechnut.enmu.edu`	192.94.216.86	4201
Spatial Wastes	`chestnut.enmu.edu`	192.94.216.74	2001
StarWars	`starwars.wis.com`	199.3.240.54	4402
SwordsMUSH	`world.std.com`	192.74.137.5	4201
Texas Twilight	`krynn.solace.mh.se`	193.10.118.130	6250
# The Awakening	`cestus.gb.nrao.edu`	192.33.116.67	9999
The Storyteller Circle	`draco.unm.edu`	129.24.96.4	6666
TinyCWRU	`caisr2.caisr.cwru.edu`	129.22.24.22	4201
TinyTim	`myelin.uchc.edu`	155.37.1.251	5440
TooMUSH	`cestus.gb.nrao.edu`	192.33.116.67	7171
Two Moons Mush	`lupine.org`	198.4.75.40	4201
XMUSH	`xmen.esi.com`	192.82.101.106	1994

TYPE oxmud (2)

No information available.

| Island | teaching4.physics
.ox.ac.uk | 163.1.245.204 | 2092 |
| Island | teaching4.physics
.ox.ac.uk | 163.1.245.204 | 2093 |

TYPE silly (1)

No information available.

| Chomestoru | dfw.net | 198.175.15.10 | 4000 |

TYPE talker (7)

A little closer to IRC than a MUD. Definitely a place to hang out and chat.

Addicted	sun1.gwent.ac.uk	193.63.82.1	6666
DS9	rivendel.slip.umd.edu	128.8.11.201	3000
Foothills	marble.bu.edu	128.197.10.75	2010
Gamma Quadrant	rivendel.slip.umd.edu	128.8.11.201	6000
MBA4	jumper.mcc.ac.uk	130.88.202.26	3214
* SomeWhere Else	kehleyr.phys.ttu.edu	129.118.41.9	2010
Surfers	muscle.rai.kcl.ac.uk	137.73.16.2	3232

TYPE teeny (2)

A tiny lookalike chat MUD.

| (EVIL!)Mud | intac.com | 198.6.114.2 | 4201 |
| ApexMUD | apex.yorku.ca | 130.63.237.12 | 4201 |

TYPE tiny (1)

The original chat MUD.

DragonMUD   `satan.ucsd.edu`   132.239.1.7   4201

TYPE uber (1)

No information available.

The Land of   `drogon.meiko.com`   192.131.107.11   6123
Drogon

Key

?   No successful connect on record—may be removed from future lists.

*   Last successful connect more than 7 days ago.

\#   Last successful connect more than 3 days ago.

List of World Wide Web Spiders and Robots

The following list of World Wide Web Robots, Wanderers, and Spiders is compiled from Martijn Koster's List of Active Robots found at `http://web.nexor.co.uk/mak/doc/robots/active.html`.

The JumpStation Robot

Home Page: `http://www.stir.ac.uk/jsbin/js`

Run by: Jonathon Fletcher,
`J.Fletcher@stirling.ac.uk`

From: `pentland.stir.ac.uk`

User-Agent: JumpStation

Its purpose is to generate a Resource Discovery database. The Proposed Standard for Robot Exclusion is supported. It is a set of stand-alone programs written in Perl 4, C, and C++. Verion I has been in development since September 1993, and has been running on several occasions; the last run was between February 8th and February 21st, 1995. Version II is under development.

RBSE Spider

Home Page: `http://rbse.jsc.nasa.gov/eichmann/rbse.html`

Run by: Dr. David Eichmann,
`eichmann@rbse.jsc.nasa.gov`

From: `rbse.jsc.nasa.gov` (192.88.42.10)

User-Agent: RBSE-Spider/0,1a

Seems to retrieve documents more than once. Its purpose is to generate a Resource Discovery database, and generate statistics. It is a stand-alone program written in C, and Oracle, WAIS. Developed and operated as part of the NASA-funded Repository Based Software Engineering Program at the Research Institute for Computing and Information Systems, University of Houston—Clear Lake.

The WebCrawler

Home Page: `http://webcrawler.com/`

Run by: Brian Pinkerton,
`bp@biotech.washington.edu`

`http://www.cs.washington.edu/homes/bp/bp.html`

From: `surfski.webcrawler.com`

User-Agent: WebCrawler/2.0 libwww/3.0

Its purpose is to generate a Resource Discovery database, and generate statistics. The WebCrawler does a breadth-first walk, and indexes content as well as URLs, and so on. The Proposed Standard for Robot Exclusion is not supported. It is a stand-alone program written in C. The WebCrawler originated as an experiment in Internet resource discovery at the University of Washington in 1994. Today, it is operated by America Online as a service to the Internet. robots.txt support is coming soon!

The NorthStar Robot

Home Page: `http://comics.scs.unr.edu:7000/top.html`

Run by: Fred Barrie, `barrie@unr.edu`

`http://comics.scs.unr.edu/people/barrie.html`

Billy Barron, `billy@utdallas.edu`

`http://www.utdallas.edu/acc/billy.html`

From: `frognot.utdallas.edu`, possibly other sites in `utdallas.edu` and in `cnidir.org`.

User-Agent: NorthStar

More information, including a search interface, is available on the NorthStar Database. Recent runs (April 26, 1994) will concentrate on textual analysis of the Web versus GopherSpace (from the Veronica data) as well as indexing.

W4 (World Wide Web Wanderer)

Run by: Matthew Gray, mkgray@mit.edu

User-Agent: WWWWanderer v3.0 by Matthew Gray, mkgray@mit.edu

Run initially in June 1993, its aim is to measure the growth in the Web.

The Fish Search

Home Page: http://www.win.tue.nl/help/help-on-fish-all.html

Written by: Paul De Bra, debra@win.tue.nl

http://www.win.tue.nl/win/cs/is/debra/

Software: file://ftp.win.tue.nl/pub/infosystems/www/

Paper: http://www.win.tue.nl/win/cs/is/reinpost/www94/

From: Not set, but it's usually run from www.win.tue.nl.

User-Agent: Fish-Search-Robot

Its purpose is to discover resources on the fly. The Proposed Standard for Robot Exclusion is not supported because of the incurred overhead. It is a stand-alone program written in C, but a version exists that is integrated into the Tubingen Mosaic 2.4.2 browser (also written in C). Originated as an addition to Mosaic for X. Available as a stand-alone program from ftp://ftp.win.tue.nl/pub/infosystems/www/fish-search.tar.gz.

The Python Robot

Home Page: http://info.cern.ch/hypertext/WWW/Tools/Python/Overview.html

Written by: Guido van Rossum, Guido.van.Rossum@cwi.nl

Software: ftp://ftp.cwi.nl/pub/python/python0.9.8.tar.Z

ftp://ftp.cwi.nl/pub/python/demo/www/

HTML Analyzer

Run by: James E. Pitkow, pitkow@aries.colorado.edu

Its aim is to check validity of Web servers. Not sure if it has ever been run remotely.

MOMspider

Home Page: http://www.ics.uci.edu/WebSoft/MOMspider

Written by: Roy Fielding, `fielding@ics.uci.edu`

Software: `ftp://liege.ics.uci.edu/pub/arcadia/MOMspider/MOMspider-1.00.tar.Z`

Paper: `http://www.ics.uci.edu/WebSoft/MOMspider/WWW94/paper.html`

From: Can run from anywhere.

User-Agent: MOMspider/1.00 libwww-perl/0.40

MOMspider is a Web-roaming robot that specializes in the maintenance of distributed hypertext infostructures. Its purpose is to validate links, and generate statistics. The program is stand-alone and written in Perl. The Proposed Standard for Robot Exclusion is supported. Originated as a research project at the University of California, Irvine, in 1993. Presented at the First International WWW Conference in Geneva, 1994.

HTMLgobble

Run by: Andreas Ley, `ley@rz.uni-karlsruhe.de`

From: `tp70.rz.uni-karlsruhe.de`

User-Agent: HTMLgobble v2.2

Software: `ftp://ftp.rz.uni-karlsruhe.de/pub/net/www/tools/htmlgobble.tar.gz`

A mirroring robot. Configured to stay within a directory, sleeps between requests, and the next version will use HEAD to check whether the entire document needs to be retrieved.

WWWW—the WORLD WIDE WEB WORM

Home Page: `http://www.cs.colorado.edu/home/mcbryan/WWWW.html`

`http://www.cs.colorado.edu/home/mcbryan/WWWintro.html`

Run by: Oliver McBryan, `mcbryan@piper.cs.colorado.edu`

`http://www.cs.colorado.edu/home/mcbryan/Home.html`

Paper: `http://www.cs.colorado.edu/home/mcbryan/mypapers/www94.ps`

From: `piper.cs.colorado.edu`

Another indexing robot that has quite flexible search options.

WM32 Robot

Home Page: `http://www-ihm.lri.fr/~tronche/W3M2/`

Written by: Christophe Tronche, `Christophe.Tronche@lri.fr`

`http://www-ihm.lri.fr/~tronche/`

From: E-mail address of the operator, usually `tronche@lri.fr`.

User-Agent: W3M2/x.xx

Its purpose is to generate a Resource Discovery database, validate links, validate HTML, and generate statistics. The Proposed Standard for Robot Exclusion is supported. It is a stand-alone program written in Perl 4, Perl 5, and C++.

Websnarf

Run by: Charlie Stross, `charless@sco.com`

From: `ruddles.london.sco.com`

A WWW mirror designed for offline browsing of sections of the Web. No longer running.

The Webfoot Robot

Run by: Lee McLoughlin, `L.McLoughlin@doc.ic.ac.uk`

`http://web.doc.ic.ac.uk/f?/lmjm`

From: `phoenix.doc.ic.ac.uk`

First spotted in Mid-February 1994. Further information unavailable.

Lycos

Home Page: `http://lycos.cs.cmu.edu/`

Run by: Dr. Michael L. Mauldin, `fuzzy@cmu.edu`

`http://fuzine.mt.cs.cmu.edu/mlm/home.html`

From: `fuzine.mt.cs.cmu.edu`

User-Agent: Lycos/x.x

This is a research program in providing information retrieval and discovery in the Web, using a finite memory model of the Web to guide intelligent, directed searches for specific information needs. Lycos also complies with the latest robot exclusion standard.

ASpider (Associative Spider)

Written by: Fred Johansen, `fred@nvg.unit.no`

`http://www.nvg.unit.no/~fred/`

From: `fredj@nova.pvv.unit.no`

User-Agent: ASpider/0.09

Currently under construction, this spider is a CGI script that searches the Web for keywords given by the user through a form.

SG-Scout

Home Page: `http://www-swiss.ai.mit.edu/ ~ptbb/SG-Scout/SG-Scout.html`

Run by: Peter Beebee, `ptbb@ai.mit.edubeebee@parc.xerox.com`

User-Agent: SG-Scout

From: Set to operator, usually from `beta.xerox.com`

The SG-Scout robot was developed for the Xerox Palo Alto Research Center as part of a project involving the development of a new form of directed Web browser. The SG-Scout is compliant with the Standard for Robot Exclusion. The SG-Scout was run in late June and again in early August 1994. In August the robot discovered over 7,250 Web servers and 250,000 html and text pages available through the HTTP protocol. It performs a "server-oriented" breadth-first search in a round-robin fashion, with multiple processes.

EIT Link Verifier Robot

Home Page: http://wsk.eit.com/wsk/dist/ doc/admin/webtest/verify_links.html

Written by: Jim McGuire, mcguire@eit.COM

Software: ftp://ftp.eit.com/pub/wsk/doc/ README.verify_links

From: Can be run by anyone from anywhere.

User-Agent: EIT-Link-Verifier-Robot/0.2

Announced on July 12, 1994. Combination of an HTML form and a CGI script that verifies links from a given starting point (with some controls to prevent it going off-site or limitless).

NHSE Web Forager

Run by: Bob Olson, olson@mcs.anl.gov

From: Usually *.mcs.anl.gov

User-Agent: NHSEWalker/3.0

Its purpose is to generate a Resource Discovery database. This robot is gathering data to do a full-text glimpse and provide a Web interface for it. The Proposed Standard for Robot Exclusion is supported. It is a stand-alone program written in Perl 5.

WebLinker

Home Page: http://www.cern.ch/WebLinker/

Written by: James Casey, casey@ptsun00.cern.ch

http://www.maths.tcd.ie/hyplan/jcasey/ jcasey.html

Paper: http://www.cern.ch/WebLinker/Paper/ Welcome.html

User-Agent: WebLinker/0.0 libwww-perl/0.1

It is a tool which traverses a section of Web, doing URN-URL conversion. It will be used as a post-processing tool on documents created by automatic converters such as LaTeX2HTML or WebMaker.

At the moment it works at full speed, but is restricted to local sites. External GETs will be added, but these will be running slowly.

Emacs W3 Search Engine

Home Page: http://www.cs.indiana.edu/elisp/ w3/w3_1.html

http://www.cs.indiana.edu/elisp/w3/ w3_toc.html#SEC39

Written by: William M. Perry, wmperry@spry.com

http://www.cs.indiana.edu/hyplan/ wmperry.html

From: Various machines

User-Agent: Emacs-w3/v*.*

Its purpose is to generate a Resource Discovery database. This is part of the w3 browser mode for Emacs, and is written in Lisp. The Proposed Standard for Robot Exclusion is not supported.

Arachnophilia

Run by: Vince Taluskie,
`taluskie@utpapa.ph.utexas.edu`

`http://www.ph.utexas.edu/people/vince.html`

From: `halsoft.com`

User-Agent: Arachnophilia

The purpose (undertaken by HaL Software) of this run is to collect approximately 10,000 html documents for testing automatic abstract generation. This program honors the robot exclusion standard and waits one minute between requests to a given server.

Mac WWWWorm

Written by: Sebastien Lemieux,
`lemieuse@ERE.UMontreal.CA`

`http://alize.ere.umontreal.ca:8001/ ~lemieuse/sebast.html`

This is a French Keyword-searching robot for the Mac, written in HyperCard. The author has decided not to release this robot to the public.

ChURL

Home Page: `http://www.engin.umich.edu/ ~yunke/scripts/#Churl`

Run by: Justin Yunke, `yunke@umich.edu`

`http://www.engin.umich.edu/~yunke/`

Software: `http://www.engin.umich.edu:80/ ~yunke/feedback/`

A URL checking robot, which stays within one step of the local server. However, the remote links can be checked for a connection. It is written in Perl.

Tarspider

Home Page: `http://www.chemie.fu-berlin.de/ user/chakl/Spider.html`

Run by: Olaf Schreck, `chakl@fu-berlin.de`

`http://www.inf.fu-berlin.de/~weisshuh/ chakl/ChaklHome.html`

From: `chakl@fu-berlin.de`

User-Agent: tarspider version

A mirroring robot.

The Peregrinator

Home Page: `http:// www.maths.usyd.edu.au:8000/jimr/pe/ Peregrinator.html`

Run by: Jim Richardson, `jimr@maths.su.oz.au`

`http://www.maths.usyd.edu.au:8000/jimr.html`

User-Agent: Peregrinator-Mathematics/0.7

This robot, in Perl V4, commenced operation in August 1994 and is being used to generate an index called MathSearch of documents on Web sites connected with mathematics and statistics. It ignores off-site links, so does not stray from a list of

servers specified initially. The robot follows the exclusion standard and accesses any given server no more than once every several minutes.

Checkbot

Written by: Dimitri Tischenko,
`D.B.Tischenko@TWI.TUDelft.NL`

`http://www.twi.tudelft.nl/People/D.B.Tischenko.html`

Run by: Hans de Graaff,
`j.j.degraaff@twi.tudelft.nl`

From: Usually `dutifp.twi.tudelft.nl`

User-Agent: checkbot.pl/x.x libwww-perl/x.x

The Proposed Standard for Robot Exclusion is not supported. It is a stand-alone program written in Perl 5.

Webwalk

Written by: Rich Testardi, `rpt@fc.hp.com`

User-Agent: webwalk

Its purpose is to generate a Resource Discovery database, validate links, validate HTML, perform mirroring, copy document trees, and generate statistics. The Proposed Standard for Robot Exclusion is supported. It is a stand-alone program written in C. Webwalk is easily extensible to perform virtually any maintenance function which involves web traversal, in a way much like the -exec option of the find(1) command. Webwalk is usually used behind the HP firewall.

Harvest

Home Page: `http://harvest.cs.colorado.edu/`

Run by: Darren Hardy,
`hardy@bruno.cs.colorado.edu`

Software: `http://harvest.cs.colorado.edu/harvest/gettingsoftware.html`

Papers: `http://harvest.cs.colorado.edu/harvest/papers.html`

From: `bruno.cs.colorado.edu`

A Resource Discovery Robot, part of the Harvest Project. Pauses 1 second between requests (by default). Note that Harvest's motivation is to index community- or topic-specific collections, rather than to locate and index all HTML objects that can be found. Also, Harvest enables users to control the enumeration several ways, including stop lists and depth and count limits. Therefore, Harvest provides a much more controlled way of indexing the Web than is typical of robots.

Katipo

Home Page: `http://www.vuw.ac.nz/~newbery/Katipo.html`

Run by: Michael Newbery,
`Michael.Newbery@vuw.ac.nz`

`http://www.vuw.ac.nz/~newbery`

From: `Michael.Newbery@vuw.ac.nz`

User-Agent: Katipo/1.0

The Proposed Standard for Robot Exclusion is not supported. It is a stand-alone program written in C.

A Macintosh robot that periodically (typically, once per day) walks through the global history files provided by some browsers (Mosaic, Netscape), looking for pages that have changed since last visited. It emits only HEAD queries and prefers to work through proxy (caching) servers.

InfoSeek Robot

Written by: Steve Kirsch, stk@infoseek.com

From: corp-gw.infoseek.com

User-Agent: InfoSeek Robot 1.0

Its purpose is to collect information to use in a "WWW Pages" database in InfoSeek's information retrieval service. The Proposed Standard for Robot Exclusion is supported. It is a stand-alone program written in Python.

Collects WWW pages for both InfoSeek's free WWW search and commercial search. Uses a unique proprietary algorithm to identify the most popular and interesting WWW pages. Very fast, but never has more than one request per site outstanding at any given time. Has been under refinement for more than a year.

GetURL

Written by: James Burton, burton@cs.latrobe.edu.au

http://www.cs.latrobe.edu.au/~burton/

Software: http://www.cs.latrobe.edu.au/~burton/Public/

User-Agent: GetUrl.rexx v1.0

Its purpose is to validate links, perform mirroring, and copy document trees. The Proposed Standard for Robot Exclusion is not supported. It is a robot written in ARexx (Amiga Rexx), which downloads a hierarchy of documents with a breadth-first search.

Designed as a tool for retrieving Web pages in batch mode without the encumbrance of a browser. Can be used to describe a set of pages to fetch and to maintain an archive or mirror. Is not run by a central site and accessed by clients—is run by the end user or archive maintainer.

Open Text Corporation Robot

Run by: Tim Bray, tbray@opentext.com

User-Agent: OMW/0.1 libwww/217

Follows robot exclusion rules and shouldn't visit any host more than once in five minutes.

NIKOS

Home Page: http://www.rns.com/cgi-bin/nomad

Written by: Rockwell Network Systems

This is an Internet resource discovery written by Rockwell Network Systems that searches only through document titles.

The TkWWW Robot

Home Page: `http://fang.cs.sunyit.edu/Robots/tkwww.html`

Written by: Scott Spetka, `scott@cs.sunyit.edu`

`http://fang.cs.sunyit.edu/Robots/spetka.html`

Software: `http://fang.cs.sunyit.edu/Spetka/tkwww`

TkWWW robots are dispatched from the TkWWW browser their results can be used to guide further browsing. It is designed to search Web neighborhoods to find pages that may be logically related. Robots can also be run in the background to build HTML indexes, compile WWW statistics, collect a portfolio of pictures, or perform any other function that can be described by the TkWWW Tcl extensions.

A Tcl W3 Robot

Home Page: `http://hplyot.obspm.fr/~dl/robo.html`

Written by: Laurent Demailly, `dl@hplyot.obspm.fr`

Software: `http://hplyot.obspm.fr/~dl/geturl.tcl`

`http://hplyot.obspm.fr/~dl/w3cli.tcl`

From: Usually `hplyot.obspm.fr`

User-Agent: dlw3robot/x.y

Its purpose is to validate links, and generate statistics. The Proposed Standard for Robot Exclusion is supported. It is a stand-alone program written in TCL.

TITAN

Written by: Yoshihiko Hayashi, `hayashi@nttnly.isl.ntt.jp`

From: Usually `nttnly.isl.ntt.jp`

User-Agent: TITAN/0.1

Its purpose is to generate a Resource Discovery database, and copy document trees. A primary goal is to develop an advanced method for indexing the WWW documents. By using libwww-perl, the Proposed Standard for Robot Exclusion is supported. It is a stand-alone program written in Perl 4.

CS-HKUST WWW Index Server

Home Page: `http://dbx.cs.ust.hk:8000/`

Written by: Budi Yuwono, `yuwono-b@cs.ust.hk`

From: Usually `dbx.cs.ust.hk`

User-Agent: CS-HKUST-IndexServer/1.0

Its purpose is to generate a Resource Discovery database, and validate HTML. The Proposed Standard for Robot Exclusion is supported. It is a stand-alone program written in C. Part of an on-going research project on Internet Resource Discovery at Department of Computer Science, Hong Kong University of Science and Technology (CS-HKUST).

Spry Wizard Robot

Home Page: `http://www.compuserve.com/wizard/wizard.html`

Written by: Spry `info@spry.com`

Its purpose is to generate a Resource Discovery database. Unfortunately neither the User-agent nor the From HTTP fields are set. It's usually run from `wizard.spry.com` or `tiger.spry.com`. Spry is refusing to give any comments about this robot.

Weblayers

Home Page: `http://www.univ-paris8.fr/~loic/weblayers/`

Written by: Loic Dachary, `loic@afp.com`

Software: `ftp://www.univ-paris8.fr/~loic/weblayers/weblayers-0.0.tar.gz`

User-Agent: weblayers/0.0

Its purpose is to validate, cache, and maintain links. The Proposed Standard for Robot Exclusion is supported. It is a stand-alone program written in Perl 5. It is designed to maintain the cache generated by the emacs w3 mode (Netscape replacement) and to support annotated documents (keep them in sync with the original document via diff/patch).

WebCopy

Home Page: `http://www.inf.utfsm.cl/~vparada/webcopy.html`

Written by: Victor Parada, `vparada@inf.utfsm.cl`

Software: `ftp://ftp.inf.utfsm.cl/pub/utfsm/perl/webcopy.tgz`

From: Not set.

User-Agent: WebCopy/(version)

Its purpose is to perform mirroring. The Proposed Standard for Robot Exclusion is not supported. It is a stand-alone program written in Perl 4 or 5. WebCopy can retrieve files recursively using HTTP protocol. It can be used as a delayed browser or as a mirroring tool. It cannot jump from one site to another. It can be used by anyone from anywhere.

Scooter

Home Page: `http://scooter.pa-x.dec.com/`

Written by: Louis Monier, `monier@pa.dec.com`

From: Usually `scooter.pa-x.dec.com`

User-Agent: Scooter/1.0

Its purpose is to generate a Resource Discovery database, and generate statistics. After fetching a page, Scooter will not contact the same host for 100 times the duration of the last fetch. The Proposed Standard for Robot Exclusion is supported. It is a stand-alone program written in C.

Aretha

Written by: Dave Weiner, `davew@well.com`

A crude robot built on top of Netscape and Userland Frontier, a scripting system for Macs.

WebWatch

Home Page: `http://www.xensei.com/users/janos/specter/`

Written by: Joseph Janos, `janos@specter.com`

From: Not set.

User-Agent: WebWatch

Its purpose is to validate HTML, and generate statistics. The Proposed Standard for Robot Exclusion is not supported. It is a stand-alone program written in C++. Checks URLs modified since a given date. Shareware.

Chapter 1

(Apple 1988) Apple Computer Inc. "Project 2000—A Knowledge Navigator." Videotape. Available from Apple Video Fulfillment Program, 1-800-627-0230, Mar 8, 1988.

(Bates 1994) Bates, Joseph. "The role of emotion in believable agents." *Commun. ACM*, 37, 7, pp.122–125, 1994.

(BDDWW 1993) Birmingham, W., T. Darr, E. Durfee, A. Ward, and M. Wellman. "Supporting mechatronic design via a distributed network of intelligent agents." In *AI in Collaborative Design, workshop notes*, J.S. Gero and M.L. Maher, Eds. University of Sydney, 1993.

(BFKM 1985) Brownston, L., R. Farrell, E. Kant, and N. Martin. *Programming Expert Systems in OPS5: An Introduction to Rule-Based Programming*. Reading, Mass., Addison-Wesley, 1985.

(Bledsoe 1986) Bledsoe, Woody. "I had a dream: AAAI presidential address." *AI Magazine*, vol. 7, no. 1, pp.57–61, 1986.

(BLR 1992) Bates, J., A.B. Loyall, and W.S. Reilly. "An architecture for action, emotion, and social behavior." In *Proceedings of the Fourth European Workshop on Modeling Autonomous Agents in a Multi-Agent World*. S. Martino al Cimino, Italy, 1992.

(Boden 1991) Boden, M.A. *The Creative Mind: Myths and Mechanisms. (Expanded Edition)*. Basic Books, New York; Abacus, London, 1991.

(Boden 1994) Boden, M.A. "Agents and creativity." *Commun. ACM*. 37, 7, pp.117–121, 1994.

(Brooks 1986) Brooks, Rodney. "A robust layered control system for a mobile robot." IEEE J. Robotics and Automation, RA-2, pp.14–23, 1986.

(Brooks 1989) Brooks, R. "A robot that walks: Emergent behavior from a carefully evolved network." *Neural Computation*, 1, 2, (Summer 1989), pp.253–262.

(Brooks 1990) Brooks, R. "Elephants don't play chess." In *Designing Autonomous Agents*, Pattie Maes Ed. pp.3–15, MIT Press, Cambridge, Mass., 1990.

(Brooks 1991) Brooks, R. "Intelligence without representation." *AI Journal*, 47, 1, 1991.

(Cheong 1992a) Cheong, F.C. "Oasis: An Agent-Oriented Programming Language for Heterogeneous Distributed Environment." Ph.D. Thesis. University of Michigan, 1992.

(Cheong 1992b) Cheong, F.C. `ftp:// ftp.eecs.umich.edu/software/oasis/`.

(Cutkosky 1993) Cutkosky, M. et al. "PACT: An experiment in integrated engineering systems." *Computer* 26, 1, pp.28–37, 1993.

(Cypher 1993) Cypher, A., Ed. *Watch What I Do: Programming by Demonstration*. MIT Press, Cambridge, Mass., 1993.

(DB 1992) Darr, T.P. and W.P. Birmingham. *Concurrent Engineering: An Automated Design Space Approach*. Tech. Rep. CSE-TR-149-92, University of Michigan, 1992.

(DBMMZ 1992) Dent, L., J. Boticario, J. McDermott, T. Mitchell, and D. Zabowski. "A personal learning apprentice." In *Proceedings of the International Joint Conference on Artificial Intelligence*. 1992.

(DS 1983) Davis, R. and R.G. Smith. "Negotiation as a metaphor for distributed problem-solving." *Artificial Intelligence*. 20, 1, pp.63–109, 1983.

(ECJS 1994) Edmonds, E.A., L. Candy, R. Jones, and B. Soufi. "Support for collaborative design: agents and emergence." *Commun. ACM*. 37, 7, pp.41–47, 1994.

(EW 1994) Etzioni, O. and D. Weld. "A softbot-based interface to the Internet." *Commun. ACM*. 37, 7, pp.72–76, 1994.

(GK 1994) Genesereth, M. and S. Ketchpel. "Software Agents." *Commun. ACM*, 37, 7, pp.48–53, 1994.

(GL 1994) Guha, R.V. and D.B. Lenat. "Enabling agents to work together." *Commun. ACM*. 37, 7, pp.126–142, 1994.

(GM 1994) General Magic Inc. *The World of Telescript Technology*. 1994.

(Greif 1994) Greif, I. "Desktop agents in group-enabled products." *Commun. ACM*. 37, 7, pp.100–105, 1994.

(Gruber 1991) Gruber, T. "Ontolingua: A mechanism to support portable ontologies." KSL-91-66, Stanford Knowledge Systems Laboratory, 1991.

(HF 1992) Hersey, G. and R. Freedman. *Possible Palladian Villas (Plus a Few Instructively Impossible Ones)*. MIT Press, Cambridge, Mass., 1992.

(Hodgson 1990) Hodgson, P. "Understanding Computing, Cognition, and Creativity." M.Sc. thesis, University of the West of England, 1990.

(HP 1989) Hewlett-Packard. "HP New Wave Agent Guide." Santa Clara, Calif., Oct 1989.

(JDMMZ 1991) Jourdan, J., L. Dent, J. McDermott, T. Mitchell, and D. Zabowski. "Interfaces that learn: A learning apprentice for calendar management." *Tech. Rep.* CMU-CS-91-135, Carnegie Mellon Univ., Pittsburgh, PA., 1991.

(Kay 1984) Kay, A. "Computer software." *Scientific American.* 251, 3, pp.53–59, 1984.

(Kay 1990) Kay, A. "User Interface: A personal view." In *The Art of Human-Computer Interface Design.* B. Laurel ed. Addison-Wesley, Reading, Mass., 1990.

(KE 1981) Koning, H. and J. Eizenberg. "The language of the prairie: Frank Lloyd Wright's prairie houses." *Environmental Plan.* B 8, 1981, pp.295–323.

(KSC 1994) Kautz, H., B. Selman, and M. Coen "Bottom-up design of software agents." *Commun. ACM.* 37, 7, pp.143–146, 1994.

(LB 1983) Loyall, A.B. and J. Bates. "Real-time control of animated broad agents." In *Proceedings of the Fifteenth Annual Conference of the Cognitive Science Society*, Boulder, Colorado, 1993.

(Lenat 1983) Lenat, D.B. "The role of heuristics in learning by discovery: Three case studies." In *Machine Learning: An Artificial Intelligence Approach.* R.S. Michalski, J.G. Carbonell and T.M. Mitchell, eds. Tioga, Palo Alto, Calif., 1983.

(LGPPS 1990) Lenat, D.B., R.V. Guha, K. Pittman, D. Pratt, and M. Shepherd. "Cyc: Toward programs with common sense." *Commun. ACM.* 33, 8, pp.30–49, 1990.

(LNR 1987) Laird, J., A. Newell, and P. Rosenbloom. "SOAR: An Architecture for general intelligence." *Artificial Intelligence.* J. 33, 1, pp.1–64, 1987.

(Maes 1989) Maes, Pattie. "How to do the right thing." *Connect. Sci.* 1, 3, pp.291–323, 1989.

(Maes 1994) Maes, Pattie. "Agents that reduce work and information overload." *Commun. ACM.* 37, 7, pp.30–40, 1994.

(MCFMZ 1994) Mitchell, T., R. Caruana, D. Freitag, J. McDermott, and D. Zabowski. "Experience with a learning personal assistant." *Commun. ACM.* 37, 7, pp.80–91, 1994.

(MGLRR 1987) Malone, T.W., K.R. Grant, K-Y. Lai, R. Rao, and D. Rosenblitt. "Semi-structured messages are surprisingly useful for computer-supported coordination." *ACM Trans. Information Systems.* 5, 2 (April, 1987), pp.115–131.

(Minsky 1985) Minsky, M. *The Society of Mind.* Simon and Schuster, New York, 1985.

(MWFF 1992) Medina-Mora, R., T. Winograd, R. Flores, and F. Flores. "The action workflow approach to workflow management technology." In *Proceedings of the '92 Computer-Supported Cooperative Work '92 Conference.* pp.281–288, 1992.

(Negroponte 1970) Negroponte, N. *The Architecture Machine: Towards a More Human Environment.* MIT Press, Cambridge, Mass., 1970.

(Negroponte 1989) Negroponte, N. "An iconoclastic view beyond the desktop metaphor." *Journal on Human-Computer Interaction*, 1, 1, pp.109–113, 1989.

(NFFGPSS 1991) Neches, R., R. Fikes, T. Finin, T. Gruber, R. Patil, T. Senator, and W. Swartout. "Enabling technology for knowledge sharing." *AI Magazine*. 12, 3, pp.36–56, 1991.

(Norman 1994) Norman, D.A. "How might people interact with agents?" *Commun. ACM*. 37, 7, pp.68–71, 1994.

(OCC 1988) Ortony, A., G. Clore, and A. Collins. *The Cognitive Structure of Emotions*. Cambridge University Press, 1988.

(Pottmyer 1994) Pottmyer, J. "Renegade intelligent agents." SIGNIDR V, Proce. Special Interest Group on Networked Information Discovery and Retrieval, McLean, VA, August 4, 1994. Presentation slides available as `http://www.wais.com/SIGNIDR/Proceedings/SA3/`.

(PYFLHCM 1992) Palaniappan, M., N. Yankelovich, G. Fitzmaurice, A. Loomis, B. Haan, J. Coombs, and N. Meyrowitz. "The envoy framework: An open architecuture for agents." *ACM Trans. Information Systems*. 10, 3, July 1992, pp.233–264.

(Quinlan 1986) Quinlan, J.R. "Induction of decision trees." *Machine Learn*. 1, 1, pp.81–106, 1986.

(Riecken 1994) Riecken, D. "M: An architecture of integrated agents." *Commun. ACM*. 37, 7, pp.106–116, 1994.

(Schneiderman 1988) Scheneiderman, B. "Direct manipulation: A step beyond programming languages." *IEEE Comput*. 16, 8, pp.57–69, 1988.

(SCS 1994) Smith, D., A. Cypher, and J. Spohrer. "KidSim: Programming agents without a programming language." *Commun. ACM*. 37, 7, pp.54–67, 1994.

(Selker 1994) Selker, Ted. "COACH: A teaching agent that learns." *Commun. ACM*. 37, 7, pp.92–99, 1994.

(Smith 1977) Smith, D.C. *Pygmalion, A Computer Program to Model and Stimulate Creative Thought*. Birkhauser Verlag, Basel, Switzerland, 1977.

(TJ 1981) Thomas, F. and O. Johnston. *Disney Animation: The Illusion of Life*. Abbeville Press, New York, 1981.

(Waugh 1992) Waugh, I. "Improvisor." *Music Tech*. (Sept. 1992), pp.70–73.

(White 1994) James E. White. "Telescript Technology: The Foundation for the Electronic Marketplace." *General Magic White Paper*. 1994.

Chapter 2

(Cerf 1992) Cerf, Vinton. "A Brief History of the Internet and Related Networks," Internet Society, Reston, Virginia, 1992.

(Chapin 1992) Chapin, Lyman (Chair). "The Internet Standards Process," RFC 1310, Internet Activities Board, March 1992.

(Denning 1989) Denning, Peter. "The ARPANET after twenty years." *American Scientist*. Nov-Dec, 1989, pp.530–534.

(Horton 1983) Horton, M.R. Standard for interchange of Usenet messages. RFC 850. SRI International, Menlo Park, California, June 1983.

(KL 1986) B. Kantor and P. Lapsley. "Network News Transfer Protocol: A Proposed Standard for the Stream-Based Transmission of News." RFC 977, UC San Diego, UC Berkeley, February 1986.

(Lottor 1992) Lottor, Mark. RFC 1296: Internet Growth (1981-91). 1992.

(Merit 1992) Merit Network, Inc. "NSFNET: Bringing the World of Ideas Together." April, 1992. `ftp://nis.nsf.net/nsfnet/nsfnet.overview`.

(Moore 1994a) Moore, Martin. "Introducing the Internet." From *The Internet Unleashed*. Sams.net Publishing, Indianapolis, Indiana. 1994.

(Moore 1994b) Moore, Martin. "The Internet Today and Tomorrow." From *The Internet Unleashed*. Sams.net Publishing, Indianapolis, Indiana. 1994.

(Moore 1994c) Moore, Martin. "The Future of the Internet." From *The Internet Unleashed*. Sams.net Publishing, Indianapolis, Indiana. 1994.

(Quarterman 1993) Quarterman, John S. *Internet Growth*. Matrix News, 3(12), December 1993. `gopher://gopher.tic.com/00/matrix/news/v3/inetgrow.312`.

(QH 1986) Quarterman, John S. and Josiah C. Hoskins. "Notable Computer Networks." *Commun. ACM*, vol.29, no.10, October 1986, pp.932–971.

(QCM 1994) Quarterman, John S. and Carl-Mitchell, Smoot. *The Internet Connection: System Connectivity and Configuration*. Addison-Wesley, Reading, Massachusetts, 1994.

(Tanenbaum 1981a) Tanenbaum, Andrew. "Network protocols." *ACM Computing Survey*, vol.13, no.4, pp.453–489, Dec, 1981.

(Tanenbaum 1981b) Tanenbaum, Andrew. *Computer Networks*. Prentice-Hall Software Series, Prentice Hall, Englewood Cliffs, New Jersey, 1981.

Chapter 3

(AMLJTA 1993) Anklesaria, F., M. McCahill, P. Lindner, D. Johnson, D. Torrey, and B. Alberti. "The Internet Gopher Protocol: A Distributed Document Search and Retrieval Protocol." RFC 1436, University of Minnesota, March 1993.

(BL 1994) Bernes-Lee, T. "Universal Resource Identifiers in WWW" RFC 1630, CERN. June 1994.

(BLCLNS 1994) Bernes-Lee, T., R. Cailliau, A. Luotonen, H. Nielsen, and A. Secret. "The World Wide Web." *Commun. ACM*. 37, 8, pp.76–82, 1994.

(BLC 1995) Berners-Lee, T. and D. Connolly. "HyperText Markup Language—2.0." Work in Progress. June 1995. `ftp://ds.internic.net/internet-drafts/draft-ietf-html-spec-04.txt`.

(BLFN 1995) Bernes-Lee, T., R. T. Fielding, and H. F. Nielsen. "Hypertext Transfer Protocol—HTTP/1.0." *Work in Progress*. March 1995. `ftp://ds.internic.net/internet-drafts/draft-ietf-http-v10-spec-00.txt`.

(BLMM 1994) Berners-Lee, T., L. Masinter, and M. McCahill. "Uniform Resource Locators (URL)." RFC 1738, CERN, Xerox PARC, University of Minnesota, October 1994.

(BF 1993) Borenstein, N. and N. Freed. "MIME (Multipurpose Internet Mail Extensions) Part One: Mechanisms for Specifying and Describing the Format of Internet Message Bodies." RFC 1521, Bellcore, Innosoft, September 1993.

(DKMSSWSG 1990) Davis, F., B. Kahle, H. Morris, J. Salem, T. Shen, R. Wang, J. Sui, and M. Grinbaum. "WAIS Interface Protocol Prototype Functional Specification." (v1.5), Thinking Machines Corporation, April 1990.

(DR 1995) December, John and Neil Randall. *The World Wide Web Unleashed*. Sams.net Publishing, Indianapolis, Indiana. 1995.

(Goldfarb 1990) Goldfarb, Charles. *The SGML Handbook*. Clarendon Press, Oxford, 1990.

(Raggett 1995) Raggett, Dave. "HyperText Markup Language Specification Version 3.0." *Work in Progress*. W3C. March 1995. `ftp://ds.internic.net/internet-drafts/draft-ietf-html-specv3-00.txt`.

Chapter 4

(BDHMS 1994) Bowman, C. Mic, Peter B. Danzig, Darren R. Hardy, Udi Manber, and Michael F. Schwartz. "The Harvest Information Discovery and Access System." Proceedings of the Second International World Wide Web Conference, pp. 763–771, Chicago, Illinois, October 1994.

(DR 1995) December, John and Neil Randall. *The World Wide Web Unleashed*. Sams.net Publishing, Indianapolis, Indiana. 1995.

(December 1994) December, John. "New Spiders Roam the Web." *Computer-Edited Communication Magazine*. 1(5), Sep. 1, 1994. `http://www.rpi.edu/~decemj/cmc/mag/1994/sep/spiders.html`.

(DP 1994) DeBra, P. and R. Post. "Information Retrieval in the World Wide Web: Making Client-based searching feasible." Proceedings of the First International World Wide Web Conference. R. Cailliau, O. Nierstrasz, M. Ruggier (eds.), Geneva, 1994.

(Eichmann 1994) Eichmann, David. "The RBSE Spider—Balancing Effective Search Against Web Load." Proceedings of the First International World Wide Web Conference. R. Cailliau, O. Nierstrasz, M. Ruggier (eds.), Geneva, 1994.

(Koster 1994) Koster, Martijn. "ALIWEB: Archie-Like Indexing in the Web." Proceedings of the First International World Wide Web Conference. R. Cailliau, O. Nierstrasz, M. Ruggier (eds.), Geneva, 1994.

(Koster 1994a) Koster, Martijn. "A standard for robot exclusion." Nexor Corp. `http://www.nexor.co.uk/mak/doc/robots/norobots.html`.

(Koster 1994b) Koster, Martijn. "Guide for robot writers." Nexor Corp. `http://www.nexor.co.uk/mak/doc/robots/guidelines.html`.

(Koster 1994c) Koster, Martijn. "List of robots." Nexor Corp. `http://www.nexor.co.uk/mak/doc/robots/active.html`.

(Koster 1994d) Koster, Martijn. "World Wide Web Robots, Wanderers, and Spiders." `http://www.nexor.co.uk/mak/doc/robots/robots.html`.

(Mauldin 1995) Mauldin, Michael L. "Measuring the Web with Lycos." Third International World Wide Web Conference, April 11, 1995. `http://lycos.cs.cmu.edu/lycos-websize.html`.

(McBryan 1994) McBryan, Oliver. "GENVL and WWWW: Tools for Taming the Web." Proceedings of the First International World Wide Web Conference. R. Cailliau, O. Nierstrasz, M. Ruggier (eds.), Geneva, 1994.

(ML 1994) Mauldin, Michael L. and John R. R. Leavitt. "Web Agent-Related Research at the Center for Machine Translation." SIGNIDR, McLean, Virginia, August 4, 1994. `http://fuzine.mt.cs.cmu.edu/mlm/signidr94.html`.

(Pinkerton 1994) Pinkerton, Brian. "Finding What People Want: Experiences with the WebCrawler." The Second International World Wide Web Conference '94: *Mosaic and the Web*. `http://webcrawler.com/WebCrawler/WWW94.html`.

(SM 1983) Salton, G. and M.J. McGill. "Introduction to Modern Information Retrieval." McGraw-Hill, New York, 1983.

(Salton 1989) Salton, G. *Automatic Text Processing: The Transformation, Analysis, and Retrieval of Information by Computer*. Addison-Wesley, 1989.

Chapter 5

(Asimov 1942) Asimov, I. "Runaround." *Astounding Science Fiction*. 1942.

(Eichmann 1994) Eichmann, D. "Ethical web agents." In *Proceedings of the Second International Conference on the World Wide Web*. Oct, 1994.

Also available at `http://rbse.jsc.nasa.gov/eichmann/www-f94/ethics/ethics.html`.

(Koster 1994a) Koster, M. "A standard for robot exclusion." Nexor Corp. `http://web.nexor.co.uk/mak/doc/robots/norobots.html`.

(Koster 1994b) Koster, M. "Guide for robot writers." Nexor Corp. `http://web.nexor.co.uk/mak/doc/robots/guidelines.html`.

(Koster 1994c) Koster, M. "List of robots." Nexor Corp. `http://web.nexor.co.uk/mak/doc/robots/active.html`.

(EW 1994) Weld, D. and O. Etzioni. "The first law of robotics (a call to arms)." In *Proceedings of the Twelfth National Conference on AI*. Seattle, Wash. 1994. Also available at `ftp://cs.washington.edu/pub/ai/first-law-aaai-94.ps`.

Chapter 6

(Alvestrand 1995) Alvestrand, H. T.. "Tags for the identification of languages." RFC 1766, UNINETT, March 1995.

(AMLJTA 1993) Anklesaria, F. , M. McCahill, P. Lindner, D. Johnson, D. Torrey, and B. Alberti. "The Internet Gopher Protocol: A distributed document search and retrieval protocol." RFC 1436, University of Minnesota, March 1993.

(BL 1994) Berners-Lee. T. "Universal Resource Identifiers in WWW: A Unifying Syntax for the Expression of Names and Addresses of Objects on the Network as used in the World Wide Web." RFC 1630, CERN, June 1994.

(BLC 1995) Berners-Lee, T. and D. Connolly. "HyperText Markup Language Specification—2.0." *Work in Progress* (draft-ietf-html-spec-01.txt). CERN, HaL Computer Systems, February 1995.

(BLMM 1994) Berners-Lee, T., L. Masinter, and M. McCahill. "Uniform Resource Locators (URL)." RFC 1738, CERN, Xerox PARC, University of Minnesota, October 1994.

(BF 1993) Borenstein, N. and N. Freed. "MIME (Multipurpose Internet Mail Extensions) Part One: Mechanisms for Specifying and Describing the Format of Internet Message Bodies." RFC 1521, Bellcore, Innosoft, September 1993.

(Braden 1989) Braden, R. "Requirements for Internet hosts—application and support." STD 3, RFC 1123, IETF, October 1989.

(Crocker 1982) Crocker, D. H. "Standard for the Format of ARPA Internet Text Messages." STD 11, RFC 822, UDEL, August 1982.

(DKMSSWSG 1990) Davis, F., B. Kahle, H. Morris, J. Salem, T. Shen, R. Wang, J. Sui, and M. Grinbaum. "WAIS Interface Protocol Prototype Functional Specification." (v1.5), Thinking Machines Corporation, April 1990.

(KL 1986) Kantor, B. and P. Lapsley. "Network News Transfer Protocol: A Proposed Standard for the Stream-Based Transmission of News." RFC 977, UC San Diego, UC Berkeley, February 1986.

(Postel 1982) Postel, J. "Simple Mail Transfer Protocol." STD 10, RFC 821, USC/ISI, August 1982.

(Postel 1994) Postel, J. "Media Type Registration Procedure." RFC 1590, USC/ISI, March 1994.

(PR 1985) Postel, J. and J. K. Reynolds. "File Transfer Protocol (FTP)." STD 9, RFC 959, USC/ISI, October 1985.

(RP 1994) Reynolds, J. and J. Postel. "Assigned Numbers." STD 2, RFC 1700, USC/ISI, October 1994.

(ANSI 1986) US-ASCII. Coded Character Set - 7-Bit American Standard Code for Information Interchange. Standard ANSI X3.4-1986, ANSI, 1986.

(ISO 1990) ISO-8859. International Standard—Information Processing—bit Single-Byte Coded Graphic Character Sets—Part 1: Latin Alphabet No. 1, ISO 8859-1:1987. Part 2: Latin alphabet No. 2, ISO 8859-2, 1987. Part 3: Latin alphabet No. 3, ISO 8859-3, 1988. Part 4: Latin alphabet No. 4, ISO 8859-4, 1988. Part 5: Latin/Cyrillic alphabet, ISO 8859-5, 1988. Part 6: Latin/Arabic alphabet, ISO 8859-6, 1987. Part 7: Latin/Greek alphabet, ISO 8859-7, 1987. Part 8: Latin/Hebrew alphabet, ISO 8859-8, 1988. Part 9: Latin alphabet No. 5, ISO 8859-9, 1990.

Chapter 7

(Fielding 1994) Fielding, Roy. "Maintaining Distributed Hypertext Infostructures: Welcome to MOMspider's Web." In *Proceedings of the First International Conference on the World Wide Web* (WWW 1994), Geneva, May 1994. Also available at http://www.ics.uci.edu/WebSoft/MOMspider/WWW94/paper.html.

(Tilton 1993) Tilton, James. "What is an Infostructure?" Available at http://www.willamette.edu/~jtilton/info-p.html.

Chapter 8

The Web Transaction Security Working Group (under the auspices of the Internet Engineering Task Force) is tasked with developing requirements and specifications for the provision of security services to HTTP. The Web Transaction Security Working Group has a mailing list at `mailto://www-security@nsmx.rutgers.edu`, as well as a home page at `http://www-ns.rutgers.edu/www-security/wts-wg.html`.

Rutgers University Network Service also maintains a home page on World Wide Web Security at `http://www-ns.rutgers.edu/www-security/index.html`.

The World Wide Web Consortium also maintains a home page listing the W3C Security Resources, and can be found at `http://www.w3.org/hypertext/WWW/Security/Overview.html`.

As an alternative, Phillip Hallam-Baker of CERN has proposed Shen as a security scheme for the World Wide Web, details of which are available at `http://www.w3.org/hypertext/WWW/Shen/ref/shen.html`.

(Bamford 1982) Bamford, James. *The Puzzle Palace: A Report on America's Most Secret Agency.* Houghton Mifflin, Boston. 1982.

(Brassard 1988) Brassard, G. "Modern Cryptography." Volume 325 of *Lecture Notes in Computer Science*, Springer-Verlag, Berlin, 1988.

(CCITT 1988) CCITT (Consultative Committee on International Telegraphy and Telephony). Recommendation X.509: "The Directory—Authentication Framework." 1988.

(ElGamal 1985) ElGamal, T. "A public-key cryptosystem and a signature scheme based on discrete logarithms." IEEE Transactions on Information Theory. IT-31, pp.469–472, 1985.

(FIPS 1988) National Institute of Standards and Technology (NIST). FIPS Publication 46-1: Data Encryption Standard. January 22, 1988. Originally issued by National Bureau of Standards.

(Garfinkel 1995) Garfinkel, Simson. *PGP: Pretty Good Privacy.* O'Reilly and Associates, 1995.

(Hickman 1994) Hickman, Kipp E.B. Netscape Communications Corp. The SSL Prorocol. `http://home.mcom.com/info/SSL.html`.

(Hodges 1983) Hodges, Andrew. *Alan Turing: The Enigma.* Simon and Schuster, New York, 1983.

(Kahn 1967) Kahn, David. *The Codebreakers.* Macmillan, New York, 1967.

(Kahn 1983) Kahn, David. *Kahn on Codes: Secrets of the New Cryptology.* Macmillan, New York, 1983.

(Kahn 1991) Kahn, David. *Seizing the Enigma: The Race to Break the German U-Boat Codes, 1939–1943.* Houghton Mifflin, Boston. 1991.

(Kent 1993) Kent, S. RFC 1422: Privacy Enhancement for Internet Electronic Mail, "Part II: Certificate-Based Key Management." Internet Activities Board, February, 1993.

(Koblitz 1987) Koblitz, N. "Elliptic curve cryptosystems." *Mathematics of Computation.* 48:203–209, 1987.

(Linn 1993) Linn, J. RFC 1421: Privacy Enhancement for Internet Electronic Mail, "Part I: Message Encryption and Authentication Procedure." Internet Activities Board, February, 1993.

(LM 1991) Lai, XueJia and James Massey. "A proposal for a new block encryption standard." In *Advances in Crytology*—EuroCrypt '90 Proceedings. Springer-Verlag, 1991.

(Miller 1986) Miller, V.S. "Use of elliptic curves in cryptography." In *Advances in Cryptology*—Cryto '85, pp.417–426, Springer-Verlag, New York, 1986.

(NIST 1992) National Institute of Standards and Technology (NIST). "The Digital Signature Standard, proposal and discussion." *Commun. ACM.* 35(7), pp.36–54, July, 1992.

(Rivest 1990) Rivest, R.L. Cryptography. In J. van Leeuwen, ed. *Handbook of Theoretical Computer Science.* MIT Press/Elsevier, Amsterdam, 1990.

(RS 1994) Rescorla, Eric and Allan Schiffman. Enterprise Integration Technologies. "The Secure HyperText Transfer Protocol." 1994. `http://www.commerce.net/information/standards/drafts/shttp.txt`. Also available via e-mail at `mailto://shttp-info@commerce.net` or anonymous ftp at `ftp://ftp.commerce.net/pub/standards/drafts/shttp.txt`.

(RSA 1993) RSA Data Security. "Answers to Frequently Asked Questions About Today's Cryptography." Revision 2.0. October, 1993. Also available at `http://www.rsa.com/rsalabs/faq/faq_toc.html`.

(Schneier 1994) Schneier, Bruce. *Applied Cryptography: Protocols, Algorithms, and Source Code in C.* John Wiley and Sons, New York. 1994.

(Schnorr 1989) Schnorr, C.P. "Efficient identification and signatures for smart cards." In *Advances in Cryptology*—Crypto '89, pp.239-251, Springer-Verlag, New York, 1990.

(SNS 1988) Steiner, J.G., B.C. Neuman, and J.I. Schiller. "Kerberos: an authentication service for open network systems." In Unix Conference Proceedings, pp.191–202, Dallas, Texas, February, 1988.

(US 1991) Comptroller General of the United States. "Matter of National Institute of Standards and Technology—Use of Electronic Data Interchange Technology to Create Valid Obligations." File B-245714, December 13, 1991.

Chapter 9

(Bauer 1994) Bauer, Paul W. "A Beginner's Guide to the U.S. Payments System," Economic Commentary, July 1, 1994.

(BC 1989) Brassard, G. and C. Crepeau. "Sorting out zero knowledge." In *Advances in Cryptology*—Eurocrypt '89 Proceedings. Springer-Verlag 1990.

(BR 1994) Borenstein, N.S. and M.T. Rose, "The application/green-commerce MIME Content-type." First Virtual Holdings Incorporated, October, 1994.

(Brands 1993) Brands, Stefan. "An efficient off-line electronic cash system based on the representation problem." Technical Report CSR9323, Computer Science Department, CWI, March 1993.

(Brands 1994) Brands, Stefan. "Untraceable off-line cash in wallet with observers." In *Advances in Cryptology*—CRYPTO '90 Proceedings. Springer-Verlag, 1991.

(Chaum 1982) Chaum, David. "Blind signatures for untraceable payments." In *Advances in Cryptography*—CRYPTO '82 Proceedings. Plenum Press, 1983.

(Chaum 1985) Chaum, David. "Security without identification: Transaction systems to make big brother obsolete." *Commun. ACM.* vol.28, no.10, pp.1030–1044, Oct 1985.

(Chaum 1992) Chaum, David. "Achieving electronic privacy." *Scientific American.* pp.96–101, August 1992.

(Econ 1994) "So much for the cashless society." *The Economist.* vol.333, issue 7891, pp.21–23, Nov 26, 1994.

(GS 1979) Garbade, Kenneth G. and William L. Silber. "The Payments System and Domestic Exchange Rates: Technological versus Institutional Change." *Journal of Monetary Economic.* vol.5, no.1 (Jan 1979), pp.1–22.

(RB 1994) Rose, M.T. and N.S. Borenstein, "The Simple Green Commerce Protocol (SGCP)." First Virtual Holdings Incorporated, October, 1994.

(Schneier 1994) Schneier, Bruce. *Applied Cryptography: Protocols, Algorithms, and Source Code in C.* John Wiley and Sons, New York. 1994.

(White 1993) White, Peter T. "The Power of Money." *National Geographic.* vol.183, no.1 (Jan 1993), pp.80–108.

Chapter 10

(Brunner 1975) Brunner, John. *The Shockwave Rider.* Ballatine, New York. 1975.

(Cohen 1987) Cohen, Fred. "Computer Viruses—Theory and Experiments." *Computers and Security*, vol.6, no.1, pp.22–35, 1987.

(Cohen 1988) Cohen, Fred. "On the Implications of Computer Viruses and Methods of Defense." *Computers and Security*, vol.7, no.2, pp.167–184, 1988.

(Cohen 1989) Cohen, Fred. "Models of Practical Defenses Against Computer Viruses." *Computers and Security*, vol.8, no.2, pp.149–160, 1989.

(Cohen 1990) Cohen, Fred B. *A Short Course on Computer Viruses.* ASP Press, 1990.

(Ferbrache 1992) Ferbrache, David. *A Pathology of Computer Viruses.* Springer-Verlag, 1992.

(Gerrold 1972) Gerrold, David. *When Harley was One.* Doubleday, New York. 1972.

(Hoffman 1990) Hoffman, Lance J. (Ed.) *Rogue Programs: Viruses, Worms and Trojan Horses.* Van Nostrand Reinhold, 1990.

(Lucas 1994) Lucas, Kelly. "Viruses and Other Nasty Things." In *Cyberlife.* pp.423–449. Sams Publishing, 1994.

(Seeley 1989) Seeley, Donn. "A Tour of the Worm." In *Proceedings of the 1989 Winter Unix Conference.* USENIX Association, San Diego, California, Feb. 1989.

(SH 1982) Shoch, John F. and Jon A. Hupp. "The 'Worm' programs—Early experience with a distributed computation." *Commun. ACM*, vol.25, no.3, pp.172–180, March 1982.

(SHF 1990) Spafford, Eugene H., Kathleen A. Heaphy, and David J. Ferbrache. "A computer virus primer." In *Computers Under Attack: Intruders, Worms, and Viruses*. Editor: Peter Dennings. ACM Press/Addison-Wesley, 1990.

(Spafford 1989) Spafford, Eugene H. "The Internet worm: Crisis and aftermath." *Commun. ACM*, vol.32, no.6, pp.678–687, June 1989.

Chapter 11

The MUD Archive by Lauren P. Burka contains lots of MUD-related resources and can be found at `http://www.ccs.neu.edu/home/lpb/muddex.html`.

A current list of MUDs can be obtained via e-mail at `mailto://awozniak@geordi.calpoly.edu` with SUBSCRIBE as the subject. The MUD list also is available at `ftp://b63062.student.cwru.edu:/pub/mudlist/` or `http://b63062.student.cwru.edu/~mudlist`.

Further information about the Loebner Prize Competition may be obtained from Cambridge Center for Behavioral Studies, 675 Massachusetts Avenue, Cambridge, Mass., 02139. The Loebner Prize Home Page can be found at `http://www.csusm.edu/loebner_contest.html`.

The Colin Source Code, written by Michael Mauldin at CMU, can be found at `ftp://nl.cs.cmu.edu/usr/mlm/ftp/robot.tar.Z`.

Julia's log of the 1993 Loebner Prize Competition can be found at `http://fuzine.mt.cs.cmu.edu/mlm/contest93.html`.

Julia's log of the 1994 Loebner Prize Competition can be found at `http://fuzine.mt.cs.cmu.edu/mlm/contest94.html`.

Julia has a home page at `http://fuzine.mt.cs.cmu.edu/mlm/julia.html`.

To carry out a conversation with Julia, try `telnet://julia@fuzine.mt.cs.cmu.edu`.

Information about the CHAT Natural Language System can be found at `ftp://debra.dgbt.doc.ca/pub/chat/chat.html`. CHAT itself can be reached at `telnet://debra.dgbt.doc.ca:3000`.

(Bartle 1990) Bartle, Richard. "Interactive Multi-User Computer Games." MUSE Ltd. Research Report, December 1990. Also available at `ftp://parcftp.xerox.com:pub/MOO/papers/mudreport.txt`.

(Colby 1975) Colby, Kenneth M. *Artificial Paranoia: A Computer Simulation of Paranoid Process*. Pergamon Press., New York, 1975.

(Curtis 1992) Curtis, Pavel. "Mudding: Social Phenomena in Text-Based Virtual Realities." From 1992 Conference on Directions and Implications of Advanced Computing. `ftp://parcftp.xerox.com:pub/MOO/papers/DIAC92.txt`.

(CN 1993) Curtis, Pavel and David A. Nicholas. "MUDs Grow Up: Social Virtual Reality in the Real World." From The Third International Conference on Cyberspace. May, 1993. `ftp://parcftp.xerox.com:pub/MOO/papers/MUDsGrowUp.txt`.

(Epstein 1992) Epstein, R. "The Quest for the Thinking Computer." *AAAI Magazine*, Vol. 13, No. 2, Summer 1992, pp. 80–95.

(Epstein 1993) Epstein, R. "1993 Loebner Prize Competition in Artificial Intelligence: Official Transcripts and Results." Technical Report, Cambridge Center for Behavioral Studies, December 1993.

(Foner 1993) Foner, Leonard. "What's an Agent, Anyway? A Sociological Case Study." Agents Memo 93–01. Agents Group, MIT Media Lab. `http://foner.www.media.mit.edu/people/foner/Julia/`. `ftp://media.mit.edu/pub/Foner/Papers/Julia/Agents—Julia.ps`.

(Gibson 1984) Gibson, William. *Neuromancer*. Ace Science Fiction Books, New York. 1984.

(Mauldin 1994) Mauldin, Michael L. "Chatterbots, TinyMUDs, and the Turing Test: Entering The Loebner Prize Competition." AAAI-94. `http://fuzine.mt.cs.cmu.edu/mlm/aaai94.html`.

(Raymond 1991) Raymond, Eric S., editor, *The New Hacker's Dictionary*. MIT Press, 1991.

(Rheingold 1991) Rheingold, Howard. *Virtual Reality*. Summit Books, New York, 1991.

(Shieber 1992) Shieber, S. "Lessons from a Restricted Turing Test," Technical Report TR-19-92, Harvard University, Sept. 1992, Revision 4.

(Turing 1950) Turing, Alan M. "Computing Machinery and Intelligence." *Mind*. Vol. 54, No. 236, October 1950, pp. 433–460.

(Weizenbaum 1966) Weizenbaum, Joseph. "Eliza: a computer program for the study of natural language communication between man and machine." *Commun. ACM*. 9, 1, pp.36–44, 1966.

(Weizenbaum 1976) Weizenbaum, Joseph. *Computer Power and Human Reason*. W.H. Freeman and Co., New York, 1976.

(Wired 1993) Spence, Kristin and Louis Rossetto. *Wired Magazine*, San Francisco, Vol. 1.6, Dec. 1993. `http://www.wired.com/Etext/1.6/departments/net.surf.html`.

index

functions (WebWalker), 169-170
    avoidance package, 175
    history package, 176
    summary package, 180-181
    traversal package, 177-178
Future Fantasy Bookstore (online
  bookstore), 348

G

gateways, 74-75
Gatherer (Harvest), 96-97
Genghis robot, 23
GET method (HTTP request messages), 131
GetURL robot, 383
Gibson, William, 249
Glimpse backend search engine, 98
global directives (WebWalker), 159
Global Electronic Music Marketplace (online
  music store), 352
Gopher, 69
    objects, storing with Harvest Object
      Cache, 98
    sites
      searching with Harvest Gatherer, 97
      searching with Lycos, 91
    versus WWW, 66
Green Commerce model (information
  commerce), 223
group agents, 13

H

hard disks (architecture), 237
Harvest, 382
    architecture, 95-99
    backend search engines, 98
    Broker, 97-98
    Gatherer, 96-97
    Home Pages Broker, 94
    Object Cache, 98
    registering, 97
    Replicator, 99
    Server Registry (HSR), 97
HEAD method (HTTP request messages), 131
headers (HTTP)
    entities, 141-146, 288-289
    messages, 128, 286
    request messages, 133-137, 287-288
    response messages, 140-141, 288

Hewlett-Packard New Wave Agent, 8-9
history package (WebWalker program),
  175-176
home pages, *see* WWW, sites
Home Pages Broker (Harvest), 94
HSR (Harvest Server Registry), 97
HTML (HyperText Markup Language), 67
    forms, 73
    levels of SGML conformance, 71
    tags, 72
HTML Analyzer, 377
HTMLgobble robot, 378
HTTP (HyperText Transfer Protocol), 67-71,
  125-126
    augmented BNF, 284-285
    character set parameters, 148-149
    client/server computing, 126-127
    content negotiation, 150-151
    content parameters, 148-150, 290
    date/time stamps, 147
    encoding mechanisms, 149
    entities, 141, 288-289
      Allow header, 142
      body, 146-147, 289
      character sets, 148-149
      Content-Encoding header, 142
      Content-Language header, 142-143
      Content-Length header, 143
      Content-Transfer-Encoding header, 143
      Content-Type header, 143
      data types, 146-147
      Derived-From header, 143-144
      Expires header, 144
      headers, 288-289
      Last-Modified header, 144
      length of body, 147
      Link header, 144-145
      Location header, 145
      URI header, 145
      Version header, 145-146
    format negotiations, 70-71
    language tags, 150
    Media Type parameters, 148
    messages, 128
      Date header, 129
      Forwarded header, 129
      headers, 128, 286
      Message-ID header, 129-130
      MIME-Version header, 130
      posting, 131
    parsing constructs, 285-286
    protocol parameters, 147-148, 289-290

O

Oasis (Object and Agent Specification and Implementation System), 31-32
Object Caches (Harvest), 98
online bookstores, 347-349
online music stores, 351-353
Open Text Corporation Robot, 383
operator identification (robots), 112
output (WebWalker), 162-167
Oz Project, 28-30

P

Pakistani virus, 242
parameters (HTTP)
   content, 148-150, 290
   protocol, 147-148, 289-290
parent documents (WWW), identifying, 112
Parry (chatterbot), 253-255, 279
parsing constructs (HTTP), 285-286
partition records (hard disks), 237
$PauseTime parameter (WebWalker), 173
peculiarity weighting (indexing Web documents), 88
PEM (Privacy-Enhanced Mail) format, 198
Peregrinator robot, 381-382
Perl programming language, 158
physical agents, 23-24
polymorphic virus, 245-246
ports (Web servers), 68
POST method (HTTP request messages), 131-132
posting HTTP messages, 131
Powell's Technical Books (online bookstore), 349
Pragma header (HTTP request messages), 135-136
precision (spiders), 101
Privacy-Enhanced Mail (PEM) format, 198
processing tasks (WebWalker program), 174
program listings
   WebShopper, 337-345
   WebWalker, 294-335
programming agents, 16, 30-32
program gateways, 74-75
protocols
   HTTP, 67, 69-71, 125-130
   IP, 39
   NCP, 38
   NNTP, 40

parameters (HTTP), 147-148, 289-290
   S-HTTP, 201-203
   SSL, 200-201
   TCP, 39
proxy servers, 67, 129
Public header (HTTP response messages), 141
public-key cryptography, 191-194
public-key cryptosystems, 193, 197-198
publishing robot Web search results, 120
PUT method (HTTP request messages), 132-133
Python Robot, 377

Q–R

queries
   rotating during robot Web searches, 114
   URLs, 68
query servers (WebCrawler), 88
question mark (?), Web address queries, 68

RBSE (Repository Based Software Engineering) spider, 83, 376
reason phrases (HTTP response messages), 137-140, 288
recall (spiders), 101
Referrer header (HTTP request messages), 136
registering Harvest components, 97
Reiters Books (online bookstore), 349
replicating indexed Web documents, 99
Replicator (Harvest), 99
ReplyTo email_address (WebWalker directive), 159
reports (WebWalker), 157
Request for Comments, *see* RFCs
request messages (HTTP), 130, 286-287
   formats, 130
   headers, 287-288
     Accept, 133-134
     Accept-Charset, 134
     Accept-Encoding, 134
     Accept-Language, 134-135
     Authorization, 135
     From, 135
     If-Modified-Since, 135
     Pragma, 135-136
     Referrer, 136
     User-Agent, 136

U

V

W

X–Y–Z

PLUG YOURSELF INTO...

MACMILLAN INFORMATION SUPERLIBRARY™

que · SAMS PUBLISHING · Hayden Books · que COLLEGE · NRP · alpha books · Brady · ADOBE PRESS

THE MACMILLAN INFORMATION SUPERLIBRARY™

Free information and vast computer resources from the world's leading computer book publisher—online!

FIND THE BOOKS THAT ARE RIGHT FOR YOU!

A complete online catalog, plus sample chapters and tables of contents give you an in-depth look at *all* of our books, including hard-to-find titles. It's the best way to find the books you need!

- **STAY INFORMED** with the latest computer industry news through our online newsletter, press releases, and customized Information SuperLibrary Reports.

- **GET FAST ANSWERS** to your questions about MCP books and software.

- **VISIT** our online bookstore for the latest information and editions!

- **COMMUNICATE** with our expert authors through e-mail and conferences.

- **DOWNLOAD SOFTWARE** from the immense MCP library:
    - Source code and files from MCP books
    - The best shareware, freeware, and demos

- **DISCOVER HOT SPOTS** on other parts of the Internet.

- **WIN BOOKS** in ongoing contests and giveaways!

TO PLUG INTO MCP: →

GOPHER: gopher.mcp.com

FTP: ftp.mcp.com

WORLD WIDE WEB: **http://www.mcp.com**

Home Page · What's New · Bookstore · Reference Desk · Software Library · Macmillan Overview · Talk to Us

REGISTRATION CARD

Internet Agents: Spiders, Wanderers, Brokers, and 'Bots

Name _____ Title _____

Company _____ Type of business _____

Address _____

City/State/ZIP _____

Have you used these types of books before? ☐ yes ☐ no

If yes, which ones? _____

_____

How many computer books do you purchase each year? ☐ 1–5 ☐ 6 or more

How did you learn about this book? _____

Where did you purchase this book? _____

Which applications do you currently use? _____

_____

Which computer magazines do you subscribe to? _____

_____

What trade shows do you attend? _____

_____

Comments: _____

_____

_____

Would you like to be placed on our preferred mailing list? ☐ yes ☐ no

☐ **I would like to see my name in print!** You may use my name and quote me in future New Riders products and promotions. My daytime phone number is: _____

New Riders Publishing   201 West 103rd Street ◆ Indianapolis, Indiana 46290 USA

Fax to **317-581-4670**   Orders/Customer Service **1-800-653-6156**   Source Code **NRP95**